Heinemann

SOCIOLOGY AS

for OCR

Warren Kidd Gerry Czerniawski David Abbott

Heinemann

Inspiring generations

Heinemann Educational publishers
Halley Court, Jordan Hill, Oxford OX2 8EJ
Part of Harcourt Education

Heinemann is the registered trademark of
Harcourt Education Limited

© Warren Kidd, Gerry Czerniawski, David Abbott
First published 2003

07 06 05 04 03
10 9 8 7 6 5 4 3 2 1

British Library Cataloguing in Publication Data is available
from the British Library on request.

ISBN 0 435 46708 5

Typeset by 🔨 Tek-Art, Croydon, Surrey

Original illustrations © Harcourt Education Limited 2003

Printed in Great Britain by Bath Press

Cover illustration by Matt Buckley

Picture research by Thelma Gilbert

Acknowledgements
Every effort has been made to contact copyright holders of material reproduced in this book. Any
omissions will be rectified in subsequent printings if notice is given to the publishers.

t= top; c=centre; b=bottom; l=left; r=right

page 30, Bridgeman Art Library/Southampton City Art Gallery; page 32t, Corbis; page 32b,
Illustrated London News; page 34t, Topham Picturepoint page 34c, University of Chicago; page
34b, Corbis; page 41, Topham Picturepoint; page 44, Photofusion; page 68, Roger Scruton; page 79,
Trip; page 80, Science Photo Library; page 86, Photofusion; page 90, Hulton Archive; page 92,
University of Chicago; page 94, Camera Press; page 98, Paul Willis; page 108, Photofusion; page
111, Valerie Hey; page 118l, Mary Evans Picture Library; page 118r, Rex Features; page 120, Derek
Layder; page 124, Popperfoto; page 126,Topham Picturepoint/Pressnet; page 127, Kobal Collection;
page 128t, Rex Features; page 128b, Rex Features; page 131, Rex Features; page 138, Rex Features;
page 140, Camera Press; page 144, Camera Press; page 162t, S & R Greenhill; page 162c,
Photofusion; page 162b, Photofusion; page 164, Hulton Archive; page 168, Camera Press; page 172,
Hulton Archive; page 174, Science Photo Library; page 180, S&R Greenhill; page 184, Corbis; page
186, Corbis; page 196, BBC; page 212, Illustrated London News; page 213, Granata Archive; page
214, Rex Features; page 216, Popperfoto; page 218t, Rex Features; page 218b, Popperfoto; page
222, Art Archive; page 225, Rex Features; page 229, North News; page 230, Popperfoto; page 234,
Popperfoto; page 238, Source unknown; page 239, Popperfoto; page 240, Professor Cohen; page
241, Press Association; page 244, Magnum; page 246, Rex Features; page 264, Rex Features; page
268, Robert Harding; page 271, Popperfoto; page 272,Topham Picturepoint; page 274, Mary Evans
Picture Library; page 283, Rex Features; page 284, Press Association; page 287,Collections/Eric
Lewis; page 289, Corbis; page 292, Popperfoto; page 294,Topham Picturepoint; page 295,
Popperfoto; page 296, Photofusion.

Tel: 01865 888058 www.heinemann.co.uk

Contents

Contents

Contents

Contents

Foreword

We hope that you enjoy this book. Our aim was to write a book that reflects what we think about how and why sociology should be taught at AS level. As teachers, we are trying to make things simple, make things up to date, and provide a structure for you the student that gives you a route through to the exam. We have broken down sociology into bite-sized chunks, dealing with all the ideas that you will need to know.

We have divided the book into the most popular topics in the AS exam, and have then broken each topic down into key questions or debates. By doing this we hope to show that sociology is essentially a series of debates and questions that can be answered by learning about and then applying the sorts of ideas sociologists have. We recommend that you read the introduction first as it explains what sociology is all about.

Warren Kidd
David Abbott
Gerry Czerniawski
2003

Acknowledgements

We would like to take this opportunity to thank the following people: Sarah Mitchell, Liz Tyler, Samantha Jackman, Marcus Bell, Catherine Hurst and Claire Walker.

Dedication

Warren would like to thank his friends, family and loved ones. Thank you for your support and continued encouragement.

David would like to dedicate this book to Rosie, Christopher and Olivia.

Gerry would like to dedicate this book to Collette, Kim, Kevin, Dave, Janine and Hedge and the sociology students at Newham Sixth Form College who have continuously supplied the inspiration for much of the writing.

We would also like to thank our colleagues and students. Thank you for making teaching sociology interesting and rewarding.

Author biographies

Warren Kidd is the Senior Tutor for Social Science at Newham Sixth Form College. He is an experienced writer of sociology textbooks and vice president of The Association for the Teaching of Social Science

Foreword

(ATSS). Warren is a frequent contributor to ATSS Conferences, and is a regular provider of teacher and student conferences and lectures. He is currently a tutor in sociology at the London School of Economics and Political Science (LSE) on the Saturday School programme for A level students. Warren wrote the Introduction, Family and Methods chapters for this book and was the editor of the overall project.

David Abbott teaches at Hills Road Sixth Form College in Cambridge. He has written several text books and articles for AS/A level sociology. David wrote the chapter on Mass Media for this book.

Gerry Czerniawski teaches sociology at Newham Sixth Form College. Gerry is an associate lecturer in social sciences for the Open University and tutors in sociology at the London School of Economics and Political Science (LSE) on the Saturday School programme for A level students. Along with producing resources for the ATSS, Gerry has provided INSET courses in sociology and is also a teacher trainer on the City and Guilds teacher training course. He is currently studying for his PhD at Kings College (University of London). Gerry wrote the chapters on Religion and The Individual, Society and The Formation of Identity for this book.

Chapter 1

Introduction

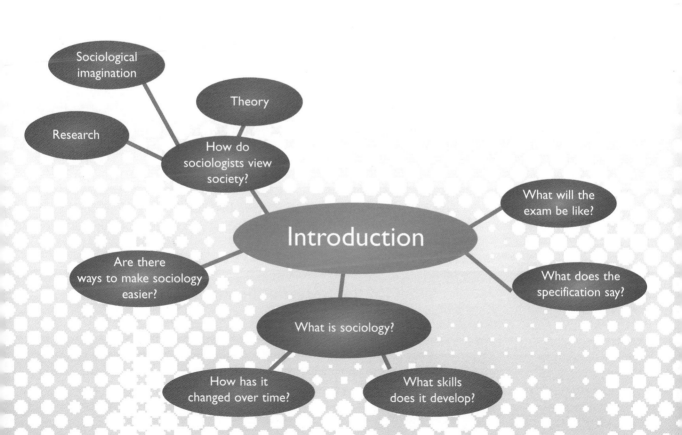

Sociological imagination

Theory

Research

How do sociologists view society?

Introduction

What will the exam be like?

Are there ways to make sociology easier?

What does the specification say?

What is sociology?

How has it changed over time?

What skills does it develop?

How to use this book

This book aims to help you be successful on your sociology course. You will find it useful in the following ways:

- It provides both classic and up-to-date sociological studies and theories.

- It focuses on the specifications from the exam boards.

- It provides a lot of knowledge, but also provides support for you for the exam. There are boxes in the margin that give you exam tips, plus sections on exams at the end of every chapter.

- It shows you what sociology is all about and what the tricks and shortcuts are to learning the subject.

- It breaks sociology down into manageable sections, focusing on the idea that there are four essential or key ingredients that you have to use in order to 'do' sociology well.

What features does this book have?

This book uses the following features:

- Margin boxes that give you tips and advice.

- Every section is a question or a key debate in sociology.

- Each section contains information to help you to think about the exam, and also to try and push your grades up as high as possible.

- Each chapter ends with some examples of frequently asked student queries and answers.

- CD-ROM symbols. This symbol directs you to the CD-ROM where you will find extra information such as case studies and revision exercises. Where the symbol appears, it is relevant to the whole chapter.

- Wider reading symbols: this symbol tells you that the section in question may be useful or interesting as wider reading for that particular chapter.

What do the boxes in the margin do?

There are different boxes you will come across in the margin. They each do a slightly different thing, and they are there to help you. Exam success is not simply a case of knowing the subject content, it is also a case of being able to apply what you know in the way the exam and the examiner wants you to.

- Thinking like a sociologist: this box allows you to get an idea of evaluation comments that you can make about a particular issue.

- Top exam hint: this box gives you some very quick exam tips.

- Synoptic link: this box allows you to begin to think about your sociology course as a whole, rather than as a series of separated topics or options.

- Key definition: this box contains a key concept or term and its definition.

- Key idea: this box contains an important sociological idea explained.

- What, when and why?: this box will help you to place the ideas and people you are reading about into the historical period that they come from. This is useful for evaluation purposes.

- Who is this person?: you will find in studying sociology that you come across many different people, many different sociologists who all have different ideas. This margin box should help you to understand a bit more about the people behind the ideas.

- Coursework suggestion: this box provides a handy hint or an actual proposed idea for linking the AS topics to coursework at A2 level.

The accompanying CD-ROM with this book gives you the opportunity to be able to print off the margin boxes in specific combinations to suit your own needs. Make good use of this facility both throughout your course and at the end for revision purposes.

1.1 Key issues in sociology

What is sociology and what does it mean?

The word sociology means the study of society and it dates back to the middle 1800s. The word is most associated, originally, with the ideas of French philosopher Auguste Comte, and then later with three important founding sociologists; Karl Marx (died 1883), Emile Durkheim (died 1917) and Max Weber (died 1920). Before the word sociology was invented people studied society. Humans have always thought about, reflected upon and evaluated the conditions under which they live, be it through painting, art, philosophy, the study of history, science or literature.

Sociology is a separate subject in its own right, with a separate way of thinking about and looking at the world, and is often classified as a social science. Like other social sciences such as psychology, politics, economics, etc., sociology is concerned with explaining what is happening in the world that humans inhabit. Sociology is not a single subject. There are different sociologies with different ways of thinking about the world we inhabit. The two main sociologies are as follows:

1   Macro sociology: this is concerned with overall patterns in society. It seeks to explain how the whole of society operates and how all the pieces work as a whole.

2   Micro sociology: this is concerned with small-scale behaviour. It aims to understand people's feelings and thoughts and how people make sense of their own lives.

Today, many sociologists combine these two sociological approaches together, looking at how the big picture relates to the small picture, how the whole of society shapes what individuals actually do, and equally, how what individuals do can shape patterns for the whole of social life.

What are the key debates in sociology?

It is possible to identify some central sociological questions, key issues or debates that all sociologists are interested in, which make the subject what it is today. The topics you study at AS and A2 level draw on these debates, and you will find many answers to these issues contained within the pages of this book.

*   Is society in harmony or in conflict?

*   Do people have free-will to make free choices, or are we controlled by society?

*   How is power organised in society? Why are some people more powerful than others?

✓ **Top Exam Hint**

In some exam questions, a distinction between macro and micro theories will help you to make quick comparisons between sociological ideas.

- Is society fair? Why does inequality exist?

- Does society shape the individual or does the individual shape society?

The value of sociology

The value of thinking in a sociological fashion, is that the subject raises lots of questions to think about. Sociology is a critical or radical subject, it is about questioning why society is as it is. It is about digging under the surface, looking at what is really going on. In order to seek answers to the above questions and debates, sociology can be seen as being made up of two essential parts:

1   Theory: these are the ideas sociologists have; how sociologists see the world around them. These ideas shape how sociologists look at issues and determine what they see.

2   Research: this is the process of gathering evidence in order to test their ideas and theories. Sociologists gather evidence that hopefully points in the direction of what society is really like.

Sociological knowledge helps the sociologist to make sense of what goes on in society. Sociology opens up the mind, it asks people to be critical of the world they live in. Sociology asks us to question how society works, and to think again about the many untested assumptions that we might have about the world. By using the tools of sociology (theory and research) you will try to understand what the world is really like, rather than how you might have been brought up to believe it is like.

Is sociology 'hard'?

It is certainly challenging. For many it is a new subject at AS level. It also takes some time before you really feel comfortable with it – lots of unusual words and new ideas. However, the value of its 'newness' is that it is fresh, it is certainly original, and it is challenging in the sense that it explores new ways of thinking. Don't worry – do what your teachers tell you, follow the advice in this book and take it one step at a time. We are sure you will enjoy it!

● Synoptic Link

The questions opposite will help you to think about how all the different views in sociology relate to each other, and how they all agree or disagree.

✍ Coursework Suggestion

When undertaking any piece of sociological research make sure you show why sociologists would be interested in the issue you are looking at.

1.2 What do we need to know about sociology?

How does the specification treat sociology?

The specification you are following breaks sociology down into a number of topic areas (see section 15). These individual topics are all related to each other, even though you will be taught them separately. All the topics link to each other as they all deal with the same issues and themes, and they all use the same tools to think about society. The same theories and the same key words will come up in each topic, as well as some ideas that are only really relevant to each particular topic.

The whole of your sociology course is interrelated, and you must see it as a whole, rather than as a series of unrelated topics. When sociologists research social life, they often cover lots of different aspects of society at the same time. For example, a study that looks at education may also look at class, ethnicity, gender, plus it might look at the family and at deviance and sub-cultures. As you can see, there are lots of links within and between the topics you will be studying, as after all, there are lots of links in society.

Within each topic that you study, you will need to know the following:

- What the main debates and issues are.
- Any key themes or key words that are especially important.
- What concepts/empirical evidence/theories are relevant.

What will you be doing on your course?

Your teachers will use a variety of teaching and learning styles for you and your class. These could include the following:

- group work
- lectures
- discussions and debates
- active learning methods, where you are asked to find things out.

No matter what style of learning you are doing, and no matter why or when in the year you are doing it, it is important to keep in mind that all sociology starts from the same point; it is all about looking at views on society and looking at how these different views try and provide evidence

Thinking like a Sociologist

In your sociological thinking, show that you understand and can see how all sociological ideas eventually fit together. This is called being synoptic and is a vital skill.

✔ **Top Exam Hint**

This list provides you with a very quick checklist for revision for any topic area that you study.

for what they state.

Your job throughout this course is to become a referee of all these different views. For example, no matter what topic area you are studying, you will find a number of different viewpoints or **theories**. These theories are how sociologists think and see the world around them. You will need to learn these different theories, understand what they say, and how they agree or disagree with each other.

Where does it all lead?

During your sociology course you will build up a good understanding of all the basic theoretical ideas in sociology. Along with these theories, you will also learn named examples of research and studies, and you will learn lots of key concepts that you will use in order to evaluate the different views on offer.

Like any subject, studying sociology ultimately leads to the exam – and then beyond into the A2 course. But, along the way you will hopefully develop some very important skills. In particular, one of the main aims of sociology is to first challenge the ideas and arguments of other people. These evaluation skills are not just important for sociology, but for many other subjects, many courses at university and many jobs. Above all else, they are important because thinking in a critical fashion allows us to really question the world we live in.

Key points to remember

- All sociology topics link to each other.
- Sociology is training you to think in a clear fashion.

❝❞ Key Definition

Theories are ideas and hypotheses put forward to explain something. They are supported by facts, observations and assumptions and can be tested.

1.3 What are the key features of thinking sociologically?

The basic ingredients of sociology

There are four important ingredients that make sociology what it is. All of these are important and will help you to understand how the subject works and how all the individual topics relates together as a whole:

1   Key words or concepts: theories have associated concepts or key words.

2   Theory: all sociology has theoretical ideas or views that can be tested.

3   Named examples: individual sociologists and groups of sociologists usually associate themselves with a particular theory or theories. They then undertake research that might support or attack other ideas.

4   Evaluation: you, as a sociology student, must learn how to evaluate all these ideas and studies, and try and find way to choose between them all.

Applying and evaluating theories

Once you learn what a theory says about society in general, it is much easier to apply the theory to a particular aspect of society, such as education, the family, the media, etc.

The sociologists you study are usually linked to a theory, and this tells you something about their values and view. Their individual ideas and studies will provide more depth on the theory that lies behind their research.

As different theories are often conflicting, and as sociologists try to criticise or support each other by the research they do, you can evaluate all sociological research yourself. In any studies you read, look for comparisons and contrasts, and which sociologists agree or disagree with the findings of the research. Then think about who you agree with and why. This is when sociology starts to come alive; when you can actually use it to think about your own life.

✓ **Top Exam Hints**

- Use the four ingredients in your exam, especially for longer mark questions, as they will add depth to your arguments.

- Make sure that you become familiar with all the key words as soon as possible. By using these you will be able to demonstrate your knowledge and understanding.

Using the four ingredients in sociology

You should try and use the four ingredients in a number of ways:

* Every time you write a long exam answer, try and include these ingredients.

* Organise your revision notes according to the four ingredient's headings.

* Use the ingredients as a checklist. Every time you write an exam answer, think about how you might combine the ingredients together in order to get more depth in your answers.

* Every time you answer a question in class, try and use the ingredients to add detail to what you are saying.

* Make index card revision notes summarising the theories and key words.

* Make a note of which theories use which of the key terms and how they use them.

* If possible link each named example you are taught to the theory they follow.

* Link each named example to a few key words that best link to their particular study.

* For every theory you learn, memorise a list of five general evaluations and apply them as much as possible.

Conclusion

These 'ingredients' are an important short-cut; an easy way for you to begin to not only learn about sociology, but to be able to actually use sociological ideas in your own thinking. This is, after all, the point of the course – developing your thinking skills.

For consideration:

1 How do you think the four ingredients might help you to learn sociology easier?
2 Which ingredients do you think will be harder to learn and apply than the others? Why do you think this might be?

⚇ Thinking like a Sociologist

Evaluation, although much more important at A2 level, is important in sociology in general. It makes the subject critical and analytical. Concentrate not just on understanding sociological ideas, but think about whether you agree with them or not.

1.4 What is the sociological imagination?

☞ **Who is this Person?**

Mills is famous in sociology for two main ideas. First, the idea that sociology can be characterised by a distinctive 'imagination', a clear way of thinking about things. Second, the radical idea of a power elite. This is a left of centre idea that society is controlled by a narrow group of elite people who operate their rule for their own benefit. We can see that his sociological imagination allows him to be critical of the world he lives in.

❝❞ Key Definition

Biography in sociology means two things. First, our life history as a person and second, the ability we might have to alter and take control over our life history and actions.

What does this mean?

The term 'the sociological imagination' is associated with American sociologist C Wright Mills who, in 1959, wrote the book of the same name. In this book, Mills tries to describe the value of the subject of sociology; a theme that many other writers have since taken up.

In his book, Mills states that:

'The sociological imagination enables its possessor to understand the larger historical scene in terms of its meaning for the inner life and the external career of a variety of individuals … the sociological imagination enables us to grasp history and **biography** and the relations between the two within society. That is its task and its promise.'

If we analyse this statement by Mills, we can deduce that the sociological imagination:

- Allows us to see our place in the world as an individual.
- Lets us see how society is connected together.
- Lets us understand how the inter-connectedness of society relates to our own life and how we live it.
- Encourages us to think about our world, and to think about what it all means.

The sociological imagination then, is both what you have to develop in order to be able to do your subject well, but at the same time, it is the end result of actually studying it. It is the means by which to do well, but it is also what the subject promises to give you for all your hard efforts. Not just a qualification written on a piece of paper, but the thinking skills you need later in life.

How does the sociological imagination work?

The job of the sociologist, using their sociological imagination, is to think about the world in new ways. By looking at new concepts within society we open up the possibility that we might be able to describe this society better. This means that studying sociology might start to deal with things that do not seem real, but it will end up very real because you will be able to take the ideas you learn and apply them to what you see around you. You will come to know yourself better.

There will come a time when you understand how sociology works and why it works as it does. When this happens your sociological imagination will be starting to develop.

The idea is that sociology contains a number of benefits for those who study it. It not only allows you to see what society is like, but may also help shape your future. Sociology might make you more tolerant of others' views as you will have to look at many different viewpoints. It will help your evaluation skills as you are required to critique and assess the ideas you are taught. Studying sociology will improve your research skills, you will be able to find, test and gather information. This will be useful for other subjects and also for many future careers. Sociology will also make you more questioning.

Finally, sociology may change the sort of person you are, or at least how you think about who you are. Sociology is about thinking about society, and as an important member of this society, you are the subject of your own sociological imagination.

Conclusion

This new way of thinking – of being able to question what happens, why it happens, and if it does happen how we think it does – is also important for the exam. Although evaluation skills are more important for the A2 level course, the nature of sociology is such that you must become as comfortable as you can, as quickly as you can, with asking difficult questions. In other words, in taking sociological ideas, 'bouncing them off each other' and using them to contradict other ideas.

For consideration:

1   Why do sociologists think the sociological imagination is important?
2   Why do you think it is important to be able to understand your life using sociological ideas?

ᵼ Thinking like a Sociologist
As you develop your sociological imagination you will become more critical and analytical of sociological research.

1.5 What is theory and why is it important?

◆ What, When and Why?

It is important that as you progress in learning about theory, you also learn the time period in which particular ideas were developed. This will help you to understand why sociologists felt the need to invent the ideas in the first place.

✓ Top Exam Hint

Sometimes you can evaluate theories in the exam by referring to when they were developed, and by saying that some ideas might now be out of date (make sure you also say why they are out of date).

What does this mean?

When sociologists use the word theory, they mean something very particular by it, but the word theory means a lot of different things in ordinary language. English language dictionaries tend to describe it as:

- An idea developed by facts and research.
- An opinion.
- A view of the world.
- The principles upon which a type of knowledge is based.

All these definitions will help us to understand what theories are. In sociological usage we use 'theory' to refer to the collections of abstract ideas that sociologists use in order to see what the world is like around them. Theories are hypotheses of what the world is like, and why it is like this.

Theoretical schools of thought

There are many different schools of thought (different views) that different sociologists collectively hold. In this book you will read about a large number of these different schools of thought or theories. They include the following:

- Functionalism
- Marxism
- Neo-Marxism
- Weberian sociology
- Interpretive sociology (also called interactionism and phenomenology)
- The New Right
- The New Left
- Feminisms (there are lots of different sorts)
- Postmodernism
- Pluralism
- Post-structuralism
- Structurational sociology.

There are many different theories to learn about in sociology as there are many different views on what society is like. We can use these theories as 'tools' to help us to think about society. Individual sociologists as well as schools of sociologists have two main ways of looking at the world:

1 **Epistemologies**: sociologists often ask the question 'what is knowledge' or 'what is the best way of getting true and real knowledge about the world?'
2 **Ontologies**: sociologists also ask the question 'what is the world like?' or 'what is real about the world?'

This means that sociologists have theories (to answer ontological questions) and they also do research (and in doing so, need to answer epistemological questions).

Types of theory

Sociologist Robert Merton (1957) talks of the existence of three different types or 'levels' of theory in sociology:

1   First order theory: simple hypotheses that we can try and test through research.
2   Middle-range theory: ideas about how society works that are not simple hypotheses, but are less than a whole world view. Such ideas are models; they explain how and why something works as it does.
3   Grand theory: described by Merton as 'master conceptual schemes' meaning a total world view about the whole of society and how it works.

Theories can also be sub divided into macro and micro theories:

*   Macro theories: these are explanations of society that look at society as a whole.
*   Micro theories: these are explanations of society that look at individuals, how they think about the world and how they relate to and interact with others.

Glaser and Strauss (1968) talk of something called **grounded theory**. This is theory that arises from research. Rather than the theory coming first, the data from research is used to formulate an idea. In this way, theories are less abstract and not totally removed from social life, but are 'grounded' in (come from) social life.

Conclusion

It would be impossible to be a sociologist without some sort of notion of what the world is like. Theories allow us to see society in different ways. As a sociology student your job is to take all the different ideas and views that sociology has and manipulate them. You can compare and contrast them; you can evaluate them; you can use them to try and think about the society you inhabit, and your place within it.

☀ Key Idea

A test that some sociologists from the micro tradition might use is to ask if the theory in question actually makes sense to those in society it is being used to describe. This means people can be critical of sociological ideas, rather than the sociologist being the expert.

❝❞ Key Definition

Grounded theory is the idea that sociological ideas and theory should be rooted or should be draw from the data we get from real people in real life situations.

For consideration:

1   Why do you think there are so many different theoretical schools in sociology?
2   Why might the large number of theoretical schools be both a problem, and a strength of the subject?

1.6 What are the problems of having theory?

What does this mean?

Many sociology students do not really see the point of theory at first. You may not understand why we have it and what we can do with it. We can summarise these concerns as the following:

- Why are there so many theories?
- Why do they disagree?
- Why do theories seem so strange and abstract?
- Why do theories use strange and difficult language and terminology?
- Why are many theories so old?

Sociology is about thinking, and thinking involves trying to see the same thing from many different views. Sociological thinking is creative and imaginative; it lets us try out and test ideas. They become the tools of our trade.

However, as there are so many theories, you may find thinking theoretically quite difficult. In this book we have tried to use theories to answer the questions in each chapter and to show how they link to each other. This means that you can start to use theory in an evaluative way; use it to think about issues, rather than simply learn it in the abstract.

What traps can we fall into with theory?

Ian Craib (1984) identifies four problems or 'traps' that theoretical, abstract thinking often leads to. He recommends that sociological thinking should try to avoid these at all costs, although it is often difficult to do so.

1 Crossword puzzle trap: some theories simply take complex social reality, and then reduce it to a simple set of ideas. To do so misses the complexity of social life in the first place. Theory simply lets us fill in the squares of a puzzle, but it does not tell us why it is patterned as it is in the first place.

2 Brainteaser trap: some theories raise interesting questions about society, but never actually try to solve them. The researcher might get bogged down by wondering what things mean, or how to define and measure something, and never actually get on with the business of explaining.

3 Logic trap: some theories contradict themselves. They try to say that lots of things are true at the same time, yet some of these things might be opposites. In this way, some theories are always right, and are unable to be proved wrong.

4 Description trap: some theories simply describe what we can already see. They do not take us beyond this, and offer no new ideas or explanations.

How can theory make society clearer?

We can break all theories down into a number of issues or questions that they are all seeking answers to:

- What is human consciousness like?

- What role do humans play in creating the society around them?

- What is power like and who has it?

- Is society in harmony or consensus?

- What causes social change?

Theory is the attempt by sociologists to try and put some distance between themselves and the world they are in. We do not simply assume that we understand how something is, but try and look at many different possibilities. At the same time, theory is also the attempt to find out about things that we do not experience; to try and understand that which does not relate to our limited experience of the world. This is an attempt to make ourselves closer to things we previously knew nothing about. Most theories also have hidden within them a political value or judgement. They may be left wing, liberal or right wing. These ideas will shape what the researcher thinks and how they express their ideas.

Conclusion

You can also use theory in your real life. Think about theories when you watch the news or read newspapers. What news items might prove or disprove particular theories? Think about your own life and ask yourself 'What would I think about this if I believed theory X'? 'What would I think if I followed theory Y'?

For consideration:

1 What do you think are the main problems with thinking theoretically?
2 Why do you think that so many non-sociologists might not see the need for theory?

✓ **Top Exam Hint**

Use the four 'traps' to help you to evaluate sociological theories.

● **Synoptic Link**

These important questions, which are behind all sociology, can be used to link ideas from different topics together.

❗ **Thinking like a Sociologist**
- Always use theory as a basis for examination answers.
- Use theory as a tool to help you organise your revision.
- Use theories in lessons; think through the eyes of theories when you answer questions.
- Use theory in your coursework; try and test theories.

✓ **Top Exam Hint**

Use theory as a way of creating links in your revision. If a person belongs to a certain theoretical school, link them to the ideas and concepts of other people from the same school of thought.

1.7 What is evaluation and why is it important?

✓ Top Exam Hint

Evaluation will give you depth and detail in any question that is not a short answer question. If you can show an awareness of why two theories or two studies disagree.

✳ Key Idea

This emphasis on evaluation is central to what Mills calls the 'sociological imagination' (see section 4); the distinctive world view that sociology gives us.

What does this mean?

Evaluation is an important skill in sociology, and involves the following:

* Making criticisms.
* Pointing out that there might be problems in evidence.
* Showing that there are comparisons between ideas.
* Showing that there are contrasts between ideas.
* Saying what is good about an idea.
* Saying what is useful about an idea.
* Having an opinion which you can back-up with evidence.

Why is evaluation important?

Evaluation is very important at AS level for the following reasons:

* You need to evaluate in order to be able to put all the ideas and theories together.
* You will find some questions in the exam that focus upon evaluation, even at the AS level.
* If you can get used to evaluating quickly, you will find it easier at A2 level.
* The more evaluative you can be at AS level, the better your exam answers will sound, and therefore the better grades you will get.

How do we evaluate?

There are different types of evaluation that you can use. The following is a checklist that you can use to think about the quality of the answers you are producing:

* Use theories to criticise other theories.
* 'Think through the eyes of theories': imagine what it would be like to think in a particular way.
* Make methodological criticisms: attack a study for how it carried out its research.

- Use real life examples. An event in the contemporary world may provide you with evidence that you can use to assess what sociologists are saying.

- Use historical examples. Support or criticise a theory for saying something when history shows that something different happened.

- Some sociologists conduct research in order to prove or disprove someone else, make sure you spell out these links.

- Use synoptic tools to think about a theory or study, i.e. link an idea to class, gender, culture, identity, power, etc. (See section 8.)

- Make a note of when the idea, study or theory was invented and think about its usefulness today.

- Do not only say what is bad about an idea, but also what is good about it.

- Point out political biases and value-judgements behind theories. Some ideas might be left or right wing, and this might cloud or affect how they see society.

♟ Thinking like a Sociologist

Use this checklist to evaluate sources in your exam, your coursework and in class. They will take time to master, but will improve your answers when you have got to grips with them.

- Assess the contribution made to sociology by a theory; say what we would miss or lack if the idea had not been invented.

Conclusion

Evaluation, although more important for the A2 course, will allow you to gain extra marks at AS level since it is a way of demonstrating that you can use sociological ideas. You can use ideas to agree or disagree with each other. You can also use ideas to attack 'common sense' or media views. This will really help you to 'think like a sociologist.'

For consideration:

1 Why do you think that evaluation is an important skill for you to have?
2 Why do you think that evaluation is a difficult skill to develop?

What is synopticity and why is it important?

What does this mean?

By being **synoptic** we mean being able to tie the whole sociology course together: being able to see how the whole six modules over the two years (at AS and A2 level) link together. It is therefore very important that you think about this right from the start, as it will be difficult to understand how AS subjects link in if you wait until A2 level to combine everything together.

You will be examined for synopticity at the end of the A2 course in the Stratification module. This is the very last exam you will sit.

How can you be synoptic?

The idea of synopticity means that as a student you should be able to see that the different units and modules you do all link together as a whole. You will therefore need to look at the things that join the individual sections up, i.e. the connections. The whole of society is interconnected, and therefore all the different parts of the sociology course are also interconnected.

In order to be synoptic (to tie everything together) the starting point is theory. Theories let us make comparisons between topics. What a theory states about one aspect of society such as family, may then affect what it states about another different aspect of society such as education or the media. Theories let us see that society is interconnected. Theories encourage us to think about the joined up bits of the course, rather than simply see sociology as a broken-down series of unrelated topics.

Building up and breaking down

Your perception of school may be that different knowledge is taught by different teachers in different rooms. The subjects all have different names and are located in different departments. You may think there are no connections between these subjects, but there are. Learning about chemicals in Science can help you in Art. Learning about art history can help you in English Literature or in History. Schools often encourage us to break down connections because otherwise how could we learn anything? It is always easier to learn something if it is broken down into smaller parts.

This is also true for this book. We are trying to pull sociology apart to show you how it all works. However, once you have pulled it apart, you then need to re-build it again, otherwise it will not work. Being synoptic will allow us to see how sociology all links together.

What synoptic tools are there to use?

In order to see how both society and sociology are connected, we can use the following 'tools':

- Class
- Gender
- Ethnicity
- Culture
- Identity
- Location
- Globalisation
- Age.

Synopticity can also be divided into two main areas:

1 Social synopticity: this means seeing the connections between the parts of society (and hopefully using sociological theories and ideas in order to do this).
2 Sociological synopticity: this means seeing the connections between sociological ideas themselves; looking at what might link different studies, theories or debates that sociologists have.

These two types of synopticity are related. As everything in society is connected together, then everything in sociology must also be connected together. Imagine the following scenario: you leave your house and you go to school one morning. You talk to your friends on the bus about what you watched on TV last night. Even in this short extract of normal life there are numerous connections; family, education, culture (telling us we must go to school), class, ethnicity (the last two might affect where we live and also what we watch on TV). As you can see, the whole of life is one big interconnected whole. In order to 'do' good sociology, you must be aware of this.

✓ Top Exam Hint

To get high marks you will need to show that you are aware of all the interconnections between the ideas in each topic of sociology. Use the synoptic tools in longer mark questions as a way to show off your understanding of how sociology is all connected together.

For consideration:

1 Why do you think synopticity in included in the AS and A2 level courses?
2 What challenges do you think this might raise for students of sociology?

1.9 How has sociology changed over time?

Sociology was invented to explain the rise of early industrial society and its effects on human life and relationships.

✳ Key Ideas

- The founders of sociology are often referred to as the 'founding fathers'. However, feminists have pointed out that by using this term we are limiting the opportunity for women sociologists to be seen to be able to make a valuable contribution.

- The 'Third Way' is the term given to the fact that New Left thinking needs to find a new third approach to thinking about society (different to the old 'right' and 'left' in politics).

✓ Top Exam Hint

If you read a broadsheet newspaper each week and keep cuttings about government plans and policies, then you will build up a good resource in order to understand sociological ideas.

◆ What, When and Why?

It is vital that you know when and why theories developed. This means you can understand why the theory might say what it does

What does this mean?

Like all subjects, sociology is constantly changing. It has its fashions and its fads, and as society itself changes so too does sociology. Equally, sociology might actually cause society to change to a certain extent. For example, the original ideas of the founders of sociology contributed to the rise of scientific thinking.

Sociology is also affected by changes in politics, as well as affecting political ideas itself. The New Right, while not a sociological view as such has been incorporated into some sociological thinking. For example, many sociologists have taken on some of the concepts and ideas of the New Right, and this view has made them think again about issues such as welfare spending. Sociology can also influence ideas in politics. Ideas on the 'Third Way' have influenced the ideas of the New Left and the New Labour government.

How did theory develop over time?

Over time we are able to chart the development of different theoretical ideas, although it is important to note that there are some problems with this. The period in which the original ideas developed, and the time they were popular or fashionable are not necessarily the same thing. For example, Marx was writing in the late 1800s, but Marxism in sociology was popular in the 1970s.

Another problem in charting the chronological development of theory is that many writers develop their ideas from other writers. To say that micro sociology was 'invented' in the 1920s in America is true, yet does not take into account that Weber was writing about these issues prior to this point.

We also have the problem that many theories have sub-branches. They can be divided into lots of different types. It is true to say that theories never really 'die out'. It is more likely that they disappear for a bit, and then reappear, maybe with a different name, or maybe combined with something new. Despite these problems, the history of sociological theorising is shown in the following table.

Theory	Description	History
The founders: Comte, Durkheim, Marx, Weber	Now we describe this as modernism. Marx was writing before the other three founders and died in 1883. Durkheim died in 1917. Weber died in 1920.	The industrial era in Western Europe. The first published use of the term sociology was by Comte in 1843.
Early action sociology	Weber and Simmel	Early 1900s
Chicago School	Seen as the development of interactionist or micro sociology	1920s–1960s
Functionalism	Sometimes known as structural functionalism	Associated with Talcott Parsons in the 1950s and 1960s
Pluralism	Associated with American sociology, and closely linked to the ideas of functionalism	1950s and 1960s
Marxism and Neo-Marxism	Although Marx himself contributed to political and economic thought, these ideas did not become popular in sociology until the 1970s	1970s. Also led to the development of what we call various different neo-Marxisms
Feminisms. It is difficult to pinpoint when and how feminist ideas developed as there are so many different sorts. They change and rapidly develop in a short space of time and still continue to do so.	Like Marxism, this was a reaction to the dominance of the functionalist view in the 1960s.	1970s. In the 1990s some writers speak of a feminist backlash; a movement away from or against feminism.
Post-structuralism and postmodernism	Associated with the views of Foucault, Baudrillard and Lyotard	1980s, but popular in the middle 1990s
Structurational sociology	A response to the postmodern ideas of the middle 1990s	Associated with the ideas of Giddens in the late 1990s

Conclusion

Modern day sociological thinking has been characterised by the following changes:

- A movement from macro to micro sociologies and to theories that try and build the middle ground between these two positions.
- A change from a concern with class to the analysis of gender and ethnicity, and to a consideration of how these link together.
- A rising concern with issues of culture and identity. Although these are present in the original ideas of the founders, there is currently a re-consideration of these ideas.

For consideration:

1 Why is sociology affected by the society it studies?
2 How does sociology in turn affect the society it is a part of?

◆ What, When and Why?

The historical pattern of the development of theories has arisen for two main reasons:

1 Theories emerge out of other theories. They either develop as a criticism of a previous idea or as a continuation of a previous idea.
2 Sociological ideas develop as a consequence of the historical context they emerge in. What this means is that sociological ideas do not exist in a cultural vacuum, but instead they are a product of the very society that they seek to explain. For example, it is no coincidence that neo-Marxism developed at a time when the UK was experiencing economic depression, as this raised issues of class in society.

1.10 What are structural theories?

✓ Top Exam Hint

If you can show the similarities as well as the differences between structural and action theories this will help with your evaluation of studies in the exam.

Emile Durkheim (1858–1917)

Karl Marx (1818–1883)

Functionalism and Marxism have had a massive impact on the structural viewpoint in sociology.

What does this mean?

Structural theories look at the big picture; at how society is patterned or 'structured'. Action theories do not look at the big picture, but instead concentrate on the small-scale level of thinking about what individuals do. The relationship between structural and action theories can be seen in two different ways:

1   Structural and action theories are the opposite of each other. In this sense there are two very distinctive and different sociologies that are in conflict with each other in how they see the world around them.

2   Structural and action theories are really two sides of the same coin, and sociology needs them both. We must, in order to get the full picture, look at both how society is structured and how people live their daily lives. Modern day sociology would not be how it currently is without both ways of thinking.

What do structural theories say?

All structural theories start with the view that society is patterned or 'structured' in a particular way. They think that beyond the surface of what society might at first look like, there is an underlying structure that shapes or moulds society in a particular way.

The clearest theories that we might call structural in AS sociology are functionalist and Marxist theories.

*   Functionalism: this theory sees society as being patterned like a living body, made-up of a complex inter-relationship of connecting parts. This is called the organic analogy; comparing society to a living body. Functionalism claims that there is more to society than the sum of its individual parts. In other words, society is the inter-connected whole, the big picture, rather than the individual parts. The socialisation of culture is what allows the whole pattern to function properly, with disorder being compared to sickness in the living body; something dysfunctional that will endanger the stability of the wider structured whole.

*   Marxism: this theory sees society as patterned by a system of inequality that shapes everything that happens. This inequality is the fact that a narrow group of people own the 'means of production', i.e. everything that is needed to make an end product. This structure is

what we call class and it shapes who has power and who is powerless. Marxists refer to this as **economic determinism**.

Structural sociologies see the surface variations and the hidden structure of society to be different from one another. What you see on the surface is the product of unseen, powerful forces. We need to use theories in order to understand these powerful forces, and to see how they control all social life. Structural sociologies see humans as 'puppets of society'. Humans are determined or shaped by these underlying forces that mould their identity, behaviour and the norms and values of the culture of a given society.

Marxists see social order to be based on **social control**, whereas functionalists see social order to be based on **social cement**.

Many sociological theories seek the big picture or the big pattern, and many sociologists do their research with the view that they will try and find out why something happens in relation to the unseen hidden structure moulding what goes on. Structural theories are 'macro' as they are trying to understand the whole of society and how it all links together.

Conclusion

It is probably more helpful to think of sociology (and of society itself) as being both macro and micro – as needing both 'structure' and, on a much smaller level, the 'action' of what people and groups actually do. Therefore, it is important that as students of sociology you pay attention to both structural and action theories – as discussed in the next section of this chapter.

For consideration:

1 What does it mean to see society as having a structure or a pattern?
2 To what extent do you think we are 'determined' or shaped by the society we live in?

❝❞ Key Definitions

- **Economic determinism** is the idea that whoever owns and controls the economy determines (shapes) the rest of how society is patterned.

- **Social control** is where society is dominated by rules laid down by the powerful. Groups in society are made to follow the rules and are punished if they are deviant. The pattern of the structure of society is maintained over time by making people follow the same rules, even if they do not all benefit from them.

- **Social cement** is where society is maintained and the structure or pattern is continued by people being 'bonded together'. We are kept together through the learning of group norms and values that shape who we are and what we do, for the benefit of all.

1.11 What are action theories?

What does this mean?

Action sociologies are those theories that try and look at the small picture. They try and understand why individuals act and interact in the ways that they do. They seek to understand how people see the world around them.

Action theories are sometimes seen as the opposite of the macro structural theories. In this sense, action theories are micro. They are called 'action' theories as they look at what people do on a day-to-day basis.

What are the ideas of action sociology?

Action sociologies start with the following ideas about society:

- Humans make society by inventing the cultural ideas that make society real.

- Humans keep society alive by interacting with each other and sharing symbols.

- Humans cannot 'act' in society without making sense of what they think society is like. In this sense they have 'meaningful action', i.e. they try to make sense of what they are doing and why they think they are doing it.

- Humans are active and creative and they have free-will. Even though the rules and ideas of a society might be laid down before they are born, they are nevertheless able to choose how to act to a certain extent within these rules.

- Humans' sense of what society is like needs to be constantly built-up and reinforced.

- Humans are constantly reflecting upon their actions, and the actions they have with others (their interactions). Humans are constantly asking why things happen; why people behave towards them as they do; what they think they should do, and how they think they should act in different situations.

Why do we need action sociology?

In one sense, we need action theories since they offer a useful 'counter' against the more structural ones, as discussed in the previous section. Whereas the structural theories allow us to see the make-up of society,

The work of Weber, Mead and Becker pioneered the action view in sociology.

general trends and historical changes, the more action theories allow us an insight into how people respond to, and work within these structural patterns. They are two sides of the same coin.

Action theories also allow us to explore more individual issues in research. They allow us to look at people's thoughts, feelings and emotions, how these are shaped by society and how they in turn affect what people do in society.

Conclusion

As we can see, this is a very different image of humans to that held by the structural theories. Structural theories are interested in what society is like, whereas action theories are interested in how and why people think as they do. Modern day theories often seek to work somewhere in between the two, looking at both the big and the small picture.

For consideration:

1 What are the main differences between structural and action theories?
2 Which approach do you think is more realistic in terms of how society is viewed (the structural approach or the action approach) and why?

❋ **Key Ideas**

- The action perspective in sociology sees humans as having a 'self', sometimes called a 'self-image'. This is the idea that humans are active in thinking about who they are.

- Action sociology is often associated with the idea of 'labelling', i.e. that groups or individuals with an authoritative role in society can affect how people might come to see themselves.

1.12 What skills are important for studying sociology?

What does this mean?

In sociology as with other AS and A2 examinations that you will be taking, it is not just simply a question of learning ideas, you also need to manipulate, evaluate and apply these ideas in various ways.

Sociology is marked and assessed according to certain skills, as set out by the examination boards. These skills are called assessment objectives. There are two sets of skills, and evaluation is very important for the second set:

* Assessment objective 1: knowledge and understanding.

* Assessment objective 2: identification, analysis, interpretation and evaluation.

The first set of skills are the main focus for the AS course, and the second set become more important as you move from AS to A2.

How do skills and the exam link together?

Answering exam questions is a skill in itself. It requires you to think in a particular way, and to do the particular things that the question requires you to do.

In the exam, different questions test different skills. Short mark questions test your skills of writing precisely and to the point. Longer mark questions at the end of the exam test your skills in more extended writing.

In order to pass exams, you will need to master the skill of revision (see section 18). Exams are about getting your knowledge out in an appropriate way, therefore revision should also be focused on getting knowledge out, rather than just trying to put it in.

The exams at AS and at A2 level will provide you with source items. Using these in the most beneficial way possible is also a skill; you will need to be able to draw out relevant ideas from the item in order to use these as a stimulus to think about the exam question in detail.

(see section 18)

✓ Top Exam Hints

* Before you answer an exam question, make sure you know what the question asks you to do. Does it want you to show knowledge and understanding, or does it want you to show evaluation and other skills?

* Always look at the author and date of the source item if it is provided. This might help you to put it into context.

It is also important that the examiner is able to read your work and to understand it. This means that exams not only test your understanding of the subject, but also your presentation, spelling and grammar skills.

What other skills are needed?

- Sociology students are often required to handle simple data in the form of graphs, statistics, etc. Such sources will be used by your teachers throughout your course.

- You will need good IT skills in order to study sociology. You will need to word-process coursework and use the Internet to look up information.

- You also need to have the skill of listening. It is very important that in the sociology classroom you are able to appreciate what other people say and their different viewpoints.

- Alongside the skill of listening, you will also need to develop the skill of expressing your own opinion, especially in group discussions or debates.

- As with any other subject at this level, keeping deadlines will be a very important skill for you. It will be important that you stay on top of your work at all times.

- You will also be required to become an independent learner and to take responsibility for your own learning.

Conclusion

As you can see, there are many skills needed to learn sociology. To be able to understand sociological ideas fully, you will need to be able to put them to good use: in lessons, in debates, in homework, for revision and finally in the exam.

For consideration:

1   Which skills do you think are the most important for sociologists to have and why?
2   Which skills do you think are the hardest to develop and why?

✓ **Top Exam Hint**

You should always express a preference over different views, but make sure that you provide reasons why, and that these reasons are linked to the evidence. Do not just give your own opinion and leave it at that.

1.13 What do I need to do throughout my sociology course?

What does this mean?

In order to be as successful as possible in your AS sociology course there are a number of important things you should try and do throughout the course. In many respects, being successful is about getting into the right habits from the start, and making sure that you can maintain these habits over time.

Practical advice

- Keep an up-to-date sociology folder, and make sure that it is organised into topics. This will help you to look back over past work and to revise properly.

- Keep a sociology vocabulary book. This could be either in a separate little notebook, or just some blank paper at the back of your folder. This will help you concentrate on the key words that different theories use, and will be a valuable aid for revision when the time comes.

- The sociology topics you will be studying are usually divided up into smaller sub-topics. At the end of every sub-topic, when you move onto something else, make sure you re-read your notes and seek help if you need it.

- At the end of every sub-topic, summarise all the key ideas so that they all make sense for you ready for revision. One way of doing this is to make a neat and colourful brainstorm diagram (sometimes called a 'mind-map') that will summarise all the ideas, people's names, and most importantly the connections between the different thinkers.

- Make sure you have lots of coloured highlighter pens with you in lessons. These will help you to focus on key information while your teacher teaches you. It is important to make the most of all your lessons and being able to highlight things while you go along will help you to achieve this focus.

- You will find that there are lots of names to remember by the end of every topic. One way of developing good evaluation skills is to make a list of who agrees and disagrees with whom and over what. Ask your teacher to check this, and do it at the end of each topic.

✓ **Top Exam Hint**

An easy way to achieve depth in your exam answers is to use key words. Make sure you do this as it means that you are 'talking in sociological language'.

- Make revision cards all the way through the course rather than leaving it until the very end. When you make your revision cards, try and divide the topics you have been taught into the four essential ingredients of theory, key words, named examples and evaluation. This will be your opportunity to learn about the topic in your own style and personalise your notes so that they work best for you.

- Try to see the connections between the topics that you are being taught. Do not see them as totally separate subjects, they are all sociology and therefore they are all connected.

- Think about synopticity all the way through your course.

Conclusion

Although this is AS level sociology, you still need to think about theory in order to do well.

Technically speaking, the AS actually focuses upon knowledge of studies and sociological language more than it does on theory. However, theory is the thing that places the other bits of knowledge into context. It unites all the studies together and it allows us to think about the ideas and assumptions that lie behind what individual researchers think and do. The words that sociologists use and the things they try and investigate are often triggered by the theories that sociologists hold in the first place.

For consideration:

1 Which of the above advice do you think is the most important to do right from the start of your sociology course and why?
2 Which of the above advice do you think will be the most difficult to keep up over the course of the year and why?

1.14 What do sociologists actually 'do'?

What does this mean?

The answer to the question 'What do sociologists actually do?' might seem obvious, but it is very important in understanding what the point of sociology is and how the subject works.

Sociologists do many different things including the following:

- Localised small-scale research.

- Large-scale research trying to seek patterns or general trends.

- Conduct research in its purest sense, i.e. collect and interpret data.

- Theorise, i.e. seek to answer the bigger questions; the 'what is it like'? questions.

- Conduct research in order to develop someone else's theoretical ideas.

As you can see, there are many possibilities but they all have in common the fact that they are thinking about what society is like and are trying to offer insights into the world we live in.

The study of sociology

Sociology is both theoretical and also **empirical**:

- Theoretical: this is about coming up with ideas that say something about what society is like and how it is made-up. It is about saying what society is really like, not what we assume it might be like.

- Empirical: this is about proving evidence and data for theories.

Sociologists may look at social problems or sociological problems:

- Social problems: these are issues that are of concern to and for society. They include problems such as crime, educational underachievement, inequality, etc. These problems are the issues that governments think about and they might use sociological ideas and data to help them to think about these issues.

- Sociological problems: these are problems that sociologists have in studying society. Sociologists spend a great deal of their time thinking and researching into social problems, but underlying these are problems of theory and method: How can we gain access? What is good data? Where can we find out information? What is truth? These are all sociological problems.

In terms of their day-to-day life, most people who would refer to themselves as 'sociologists' work for a university, a research group, or conduct freelance independent research. Most of the time these people have ideas and insights and test them.

What is sociology for?

A number of criticisms of sociology include the following:

* It is all pointless, it has no real use.

* It is just a lot of long words.

* It is all common sense.

* It just complicates things.

It is certainly true to say that some sociology is quite complicated; but the point of sociology is to look into society in depth, and this is rarely going to be a simple matter. Sociologists do use long words as, like all subjects, sociology uses a technical vocabulary.

The point of sociology is to tell us things we either do not know, or to explain why things happen that we do know about. Even if it does just tell us about things we know, at least this means we are actually right. The point of sociology is to spend time thinking in the first place, not just to assume.

Conclusion

Although different sociologists do things differently, they are all still doing sociology. They are all involved in the production of knowledge for a better understanding of the world around them.

Do sociologists theorise or do they gather data?

For consideration:

1 What do you think the point of sociology is?
2 How useful do you think sociology is?

1.15 What is the specification like for OCR sociology?

It is important that you get yourself a copy of the specification you are following. Ask your teacher or use the OCR website and look up sociology. This will contain everything you need to know about the course you are doing both at AS and A2 level.

What is the difference between AS and A2 level?

The AS is a half way point between the GCSE qualification, and the A2 course. It build on skills and exam techniques developed at GCSE, and it sets the scene for the harder A2 course, and the demands on essay writing that this asks for.

The AS qualification is designed to introduce to you the basics of the subject; the key ideas and the key debates. It places more importance on knowledge and understanding, and less importance on evaluation skills, which become important at A2 level (see section 17).

What themes run through AS and A2 level?

The specifications ask you to think about a number of key themes that run throughout the whole course. These are:

- Socialisation, culture and identity.
- Social differentiation, power and stratification.

These ideas appear in every topic area, and they are some of the most important tools you will need to link all the topics together. This means that in each topic area you study, you will be asked to think about power and about inequality. You will also be asked to think about how the topic treats the idea of how people form identity and what culture does to people.

The skill of knowledge and understanding covers your awareness of what is called 'the nature of sociological thought'. This means your knowledge of the following:

- Theories.
- The relationship between theory and methods.

● **Synoptic Link**
Use these themes and apply them to the different studies that you have been taught in each topic area.

- What sociologists think about social order and social control.

This skill of knowledge and understanding also covers a theme called 'methods of sociological inquiry'. This means that you also need to know the following:

- How sociologists collect data.

- Problems in social research.

- Ethical and moral problems in research.

- How certain topics raise specific problems for research.

What topics come up at AS level?

For the AS exam, you will be studying the following:

- The introductory module on the individual and society.

- Either Family, Media, Religion or Youth culture.

- Methods. There is a coursework option or an exam. Both require knowledge of methods that sociologists use, and the practical applications of how they could be used.

For consideration:

1 What do you think the differences are between the AS and A2 level?
2 How do the key themes link the whole subject together?

♟ Thinking like a Sociologist

Think about the ethics of each piece of research you study. Was the sociologist justified in finding out what they did and how they did it? Often this is a good way to begin to evaluate studies.

✓ Top Exam Hint

As all sociology is about ideas and research, you can bring methods into every topic because each topic poses very particular issues and problems for the sociologist wanting to research them. This is a good way to increase depth in your answers and evaluate the methods used.

1.16 How will I be examined for OCR sociology?

It is never too early to be focused on the exam.

At the end of the AS course you will be sitting either two or three examinations for the AS in sociology.

These exams could be any of the following, depending on what topic areas your teachers have decided to teach you:

*   Unit 1: The Individual and Society. This is made up of two parts:
    *   Introducing the individual and society.
    *   Culture and the formation of identities.
        (In this book these two parts are combined into one single chapter.)

*   Unit 2: Culture and Socialisation. This is made up of the following:
    *   Family
    *   Mass media
    *   Religion
    *   Youth and culture.

    You will be asked to answer two questions in this exam. They can either come from the same topic or from different topics. This decision might be made for you by your school or college depending on how many topics they have taught you.

*   Unit 3: Methods. You will either be asked to sit an exam paper or to conduct a piece of coursework based on evaluating a research report and evaluation. The emphasis is on practical research skills rather than the theoretical basis behind research, although an understanding of both are needed.

How does the qualification work?

All AS qualifications are made up of three units, and all A2 qualifications are made up of a further three units, making a whole two-year course of six units in all.

The points or marks that you get for each unit are weighted by the exam board, and are added together to make a final score for the AS grade. These marks are then added together with the weighted A2 marks for an overall grade. This means that if you take re-sits you can increase your grade (if your school or college allows you to do this).

When are the exams?

Exams take place in January and also in May/June. This means that you may be taught a topic and then sit the exam in it, or sit all the exams at the end of the year.

What does the exam look like?

The exam paper follows the same format for each of the three exams.

- The unit 1 exam is 1 hour long.

- The exam for unit 2 is 1 hour and 30 minutes long.

- If you are doing the research unit exam (and not the coursework) then this paper is 1 hour long.

Papers 1 and 3 are worth 30 per cent of the AS mark, and paper 2 is worth 40 per cent.

Each paper is presented in a slightly different way, and asks you to do different things:

- Unit 1: this paper is made up of two 4-part structured questions. You are asked to choose one question and answer all 4 parts.

- Unit 2: this paper has eight 2-part structured questions. Each of the four optional topics has a choice of two questions. You are asked to answer any two questions. They can be from the same topic, or from two different topics.

- Unit 3: Exam: if you sit the exam you are asked to answer a data response question on the practicalities of research. This is a compulsory question, using the source/stimulus material provided. Research report: if you are doing the report, you are asked to outline and evaluate a sociological study of your choice. This involves reading, analysing and evaluating an existing piece of research and writing a 1000 word report.

For consideration:

1 Do you know what topics you will be sitting?
2 Do you know how your teachers have decided you should approach the course. Will you be doing exams in January or May/June or both? Will you be able to take re-sits?

1.17 What is OCR sociology like at A2 level?

A2 sociology

As well as the AS qualification, you also have the opportunity to take the subject further and do the A2 course in sociology for a further year. The A2 qualification extends the knowledge you gained at AS level. The final exam you sit at A2 level is referred to as the synoptic paper, meaning that it is an opportunity to draw together all that you have learned across the full two years of the AS/A2 course.

At A2 level, you have a choice from the following:

- Unit 4: Crime and deviance, Education, Health, Popular culture, Social policy or Protest and social movements.

- Unit 5: Methods (either a piece of coursework or an exam).

- Unit 6: the synoptic unit (Social inequality and difference).

What are the exams like?

The A2 exams have less short answer questions than at AS level, and ask you to develop full essay writing skills. The A2 year also places a joint emphasis on evaluation and knowledge and understanding.

- Unit 4: this lasts for 1 hour and you have one structured question from a choice of two in each of the optional topics available.

- Unit 5: if you are not doing the coursework option, this exam asks you to answer a compulsory five-part data response question, which includes devising a research strategy. The emphasis is on applying your methodological understanding to a given report. This exam is 1 hour and 30 minutes long.

- Unit 6: this asks you to choose one from a choice of two multi-part data response questions. This exam is also 1 hour and 30 minutes long.

What is the A2 coursework like?

The coursework option at A2 level asks you to conduct an original piece of research using an appropriate sociological tool in order to gather your data. This research could produce primary data (your own) or use the primary data of someone else (making it secondary data for you). It could link to the research report at AS level (if you did it) or could be on something separate.

What is the synoptic unit?

For OCR sociology you will be doing Social inequality and difference as the synoptic unit. This exam asks you to think about sociology as a whole and to spell out links between the following:

- The topics themselves.

- Theories within and between topics.

- Methods and topics.

- The AS and the A2 year.

Is A2 more difficult than AS level?

The answer to this question is yes and no.

- Yes: there are another two topics to learn, plus you might still be taking some AS re-takes. You will also be required to further develop essay skills and your evaluation skills. The A2 exam has some complicated theories to learn, which reflect more about sociology today than those that you may have learned at AS level.

- No: you already have a good understanding of theory and basic sociological ideas. You will also have the basic skills which you will be building on.

For consideration:

1   What do you think will be the most difficult issues at A2 level?
2   How do you think that sociology can help us to better understand social problems?

● **Synoptic Link**
Try to link what you are studying in each topic to issues of inequality and power.

✓ **Top Exam Hint**
Use the theory from the AS year in the A2 year.

1.18 What is successful revision?

What makes good revision?

Many students take revision for granted. They assume that they know what to revise and how to do it. You should think hard about revision; what is the purpose of it, and what are the best ways of going about it?

In order to make the most of your revision, think about how best you learn:

* Do you find writing things down makes them easier to remember?

* Do you need to colour-code revision notes to help you to think about them?

* Do you need to shorten your notes?

We are all different learners, and it is important to find out what works for you by experimenting with different types and techniques of revision.

Some do's

* Undertake active revision, i.e. write things down; do not just read passively.

* Shorten all your notes from your folder and put them onto little index cards ready to revise from.

* Think about evaluation skills while you revise. Practice making lists of how theories and thinkers would criticise each other.

* Practice past paper questions. Get these from your teachers.

Some don'ts

* Do not rely on reading as revision. It is not effective as it is too passive.

* Do not leave sorting out and shortening your notes until the end of the course.

* Do not see revision as a process of putting things into your head. See it as a process of taking things out of your head and putting them onto paper. This is what you will be doing in the exam, so it is what you should be doing in the revision too.

✓ **Top Exam Hints**
* In order to revise, make sure that you link theories to studies and key words or concepts.

Experiment with all these ideas and try and find what works best. Make sure you do this early on in your course. Do not leave revision until the very end of your course. You do not want to be experimenting with revision before the real exam. You should already know what works best for you.

Conclusion

Revise early – don't leave it until the last minute. Usually the AS exams take place from the middle of May onwards – much earlier than the GCSE and A2 exams. This means that you basically have a shorter year to learn AS Sociology than you might think. Given this fact, organise your notes early: make revision notes and, most important of all, make sure you talk to your teachers early on about things you might be a bit unsure about.

Use the CD-ROM with this book to kick-start your revision and you'll be okay. Make sure you also pay attention to the 'top exam hint' boxes in the margins of this book.

For consideration:
1 What advice do you think would work best for you and why?
2 How do you already revise, and how does this link to the dos and don'ts above?

1.19 Examination advice

You might think that the start of your course is too early to start to think about the final exam. However, it is important to be as prepared as possible in order to maximise your chance of getting a good grade. The following general advice will help you to work towards the exams throughout the whole of your course.

- Get a copy of the specification you are following at the start of your course. Make sure that your folder is divided into the relevant topics, and that you have checked with your teachers what topics or units you will be sitting in the exam. Be as clear as possible from the very start.

- Keep a vocabulary book and refer to it throughout the course. This will help you to keep a track of all the technical language that sociology and sociology teachers use.

- Practice past exam questions all the way through your course. You can get these from the website for your exam board. This will help you to focus on what will be expected of you.

- Think about the synoptic links all the way through your AS course. You could colour-code or highlight topics and ideas that link to the A2 topics that you will study.

- Do not throw your AS notes away as soon as you sit the exam. You might need them for re-takes, coursework and for the synoptic unit.

- Put your studies and named examples onto cards. Bring them into lessons as a memory aid.

- At A2 level, go through your cards from the AS course and pick out those that link to the topics you are doing.

- Use the internet and the CD-ROM that accompanies this book to build-up a series of statistics, studies and other information that you can add to relevant lessons and sections of your folder.

- Read a broadsheet newspaper every week and keep a cuttings file of information and stories that are relevant to your course. This will help keep your answers up-to-date, but will also help with your coursework as you will have a ready-made context for your research.

- Word process all your essays/exam answers/homework if you can.

- Read the relevant pages of this book alongside any lessons you have for added depth and detail.

Conclusion

Probably the most important and useful type of revision you can do is practising exam-style questions. You might, nearer the exam, try and time yourself as if it was the real exam. This will avoid you getting a nasty surprise in the exam itself. It doesn't even matter if you re-do old exam questions that your teacher has given you previously. The point is simply that you take the time to practice writing.

Some ideas you could use include:

* Time yourself to make plans for the longer mark questions – 10–15 minutes each. You could do four in one hour.

* Practice whole questions and ask your teacher to mark them.

* Get a friend to choose questions for you at random (you could do the same for them) so it really is an unseen test – just like the exam will be.

Key points to remember

* It is never too early to think about the exams.

* It is never too early to be organised.

* It is never too early to make revision notes.

1.20 Pushing your grades up higher

This section provides some practical advice in order to get the best possible grade you can in your sociology exam. These are general ideas that you can apply to whatever topic areas you might be studying.

1   Start your course with an organised sociology folder and keep it this way. You will be surprised just how important this organisation might be; AS and A2 levels are as much about being organised as they are about hard work.

2   Keep a vocabulary book and always up-date this at the end of each week. Ask your teacher for definitions if you are not clear.

3   Do not just collect key words, use them in homework and in class to make sure you understand them and can use them in the right context.

4   Print off the definitions and key ideas from every chapter (even if you are not studying it) from the CD-ROM that accompanies this book, and keep them as a reference guide in your sociology folder.

5   At the end of each topic, spend some time making revision notes (little index cards are often best for this). You will have to be organised and well disciplined to keep this up, but it will really help when you come to revise at the end of the year. Rather than have to spend time making notes, you can actually get on with the business of learning them instead.

6   List evaluation points for each topic you study. If you put these onto cards at the end of each topic then you can start to learn them.

7   Put all your named examples for each topic onto separate revision cards. You should include what the sociologists did, what they said and what theory they follow (if you know). You can then use these to revise from.

8   For every theory you learn you might:
    *   make 10 bullet-pointed statements about the theory;
    *   identify ten key words the theory would use;
    *   think of four studies to support the theory;
    *   think of four criticisms of the theory;
    *   think of comparisons and contrasts with other theories.

If you do this then you will be able to answer any exam question in-depth.

✓ Top Exam Hints
*   For each study or named example you learn, try and remember the theory and method used, and also the time the study was done.

Key points to remember

- Make sure you are organised right from the start.

- Keep a vocabulary book and use key words as a way of writing in depth.

Frequently asked questions

Q. Why is there so much theory in sociology?

A. Sociology needs theory so that we can try and think about society in new and interesting ways. Theory enables us not to be confused or mislead by what we think is true. We use theories, and 'bounce them off of each other' and by doing this we can try and open up our minds. We all have views; theory is just a way of making them more detailed and then testing them.

Q. What use is sociology in the 'real world'?

A. You have two options open to you; believe what you are told about the world, or find out for yourself. Sociology helps you to do the later, to think about questions and issues you might never have had to think about before. It might seem that all this has nothing to do with the real world, but what you see as the real world might not be 'real'.

Q. Why do sociologists disagree?

A. It is very frustrating when you realise that there are all these theories and they all seem to be saying different things; surely one must be correct? This is how it is with most subjects; there is usually more than one answer and more than one interpretation. It is just that sociology starts people thinking like this much earlier than other subjects do. The disagreement allows us to think about lots of different ideas and this is how the subject moves forward, by disagreement and discussion.

Chapter 2

Sociological research skills and methods

Key issues in research and methods

Why are sociologists interested in research?

Sociology is not just about ideas or ways of thinking about the world; it is also about testing ideas and trying to uncover evidence that might show that some ideas are better than others. In this sense, sociology is not just about theory, but it is also about research. The value of sociology is that it seeks out observations that might not at first seem apparent.

Different sociologists use research in different ways and carry out research for very different reasons.

* Some sociologists collect what we call quantitative data (e.g. numbers, statistics or anything that can be measured). For them, research is about looking at the big picture, making generalisations and trying to find out facts that might relate to a large proportion of society.
* Other sociologists might produce qualitative data (e.g. in-depth meanings or descriptions of peoples' thoughts and feelings). These sociologists are interested in the smaller picture, such as how something is perceived by an individual or a small group of people at a particular moment in time.

What are the key debates in research and methods?

The key debates in understanding why and how sociologists use methods include the following:

* What is data? Why do sociologists want to produce data?
* When should quantitative/qualitative data be collected/used?
* Is sociology a science?
* Is social research value free?
* Should research try and identify trends, or should it look at individual thoughts and feelings?
* What decisions affect research design?
* Why and how do sociologists choose the methods they use?
* What is sampling and why is it important?
* How can sociologists use secondary sources of data?

What are the key ideas and concepts?

There are three key concepts that need to be understood when undertaking research:

✍ Coursework Suggestion

If you do coursework either at AS or at A2 make sure that you use the evaluative tools (is the research valid, reliable and representative?) and be highly critical of what you are doing. Predict any problems you might have in advance, and explain how you will solve them.

1 Theories: ideas and hypotheses put forward to explain something. They are supported by facts, observations and assumptions and can be tested.
2 Methods: the individual tools or techniques of data collection, for example, questionnaires or interviews.
3 Methodologies: the underpinning reasons and philosophies behind how and why a particular sociologist follows the research tradition they adopt.

Positivists such as Comte are interested in looking at research in a scientific way. They aim to uncover social facts and make generalisations or laws (see section 18). Phenomenologists (or interpretivists) such as Weber are interested in **verstehen**, a German word meaning to try to 'see the world through the eyes of those involved' (see section 19).

Many researchers adopt a position half way between these two extremes.

What are the key problems in the sociology of research and methods?

In order to do well in research you must critically evaluate everything. There is no such thing as a perfect method; think about how the research was undertaken and if the claims being made match the evidence and the conditions under which the research was carried out. In order to evaluate research and methods, you can use the following tools.

• Is the research valid? (How true to life are the data collected?)
• Is the research reliable? (Does the research always yield the same results when carried out by different researchers on different occasions, using the same method?)
• Is the research representative? (Can the results of the research be extended to the whole of society?)

There are many problems that a researcher might encounter when undertaking research:

• Practical problems
• Ethical problems
• Theoretical problems
• Sensitivity problems.

These problems are known as PETS. Some might affect the research results, but some might be overcome. You will need to consider any possible problems when making judgements about how successful you think a piece of research is. Remember, as research is about dealing with people, and sometimes a lot of people, it often does not go according to plan, and it is often not perfect.

66 99 Key Definition

Verstehen is the term used by Max Weber to refer to the fact that whereas natural science seeks to test laws and predictions, social science is very different as it tries, in his view, to 'see the world through the eyes of those involved'. Weber was German and *verstehen* is the German word for understanding, or for empathy. In modern-day sociology this idea of verstehen is the aim of micro sociology.

✓ Top Exam Hint

Use the evaluative terms (is the research valid, reliable and representative?) as tools to help you to think about the successfulness of research.

What do we need to know about sociological research?

What does the specification say about methods?

The OCR specification identifies three main aspects of research methods that should be understood:

1 Why would a sociologist undertake research?

2 What types of methods are useful in sociological research?

3 What problems might the sociologist encounter when doing research, and how might they be solved?

You will need to be able to discuss these issues and to use examples of studies made by sociologists to illustrate your points.

How will I be examined in this topic?

There are two options:

1 Examination. This will last for 1 hour. There will be four parts to each question worth 6, 8, 16 and 30 marks, asking you to use the sources provided and to add your own understanding from what you have revised. The questions will ask you to consider a key methods term, to draw ideas from the source and then to evaluate the source.

2 Coursework. This will involve you writing up a research report.

How well does this topic relate to coursework?

All the ideas, skills and concepts you learn in this topic will relate directly to your coursework. Equally, all the ideas about methods you learn at AS level will link to A2 level as well.

How well does this topic help with synopticity?

At A2 level you will be required to 'think around the subject', i.e. to make links between all the different topic areas. Learning about methods is an ideal way to do this as the methods used will be common to all branches of sociology. All sociologists are faced with the same set of problems, the same challenges, the same need to find out about society in a convincing way. This means that the act of research raises common issues that can be used as a way to think about studies and will allow you to compare them.

Conclusion

For the exams, not matter what subject, you might like to think about trying to use methods issues – but only if they are actually relevant! Try and think about *why* sociologists say what they say, and *how* they might come to the conclusions that they do. In other words, try and think about both theory and methods. After all, the whole of sociology is based on them.

Key points to remember

*   At AS level the topic of methods focuses on how to carry out research.

*   You are required to understand how all research contains problems and challenges to be solved.

2.3 How can we find out about the world through research?

How have sociologists used methods to measure the world?

Sociology is not just about having ideas but also about testing them. In order to test ideas, and in order to find out about the world, different methods are used by different sociologists at different times for different reasons.

- Some methods are better suited to studying certain aspects of society than others. For example, participant observation, where the actual process of research is hidden, might be used to study people's everyday behaviour or crime.

- Specialist methods such as content analysis or semiotics are needed to study the media's content.

- Sensitive issues might be best studied using an interview in order to build up trust, or an anonymous questionnaire might mean people do not feel embarrassed to answer questions truthfully.

Using methods to find things out about society involves lots of difficult decisions, and often the method chosen ends up shaping the direction that the research takes. Methods that produce quantitative data (based on numbers) such as questionnaires, will produce different results to methods that are qualitative (in depth discussions).

What methods do sociologists use?

We can identify a wide range of methods that sociologists use in order to try and investigate what society is like:

- Questionnaires: these can be postal, face to face, by telephone or by e-mail.

- Interviews: these can be structured or semi-structured, allowing the researcher to 'go off the point' and allow the person being interviewed to raise issues of their own.

- Group interviews: these are called focus groups, where people are asked to participate in a group discussion about a focused topic.

- Content analysis and semiology: this is where media text and pictures are analysed in order to try and understand the messages within them and meanings behind them.

- Observation: this can be either covert (hidden) or overt (open) and the observer can either participate with those being studied, or can stand back from them.

Many sociologists today mix methods together, using one main method and backing it up with a second method, carried out in less detail, in order to help support or evaluate the findings of the first. Sociologists often make good use of secondary sources which can be either quantitative, such as official statistics from the government, or qualitative such as diaries, letters, etc. A researcher might try and combine both quantitative and qualitative methods together in order to get a much fuller picture, adopting a scientific and also a more interpretive approach within the same study. Much modern day research is undertaken from a position in between the two extremes of sociology, namely positivist and phenomenologist.

Key points to remember

- All methods have both their strengths and weaknesses.

- Good research involves predicting problems and trying to solve them, and making sure that the best, most suitable method is chosen in relation to the topic studied.

- Many sociologists today mix methods together.

✴ Key Idea

Mixing methods together is sometimes called 'methodological pluralism' or 'triangulation'. In other words, it is about using one set of results to compare with, support and evaluate another set. A great deal of modern research works like this, to the extent that the traditional divide between being either 'scientific' or 'non-scientific' is often blurred.

✍ Coursework Suggestion

During your coursework always try to predict problems you may encounter before they happen. Then explain all the possible solutions you can think of to these perceived problems. Good sociological research will comes up with inventive practical solutions to the problems of finding out about people and their lives.

2.4 Why do we do research in sociology?

What does this mean?

Research is the process of exploring and gathering evidence. There are two main reasons for a sociologist to undertake research:

1 To build theories: in this type of research the sociologist seeks to uncover data that will help in the creation of an idea of a theory. The sociologist usually has an idea about what is going on, but they will seek data that point towards an explanation for why things are as they are.

2 To test theories: in this type of research, the theory or idea has already been suggested, and the data are gathered in order to see if the idea is true.

Theories allow us to think about the world we inhabit. They allow us to think through why things are as they are, or why things might be different from how they actually seem. Theories are critical; they seek to question, to assess and to ask why. Sociologists undertake research in order to support theories, to prove them, disprove them, and to find out why and how society works.

What is the role of the sociologist in research?

If we consider the role of the person undertaking the research, there are two broad approaches to sociological research:

1 The sociologist as 'expert': in this approach the sociologist gathers the data and is able to uncover the truth as to why things are as they are. The sociologist sees what others in society cannot see because they have the big, overall picture. The sociologist in this view is often seen as a scientist or a detective, trying to find out what is really going on, despite what people in society might think.

2 The sociologist as 'reporter': in this approach the sociologist allows those studied to be the experts on their own lives, and the sociologist takes a back seat, promoting, asking questions, and letting people explain how they see their own lives and the world around them.

Is the sociologist inside or outside?

When undertaking research, you must think about the relationship of the researcher to those they are researching. Is the sociologist 'inside' the group, i.e. part of them and their lives, or is the sociologist separate, i.e. researching from a distance?

- Inside: the sociologist is part of what is being studied. Sociologists are human, and they study humans, so they cannot detach themselves totally from their customs, values and culture. This is often helpful as it means you are quick to understand those being studied and can build relationships with them. This might also be a problem since you might let your own up-bringing affect how you view the evidence.

- Outside: the sociologist is often described as 'outside' as they are researching people from different backgrounds to themselves. This can be helpful as you have to sit back and let your subjects tell you what they think. However, can anyone ever truly understand someone else's life? People are often too distanced to fully be able to appreciate how others live and feel. Equally, if you are too dissimilar to those you are studying they might not trust you, and you might not be able to build up the sort of relationship needed to fully understand them.

The central problem to overcome is whether to be inside or outside your research. It should be easy to find out what others think because you are human like them, but it is often difficult for this very reason.

Conclusion

All sociological research rests ultimately on the assumption that the world of society, of other people's thoughts, of what people do in their daily lives is worth investigating, and also that it is actually possible to 'know' what the world is like. In order to investigate the world, different sociologists adopt very different ways of finding things out, i.e. they use different methods in their research.

For consideration:

1 How does research make sociological ideas more justified?
2 What do you think the problems of research might be for a sociologist, given they are part of the world being studied?

※ **Key Ideas**

- Sociologist Ray Pawson talks of the existence of an 'imposition problem' in social research, i.e. you might end up interpreting what you want in your data without realising it. This is because it is very difficult to distance yourself from the process of research. You set the questions, decide who to talk to, and in the end, because of this, decide in part on what the results will look like.

- We use the word 'epistemology' to refer to the idea that something can be 'known' and that there might be a wide range of different ways to find out about it.

2.5 What are validity and reliability?

What is validity?

When sociologists talk of research being 'valid' they mean that the measurement or technique (method) used to collect the data actually measures what it sets out to measure. Some sociologists make a distinction in research between two types of **validity**:

1 Criteria validity: this is when a concept used in a piece of research should closely link to the real life events it is supposed to relate to. For example, if you were to study 'class' and ask people about their levels of income, this would be valid since these two factors (class and income) would sensibly be related in the real world. However, if you were to measure class by asking people about their favourite football team, this has no validity since football supporting is not a sensible measurement of one's class.

2 Construct validity: this is when measurement of an aspect of social life allows you to make correlations between this and other aspects of social life that you would think are related. For example, you might predict that it would be possible (if your data and measurements were valid) to correlate class with one's lifestyle, type of house and type of car, as class would cause (determine) these things.

In order to check for validity, it is vital that **operationalisation** of concepts takes place early on in the research process.

A key problem with the validity of any piece of research is that often the same question asked to different people (be it from a questionnaire or an interview) might be interpreted to mean a different thing. Can you therefore guarantee that you are comparing the same thing? Are you studying the same thing, or are you assuming a likeness that does not exist in real life?

What is reliability?

If something is 'reliable' it means that the results would have been produced in the way they were no matter who did the actual carrying out of the research. In other words, the research could be carried out again by someone else and the same results produced. As with validity, there are two ways to measure **reliability**:

1 Temporal reliability: this is when the same research is carried out after a period of time, and the same results are produced.

❝❞ Key Definitions

- **Operationalisation** is the process whereby key concepts are clearly explained and defined so that it is obvious to other people what the sociologist means by the concept. For example, if you were to study class, what do you mean by this? What you mean by the term will shape how you study it.

- **Reliability** means a piece of research that can be repeated with the same results.

- **Validity** means true to life.

2   Comparative reliability: this is when two different studies are compared using the same method on the same or different samples, or different methods are used on the same or different samples, and yet still the results are the same.

How do reliability and validity relate to data gathering?

In general, quantitative data are presumed to be high in reliability and low in validity, whereas qualitative data are usually high in validity and low in reliability. In other words, methods that seek to produce a large amount of data tend to be best judged by the replication of the data to see if it holds true, whereas methods that seek small-scale but high depth data tend to be best judged as to whether or not the research is a true reflection of the lives of those involved at the time.

Conclusion

Many sociologists seek to combine methods in order to produce both quantitative and qualitative data, thus trying to make their research stand up to both standards of validity and reliability.

For consideration:

1   Which do you think is more important, validity or reliability?
2   What issues or aspects of society do you think would create the most problems for validity and reliability?

✓ Top Exam Hint
Use the ideas of validity and reliability to raise evaluative questions about a study or a piece of research. Also use them to evaluate different research methods; how valid or reliable might different methods be and why?

What types of data do sociologists produce?

What does this mean?

Data are simply pieces of information. This information is gathered through the act of doing research; it is the end product of using a research tool such as a questionnaire or an interview. There are two different types of data that research might produce:

1   Quantitative data

2   Qualitative data

When applied to research traditions, quantitative data are used by positivists (who look at society at a macro level), and qualitative data are used by phenomenologists (interpretivists) who look at micro sociology.

Using different types of data

As we have seen, quantitative data are associated with techniques that are high in reliability and low in validity, i.e. techniques that produce results that can easily be repeated by another researcher. Since these data are produced in number form, they are often associated with what positivists call 'social facts' (underlying patterns of social reality that exist as real things). Quantitative data are produced by techniques such as questionnaires and structured interviews and often sociologists use official statistics produced by the government to back-up their research. **Sampling** is very important in this type of research as the researcher needs to be able to generalise from their findings.

Qualitative data are associated with techniques that are high in validity and low in reliability, i.e. techniques that explore the world 'as it is' and discover meanings and motives.

Many sociologists try and combine the use of both quantitative and qualitative data together. This approach is often called methodological pluralism or **triangulation**. The benefits of this are that a sociologist can use one type of data to support their findings from the other type. For example, in a famous study looking at the Moonies (a religious movement) Eileen Barker (1984) mixed together the methods of questionnaires, in-depth interviews and observation. Equally, sociologist Valerie Hey's (1997) work on female friendship groups in school uses a mixture of focus group interviews, participant observation and the use of qualitative secondary sources such as life documents (diaries and classroom notes).

66 99 Key Definitions

- **Sampling** is the process of selecting a part in order to judge the characteristics of the whole.

- **Triangulation** is the idea that sociologists can mix methods together from different traditions in order to achieve a fuller, more rounded picture of society.

✳ Key Idea

Meaning and motives are major elements in the micro sociology. All human action is seen to be meaningful or based upon an underlying motive (a reason behind the action). The aim of qualitative sociology is to get at these meanings and to see how people make sense of their world.

Evaluating types of data

Feminist sociologists place a great deal of importance upon the creation of qualitative data. Many feminists such as Anne Oakley have argued that in order to make sure we support what we study, we should reject quantitative research in favour of more qualitative research. This is because quantitative research reduces individual people to numbers and statistics rather than trying to genuinely understand each person's experiences in their own right.

Some qualitative techniques raise ethical and sensitivity issues in a way that quantitative methods might not. For example, in-depth interviews might explore the private feelings of an individual, making them feel open, vulnerable and even exploited.

Conclusion

Data is essential and central to all that sociologists do. Data is what we use to think about the world. Our data might either be used to create new ideas, or to test existing ideas. Often, as social research is a 'messy' business, the data we get isn't quite what we expected it to be. On the other hand, sometimes we find what we went looking for since we have structured the research in the first place.

For consideration:

1 Which do you think is the best type of data to produce, quantitative or qualitative? Why?
2 How might the nature of the topic being studied affect the type of data a sociologist produces?

● Synoptic Link

Using the feminist view on quantitative data you can make some important evaluations of macro theories in whatever topic area you are studying. This will not only improve your evaluation skills but also allow you to link different parts of the course together.

✓ Top Exam Hint

Evaluate research studies by thinking about the ethical and sensitivity issues they might raise.

2.7 How and why do sociologists use questionnaires?

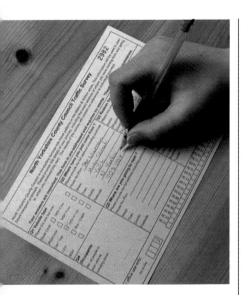

Why do sociologists use questionnaires to gather data?

What does this mean?

Questionnaires are lists of questions administered either face to face with an interviewer, by telephone, by e-mail or by post. Sometime questionnaires might be given to people to complete on their own, or sometimes an interviewer might ask the questions and the responses are written down on a standardised form. All the people taking part in the research will be asked the same questions so that comparisons can be made. Postal surveys have a high non-response rate, whereas questionnaires where interviewers need to be employed cost more money but have a higher response rate.

There are four main types of questionnaires in social research:

1 Factual surveys: these gather information about features of people's lives, rather than asking for opinions or thoughts.
2 Attitudinal surveys: these ask people about their views on certain issues.
3 Social psychological surveys: these developed out of attitudinal surveys and concentrate on asking people about their thoughts in order to try and group people into personality types.
4 Explanatory surveys: these are surveys that are designed to test a **hypothesis** which suggests a relationship exists between two factors. This type of research tries to use questionnaires to show how one set of factors causes something else to happen (causality).

Why are questionnaires used to collect data?

There are six main reasons why questionnaires prove popular with sociologists who want to produce quantitative data:

1 Questionnaires can be used to test theoretical ideas using a hypothesis.
2 Statistics can be produced and analysed thus making sociology more 'scientific'.
3 Generalisation from the sample can take place.
4 Causality between variables can be measured.
5 Standardisation of question allows for measurement and comparison between responses.
6 The findings can be replicated and bias can be checked.

What types of questions can be asked?

Different questionnaires use different types of questions:

- Open questions are where people are asked for their view and have a blank space to say/write what they feel.
- Closed questions are where people are restricted in the type of answer they can give. The question may require a simple 'yes' or 'no', or it might ask for a 'graded response' for example, strongly agree/agree/disagree/strongly disagree, etc.

There are four main types of questions asked in questionnaires, and they are used for different reasons:

1 Classification questions: these are questions about who the person is, so that they can be classified and their answers compared with others of a similar type. These questions might ask about occupation, age, income, etc. and allow the sociologist to gather information for their **explanatory variables**.
2 Factual questions: these are questions that ask for answers that do not involve an opinion, i.e. How many times do you go to church each week? What TV programmes did you watch last night? etc.
3 Opinion questions: these are questions that ask someone what they think about something, i.e. Which TV programme do you think is the best? What clothes do you like the most?
4 Attitude scales: these are statements that the respondent can agree or disagree with. They are used in order to test and compare views and attitudes to certain issues.

Questions should be simple to understand, clear and well laid-out and should only ask about things that can be accurately measured.

Weaknesses of questionnaires

- Questions are set by the sociologist and so might 'impose' their biases onto the research.
- The questions used might simplify important issues by reducing thoughts and feelings to a 'tick box' answer.
- Questionnaires might not be returned if they are self-completion without an interviewer present.
- People might interpret the same question differently; one person's 'strongly agree' might be very different to another's.

66 99 Key Definition

Explanatory variables are characteristics that might cause or explain why the person answers a question as they have. These are key sociological concepts such as class, gender, age, location, ethnicity, etc. This type of data is collected through the type of questions we call 'classification questions'.

✳ Key Idea

Questionnaires often suffer from an 'imposition problem'. This is because as the sociologist chooses the questions in the first place, they are imposing their own views on the answers people can give. They are limiting some responses, ignoring others by simply not asking questions about certain things, and therefore they are finding the answers they want because they are asking the questions they want to in the first place.

For consideration:

1 Do the strengths outweigh the weaknesses of the questionnaire method?
2 What areas of social life would most suit using questionnaires?

How and why do sociologists conduct interviews?

What are interviews?

An interview involves someone being asked questions. They are usually taped as the answers might go into a lot of depth. Different types of interviews can be classified as follows:

- Structured interviews (formal interviews): a formal set of questions are asked and the interviewer cannot ask extra questions. This means that comparisons can be made because there is standardisation of questions.
- Unstructured interviews (informal interviews): no lists of formally pre-arranged questions exist, and the interview itself is open and flexible. The person being interviewed (the interviewee) is able to say what they feel, as directed by the interviewer. This type of interview usually lasts a long time, and might occur over more than one session. These interviews must be taped in order for the researcher to be able to fully concentrate on what is being said at the time, thus making sure that they can keep the questioning relevant.

   It is debatable that a totally unstructured interview can actually exist as the researcher will usually have some initial idea of what sorts of things to listen out for. They will also have decided which question to ask first, in order to start the interview in the first place. Many researchers use semi-structured interviews; a set pattern of questions are asked, but the interviewer can allow answers to bring up new questions not previously thought about.

- Focus groups: a number of people are interviewed at the same time, forming a group discussion. A focus is given to the discussion and an interviewer is usually present to direct and guide participants.

Structured interviews are usually associated with quantitative data and the standardised approach means that patterns can be identified. Unstructured interviews are more qualitative, and they are more difficult to analyse as it is often tricky to isolate key variables. Computer programmes are currently available that can turn qualitative interview data into quantitative data by searching for key words or phrases used in answers.

Why are interviews used?

- Many researchers use interviews as a way to generate qualitative data, exploring in more detail people's thoughts and feelings.

- Feminist sociologists often use interviews as they feel that questionnaires are too **masculinist**, i.e. they categorise people and reduce complex personal feelings to statistics.
- Feminist and more interpretive sociologists use interviews as a form of empowerment, i.e. as a way of helping people to understand their own lives and helping them to reflect upon their own experiences.
- Interpretive sociologists use interviews in order to try and achieve *verstehen*, (to see the world from other people's eyes).
- When dealing with sensitive issues, a degree of trust might need to be established between the interviewer and the interviewee (this would not be achieved with a questionnaire).
- Interviews are often used to support other methods of research: more quantitative methods might be supported by interviews which add a bit more depth to the research.

Strengths and weaknesses of interviews

Interviews are a useful research tool as the interviewer might be able to explain questions to the interviewee and ensure that all the questions are answered. People can have their own say, i.e. they can say what they think is important about their lives, rather than their answers being guided by a researcher.

The interviewer and interviewee can develop rapport, allowing for an honest exchange of material based upon trust. Interviewing should be about building an equal relationship between both the interviewer and the interviewee. There should be a bond of trust that breaks down the obvious unequal power relationship within the interview situation, where the interviewer traditionally has power over the interviewee. The interviewee should also be allowed to ask questions as well as the other way around.

Interviews may be less useful where there is interviewer bias, i.e. where the interviewer directs answers with leading questions, ensuring they get what they wanted to find. Interviewers may 'bully' the interviewee into providing the answer they want to hear. In addition, the ethnicity of the interviewer has been shown to have a dramatic effect on the interviewee. Interviews might not be comparable if different questions are asked as there would be no standardisation. As it takes such a long time to conduct an interview, they are often expensive and this means that not many interviews can actually take place (when compared with numbers of questionnaires that can be collected).

For consideration:

1 Why are interviews a useful research method to use?
2 Do you think that interviews allow sociologists to give power to those they study?

66 99 Key Definition

Masculinist is a word used by feminist sociologists to describe non-feminist sociology that is often quantitative and positivist in nature. It is research that categorises people and tries to see patterns in society beyond the experience of the individuals who make up the sample used in the research. Feminist sociology tries to build up personal relationships with those they study since this is seen as less exploitative.

Coursework Suggestion

You can use interviews for coursework at A2 course. If you do, make sure you give consideration to any power inequalities in the interview; are you really letting people speak for themselves? This will help you to evaluate what you are doing.

Thinking like a Sociologist

When you conduct or use interviews in your research, discuss the following points:

- The way the interviews allow for *verstehen*.
- The feminist use of interviews.
- How ethnicity might affect the outcome of the interview.

How and why do sociologists observe?

What does this mean?

Observation is the term given to the situation when a sociologist watches what goes on, and makes notes about the relationships, actions and events that are seen. Observations can be either quantitative or qualitative.

*   Quantitative observation: this is where use is made either of a pre-coded checklist or the creation of a **sociogram**. A record is made of what happens and this record is linked to categories that the researcher has pre-decided upon. These observations can then be presented as quantitative data, and observations can be compared. The danger with this method is that different observers might 'see' the same observations in different ways, making comparison less objective.
*   Qualitative observation: this is where a narrative or story of the situation is created, often associating events with the time they took place.

Traditionally observation is associated with the interpretive sociological perspective. This form of sociology aims to understand, from people's own view points, what they do and how and why they do it. Interpretivists feel that since society does not exist separately from people (but is actually created by people's thoughts and feelings and how they interact with others) this interaction should be studied first hand.

Types of observation

Different sociologists use observation in different ways:

*   Participant observation: this is where the observer joins in with those being studied.
*   Non-participant observation: this is where the observer steps back and observes those being studied from the outside.
*   Covert observation: this is secret observation where those being studied do not know that they are being observed. This is often seen as an unethical research method as those who are taking part are not aware that they are doing so, and as a consequence cannot give their **informed consent** to the research.
*   Overt observation: in this situation, those being studied are aware of the fact that they are being observed. The researcher may take the part of a member of a focus group (this often happens with ethnographic research), or may remain at a distance making notes such as in classroom observations. A well known problem with overt observation is what we call the **Hawthorne effect**.

❝❞ Key Definitions

*   A **Sociogram** is a diagram that shows the lines of interaction and communication between people. It allows you to see who talks to who and how often.

*   **Informed consent** is when people know that research is taking place and are aware of what it is about, what it will be used for and what their level of involvement will be. They have the right to refuse to take part.

*   The **Hawthorne effect** refers to the idea that the presence of an observer will alter the outcome of that being observed, if those being observed are aware of it. This problem has been given this name after a piece of research on the Hawthorne factory plant in the USA by sociologist Elton Mayo (1933) who found that workers' productivity increased dramatically when they knew they were being observed.

✳ Key Idea

The British Sociological Association (BSA) state that research should involve informed consent. They also state that researchers have a responsibility towards research participants to ensure that their well-being is protected at all times. The problem with covert methods of observation is that after the event, some people may feel lied to, spied on and cheated. In all types of research, sociologists enter into personal relationships with those they study. These relationships should be genuine and not based upon deceit.

- Experimental observation (artificial): this is where the situation being studied is created by the researcher themselves, with the sole purpose of allowing observation to take place. This might involve the use of two different groups to observe; the control group who are allowed to act freely, and the experimental group who have been controlled or changed in some way. A comparison can then take place between the two. This observational situation is often criticised for being too artificial as it does not tell us about how people behave in the real world.
- Field observation (natural): this type of observation occurs in social situations where the sociologist makes use of interactions and group encounters that would normally exist in society, without the sociologist having to actually create them in the first place. This gives the sociologist a direct understanding of real life situations, although the nature of what takes place might still be influenced by the presence of an observer if the method is overt.

Strengths and weaknesses of observation

The strengths of observation methods include the following:

- They provide a means for the sociologist to see first hand what people do and how they do it.
- Sociologists can achieve a sense of *verstehen* through observation. They can feel what it feels like to be a member of a group.
- If using covert methods, researchers can observe natural behaviour.
- The methods usually produce valid data.

The weaknesses of observation methods include the following:

- If the method is covert in nature, some observation might be dangerous for the researcher (especially if those in the group are engaged in dangerous or criminal behaviour).
- The researcher might 'go native', i.e. it might be hard to distance oneself from the group and therefore not be able to observe in an independent way.
- It might take time and lots of funding to maintain observation.
- The method raises serious ethical questions, do we have the right to observe particular situations?
- It might be very difficult to record information (especially if covert methods are used).

✍ **Coursework Suggestion**

If appropriate in your coursework, discuss the BSA ethical guidelines as part of your evaluation of observation methods.

For consideration:

1 Why is observation a useful method for sociologists?
2 Do you think that informed consent with covert observation is an important ethical rule or not?

2.10 How and why do sociologists use secondary sources?

What does this mean?

There are two types of data:

1   Primary data: these are data collected by the sociologist themselves; without this original research the data would not exist.
2   Secondary data: these are data that exist prior to and independent from the sociologist's own research, and that would still exist even if the sociologist did not do their own research in the first place. Secondary data can be either quantitative or qualitative in nature.

Secondary data can come from a variety of sources:

*   Official statistics: these are statistics produced by government bodies.
*   Unofficial statistics: these are statistics produced by charities etc.
*   The mass media: news stories can be used as a source of information, or research can be conducted into the content of the news and media in general.
*   Life documents: these are personal records of thoughts and feelings such as diaries, etc.

Why are secondary sources useful?

Secondary sources can be used as a source of data to support the findings of a piece of research or can be studied in their own right as the sole purpose of a piece of research. Secondary sources can offer a quick and easy way for sociologists producing one type of data to compare their findings with other data, either more quantitative or more qualitative than their own study.

Some sociologists use secondary sources because it is interesting to explore how and why they were created as data in the first place. For example, interpretive sociologists associated with an anti-positivist, phenomenological methodology might use secondary statistical data, but they would use it in a very different way to quantitative positivists. While the positivists would use the data as facts to indicate general patterns and trends, the phenomenologists would ask critical questions of the data, such as the following:

*   Where does the data come from?
*   How was it collected?
*   Who collected it and what did they intend to do with it?

- Why did the sociologist draw the conclusions they did from the data they had?

Phenomenologists would agree that statistical secondary data does tell us something useful about society; they allow us to see how people construct data. This tells us about what the people who made the data were thinking.

Most, if not all research uses secondary data of some sort, since most research is not done in a vacuum, either a vacuum from society or from sociology:

- **Society**: all sociologists start with a problem or research question they wish to explore, these thoughts do not just simply appear out of nothing. Media, statistics from the government, etc. would point towards an interesting topic for investigation, therefore secondary data and sources provide the initial idea to start a piece of research.
- **Sociology**: all sociologists think about what research other people have done into the topic that they themselves are researching into. A major requirement of all research (and of your coursework) is to undertake a 'literature review' which forms the context or the background to what you do. In this sense, therefore, all research involves a consideration of other research, i.e. of secondary data.

Strengths and weaknesses of secondary sources

The strengths of using secondary data sources include the following:

- They are cheap and easy to collect.
- They are a useful way to obtain a historical perspective on research you are doing.
- You can use these data to compare with your own primary data for added depth.
- They may help to make cross-society comparisons with your own data.

The weaknesses of using secondary data sources include the following:

- If you do not know how the data were collected, then it is very difficult to know how valid and reliable the data is.
- You will not know how biased the researcher might have been.
- You will not know if personal life documents really are true or are simply one interpretation of events that might have happened.
- Much research takes place with its own political biases; you may not know if the research was originally intended to attack the government or support them.
- You may not know who funded the research and how this might have influenced its creation.

> ### For consideration:
> 1 How useful do you think secondary sources really are?
> 2 What warnings come with the use of secondary sources?

✓ **Top Exam Hint**

The critical questions that interpretive sociologists ask of quantitative secondary data highlight the sociologist's mistrust of data, and the idea that sociologists should question everything around them, including so-called facts produced by other sociologists. Try to be this critical in your exam; question everything, every piece of research and every piece of data you come across.

● **Synoptic Link**

Use the idea that you can question how statistics are created in the crime and deviance or stratification topic area at A2 level.

✍ **Coursework Suggestion**

Use a secondary source in your coursework to 'sell your idea' to the examiner, i.e. to make it seem like it is an up-to-date and worthy idea for research in the first place. Make it link to the real world in some way.

What are the problems of official statistics?

What are official statistics?

Official statistics are statistics that have been produced by an official body, usually a government department, or an organisation associated with the government. Non-official statistics might come from such organisations as pressure groups, charities, etc. Sociologists themselves may be involved in the creation of these official statistics, since they might be funded by and employed by the government. Many sociologists use official statistics as a secondary source.

How can sociologists use official statistics?

There are a number of reasons why sociologists might need official statistics as a secondary source:

* Sociologists use official statistics as a comparison with research they themselves have produced. It might help to be able to compare the findings of a micro piece of research with a larger macro set of results.

* Sociologists use official statistics as a way to compare their own quantitative research with that from another source.

* Official statistics can be used in the comparative method; sociologists can obtain data from a wide variety of nations and can then seek trends and patterns between them.

* Many qualitative sociologists use official statistics, but in a very particular way. They argue that since these statistics are not facts, but are **social constructions**; we can use them to understand more about the assumptions behind their making, but they do not tell us anything about society. They tell us about the views of the people who made them and who claim they are real in the first place.

Strengths and weaknesses of official statistics

The strengths of using official statistics include the following:

* They are often easily available.

* They can give the sociologist a sense of historical perspective.

* They are inexpensive to use.

* They will allow easy comparisons to be made between different societies.

66 99 Key Definition

A **social construction** is not a fact, it is not real, it is something that only seems real because it has been made to appear so in the first place. Things we take for granted in society and see as normal only seem this way because society and culture says it should be like this in the first place.

- They allow hypotheses to be tested.
- Sociologists might be able to get information about aspects of society that they would otherwise not have any information about.

The weaknesses of using official statistics include the following:

- You do not know the circumstances under which the statistics were created (this is often true for secondary sources).
- Statistics which come from governmental sources might be politically motivated, for example, the figures might be changed in order to make the government look better than they are.
- Statistics do not readily show us how they were constructed in the first place. How valid and reliable are they?
- You do not know how the statistics were collated, how large the sample was, or even how the sampling took place.
- The method used to measure official statistics might change over time. This might alter the patterns and trends being claimed. This is especially true of government statistics, for example, unemployment figures or crime figures.

Qualitative (interpretive) sociologists make the point that official statistics are in fact useful, but only if we use them in the right way and for the right reasons. They do not tell us about 'factual social reality'. Instead, they give us an insight into the complex basis upon which such statistics are actually created in the first place, and how and why they are created.

Conclusion

Official statistics, like any secondary source, have advantages and disadvantages to their use. As long as you are aware of these, they will provide a useful tool for the sociologist. In fact, the many problems with such statistics are themselves objects of sociological investigation.

For consideration:
1 Why are official statistics criticised by some sociologists?
2 Why are official statistics still potentially useful to the sociologist, despite the criticisms?

2.12 How can sociologists use life documents?

What does this mean?

Life documents are secondary sources that involve the expression of feelings, emotions and thoughts that are used in everyday life. They are personal documents and sources that have been created not for the purpose of research, but during the course of ordinary life. Examples of life documents include the following:

- Diaries
- E-mails
- Love letters
- Post cards from holidays
- Shopping lists
- School-children's classroom notes
- Photographs
- Graffiti
- Letters from readers written to newspapers and magazines.

Life documents tend to be qualitative in nature as they are about what people think, and often how they feel. They are expressions of ideas that might allow a researcher to understand what it means to be someone. In this way, using life documents might be seen to allow *verstehen*.

Strengths and weaknesses of life documents

The strengths of using life documents include the following:

- They are an interesting and unusual source, adding variety to a piece of research.
- They are valid. They are a rich and ever-present source of documentation of ordinary social life that allows a researcher to see 'how it really is'.
- They pre-exist the sociologist, and therefore are not expensive to collect.
- They are created normally in social life, not simply as part of a piece of research. They are therefore authentic, not artificial.
- They are a good source of qualitative data, they tell us about emotions.
- They allow for *verstehen*, i.e. to see how people think about the world they live in.
- If combined with other methods, they help to provide a fuller picture. For example, if combined with questionnaires, they add a sense of personal feelings and depth not obtainable through questionnaires.
- They allow historical comparison.

The weaknesses of using life documents include the following:

- They may be difficult to obtain.
- You might not know the conditions under which they were written.
- They might not be true (sometimes people write fantasies in diaries rather than actual experiences).
- They are a selective perception. Did it really happen in the exact way expressed, or is it a matter of interpretation?
- Since they are so individual it is difficult to use them for generalisation.

Using life-documents

Max Weber (1905), in his study of Calvinist Protestants, made good use of diaries in order to try and explore the feelings and thoughts of this religious group. This allowed Weber to gain some important historical data, which may otherwise have been lost. In *The Protestant Ethic and the Spirit of Capitalism* he concluded that this group accidentally laid the foundations for the creation of capitalist values in Europe. They believed that through hard work people would receive signs from God suggesting that they were chosen to go to Heaven. They also thought that Catholic groups were too decadent, i.e. they spent too much money. This combination of hard work, seeking profit in business, and then re-investment into the business to avoid spending on personal luxury, created the capitalist values of profit-seeking and reinvestment. Weber explored these ideas by being able to 'get into the minds' of this historical group through their diaries.

A more contemporary use of life documents can be found in the ethnographic study by Valerie Hey (1997) *The Company She Keeps*. Hey was interested in exploring the ways in which school girls thought about and created friendship groups. She wanted to understand how gender and sexual identities were expressed and created through interaction and the sharing of thoughts and feelings amongst 'friends'. In order to explore this very personal issue, Hey used a mixture of methods including participant observation, interviews and the collection of notes passed between girls in lessons behind the teachers' backs. Hey suggests that these notes were important as they were the physical expression of how the girls tried to explore and think about sexuality, gender, being a girl and friendship (these were the most common themes found in the notes). In order to be able to collect these data Hey had to gain the trust and friendship of the girls, and even swapped her own personal diaries in order to share thoughts and feelings.

Secret notes might make interesting life documents

✍ **Coursework Suggestion**

You can use life documents to investigate school-children's thoughts about school. Use diaries, graffiti and classroom notes to see what images of life at school children have. What are their concerns? What themes can you identity? How will you collect your data?

For consideration:

1   How useful do you think using life documents are?
2   Do you think life documents really tell us anything? Are they just meaningless or are they important pieces of data?

2.13 Is sociology a science?

Is it realistic to think of sociology as a science in the same way as we think of chemistry and physics?

66 99 Key Definitions

- A **causal relationship** is a link between two things (variables). One variable is seen to be independent and to affect or cause the other, which is dependent upon the first. This is a basic scientific law; 'if this happens, then this will also happen as a result'. Some sociologists think that with enough quantitative data, these relationships can be uncovered in society. We can identify social facts that cause other things to happen, for example, high unemployment might lead to increased suicide rates. Spotting these links is the aim of positivism.

- **Malestream** sociology is a feminist idea that means the mainstream in sociological thinking, the normal way of going about things, is from a male perspective. Feminists claim that sociology traditionally focuses on male concerns and if women are thought about, it is usually as an afterthought.

✓ Top Exam Hint

Use the idea of malestream as a way to evaluate macro sociology, in particular the methodology of positivism. Try and remember the following short quotes, and use them in the exam:

Ann Oakley (1997): 'Sociology is by men, for men and about men.'

Abbott and Wallace (1997): 'Sociology is at best sex-blind and at worst sexist.'

What does this mean?

The philosopher Paul Feyerabend (1993) argues that there is simply no agreed method that research follows, despite what sociologists and scientists might tell you. Most of the time, research is about solving unexpected problems and rarely ever goes smoothly or according to plan. This means that our search for the 'truth' of society is solely dependent upon the methods we use in the first place; what we find out is a product of how we look, and where we go looking. As long as we recognise this, and as long as we are open about what we did and how we did it, then this is all that matters.

The science of sociology?

The question 'Is sociology a science?' is a long running debate in sociology. There are a number of opinions on this issue:

- Sociology is a science. It can test theories and create laws, and it can seek to uncover **causal relationships**. This view is associated with sociological positivism.

- Sociology cannot be a science because the subject matter of sociology, humans, is very different from the natural world of matter and gases etc. Humans have consciousness and as such they cannot be generalised about. Phenomenologists tend to hold this view.

- Sociology should try and be scientific since science is the best form of knowledge. However, it is impossible for sociology to be so as it tends to simply prove its theories right, and it is reluctant to reject its ideas in the face of the evidence. This view is held by the positivist Karl Popper who argues that sociology is not a science because it does not falsify (reject) theories and seek to disprove them (see section 18).

- Sociology should not be a science as science is a masculinist form of knowledge concerned with categorisation and generalisation, not with trying to understand people (and in particular women) and in doing so, help them and their life situation. This is a feminist view; feminists often reject science as being **malestream**.

- Sociology can be considered scientific, but it depends on what you mean by the idea of science in the first place. Sociology provides a method of choosing between theories by matching theories to evidence and research. As long as research allows you to test theories against each other and it is done in a systematic way, then sociology can be scientific. This is a **realist** position.

Do scientific facts actually exist?

For positivists, scientific sociology is about finding laws, patterns and generalisations. This is done in a detached or value-free way (see section 18). The sociologist is often seen as a detective, seeking to uncover trends and relationships, but one who tests ideas fairly and is not involved with those being studied.

Many sociologists have criticised this positivist approach. For example, phenomenologist or interpretive sociologists argue that facts that cause others things to happen do not exist in society, and they cannot be studied as if they are external to the people in society. Instead, what exists in society are simply ideas which we have as people in the first place. Therefore, it is nonsense to seek causality as if it is separate from people. People think about life and come up with the ideas that we think are 'real' in the first place. Therefore, we should give up macro ideas of generalisation and prediction and concentrate on describing what people make of their own actions, thoughts and their feelings.

A recent, popular view, is that of postmodernism, which argues that the idea that sociology should be a science, and even the idea that being 'scientific' is somehow of value, is a left over idea of a past age. This view says that claims of science being able to seek out a 'truth' that is absolute is a false idea. There are many truths, many viewpoints, and it is impossible to point to one explanation for things happening in society and say that this is the only real reason. If we agree with this idea, the question is what is there left to do? Why do research at all, if its just a matter of interpretation and opinion?

66 99 Key Definition

Realism is the view that sociology can be a science, but only if this means finding ways to test theories against each other. Realists argue that there are real, unseen structures that shape society, but action must be studied as this is what we see. They see sociology as an open system science, i.e. society is unpredictable so generalisations and certainties are difficult to create.

For consideration:

1 If postmodernists are right, and there are no 'facts' then what is the point of research and what is the aim of sociology?
2 Why do you think the debate on whether sociology is a science is so popular for sociologists?

2.14 Is sociology value-free?

What does this mean?

If a sociologist (or anyone) is 'value-free' it means, quite literally, being free from values, views or beliefs. A more detailed, sociological way of saying this would be to say that they would not allow their views and beliefs to alter or affect the research they do. So, being value-free is the same as making sure your research is as unbiased as possible.

If your research is not value-free, your results may be incorrect. The whole point of sociology is to try and uncover or get to the reality of social life. You cannot do this if you are not sure that the results of your research are true and genuine.

Types of values

There are different types of values and beliefs that might affect a sociologist when they do their research:

- Personal values: these are the beliefs you have as an individual; beliefs and ideas that are special to you.

- Cultural values: these are the norms and values you have as a member of society. They might affect how you see your results and even what you think might be worth studying in the first place.

- Political values: many sociological theories are based on political views. They are either left wing (e.g. Marxism) or right wing (e.g. functionalism).

- Academic values: sociology has its fashion and trends just like anything else. Things popular to study in sociology today are different from the past, and will be different again in the future. The sociologist will probably try and fit in with the current trends of sociology, otherwise they may not be funded.

- Research values: as a sociologist you might have a personal preference for a particular method over another. Alternatively, you might belong to a group of researchers who all favour a particular approach that you would then need to follow.

As you can see, there are many types of values to try and be free from and this clearly makes it very difficult to undertake objective research. The image of research as being true and correct is not always valid as there are many influences upon research. There is a belief in our society that science is always right as it is based on research and it tests its ideas. However, how do we know that such research is value-free?

Sociologists have particular problems in trying to be value-free, more so than natural scientists such as chemists, since sociologists are part of the thing they are studying. Sociologists seek to understand society, yet they are members of that society. This makes it hard to be objective, detached or distanced from the values of the culture they were socialised into.

Is it possible to be value-free?

All sociologists want those who do research to be honest about their results. Personal values and cultural values concern sociologists the most. This is because they are often hidden. We can see the methods sociologists may have chosen, and if different sociologists use different methods, this gives us a variety of results to compare. However, the reasons behind why the topic was chosen in the first place, and how and why the research ignores some results and interprets others changes what the research means, but it is a process that is hidden to us.

Conclusion

Howard Becker in an essay called *Whose side are you on?* argued that sociologists should give up the idea of trying to be neutral, and instead should try and actually help the disadvantaged in society. He says we should 'side with the underdog' as he feels sociology should help those who lack power. This view has been adopted by those who follow the theories of Marxism and feminism. They seek to identify who the disadvantaged are and to support them. This is clearly not value-free research.

For consideration:

1 Do you think it is possible to be totally value-free in research?
2 Why do you think many sociologists would want to be seen as being value-free?

✓ **Top Exam Hint**

It is a good idea to focus on practical issues when trying to evaluate sociological research. Time, money, bias, funding, resources, etc. might all affect what you choose to do and how you do it.

✳ **Key Idea**

Max Weber suggests that values come into play the most when the sociologist tries to identify what to study in the first place, and at the end of research when they try and figure out what it all means; to interpret their results. He suggests that all we can do is to announce clearly at the start of our research what our personal values or views might be, and be open about these.

✎ **Coursework Suggestion**

Think about the issue of value-free research when you do coursework. It is a good way of evaluating sources and is vital for good marks.

2.15 What ethical problems do sociologists face?

What does this mean?

Ethical problems in research are problems of morality, where the sociologist doing the research potentially violates or breaks people's trust or affects them through the research in some way. Examples of ethical problems include the following:

- Lying to gain access to people to include in research.
- Not telling the truth about the research you are conducting. This is particularly true for covert research where the sociologist is 'undercover'.
- Putting those you study at personal risk and harm.
- Causing upset and emotional trauma.

Ethical problems are more serious than sensitive issues. For example, a sensitivity problem might involve asking people personal questions that may upset them, whereas an ethical problem would be putting people in danger, or exposing someone's private life to their family.

The problem with informed consent

Sociology would not be possible without people to study as it is the study of society. If society is unwilling to be studied, or if society ends up not trusting sociologists, then damage has been done, to society and to the aims and goals of sociology. The BSA suggests that all research wherever possible should be conducted with informed consent, and those involved in research should:

- Choose freely to be involved.
- Not be harmed in any way.
- Have their privacy respected.
- Understand what they are volunteering for.
- Understand they can say 'no' at anytime.
- Understand what the point of the research is.

The problem with this is that sometimes, by knowing you are being studied, you might behave very differently. This creates a real tension in research; having to inform people what you are doing will contradict with not letting them know so you can obtain the 'truth'.

Do we have the right to know?

The problem with ethics in sociology is that sociologists are self-appointed searchers for the truth. Someone usually funds research, and sometimes charities and the government might ask a sociologist to find something out for them, but society as a whole has not asked the sociologist. You have chosen to study sociology, but why should this give you the right to uncover people's personal and private lives? Why should you be allowed to pry? Do you have the right to find out what you want to know?

✔ **Top Exam Hint**

Discuss ethical issues in order to evaluate any research that uses covert methods such as observation. This will help you to score evaluation marks in the exam.

✍ **Coursework Suggestion**

Make sure you include a discussion on ethical issues when you do coursework. Think about the idea of informed consent. How will you manage this?

Covert research methods have particularly been criticised for their lack of ethical consideration. To find out some things, sociologists might have to ensure that those being studied do not know about it, to gather the clearest data. But is this morally right? Why should someone use other people (without asking) in order to further their own career? Sociologists who use covert methods respond by arguing that sociology makes a positive contribution to the knowledge society has about itself, and therefore as long as anonymity is maintained the ends justify the means.

Other sociologists suggest that if informed consent is not present at the start of a study, then a full de-brief should be present at the end. But is this good enough or has the damage been done already?

What do you think?

Consider the following study, published in 1970, by American researcher Laud Humphreys. Humphreys conducted an infamous study that created a lot of press attention at the time called *The Tea Room Trade*. 'Tea-room' was, at the time, a sub-cultural word used by gay men to refer to the public toilets where gay men would meet each other and engage in sexual activity. At the time, homosexual acts were illegal in the USA. Humphreys covertly studied these activities, at the same time taking on the role of the 'watch-queen', the lookout in case the men got caught. He also noted the men's car number plates, managed to find out where they lived, followed them home, interviewed them on the pretence of it being about something else and published his study.

There were a number of different responses to this research:

- Humphreys gave a voice to people whose sexuality was illegal and in doing so, raised attention to this discrimination.
- Humphreys should not have lied to these people since he was studying them breaking the law.
- Humphreys should not have taken it on himself to help these people, they did not ask him.
- Kimmel says about Humphreys' research 'the research was applauded by members of the gay community and some social scientists for shedding light on a little known segment of society, and for dispelling stereotypes and myths'.
- Warwick says about Humphreys' research 'social research involving deception and manipulation ultimately helps produce a society of cynics, liars and manipulators, and undermines the trust which is essential to a just social order'.

Do you think Humphreys conducted his research in an ethical way?

For consideration:

1 Why might ethical problems affect research that is more qualitative than quantitative?
2 Do sociologists really have the right to find out? Should covert methods ever be used?

2.16 What is sampling and why is it important?

How are people selected to take part in research?

66 99 Key Definitions

- A **sample** is a small part taken from the whole by which the characteristics of the whole can be deduced.

- The **relevant population** is all those who are relevant to the study; those that the sample comes from and stands for.

- **Non-response** is what happens when people do not agree to take part in research. The people in the sample who do take part are called the respondents. Postal questionnaires usually have a high non-response rate. When this happens, the process of sampling might need to be done a second time in order to obtain more people to study.

- A **sampling frame** is a list of people in the relevant population from which the sample can be drawn.

✳ Key Idea

Quantitative sociologists are usually trying to generalise from their findings, which is why they are interested in gathering large numbers of people to study. A concern for this type of research is that the sample choice must actually represent the relevant population, otherwise the generalisation would not be true. These sociologists are trying to say 'if it is true for these people, then it must also be true for these as well, since they have the same characteristics'.

What does this mean?

Sampling is the process of selecting those who you will study in your research. The **sample** refers to the selection of people who actually take part, and is seen to represent those in the rest of society who share the same characteristics as those selected to study. Everyone else not studied but to whom the research will apply, are called the **relevant population**.

Sampling occurs because sociologists simply cannot study everyone. They need to make choices as to who to look at, how many people to study and how long the research will actually take. The size and type of the sample will depend on a number of factors such as the following:

- How long the research might take.

- How much funding the research has.

- Whether interviewers/deliverers of questionnaires need to be trained and paid or if the sociologist is going to have to see every person in the sample themselves.

- The method used; questionnaires can be delivered to many more people than in-depth interviews can in the same period. However, questionnaires may have a much higher **non-response** rate than interviews.

- Whether the sociologist wishes to generalise or not.

- Whether qualitative or quantitative data are being collected. If quantitative data are required then the sample size is usually much larger, as generalisation is being attempted.

Sampling methods

- Simple random sampling: in this method, everyone has an equal chance of getting asked/involved in the research. For example, names are chosen at random from a **sampling frame**, maybe by a computer program that is designed to generate random numbers.

- Systematic sampling: in this method a sampling frame is used, and names are chosen at regular intervals, for example, every tenth name.

- Quota sampling: this is when people are selected according to specific characteristics they have, but the way they actually get chosen is still random. For example, you might need 10 males under the age of 30 and 10 females under the age of 30. Often the amount of people studied in each category (each quota) represents the amount of that type of person there is in the relevant population in the first place.

- Stratified random sampling: this method divides people from the relevant population into layers or groups, and then specific names are chosen. Like quota sampling people are put into categories, but like systematic sampling, actual individuals are identified, rather than being selected randomly.

- Snowballing sampling: this method is usually favoured by qualitative sociologists who are not trying to generalise or to have a representative sample. It refers to the way that if you roll a snowball down a hill it gets bigger and bigger as time goes on. In this method, each respondent introduces you to another, and so the sample gets bigger. This is useful if you need access to a difficult group, or if you are researching a sensitive issue where you need to build up trust and personal relationships. This is a 'self-selected sample' which means that people volunteer.

Conclusion

Sampling is important for quantitative sociologists so that generalisations can be made. Clearly, the whole of the relevant population cannot always be studied, and research is usually limited by time and funding. The process of sampling makes the collection of meaningful data manageable, and more data can be collected on less people because you have time to do so. If a sociologist is going to generalise from their sample, then standardisation of the method is important, i.e. the same questions must be asked to the same sorts of people in the same way, otherwise comparisons will not be possible.

For consideration:

1 Why is sampling important in research?
2 Why is generalisation more important for quantitative research?

> ☀ **Key Idea**
>
> Sometimes, if sampling goes wrong, you might have an unrepresentative sample that does not represent the relevant population. When this happens, any generalisations you make may be incorrect, as those you have studied are not like those you want them to represent. This is a problem for random sampling and for self-selected samples.

2.17 How much personal involvement is there in research?

What does this mean?

We can think of sociology as one of two extremes:

1 Sociologists should be experts, detached from personal involvement in those they study

2 Sociologists need to get involved to be able to truly explore what people think.

Some argue that the sociologist must get involved personally with those they study, in order to be able to build up the sorts of relationships needed to explore in-depth what people think. This argument is often used by feminists who argue that qualitative methods allow female researchers to build-up bonds with female respondents. For example, Ann Oakley (1999) states that involvement is necessary to develop the bond of trust '…personal involvement is more than a dangerous bias – it is the condition under which people come to know each other and admit each other to their lives'.

Feminists feel that so-called 'detached' methods are masculinist, i.e. too clinical, and involve the researcher acting as an expert having power over those they study. Many interpretive researchers and feminists wish to **empower** those they study.

In the study *The Company She Keeps* Valerie Hey (1997) built up bonds of friendship with the school girls she studied that went beyond the traditional researcher-respondent relationship (see section 12). She visited their houses, and they visited hers, she went out with them at the weekend and exchanged notes and personal letters with them to explore each others' feelings. She even skipped school with them. The point of her research was to explore what being at school and making friends meant to these girls. Hey judged that in order to best do this, she would need to develop close relationships with the girls.

Personal experience and research

Sometimes the decision to start a piece of research is due to personal involvement, or a personal experience. Some sociologists argue that this enables the researcher to explore in detail an aspect of society that allows us to develop a detailed understanding of people's emotions, thoughts and feelings by being able to identify with those we study.

❝❞ Key Definition

Empowerment means making the process and experience of being involved in research beneficial to those taking part. This is called 'action' research and is associated with qualitative methods, where those being studied, by reflecting on their lives, are moved forward in their lives from where they started.

Others ague that this makes us too involved in the research, and not detached enough to be able to 'step back'. Potentially this can make the research biased, and the observations and conclusions from the research may be suspect. They may be a fair reflection of reality, but they may be the sociologists' personal view.

An example of research that was triggered by a personal experience is the book *The Making of Men* by Mairtin Mac an Ghaill (1994). This study was ethnographic, exploring how male gender identity was created by boys in school, and the role heterosexuality, homosexuality and homophobia played in the creation of these identities. The study opens with a description of an experience Mac an Ghaill was involved in.

Early on in his teaching career, prior to becoming a researcher, Mac an Ghaill worked at a school where a pupil gave him flowers as a present in the way that pupils often do to thank teachers after exams. The difference in this case was that it was a male pupil giving flowers to a male teacher. Having seen this, some of the other pupils in the school bullied the pupil and this resulted in a fight. Mac an Ghaill was called into the head-teacher's office to explain his role in this situation. It turned out that the head-teacher knew nothing of the fight, he was telling off Mac an Ghaill for receiving the flowers. The fight was ignored. This led Mac an Ghaill to conclude that schools are heterosexual institutions and that they allow homophobia to develop. This incident led him to consider issues of masculinity, sexuality and homophobia. He may not have conducted this research if it was not for this personal experience.

Quantitative (positivist) sociologists would be critical of using personal experiences in research. They would argue that if the researcher is not detached from the study, then their ability to see the facts will be clouded. However, what positivists say, and what actually happens can be very different. For example, Durkheim is considered to be a 'scientific' sociologist; detached and value-free. His study on suicide (1897) is often presented as a scientific study, as it deals with facts in a detached fashion. He even says in the introduction that his study will make people see sociology as a true science. He might have been detached, but what he does not tell us is that a close personal friend of his committed suicide just prior to him making the decision to carry out the study. So, how detached and scientific was he?

Coursework Suggestion

In your coursework, think about how personally involved you might get with those you study. Is it a good thing or not? Does it aid research, or get in the way? If you discuss these issues you will gain evaluation marks.

For consideration:

1 Should sociologists be allowed to draw on personal experience in research?
2 How attached should sociologists become to those they study?

2.18 What is positivism?

What does this mean?

Positivists are sociologists who believe that sociology is a science. They produce quantitative data and seek generalisation from these data. It is usually seen as the opposite of the interpretive approach that focuses on individual meaning rather than on external facts that are seen to affect how society works, creating patterns and trends that can be analysed over time.

Positivism is first credited to have started with Auguste Comte and then later, with his student, Durkheim. For Comte, writing during the Industrial Revolution in Europe, as societies progress, the basis for knowledge used in society changes. He believed in a 'law of three stages':

* Stage 1: the theological stage where knowledge is based on magic and superstition.

* Stage 2: the metaphysical stage where knowledge is based on the belief in abstract forces that might shape the world, i.e. the idea of gravity; we can not see it, but it has a measurable effect. This second stage is a criticism of the first type of knowledge and represents the rise of early science.

* Stage 3: the final stage is a continuation of the second; the rise of scientific thinking. This means it is not a negative development, but it is 'positive' hence positivism.

How does positivism work?

Positivists today try to undertake the following:

* Produce quantitative data.

* Generalise from findings, looking at patterns and trends.

* Seek laws.

* Be 'value-free'.

* Prove or disprove hypotheses.

* Believe facts exist and the process of research is to uncover the facts that are 'out there'.

* Ignore the small-scale world of people's thoughts and feelings which they feel are unable to be measured in a reliable fashion.

* Make sure their findings are representative of those in society they are studying.

Auguste Comte (1798–1857)

☞ Who is this Person?

Auguste Comte, the French philosopher usually credited with coining the term 'sociology' was originally going to call this new subject 'social physics' in order to emphasise its scientific nature.

66 99 Key Definition

Positivists are sociologists who believe that there is 'a single common method that all scientific subjects follow'. Positivism is the belief, therefore, that in sociology, the social world can be studied with the same approach we might use to study the natural world.

◆ What, When and Why?

Positivism had its origins in the Industrial Revolution in Europe in the late 1800s and is very much a product of its time. During the Industrial Revolution many thinkers came to believe that science was the solution to all of humankind's problems. Science would be able to predict and solve the governing of society. Comte stated that sociology was both a way of measuring the world, and a way to control it. He thought that social scientists would run society as they were best placed to understand what was happening in it.

We call positivism a scientific approach to sociology as it is concerned with approaching research in a systematic way. Positivists have a clearly identifiable approach to research that seeks to test ideas and be value-free, just like scientists.

Positivists use methods that allow for the collection of large amounts of data, but with limited personal involvement on behalf of the researcher with those being studied. They believe that in this way trends can be identified, but that the research will be detached from their own values. For example, questionnaires might be given to thousands of people all over the country and the same questions allow easy comparisons. Interviews are also used, but they would have to be highly structured to allow for a standard set of questions to be asked.

Conclusion

The word 'science' (associated with positivism) might at first seem simple to understand, but sociology has tried to show that science is a very powerful idea. If you can claim that something is scientific in today's world, then lots of people will believe you. Science has what we call a powerful legitimisation claim. This might be one reason why the 'is sociology a science' debate is so important to some sociologists; if your subject is seen as a science it might make people believe you more.

For consideration:

1   Why might sociologists wish to be seen as scientific?
2   How would you criticise the idea that we can apply scientific methods to the study of humans?

2.19 What is interpretive sociology?

Mead and interpretivism

Interpretivism is one of the many names given to the micro approach to sociology. This micro approach determines how sociologists think about what society is (theory) and how they might try and find out about society through research (methods). Other names associated with this view are interactionism, symbolic interactionism and phenomenology. The key point behind this view is that the social world is not seen to exist as a 'thing' having independence from humans and shaping their actions, but instead, society is the sum of the interactions between those who make-up society. All such interactional encounters are motivated by thought, meanings and motives. Therefore, in order to study society from this viewpoint, we should seek to try and understand how people think and how they see themselves. We can then interpret their actions and make sense of the situations they find themselves in.

George Herbert Mead (1863–1931)

☞ Who is this Person?

American philosopher, George Herbert Mead was one of the key founders of interpretive sociology.

✍ Coursework Suggestion

Try to follow the interpretive approach in your coursework. You could adopt the aim of developing *verstehen* and use an in-depth interview technique to do this. Like all interpretivists you would be trying to understand how people themselves understand their life.

How does interpretivism work?

Interpretivism is often seen as the complete opposite of positivism. Interpretive sociology is anti-scientific in the sense that it wishes to explore in detail people's feelings and emotions rather than trying to explore large-scale laws, patterns, generalisations and causality. One of the original sources of the interpretive view is the notion of *verstehen* used by founder Max Weber. This is the idea that the aim of research is to see the world through the eyes of those involved. This approach is highly qualitative and it tries to be valid rather than reliable (see section 1). It deals with depth and detail; words, quotes and observations rather than numbers.

Interpretivism recommends the use of techniques that provide ways of getting people to open up and to explore what they do, and why they think they do it. Researchers use semi-structured and unstructured interviews, focus groups and observational methods. The method most associated with this view is that of participant observation where the researcher joins in with the 'real life' activities of a group (either openly or in secret) in order to try and achieve a degree of empathy, i.e. to try and understand how groups work and how they interact with each other.

Interpretive sociology criticises the positivist approach for seeing patterns that do not exist. For example, positivists, because of their use of statistical data would argue that large-scale data provide us with patterns and trends that give us an understanding of how society as a whole works.

These statistics provide us with an insight into social facts, i.e. truths about society. On the other hand, the interpretive view suggests that these so-called facts are really the made-up **social constructions** of those who put the statistics together in the first place. They do not reflect reality, but might come, in time, to be seen as reality. These facts are really human-made. They are highly selective and the product of people using their meanings in the first place, e.g. sociologists writing questionnaires, governments choosing what statistics to look at and publish and people filling in questionnaires when stopped on the street. Instead, interpretive sociologists look at how people behave.

Is interpretivism better than positivism?

This is an unanswerable question. Both approaches do very different things and are therefore both very useful. Many sociologists today combine both approaches together.

Conclusion

The strength of the micro approach in sociology is to focus our research on the small and 'ordinary' things in life – the ordinary ways in which ordinary people go about their lives. This is often missed by the more macro approach.

For consideration:
1 What do you think are the main strengths of the interpretivist approach?
2 Which do you favour, interpretivism or positivism and why?

66 99 Key Definition

Social construction is is an interpretive word meaning the way in which society is created by people and their thoughts and culture. Things that appear real are only real because society says so.

✓ Top Exam Hint

Although textbooks present positivism and interpretive sociology as total opposites it is important to remember that many sociologists combine both approaches together (see section 3). The reality of current research is that people do interesting and exciting research in a structured way. They do not necessarily follow a trend or a narrow position.

2.20 What is the link between theory and methods?

Sir Karl Popper (1902–1994)

☞ Who is this Person?

Karl Popper was born in Vienna in 1902. A famous philosopher and positivist, he was a Marxist in terms of his political views. He invented the idea of **falsification**, the idea that we can only prove things wrong, allowing us to reject theories. Popper was very critical of both Marxism and sociology claiming they were unscientific since they never tried to genuinely test their theories, but held on to them as if they were untestable truths. He was knighted while resident in the UK in 1965 and was professor of Logic and Scientific Method at the London School of Economics. He died in 1994.

❝❞ Key Definitions

- **Falsification** is, according to Popper, the process of proving ideas and theories wrong. Popper uses the example of the hypothesis 'all swans are white'. We could never prove that this is true because how many observations are enough? Even if we saw 100 or 1000 swans, we could never say for certain that the next one will also be white.

- **Conjecture** and **refutation** is the twin process of creating a theory to test and then trying to prove the theory wrong.

What does this mean?

Theories are ideas that we have, ways of thinking about the world and society around us, whereas methods are the ways we go about collecting evidence or data. Methods are used to do the actual research in order to test if theories are correct or not. In this sense, both are important, we cannot really have one without the other:

- Theory with no methods means we have not tested our ideas and assumptions. How do we know if our theory is correct? How do we know if our image of the world is true or not? Are we just choosing theories because they are our favourites, not because we can find evidence to support them?

- Methods with no theory behind them become an exercise in collecting data for no real reason and not being able to do anything with it.

Which comes first, theory or method?

- Some sociologists who adopt an empiricist approach to research argue that we can do research without theory and that after collecting data the 'facts will speak for themselves'. In other words, data collection will point towards the theory and conclusions rather than needing them first.

- More sociologists adopt a position called rationalism. This means that we think about social life first, come up with theories and then we test them with research.

Some have suggested that it is impossible to collect data without some sort of theory. It is impossible to be so detached and value-free that we can simply go out and find facts. All research is directed in some way, from the questions asked to those who get chosen to take part. This means there must be something guiding research, some idea of what is interesting to look at, or some idea of what the researcher might wish to find out. Therefore, theory will exist before the method in this case.

Testing theories

Karl Popper argued that research should take place through a twin-process of what he calls **conjecture** and **refutation**:

- First, an idea or theory is devised. This is a conjecture, i.e. making interesting and bold statements to then test.

- Second, you should seek to test the ideas and try and prove them wrong (refute them). This is because, Popper argues, you can only ever say for certain that 'so far you have found something out'. You can never for certain ever say 'this is always true' because you never know what the next test might show.

In this way, it does not matter where the theory originally comes from or even how biased it might be as if it is wrong you have to say so. This will still help your research, because knowing something is not true is still knowledge. The methods allow us to test theories and to discard them away if we need to.

Macro or micro?

Traditionally, sociologists have adopted either a way of looking at society on a large-scale (macro) or a way of looking on a much smaller-scale (micro). The theory adopted then directly influences the methods chosen. For example, those who wish to study the whole of the social structure, the way society links together as a whole unit, would use large-scale methods that produce quantitative data. Those who are interested in the small-scale level of individual actions and in trying to explain what and how people think would wish to adopt micro methods that produce qualitative data such as interviews and observation. In this way, the type of theory and the approach the sociologist uses to understand what is real in society links directly to the methods used to find out about social life.

It could also be the case that rather than theory influencing methods, methods may influence theory. For example, for some, only methods that give power to the individual to express themselves should be used in sociology as this is more humane and ethical. We should not see research as something we do to people, but as something they join in with in an active fashion. If you think this, as many feminist sociologists do, then you are drawn to a very micro set of methods, which in turn will shape what you can and cannot actually find out. This will then ultimately affect the theory you adopt.

A great deal of research today mixes both macro and micro approaches. In these cases, the links between theories and methods are still there, but can be much more open than the rigid and rather unrealistic macro/micro divide of traditional sociology.

For consideration:

1 Do you agree that facts can speak for themselves without theory to direct research? Explain your view.
2 Why might the traditional link between theory and methods be limiting for sociologists?

How has sociological research changed over time?

What does this mean?

Like everything else, sociology has its fashions and fads. It changes and evolves over time, and the ways of doing social research also change. Different techniques and issues popular at one particular time will be replaced with other ideas over time.

Late 19th century

When sociology was developed by Comte as a distinctive way of seeing the world, it was associated with the ideas Comte himself had on positivism. This was a very macro, very scientific approach. General laws about human behaviour were made. This is the same image that Durkheim held in his classic study on suicide (1897). Sociology was seen as a means by which the truth about the whole of society could be uncovered.

Early 20th century

The ideas of Weber on *verstehen* sociology were first developed in the early 1900s, but became popular in sociology during the 1920s when taken up by the Chicago School, a group of sociologists associated with the more interpretive approach. This change from macro sociology to micro sociology has developed a key debate within modern-day sociology, and a debate that still exists today: what is the best type of data to produce? What are the most useful techniques to use to understand society?

The ideas associated with the Chicago School, the use of participant observation in particular and their view of people as active and creative, seeking the meaning of their actions, challenged the previously dominant macro approach of early sociology. These views claimed that sociology is not value-free and not scientific. Instead, the sociologist is part of what they study, and seeks to try and explore how people make sense of what they do.

Late 20th century

Since the 1960s and 1970s the aims of positivist sociologists became significantly different from the early positivism associated with Comte

◆ What, When and Why?

When sociology was first invented it was heavily scientific in nature. It was believed that sociologists could obtain absolute truth and that facts could be established about the social world. Since this time, many sociologists have questioned the ability for anyone doing any sort of research to be able to certainly say that facts exist.

✳ Key Idea

The Chicago School are closely associated with the development of both the theory of symbolic interactionism, and the use of the method of participant observation. As the name suggests, the Chicago school was the sociology department at Chicago University in the USA in the 1920s. It was heavily influenced by the ideas of Max Weber on *verstehen*, plus it was the first official English speaking sociology department in the world. The aim of the Chicago School was to use the local micro environment as a tool for research; to study how the city worked and how its people lived their day-to-day lives. In doing this the School pioneered the development of micro methods, and also made some major contributions to the subject of geography; in particular the idea that cities are based upon a series of concentric circles of land use.

and Durkheim. Rather than seeking absolute 'truths' or general laws of society, the aims of quantitative sociologists today are much less absolute. Many seek to produce statistical overviews and to seek causality, in other words to try and find a connection between two variables, such as class and health. This is called a **correlation**, where two or more things have a relationship to each other that can be identified. This is usually the point of those pieces of research that try and use quantitative methods such as questionnaires.

Feminists have greatly contributed to the methods debate in modern times. Feminists have tended to adopt more qualitative approaches in social research as they see these as not being 'masculinist' in the ways that quantitative methods are. Feminists have argued that quantitative methods objectify the research participants, i.e. take advantage of people and then throw them to one side once they are finished with.

Most modern sociologists are not interested in the macro/micro divide. Researchers are interested in ways that they might combine both quantitative and qualitative methods together, using them to support each other's findings. Modern sociology is also less scientific than that of the founders. Definitions of what science is and how it works are continuously changing over time. For example, realists argue that sociology can be scientific, but only in the sense that theories can be combined together and can be tested; not in that absolutes can be established. Another trend that realists often adopt is 'grounded theory': the idea that theories can come from research data, but through using these data we can locate or 'ground' what sociologists find in the ideas and reality of people themselves.

Conclusion

In all, much research today is about practical considerations. Research is about problem solving; how can sociologists get the data they need? What methods are the best? Remember, there is no such thing as a perfect method, it depends what you do, and how you do it.

For consideration:

1   Why do you think sociological ideas change over time?
2   Why might it be important to know the time that an idea was popular?

66 99 Key Definition
Correlation means the degree of relationship between two variables.

2.22 How and why do some sociologists mix methods together?

✳ Key Idea

Methodological pluralism is the term we use to describe mixing methods. These methods could produce both quantitative or qualitative data or could both produce the same type of data. Alternatively, you might mix both primary and secondary sources or have a main method and then a secondary method that you can use to test the first.

Paul Willis

☞ Who is this Person?

In his classic study *Learning to Labour* (1977), Paul Willis mixed a number of methods together in order to understand what it meant to be a working-class boy in an education system set-up to disadvantage you in the future.

❝❞ Key Definition

Ethnography is an approach to sociological research that concentrates on the collection of small-scale data through a number of qualitative techniques. These allow the researcher to understand what it means to be a member of a small group, usually a sub cultural group. It is used to try and allow the researcher to fully 'submerge' themselves within the strange new world they are studying, yet unlike covert participant observation, it still allows the researcher to ask questions from the viewpoint of someone who is an outsider, trying to understand enough to become an insider.

What does this mean?

For many modern-day sociologists, the traditional divide between being either a positivist or an interpretivist is not realistic nor is it sensible. For many, good sociology, and good sociological research is simply that which works, that which gets meaningful results. Often, to get an interesting result, to find things out about society that you would not have known before, you have to adopt an interesting approach. Sometimes mixing methods (methodological pluralism) is the only way to get a fuller picture.

Examples of methodological pluralism

A classic example of a study that has combined methods together is by Paul Willis' *Learning to Labour*, originally published in the late 1970s. Willis combined a number of qualitative methods together (observation and interviews). These methods, added within the method of 'hanging around' with people and groups (a much used approach to qualitative data gathering) is known as an **ethnographic** approach.

A more modern mixed approach that focuses upon the qualitative, is the research entitled *The Making of Men* by Mac an Ghaill (1994) (see section 17). He was interested in how a sense of masculine identity was created within schools, and to investigate this conducted a three year piece of research using daily observations at a school he worked at. He also used questionnaires and diaries, plus formal and informal group interviews with both pupils and staff at the school.

Is mixing methods a good idea?

French sociologist Pierre Bourdieu has suggested that ethnographic data collection is not enough on its own. We need to see the general trends (often presented as a series of statistics) and use the ethnographic data to explain what the statistics mean, how they were created, what they mean for ordinary people and their lives and how the broad trends operate in day-to-day practice.

It is dangerous to assume that mixing methods is always a good thing. It has become very fashionable in social research to mix methods, but like anything fashionable, you should do it because it is the best thing to do, not simply because everyone else is. A weak method and a poor research plan will still have their problems no matter how many methods you use. Mixing methods can have real benefits, but only if it is planned and thoroughly executed.

The reality of going out and getting data is often very different from the simple, neat and clean way in which methods are presented in textbooks. There are always problems, and the solution to the problem might take the researcher off in a very different direction to the original aim of the research. When mixing methods you might be led along very different paths, and the different methods might produce very different results to each other.

Conclusion

What happens if your different methods produce results that do not support each other, but actually contradict each other? The study *Negotiating Family Responsibility* by Finch and Mason (1993) starts with the view that the results you get are a product of the methods you use in the first place. This means that different methods will naturally produce different results, but this is fine as it allows us to compare results and account for the differences. In this case, research becomes about exploring the differences between data rather than simply having one viewpoint only.

For consideration:

1 Why should you not always use methodological pluralism?
2 How and why might research be different to the way it is presented in textbooks? What does this mean for how research actually happens?

Examination advice

This section provides some practical advice in order to get the best possible grade you can in your sociology exam.

Learn key terms and know when to use them

- In the AS research methods exam, the first question will ask you to define a key methodological concept and explain it. This means that you can arm yourself before you go into the exam with definitions of key concepts. Keep a key vocabulary dictionary throughout your course to help you to revise this aspect.

- Use key terms in longer exam answers, especially those at the very end of the exam (which you must leave enough time for). Using key terms adds important depth and detail to your answers and it demonstrated your knowledge to the examiner. Question c) and question d) will be based on designing and evaluating a research strategy. It is important to contextualise your answer; in other words, use your knowledge of methodology but make it applicable to your research strategy.

- Refer back to the guidelines on page 45 if you are doing the coursework option.

Evaluate sources critically

- Some key ideas in the methods topic area can link well to evaluative points you might like to make. For example, consider the following list:

  - Validity
  - Reliability
  - Representativeness/Generalisability
  - Malestream
  - Verstehen

  All these key ideas can be used to assess the worth of a piece of research or a study. If you can comment on each for a particular source you will be successfully evaluating the usefulness or success of the study.

- In any longer methods exam questions (and in your coursework as well) there are always assessments to be made about studies and methods regarding practical issues, ethical issues, theoretical issues and sensitivity issues (PETS) name these and try and use them.

✓ **Top Exam Hint**

PETS is a good tool to use to assess methods:

P = practical problems/issues
E = ethical problems/issues
T = theoretical problems/issues
S = sensitivity problems/issues

Always use this as a tool to evaluate sources.

✍ **Coursework Suggestion**

When writing coursework for A2, make sure that you give a lot of attention to PETS and to issues of validity and reliability of the methods that you are using. Also make sure that you give some thought to how value-free your research may or may not have been.

- Every method has both strengths and weaknesses. Make sure that you always present both of these, this is an easy way to be more evaluative in your work.

- Value-freedom is an important debate within methods, and again, provides a way of evaluating a source. You might like to explore the extent to which a study might be value-free or not, and why this might be a problem. You could also look at how a particular method might present issues of value-freedom. You could link this to quantitative and qualitative methods; how do different methods that produce different types of data have different types of problems?

- Some methods raise ethical issues, especially the more qualitative methods based upon observation. Use these ethical issues as a way to think about whether sociologists have the right to do their research or not.

- You could evaluate a study by asking yourself the question 'What value has this study contributed to sociological knowledge?' In other words, why has a study been useful?

- Try to think about the 'influences' on research. These will help you to consider why a piece of research was done the way it was.

- Think about the relationship between theories and methods. What people do and how they do it is often a consequence of what they think about society in the first place.

Key points to remember

- Use PETS.

- Learn key words and key ideas relating to methods off by heart.

- Always think about both strengths and weaknesses of sources.

Pushing your grades up higher

This section provides some practical advice in order to get the best possible grade you can in your sociology exam.

1 Refer to methods used in other exam questions if you can make a link to the method in the source you are studying. If you know the research technique used in a particular study, you can make evaluative points about the findings of a study.

2 Use the idea of macro/micro sociology or positivism/phenomenology in exam questions on methods. Most research techniques, types of data, etc. can be related back to these opposite approaches to sociology, and by talking about them then you can achieve a more detailed answer.

3 Use the idea of malestream sociology in order to evaluate positivism and quantitative sociology from a feminist viewpoint. Feminists argue that quantitative sociology is masculinist as it is about facts and not about feelings. As such, feminists use micro methods since they are interested in supporting and respecting those they study.

4 Discuss the idea of *verstehen* when you discuss qualitative techniques. It is a very important idea and one that will allow you to analyse qualitative techniques in a clear and concise way.

5 Learn some case studies that will enable you to use them more than once in your exam. For example, if you learn about a particular study relating to Family and households about housework, learn about the methods used in the study as well, then you can use it in questions relating to both topics.

6 Learn a case study for every method possible and learn a list of strengths and weaknesses for each one.

7 For the A2 course you will be required to be synoptic; this means making lots of links between all the different topics. Talking about methods is an excellent way of doing this.

   • Make sure you are able to describe the macro and micro traditions in-depth – you will probably use these in most exams.

   • Make sure you can demonstrate that research is 'messy' – that there are lots of problems and the challenge of research is to find ways to solve these problems.

✓ **Top Exam Hint**

Do not forget that methods and theories are always linked; you can discuss both in every topic in order to show how sociology really works.

🛢 Thinking like a Sociologist

In order to evaluate a source discuss the following key ideas in relation to it:

• Reliability
• Validity
• Representativeness.

Key points to remember

* Learn the methods used in case studies for all topics.
* If possible discuss both positivism and phenomenology in your answers.
* Use the idea of malestream sociology as a good way to evaluate sources.
* Apply your knowledge to the specific task – how do sociologists use methods in research?

Frequently asked questions

Q. Why are methods so important?

A. Methods are vital to research. Without them we would have only theory, and no evidence. Methods allow sociologists to seek answers, whereas theories allow them to imagine what society might be like. Sociology is both a theoretical and an empirical discipline. It needs to undertake research in order to find out what society is really like, rather than taking for granted what others might tell us, or what we might have been socialised to believe.

Q. Should I try to discuss methods in all my exam answers?

A. Yes, if it is relevant. You must make sure that you answer the question you were originally asked, but methods are a good way of evaluating sources. You could question the usefulness of a method, or argue that a study is out of date so more research is needed. Also, you could say that generalisations are not possible from small-scale research. All these methods-related comments would help you to be more critical of the named examples and theories you learn in all topics in both the AS and A2 course. Discussing methods in the A2 exam will help you be synoptic, allowing you to pull all your sociology knowledge together.

Q. Which method is the best?

A. This is impossible to answer. It is important to remember that all methods have their strengths but also their weaknesses. Your choice of method depends on who and what you are studying, what data you wish to collect and also what type of theory you have. Some sociologists might have favoured methods, but they would only use them if the topic in question was relevant.

Chapter 3

The individual, society and the formation of identity

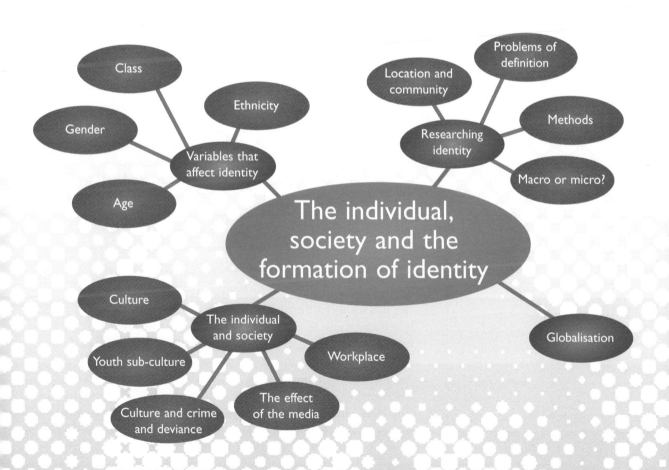

 CD-ROM 3.1

Key issues in the individual, society and the formation of identity

Why are sociologists interested in the individual, society and the formation of identity?

For sociologists the relationship between an individual and the society in which they live is a fascinating one. Asking questions about the formation of different types of identities (e.g. class-based or gender-based) allows the sociologist to explore the role of family, education, the world of work and other 'institutions' to find out how these affect somebody's identity.

The concept of identity is not a straightforward one. For some, our identities are based on how we define our class background – for others, it might be our gender, sexuality, the job that we do or even which football team we might support. Sociologists also ask questions about why some identities seem to be more important at particular moments in time than at others (e.g. national identities – what does it mean to be a Muslim in the United Kingdom post '9/11'). You might like to consider the following questions surrounding identity to see how complex these issues are:

1   How might the issue of identity and ethnicity be a confusing one particularly at a time when many societies are seen to be becoming more 'Westernised'?
2   Are terms like 'class', 'gender', 'ethnicity', 'nation' or 'age' becoming outdated?
3   Do the lifestyles that many people live today bear any similarity to the lifestyles of those who lived in an earlier historical period?

What are the key debates in the individual, society and the formation of identity?

1   The relationship between the individual and society is at the heart of the 'macro/micro' discussion that rages within sociology. This debate is between those who say institutions (e.g. the family, education, religion and the media) shape our identities (the macro argument) and those who argue that it is individual identities that shape the institutions and ultimately the society around them (the micro argument).
2   The 'nature/nurture' debate can also be applied to the individual, society and the formation of identity (see section 4). On the 'nature'

side there are those who argue that our identities are formed by what is biologically within each individual, e.g. our genes, our personalities, and so on. Those that support the 'nurture' side stress the importance of how outside institutions shape and determine our identities, e.g. the media, our peer groups, or the area where we live.

3   A final debate exists between those who argue we are living in a 'modern' world, and those who argue that this is a postmodern one. Many postmodernists argue that terms like class, gender and many other classifications are outdated. Instead they argue that we can choose whatever identity we like. We can 'buy' our way into an identity in much the same way that we choose groceries in a supermarket.

What are the key ideas and concepts in the individual, society and the formation of identity?

When answering exam questions you need to be able to talk about and use the *key terms* correctly. However, you will also need to be able to discuss the various *processes* that many sociologists argue are taking place. You will need to be able to make distinctions between what we mean by 'individual', 'society', 'identity' and 'culture'. However, you also need to be able to explore them by relating them to issues connected with class, ethnicity, gender and age.

When focusing on the many processes that individuals in societies come up against, you will need to explore those of the community, location, workplace and the media and also explore how identity is affected. In the interconnected world that we all live in you will also need to be aware of how the processes of 'globalisation' may shape and determine our identities (see also section 17).

What are the key issues in the individual, society and the formation of identity?

Sociologists are interested in *four* issues when examining this fascinating branch of the social sciences:

1   What is the relationship between the individual and society?
2   How do we learn our identities?
3   What are the processes that shape identity?

☀ Key Idea

'Postmodernists' represent a branch of sociologists who have emerged over the last thirty years. They argue that the type of society we live in today is very different from any previous historical period (you will examine this in more detail later on in this chapter). They also argue that the more traditional sociological theories such as functionalism and Marxism cannot adequately explain today's rapidly changing world.

● Synoptic Link

Identity forms one of the central concepts in sociological theory by which all others can be connected. This means that you can use identity wherever you feel a connection can be made with the synoptic subjects in A2. Issues surrounding why or why not a particular identity may be branded 'deviant', i.e. not conforming to what members of a particular society might consider to be 'normal' behaviour (e.g. AIDS victims, anti-capitalists, 'crew' members and 'New Age travellers').

✎ Coursework Suggestion

Set up interviews with two different groups. This could be a group of teenagers and a much older group – perhaps in their fifties or sixties. Taking the key sociological concepts of class, gender and ethnicity, construct a set of questions to be posed to both groups. This will enable you to explore whether these concepts are as important today as they once used to be.

3.2 What do we need to know about the individual, society and the formation of identity?

How individual is it . . . to want to be an 'individual'?

What does the specification say about the individual, society and the formation of identity?

The OCR specifies that you will be expected to know about:

*   *The individual and society* – i.e. the role of values, norms (acceptable forms of behaviour) and agents of **socialisation** (e.g. the media) in the formation of culture. You will also be expected to understand how social roles are learnt and, in particular, how expected patterns of behaviour regulate social life.
*   *Culture and the formation of identities* – i.e. the formation of gender identities, national identities, ethnic identities, class identities and how all of these impact on social behaviour. You will be expected to understand how institutions shape and reinforce national identity. You will also be expected to understand how contemporary social change might impact on all of the identities mentioned above.

How will I be examined in this topic area?

The exam for this unit will be 60 minutes and you will answer one from two 4-part structured questions.

As with all of the OCR units you will have to show competency or ability in the assessment objectives of AO1 (*knowledge & understanding and presentation & communication*) and AO2 (*interpretation & analysis and evaluation*). For AO1 you will need to show *knowledge and understanding* of: the names of sociologists and their case studies; the relevant theories; the key concepts; evidence to support the claims that sociologists make (e.g. interview data); and show a keen awareness of the research methodologies used within this topic area.

For AO2 you will need to show how you can actually *interpret and apply* this knowledge when putting forward a particular argument and *evaluate* continuously throughout any answer you are writing. For example, this might mean that you draw on the ideas of a theory or case study that was carried out thirty years ago and see how it might (or might not!) be relevant to this topic today. You might also identify trends from the past and see to what extent these trends still exist today.

How well does this topic relate to A2 coursework?

As you will see when reading through the chapter, this area of sociology offers a wide variety of possibilities for coursework. You might like to explore how a particular identity, e.g. gender, class or even professional, might change over a period of time. You could also explore to what extent the variables of age, class, gender and ethnicity could impact on the life chances of a group of adults who were teenagers during the 1950s or 1960s. By 'life chances' sociologists mean the type of job, accommodation, overall health and life expectancy of a person or group of people under examination.

Explore notions of female or male identity by showing a focus group pictures of a wide variety of very different male or female 'role models'. Explore what 'being male' or 'female' means in the 21st century and how that might have changed over time. Carry out analysis of any branch of the media to explore the social construction (the way we create categories to describe people, theories and concepts) of teenagers or how a particular national identity is expressed in British newspapers.

How well does this topic help with synopticity?

Identity is an ideal synoptic concept. Synopticity examines the themes of social differentiation, power and stratification. This means that identities, whether they are those of class, gender, sexuality, ethnicity or nation, can be linked to issues surrounding 'power'. All you have to do is to be able to identify why and by what processes different identities possess different levels of power in society. Once you have done that, then any institution (e.g. the family, education, the media or religion) can be used to explain how different identities possess different levels of power.

Key points to remember

*   This topic not only requires that you understand how these different terms are used by sociologists but also expects you to be able to explain the processes that form different identities (such as socialisation).
*   By combining the concepts of identity and power all units in sociology can be synoptically linked in an easy and yet sociologically sophisticated way.
*   Identify, practise and perfect the skills required for AO1 and AO2 described above (the many examples in this chapter will help you do this).

✍ Coursework Suggestion

Using the media as a source for research, examine how 'identities' have changed over time. By taking a particular identity such as 'class' or 'gender', examine photographs taken during the twentieth century to see how those images have changed (e.g. look at how working-class people may have been portrayed in the media in the 1920s and see how this compares to now). Your photographic research may either go to prove or disprove the debate as to whether these identities have changed.

● Synoptic Link

When you have completed this unit spend one hour labelling any connections you can think of with this chapter and the synoptic unit that you will study in A2. By doing this work now you will save enormous amounts of time in your second year. Use post-it notes every time you come to such a connection e.g. the media, the family, religion, and so on, to identify these connections. You can then make a list of the connections, each with one sentence explaining how they connect with identity. Keep this list for when you revise for the synoptic component in your exam (make sure you show it to your teacher first!).

How can we find out about the individual, society and the formation of identity?

✳ **Key Idea**

Symbolic interactionism is a theory which focuses on the way that meanings emerge when human beings interact with each other. It examines 'close up' the everyday interaction of people in an attempt to analyse the meanings of everyday life. Popular methods of research used by symbolic interactionists are observation and in-depth interviews

How have sociologists tried to measure the individual, society and the formation of identity?

Sociologists choose their methodology depending on:

*   *The traditional research strategies, methods and data sources* thought to be appropriate for a particular problem (e.g. in-depth interviews with people over a period of time to see if their identity changes).

*   *How available or accessible the data is* that the sociologist requires (e.g. when exploring subcultures, how difficult would it be for the sociologist to be 'accepted' by the group they are studying?)

*   *What are the resources at the researchers' disposal* – funding, time, equipment and assistance?

Values also determine how a particular sociologist approaches any area of research. The aim or particular focus of their research will reflect the theoretical interest of the sociologist carrying out the study i.e. are they a Marxist, or feminist or symbolic interactionist? The fact that the researcher may be working-class or middle-class will also affect what they research and how they interpret their research.

Such values will also determine whether or not the researcher is gathering quantitative data or qualitative data and this might depend on whether they consider themselves to be 'positivist' (i.e. scientific) or 'interpretive' (trying to imagine what it must be like to be the person they are researching) in their approach to the area being studied.

What methods do sociologists tend to use to study the individual, society and the formation of identity?

Here are three sociologists who have used a variety of methods:

*   Marxist Paul Willis (1977) used in-depth interviews with groups of young people in the Midlands to explore the ways in which language,

clothes and music created new cultural meanings other than what was intended by the manufacturers, e.g. the use of the BMW logo as a fashion statement.

- Ken Pryce (1986) used participant observation to study institutionalised racism in the West Indian community in St Pauls, Bristol.
- Valerie Hey (1997) in her study of girls' friendships in school not only used participant observation but also gathered girls' notes that she had 'confiscated' in class and also examined their diaries. She referred to both of these as a 'pocket ethnography'.

What problems with definition are encountered in studying the individual, society and the formation of identity?

This chapter will show how 'identity' and 'society' can have a number of different and often confusing meanings. You will see that 'class' and 'gender' are just *some* of the ways that we can describe identities. Other ways include the jobs we do, the religion we may or may not belong to and the youth cultures that some look up to. Also, do not forget how important 'age' is when talking about identity. As already shown (see section 1), 'postmodernism' even focuses on the importance of 'consumerism', i.e. what we buy as a way of marking out who we are.

Nevertheless while definitions come and go (and sociology is full of definitions!), what *is* important to realise is that good sociology always 'operationalises' concepts (i.e. defines what they mean) so that research cannot be misinterpreted.

Key points to remember

- There are a variety of reasons why sociologists choose the methods they do.
- The difference between 'quantitative' and 'qualitative' research methods.
- The importance of 'definition' or 'operationalisation' when discussing any research that takes place. You cannot talk about *how* identity is formed until you have defined what you *mean* by identity.

What ethical problems do you think Valerie Hey's (1997) research poses?

✳ Key Idea

Remember that different 'regions' (e.g. the West or the East; Greater London or Kent; or even Europe and South East Asia) will have enormous significance when we are talking about individual identities based around class, ethnicity or gender. The experience of being 'female' will vary enormously depending if you live in or out of London, in the north or south of England, or in South America! Regions will also have a huge impact on how we see religious identities and national identities. As a 'sociological variable' make sure that you remember region when discussing the difficulty in defining identities.

3.4 What do we mean by the 'individual'?

Key Ideas

* The 'structure versus agency' debate is another way of referring to 'macro sociology versus micro sociology'. The idea is that some sociologists (called 'structuralists') say that we are shaped by 'structures' which can include the family, religion, education, the media and even the language we speak. These structures shape or determine who we are, i.e. our identities. Other sociologists say that we have 'agency', i.e. we have the ability to shape and determine events around us and even those very same institutions that structural sociologists say shape us!

What does this mean?

At the heart of the 'structure versus agency' debate is the notion of 'society' on one side and 'the individual' at the other. Society, after all, is made up of individuals. However, if we point out somebody as being individual are we therefore not admitting that *the rest* of society is made up of people with similar sets of norms and values (otherwise, why would we point out somebody as 'individual')?

For post-structuralist Stuart Hall (1996) the concept of identity manages to link 'structure' (macro sociology) and 'agency' (micro sociology) together. He believes that culture and identity meet society and the individual at the 'point of suture'. By this he means that all four elements are inter-linked. As a 'student' you behave in a way that society expects you to behave. Thus your student identity owes much to your own behaviour *and* what you expect society expects from you! Who you are (your 'individuality') is a product of the relationship between society and the individual.

How 'individual' are you?

Certainly your thoughts are your own – or are they? If you accept that you express your thoughts in words, then surely the words you use are created before you entered the world. Your thoughts are limited to the words that existed before you were born. As we shall see later on in the chapter both structuralists and post-structuralists refer to the ways language can impact on our 'individuality'.

The 'nature versus nurture' debate is at the heart of sociological, philosophical, political and even medical theory. It refers to a debate concerning whether or not human beings are more the product of their biological inheritance (their genes) or the cultural environment they grow up in. Put more simply – are you like your parents because you share their blood and genes, or are you like them because you may have spent so much time with them?

Many Marxists, feminists and even interpretive sociologists challenge the notion of 'free will'. Even your choice of clothes and food may actually reflect the economic decisions of others or the cultural expectations of your religion, family, age, gender or sexuality.

Free will versus determinism

The ideas of 'free-will' and 'determinism' are like two opposite colours at either end of a rainbow. 'Free will' refers to the idea that you have complete choice in all areas of your life – from the clothes you wear to the food you eat. 'Determinism' refers to the idea that far from being free, everything is determined for you by others (or sometimes even the weather). If you are a determinist you believe that your identity is shaped by all the structures in society, e.g. your language, your family and your education.

You chose the CD that you listened to this morning (or so you thought). You bought it and played it. However, how did you choose your CD? You heard it on the radio, an event that was 'determined' by the station's play-list, which was 'determined' by the record company marketing people sweet-talking the radio station into playing it in the first place. The artist, one of hundreds that had sent their demos to the record company, was signed up for a large sum of money. The hundreds of other artists were never heard by you or anybody else. Did you really have the free will to choose your CD or was it chosen (or 'determined') for you? Is your 'individuality' a product of free will or determined by others around you, for example in this case by those in the music industry?

As you can see already the individual is always tied up to the culture that they may be part of.

For consideration:

1 What activities can you think of where you can truly describe yourself as being individual?
2 Where would you place yourself in the debate about nature versus nurture?

☞ Who is this Person?

Thomas Hobbes (1588–1679) was an English philosopher of the Enlightenment period. His writings span the period of the English Civil War and are still reference material for any social science student at university four centuries later. Praised by both Marxists and the New Right today, Hobbes managed to make himself acceptable to both Royalists and Parliamentarians when he was alive – no mean feat! For top marks in the exam no discussion about 'nature versus nurture' is complete without reference to Hobbes.

3.5 What do we mean by society?

What impact on society does tourism hold for both the visitor and the visited?

What does this mean?

Different sociologists interpret the idea of society in different ways. However, we can understand it to mean any grouping of people who are probably associated with a particular territory and who possess their own distinctive culture, institutions and sets of norms and values. The concept allows sociologists to explain how people are 'socialised' into being the people they are.

Society and social order

Sociology, when it first emerged at the end of the 19th century, was critical of older, more traditional views that said we were either created by God in 'his' image or else that nature/biology created us, as was believed by scientists at the time. Sociology claimed that *society* created us through the processes of 'socialisation' and made us become 'individuals'.

As a result of the many political revolutions that took place in the 18th and 19th centuries, key 19th-century writers like Auguste Comte (1798–1857) and Emile Durkheim (1858–1917) were obsessed with one major question: 'How is social order possible?' In the 20th century this fascination with social order continued in American sociology with the writings of functionalists Talcott Parsons and Robert Merton.

Society and 'classical sociology'

Classical sociologists argued that society was a system where every part was interconnected. It did not matter whether these 'parts' were individuals, their moral beliefs or their institutions (e.g. the media, family or religion). If one part changed, then all other parts would be affected. As a system, each society worked towards promoting its own internal social order or equilibrium while protecting itself from disorder.

Classical sociologists argued that societies should be consensus-based systems of moral values and beliefs that guide and determine each individual's activities and roles in two ways.

1   Individuals are created from social structures. Society creates the types of individuals that meet its needs. Each society ensures that its individual members acquire their identity through the socialisation process.

2   Successful socialisation ensures that people fill their social roles and realise the functional needs necessary for social order and the survival of society as a system.

Society and conflict

Society may well, in the 1950s, have been conceived ideally as that of the 'American dream' where shared norms and values (of people who were male and white) produced a prosperous view of society that much of the world wished to copy. And these ideas are reflected in the theories of **structural functionalism**. However, much was to change in the 1960s.

With the Vietnam War (1964–1975), the Black Civil Rights movement (1954–1968) and the rise of a new generation of women, many of whom were to become university students (they were able, for the first time, to control their own futures with the advent of the birth control pill), a new wave of sociological theories were to describe society in a very different way:

Neo-Marxists updated the ideas of Karl Marx to explain why his predicted revolution had not taken place despite the existence of societies where large proportions of working-class populations in one part of the world were either being killed, or being exploited to serve the needs of middle-class populations in different parts of the world.

Feminists re-evaluated the 'social construction' of being female and comment on the *lack* of attention paid to women in official statistics, their apparent *lack* of any role in the construction of 'history' and their *lack* of representation in the political institutions that make up democratic society.

Postmodernists challenged the concept of society mentioned at the beginning of this section, i.e. that one word can describe any grouping of people associated with a particular territory, or who possess their own distinctive culture, institutions and sets of norms and values. The process and pace of global change involves the movement of people (migration), a mass media that connects us all to events around the world, and the Internet that means any single conception of an identifiable 'society' is outdated.

For consideration:

1   What examples can you think of that prove that Thomas Hobbes' fears about humankind are correct?
2   How might the institutions of the family, education, religion, and the media go some way to solve Hobbes' fears?

3.6 What do we mean by 'identity'?

What does this mean?

If anyone talks of somebody's 'identity' they are usually referring to a description (what sociologists refer to as a 'marker'), such as: 'musician', 'student', 'white', 'woman', 'unemployed' or 'Muslim'. These markers help us describe our social existence and how we (and others) see and feel about ourselves.

Some of these markers can be quite individualistic, e.g. 'he is fat'. However, these markers can also refer to being part of a group, e.g. 'he is a family man'. The most common markers include: age, family, parental status, friends, sex, gender, occupation, class, status, leisure activities, religion, ethnicity, race and education. They are used in constructing a sense of 'self' (who we are) and help shape the ways people act, think or feel in a given situation.

Why is this important?

As in all sociological research it is important to 'operationalise' (define what we mean) concepts so that research cannot be misinterpreted. Identity can have a number of different and often confusing meanings. By asking questions about what identity means, sociologists can not only spotlight the social structures that shape identities but also ask questions about what processes are involved when new identities are formed.

Is it possible to have more than one identity?

Yes! Our 'self' is made up of numerous identities, e.g. I may describe myself as Indian, male, a teacher, and heterosexual all at the same time. Sometimes these numerous identities that we possess can come into conflict with each other. Consider how your role as a friend might sometimes come into conflict with your role as a student, daughter or son.

Below are some of the different types of identity that sociologists look at.

- *Primary identity* develops from birth largely as a result of the interaction with the child's family.
- *Secondary identity* develops through involvement at work and also through leisure activities.

✳ Key Ideas

- When you are evaluating writers and research, it really helps to remember the concept of 'cross-cultural perspective'. This means that what one thing means in one culture may be completely different in another. This is really useful when discussing identity in the exam. For example, what it means to be a 'man' or a 'woman' can change enormously depending on what country you come from or even the part of the country you come from.

- Symbolic interactionist George Herbert Mead (1934) connects concepts of identity to social control, i.e. how identity can be controlled by forces within society. Mead argues that social control is the expression of the 'me' over and against the expression of the 'I'. Individuals possess an 'I' and a 'me', which George Herbert Mead refers to as the 'Self'. The 'I' is capable of doing whatever she/he wants to, whereas the 'me' contains all the norms and values learnt and helps 'control' the 'I' in each of us. Our identities (and behaviour) vary depending on how much of the 'I' and 'me' we possess.

- *Personal identity* refers to those 'markers of individuality' which identify people as distinct from others, e.g. personal name, nickname, signature, national insurance number, and so on.
- *Social identity* refers to the personality characteristics that particular cultures associate with certain social roles, e.g. in some cultures mothers are supposed to be loving, nurturing and selfless.
- *Gender identity* refers to the way in which our identity connects to the culturally learned characteristics of being 'masculine' or 'feminine'.
- *National identity* refers to the way our identity can be connected to our nationality and the existence of the 'nation state'.

Sociologists refer to many other types of identities that this chapter will look at. However, it is important to remember that as much as these categories help social scientists understand the lives of different groups of people, sociologists cannot assume all of those identified as belonging to a particular social category, like 'woman' or 'elderly' people, share a common existence (this type of thinking is called '**essentialism**').

In Erving Goffman's (1959) *The Presentation of Self in Everyday Life*, he explores how we present our identities in the same way that actors act out a play. The roles are already written before we act; however, these roles are open to improvisation or interpretation. Goffman's approach shows that there are links between the society in which we live, our identities, and the limitations offered by the roles or parts we play in society. In other words, we have a certain amount of 'free will' in the formation of our identities but at the same time we are constrained by institutions that 'determine' who we are.

Identity also involves relations of similarity or difference. This means that a person cannot be identified as a mother without first having had a child. This allows us to talk of all mothers (similarity) and mothers and children (difference). Some sociologists argue that identities are fluid, changeable and fragmented. For example, you may describe yourself as a 'Muslim' at school but when you get your A-levels and people ask you what you are, you may actually refer to yourself as a 'student at uni'. Later on, you may emphasise the fact that you are 'engaged' or 'married'.

As you can see, like so many other concepts in sociology, the concept of identity is far from clear. This is why sociological theory can help us unpack the very different notions of identity this section has looked at.

6699 Key Definition

Essentialism – is used to describe a concept that claims to represent an 'absolute truth', i.e. something we cannot argue with. Many traditional theories of identity argue there is a basic 'set of ingredients' that determine a person's identity – identity is 'essentially' unchangeable. Increasingly sociologists argue that nothing is 'unchangeable' and that therefore 'essentialism' is quite often viewed negatively.

✍ Coursework Suggestion

As a starting point for your research, brainstorm as many different kinds of identities you can think of to decide which particular definition of identity you might like to explore when carrying out your own research. Perhaps you might like to study how identities can (or cannot) change over time.

For consideration:

1   Do you think it is possible for a person's identity (or identities!). to change?
2   Do you think that you can choose your own identity or is it determined (shaped) by the society you live in?

What do we mean by 'culture'?

What does this mean?

By 'culture' sociologists mean the set of shared values, norms and beliefs of a society or group of people. The word also refers to the shared meanings and symbols (e.g. language) which people use to make sense of the world they live in. The problem with this definition, however, is that different people see the world in very different ways, and the moment we start to talk about class, ethnicity, gender, age and all the other sociological variables, we need a more sophisticated way of talking about culture.

How do sociologists use the word 'culture'?

Below are some of the different ways sociologists use the word 'culture'.

Dominant culture refers to the main culture in a society whose norms and values are seen to be the most powerful and generally accepted. Feminists might argue that this dominant culture could be patriarchal; Marxists might argue that this culture could be capitalist; sociologists writing about race could argue that the dominant culture in the western world represents white, middle-class values.

Subculture refers to the culture of a social group that is distinct from the dominant culture of a society. Quite often associated with 'youths', 'subcultures' are often groups operating within a larger group but possessing cultural norms which are very different.

High culture is perceived as the culture of the elite, for example what counts as a good cultural experience. This usually refers to classical music and literature and generally more traditional types of painted art.

● **Synoptic Link**

Write one sentence on each of the types of culture described in this section to make synoptic connections with social differentiation and power. Create a section called 'synopticity' in your folders and place these notes in that section ready for the exam next year. By doing it now, while the subject is fresh you will save yourself an enormous amount of work for next year.

Who decides which is 'high' or 'low' culture and why?

Folk culture is often associated with Western ideas about the lives of working-class people (the word 'folk' means 'people'). This concept referred to the music, food and patterns of behaviour that would have existed in 'pre-modern' societies, for example to be found in pubs, churches or market places today.

Mass culture is associated with Marxists from the Frankfurt School who argue that the commercialised popular culture we have today is created by the media. This mass culture helps create false needs and continues the **false consciousness** that most working class people possess (see section 16 for more about the mass-culture debate).

Popular culture – sociologists usually include most forms of television, football, bingo, pop music, and tabloid newspapers when using this concept; however, this concept is problematic or oversimplified.

Popular culture is often viewed as being 'commodified'. By this, sociologists mean that some types of culture can be bought or sold by an audience of customers. Many postmodernists argue that this makes concepts such as 'high' and 'popular' pointless – what is the difference between the two (think now about how easy it is to collect magazines with jazz or classical CDs by buying them in branches of big newsagents, making this no longer such an elitist choice of music.

False consciousness

This Marxist concept refers to the way in which (Marxists argue) most working-class people fail to see the fact that they are exploited by those in power above them, i.e. the middle classes. By being 'distracted' with newspapers, films, music and theatre, the failings of the capitalist society in which we live are conveniently 'ignored', i.e. those of poverty, homelessness and rising crime. False consciousness 'tricks' people into believing that society is fair and stops the working-class revolution that Marx predicted one day would happen.

Conclusion

The deterministic view that many Marxists hold completely ignores the wealth of young artists, writers, filmmakers and musicians who do criticise contemporary society (e.g. the poetry of Benjamin Zephaniah, the lyrics in black rap music; the street art of New Orleans and Paris).

◆ **What, When and Why?**

The Frankfurt School for Social Research was founded in 1923 as a centre for Marxist research. Its leading figures (Theodor Adorno, Max Horkheimer and Herbert Marcuse) emigrated to America with the rise of Hitler. These writers and the many that have followed in their footsteps have attempted to 'update' the traditional Marxist ideas they were so very critical about. The theory associated with this school is referred to as 'critical theory'.

For consideration:

1 Who decides what is high, low, or popular culture?
2 What implications has this got for who has, and who has not, got power in society?

3.8

What is the relationship between the individual and society?

✳ Key Idea

Sociologists talk about primary, secondary and tertiary **socialisation**, i.e. the kind of socialisation you receive in the family, education and the workplace. But, Sociologists are also interested in the variety of identities people are socialised into such as those of class, age, ethnicity, gender and sexuality, for example. As sociologists we also look at the importance of institutions within the socialisation process, e.g. those of education, religion and the media. As with all sociology there is no one broad agreement as to how these processes happen. Rather, there are different theories that offer explanations about how the socialisation processes work.

66 99 Key Definition

By '**institutions**' sociologists mean a variety of 'patterns' of behaviour that constrain how individuals may or may not work. Quite often institutions contain 'value systems' that tell us what the 'norms' and 'values' of society are. Examples of institutions include: education, religion, the media, the family and the law.

✳ Key Idea

'Discourses' are sets of related statements or systems of knowledge which define how we think and perceive the world around us. Michel Foucault (1977), in his theory of 'post-structuralism', uses the concept of discourse to show how knowledge can be used as a form of power over others. Those who control the discourse have the power to control others. One example would be that if you were a psychiatrist you would have the specialised knowledge (and language) to determine if somebody else was 'sane' or 'insane'. Three hundred years ago no such profession existed and therefore no such power could be used over others.

What does this mean?

When trying to work out how we are **socialised**, how we develop our own selves, or identities or how we become individuals, it helps to think of the different ways we can connect people to **institutions**, other societies and events and even different points in time.

How do conventional theories view the relationship between the individual and society?

*   Functionalists believe that the individual is shaped or determined by the society they live in. Individual identities are formed as a result of the interaction between the individual and the social institution to which they belong. The institution (e.g. education, family or religion) produces a moral consensus (shared set of ideas) which most of us follow.

*   Marxists both agree with but also challenge this functionalist perspective. They agree with the idea that institutions and society as a whole have the ability to shape and determine the way we think. However, they see this as something negative. They argue that the unequal distribution of power in society is something that functionalists not only overlook but actually accept as positive.

*   Post-structuralists develop some of the ideas of Marxism in their explanation of the relationship between the individual and society but also put some of the blame on us as individuals. They argue that 'discourses' such as 'competition' or 'survival of the fittest' are things that we accept as being normal (or internalise). This then stops us from looking for alternative solutions. As individuals we are trapped by these self-created ideologies that we no longer question.

*   Interpretivists disagree that society has the ability to shape and determine the way we think. They argue that society has been 'socially constructed' by the individuals that live within it. The nature of the interaction between individuals creates the society we live in. By using labelling theory they argue that identities of individuals are constructed by the reaction of others in society to those labels and by the 'self-fulfilling prophesy' that some individuals experience. This is when people believe the label that has been applied to them and start to act accordingly.

How can this 'relationship' be analysed?

The problem with some of the more conventional theories that look at the relationship between the individual and society is that they each have their favourite way of looking at things. Functionalists and Marxists tend to see this macro relationship as one where the individual is shaped or determined by conditions beyond their control. A more 'micro' sociological perspective is one where interpretivists focus more on the importance of the individual in the creation and maintenance of certain types of society.

An alternative approach is offered by Derek Layder (1993) who argues that when analysing the relationship between the individual and society it helps to think of five different concepts or 'research elements' that can be combined to look at the whole picture. These elements are:

1   *The self* – this is the self-identity of the individual, made up of their own social experience. It involves looking at their life story, i.e. what they have done in the time they have been alive.
2   *Situated activity* – this refers to the symbols of communication and meanings and understandings that take place when two or more people communicate with each other.
3   *Setting* – this allows the sociologist to focus on the location where people interact, e.g. their work place, their school, their home, their sports place or social club and even the church, temple or mosque they might attend.
4   *Context* – this looks at the social, economic or political sets of power relationships that may exist in any society. It might look at the type of government, the legal system, the sets of values and traditions that a particular society may hold sacred or even whether or not the society is patriarchal or matriarchal.
5   *History* – history is really important when considering any relationship between the individual and society. Think how any of the issues discussed in this book have changed with time – sometimes in as little as a few years.

Derek Layder combines macro and micro approaches to sociology when looking at the relationship between the individual and society.

✍ Coursework Suggestion

Use Derek Layder's five research elements discussed in this section to help you generate ideas for coursework. Try doing a spider diagram covering any issues you are thinking of. You will be amazed at how quickly you come up with a theoretical framework that will impress the coursework examiners.

For consideration:

1   When making decisions about what you wear, what you listen to, to what extent do you feel you have free will or your choices are determined by others?
2   How could you use the ideas of Derek Layder to explain the answer to the question above?

What role does 'class' play in the formation of identity?

● Synoptic Link

By linking discussion about identity to class you are automatically making a synoptic link with stratification. Make notes from this section and attach it to your synoptic section in your folder and you will save a lot of work for the exam by having a ready-made set of synoptic links.

✷ Key Idea

Pierre Bourdieu's (1990) concept of *habitus* is an essential concept to use when talking about identity and class. It refers to the thoughts, behaviour and tastes associated with an individual or groups of individuals. As a student think about the lifestyle, language and culture that surrounds you – your 'habitus'. How might the habitus of a full-time cleaner vary to that of a college professor? It also allows a way to connect structure and agency by implying that while we carry out actions we believe to be independent (agency), these actions nevertheless reflect the habitus of the social group we associate with (structure). In other words, we act in ways that fit in with our peer groups.

✓ Top Exam Hint

As a point of evaluation you can mention briefly that many sociological academics, particularly during the 1950s and 1960s came from middle-class backgrounds. While the studies they write about are fascinating and offer extremely useful ideas there is a hint of 'cultural superiority'. In other words – that middle-class culture is somehow better than working-class culture. Be aware of this when writing in the exam; by mentioning this, you will score evaluation marks.

What does this mean?

In the Tudor times of the late 15th and 16th centuries 'laws of sumptuary' required people to dress appropriately according to their social position, i.e. their class. By the beginning of the 21st century many commentators give the impression that we are living in a 'classless' society. It is up to you, as a sociologist, to decide if that is the case.

Class identities and their impact on social behaviour

Many people describe Britain as a class ridden society – meaning that class dictates people's life chances.

- Writing in the mid-1970s sociologist Herbert Gans (1974) claimed that culture and taste were directly linked to social class. Certainly until the 1950s the cloth cap identified those wearing it as probably coming from the working class industrial cultures. Today we know that there is a direct link between class background, diet and health problems.
- Traditional Marxists argue that the economic infrastructure shapes the culture of all classes. The jobs, property and money you have (or don't have!) determine the life you will lead. This would include your peer group, in that you are likely to relate to those in the same position.
- Goldthorpe and Lockwood (1968) argued that the industrial working classes had a specific culture that meant they lived for the present. This reflected the very difficult lives that many working-class families endured during much of the late 19th and early 20th centuries. It was far more important to work from an early age than stay on in education. The immediacy and urgency of money from work outweighed any long-term gain from staying on at school.
- The above idea of 'immediate gratification' (i.e. getting something now) is echoed in education as one explanation for why working-class children have not achieved (in formal education) as well as those from the middle classes. The latter are said to 'defer their gratification', i.e. instead of leaving school and earning money now, they stay on at university in the knowledge that the extra time spent will mean greater rewards later on.
- Many Marxists are fascinated by the reproduction of the class system from one generation to the next. Neo-Marxist Bourdieu (1990) has a concern over 'cultural capital'. By this he means the knowledge and habits (or socialisation) that we pick up from our families and groups of friends that can also signify a particular class background (e.g. knowledge of certain types of music or certain ways of using cutlery).

The transference of this cultural capital from parents to children is referred to as 'class structuration' and is said to determine the life chances of these children when they grow up.

Can we really use class as a useful concept?

Postmodernists argue that class is an outdated concept because culture and identity are dependent on what we buy (e.g. clothes and music) and not our class backgrounds. Class identity is said to have fragmented into numerous separate identities which are affected by gender, location, family, education, etc. Savage (1995) argues that even middle-class culture has fragmented. For example, consider teachers, managers and executives – all have very different lifestyles but all can be described as middle-class. See section 17 (postmodernism).

A classless society?

Much has been written about the erosion of class culture. Zweig (1961) argued that because of rising living standards many affluent workers were in a position to take on middle-class lifestyles. This idea is reflected in 'the embourgeoisement thesis', which refers to when successful working-class people start to adopt the tastes and culture of the middle classes.

In many countries in the West today it is harder to spot somebody who is either working-class or middle-class. The changing nature of production and employment patterns mean that it is difficult to identify working-class or middle-class jobs. Manual jobs were traditionally working class types of employment with office jobs being carried out by members of the middle classes. However, today technology has reduced the amount of manual labour needed and increased the variety of office jobs that are available.

Some therefore argue that European societies are becoming more 'meritocratic' and less class-based, i.e. a person's identity is based more upon what they have achieved through education or the workplace for example, rather than their class. While this is a debate you might like to consider, perhaps another more crucial discussion relates to changing patterns of production.

As the West becomes richer and the production of consumer goods is increasingly carried out in other poorer parts of the world, we need to rethink what class means. Many of the disappearing Western working classes are being re-created in poorer parts of the world to produce goods for Western consumption. Is this not Marxist exploitation of a new kind? If it is, then class as a determinant of culture and identity is still with us.

For consideration:

1   Postmodernists argue that we construct our own identities through the popular cultures we are surrounded by and that class is no longer significant. To what extent do you agree with this?
2   Ask your friends, family members and acquaintances to what extent class has affected their lives.

● **Synoptic Link**

Use the synoptic concept of 'identity' with education to show how education can lead to social stratification. Paul Willis (1977) looked at how working-class 'lads' reject the school system. Their lack of status results in the formation of subcultures outside of school, leading to the social differentiation of such groups and adding to the stratification experienced by the working classes.

◆ **What, When and Why?**

Britain in the 19th and first half of the 20th century was described as a 'manufacturing economy'. Britain had steel, coal and copper industries and produced cars, fridges and a range of industrial and domestic goods. Today, Britain is described as a 'service economy'. It has a large financial sector and a leisure and tourism industry. This means that traditional working-class jobs no longer exist to the level they once did and most working-class adults work within the service sector.

✎ **Coursework Suggestion**

Explore to what extent class has changed over the years as a significant determinant of life chances. Carry out a small-scale study. Interview three people who are in their sixties and three who are in their thirties. Examine to what extent class background has had an effect on their education, health, job prospects, choice of partners and any other factors you perceive to be relevant. Use the sociological theories you read about in this chapter to analyse your findings.

3.10 What role does 'ethnicity' play in the formation of identity?

The Bradford Race Riots: an example of 'hybridisation' or class conflict? You the sociologist must decide!

◆ What, When and Why?

British ethnic identity

There have been well-established black, Chinese and Indian communities in Britain since the nineteenth century, in London and some of the bigger seaports such as Liverpool and Cardiff, not to mention the Midlands and Yorkshire. In response to British shortage of labour during the 1950s and 1960s, people from other destinations arrived including West Africa, the Caribbean, Hong Kong, India and Pakistan. After the Eastern European revolutions of 1989 and 1990, the former USSR provides the latest significant source of migration into Britain. In more recent years many refugees have emigrated from Afghanistan to the UK because of the religious persecution they face at home.

✳ Key Idea

The word 'diaspora' is used to describe the process of cultural dispersal of norms and values that produce new ethnic identities. The evidence for this can be seen by the influence of ethnic minorities on the British film and music industries along with the enormous change in eating habits in the UK over the last thirty years. Such ideas can also be linked to the postmodern view that we are living in a rapidly changing and diverse society. See also section 17 (postmodernism).

What does this mean?

Elements of the nature versus nurture debate (see section 4) are reflected in any discussion about ethnicity. While members of an ethnic minority group may share biological racial traits (e.g. skin colour), they also share other cultural characteristics, e.g. their religion, food, education, family life, language, politics and the experience of being a 'minority' where they live (see Key idea box, Section 9). This is what sociologists mean by 'ethnicity' and it is this experience that can shape what sociologists refer to as 'ethnic identities'.

Why is this important?

While ethnicity is an important source of social identity, it can also be a source of conflict (e.g. the 2002 Bradford riots). People often make stereotypical assumptions about other ethnic groups. One example of this is when ethnic minorities are blamed for the poor housing conditions many live in. Such assumptions may be racist and result in prejudice and discrimination. Today the issue of 'nationalism' is once again a source of potential conflict in many parts of the world (e.g. the success of right wing extremist Le Pen in France in 2002) and sociologists can provide answers to many of the false misunderstandings that take place in multi-cultural societies.

Can we identify patterns in ethnic identities?

Yes! The experience of racism can unify different ethnic groups when they enter the country for the first time. Cashmore and Troyner argue that on arrival, minorities often live and work in similar areas and under similar conditions. These conditions include the poor housing in which the *ethnic majority* of the 'host' country has no desire to live in.

- Marxists argue that ethnic minorities effectively become the 'new' working class as native working-class populations move further up the class ladder. The experience of living in areas where native populations no longer have a desire to live can strengthen traditional forms of ethnicity and identity by recreating the temples, mosques, churches, businesses, shops and other recreational activities of the home country.
- Traditional gender identities may be maintained with wives entering the country after their husbands and assuming traditional domestic roles. Such roles do not easily allow the wives to learn the new language of the 'host' country (husbands will learn language in the work place).

- Many traditions that families maintain are connected to the point in time they left their country. Some Asian arranged marriages are still forced despite the fact that most Asians today are against this. Such traditions may have changed since leaving and are a source of conflict for many children of families caught in a clash of cultures both in time and location.

What is 'hybridisation'?

- 'Hybridisation' refers to the merging of different types of cultural traditions. This idea fits the postmodern concept of cultural diversity and the usefulness of such terms as 'ethnicity' in the first place.
- Johal (1998) argues that second- and third-generation British Asians inherit an Asian identity but adopt a British one. In an attempt to fit into peer groups at school or college they assume a 'white' mask.
- However, a real debate exists as to whether this hybridisation process actually takes place. Writers argue that there is 'cultural resistance' from certain ethnic groups who are afraid of losing their own identities. Some members of ethnic groups may resist 'white' culture by reclaiming their ethnic identity (e.g. embracing Islam).
- Writing in the 1970s, Stuart Hall blamed capitalism for directing young British black males into low-paid work (e.g. street cleaners, security guards or night portering). A reaction from them to this can be seen in the distinct styles of dress, forms of music and cultural beliefs that assert an identity that criticises what can be seen as an oppressive white society. Some religions provide a sense of support and positive identity to ethnic minorities denied by much white, middle-class culture (such as the national curriculum, for instance).
- But while the cultures of ethnic groups tend to reflect their different origins, Stuart Hall (1996) later argued that the entertainment industry has managed to combine ethnicity with other sociological variables, e.g. religion, gender, sexuality and class. This can be seen with the explosion of Asian influence on the music and film industries along with the commercialisation of rap music. He highlights how ethnic identities are becoming harder to identify. One example is the way in which African-Caribbean music and dress are particularly popular amongst Punjabi and Bengali males.

Conclusion

Sociologists also look at how American culture is changing the way ethnicities can easily be recognised, through music, films and fashion (see also section 21 in chapter 5). Whether the process of ethnic identity formation is one of hybridisation or 'Americanisation' is something you can debate in the exam.

For consideration:

1 When discussing ethnic minorities what skin colour do you automatically consider? What are your reason for this?

✳ Key Idea

Ballard (1979) has questioned to what extent young people do experience this clash in cultures. He argues that research showed that young southern Asians in the UK produced their own 'synthesis' of Asian and British values. This is referred to as 'hyperethnicity' where younger members of ethnic minorities can switch from one cultural form to another – at school, at home and in the work place.

✓ Top Exam Hint

When writing a conclusion to any question on ethnicity, remember to point out that issues such as class and gender must be taken into consideration when discussing what it means to come from an ethnic minority. A good exam answer will recognise how these variables affect ethnic identities.

What roles does 'gender' play in the formation of identity?

How does David Beckham challenge conventional expectations of male behaviour?

What does this mean?

Historically, in most societies, power relationships in the family, socially, or within the political framework have been unequally in favour of men. Sociologists refer to these unequal power dynamics as 'patriarchy'. But in today's rapidly changing world, what are the cultural expectations of the two genders? Do 'traditional' gender roles exist? With famous celebrities like David Beckham challenging traditional male forms of behaviour and fashion, and the rise in girl 'laddishness', sociologists are questioning what exactly we mean by gender identities.

How are gender identities socialised?

Are we biologically determined into being 'masculine' or 'feminine' or are gender roles socially constructed? This essential debate within sociology underpins much of the discussion on socialisation. If we adopt the first viewpoint then things are pretty simple: how you behave and how other people react to you depends on whether you are either male or female.

However, sociologists argue that gender is a social construction and that we learn to behave in certain ways that reflect the physical differences between the sexes. These expectancies are then 'culturally transmitted' from one generation to the next through institutions such as the workplace, family, religion, peers, education and the media. Feminists argue that this reproduces patriarchal processes and relations, with female subordination achieved through 'sex role socialisation'.

Is there a 'crisis in masculinity'?

Mac an Ghaill (1994) argues that changes in the economy are leading to a 'crisis in masculinity'. As women become more successful in the work place (e.g. fund manager – Nicola Horlicks; news correspondent – Kate Adie; chief executive officer – Marjorie Scardino), they are also becoming more economically independent. This greater participation in the labour market is eroding traditional notions of female and male identity. The traditional notion of the male 'breadwinner' is increasingly being undermined.

In addition to this, boys' under-achievement in education and the increasing suicide rates amongst, and levels of crimes committed by, young men are leading to a crisis in masculinity – an insecurity in the expectation of what being masculine is. At the same time Winship (1986) suggests that because women's magazines push the notion of the strong independent woman, young females are becoming more assertive about their rights to education and careers. The very existence of girl laddishness and the rise in girl gangs, female sexual liberation and girls increasingly having strong role models in the media adds to the male dilemma of what being a 'man' actually means.

What are 'sexual' identities?

If we accept that gender roles are learnt through the socialisation processes described above, then it follows that sexual orientation is also learnt and that the classifications of 'heterosexual', 'homosexual' and 'bisexual' are themselves social constructions. Such identities are further confused by the need for markets to find new 'customers'. Images of perfectly-toned male bodies are increasingly being used to sell products. The fashion industry, magazines, cosmetics are increasingly selling to men now as opposed to just targeting women. Economists even refer to the 'pink pound' recognising that there is money to be made from commercial products targeting middle-class gay men. With mainstream cinema and television increasingly showing homosexuality as socially acceptable, what are the implications for the gender socialisation processes looked at above?

How can theories help untangle gender identities?

The view that we are biologically determined is challenged by many theories within sociology. Postmodernists argue that identities are simply 'performances' where gender and sexual identities are constructed, learned and performed (see also section 17). This concept is actually very similar to that of interactionist Erving Goffman's (1959) idea that we perform particular roles in the same way that actors perform to a script already written (see also section 6).

Feminists argue that a combination of capitalist and patriarchal ideologies mean that women's bodies are used to sell magazines, films and other cultural products even when the editors of those same magazines may well be women themselves. Post-structuralists argue that we 'internalise' discourses around what it is to be 'male' or 'female' and once internalised we 'imprison' ourselves in these patterns of expected behaviour. If as a male you grow up expecting to behave in a 'laddish' way, the mere fact that you might not *choose* to do so can result in your peer group attacking your 'masculinity'. You therefore behave laddishly even if, perhaps, you do not desire to.

For consideration:

1   What values do male and female role models offer to society?
2   To what extent are role models a creation of the media?

✳ Key Idea
Feminist Ann Oakley (1979) describes the construction of gender identities using two concepts: *manipulation* (the role of parents in encouraging the 'correct' behaviour for girls and boys) and *canalisation* (choosing the right toys and activities for their boys and girls to involve themselves in). To what extent is this view valid today?

Is 21st-century masculinity about power or sensitivity?

✍ Coursework Suggestion
Explore the changing nature of male identity. Hold a focus group of friends and show them two pictures of male role models (e.g. one of David Beckham and one of Russell Crowe's 'Gladiator' character). Using issues raised in this section put questions to the group and then stand back and let them discuss these issues. You can do two follow-up interviews with members of the group and then compare these findings with the theoretical views raised in this section.

3.12 What role does 'age' play in the formation of identity?

How do these images challenge our perception of old age?

✓ **Top Exam Hint**

Remember when discussing issues around age and identity to always use the ten sociological variables (age; class; cross-cultural perspectives; ethnicity; gender; globalisation; historical perspectives; region; religion; and sexuality). You can apply all of these (obviously leaving out age) variables to discussions around age and impress the examiners with your superb evaluation skills!

What does this mean?

This question can be interpreted in two ways.

1 How old you are has a direct bearing on how identity is perceived by you and those around you.
2 The age (or era) that you are born into has enormous implications on how different types of identity are perceived (e.g. identities based around class, gender, ethnicity and sexuality).

Is age a social construction?

By 'social construction' sociologists mean the way that classifications (e.g. 'deviant'; 'white'; and 'old') are not naturally occurring but are categories that we create. It is important to realise that age is viewed differently by different cultures, e.g. in many traditional societies older people are treated with respect and kept within the family, often playing a key role in the upbringing of children. Compare this to the Western nuclear family where the tendency is for the old to be placed in care, often with minimal contact with immediate family members. Such enormous cultural differences in how age is perceived support the argument that age is indeed a social construction.

Significant too is the role of the media when we think of popular portrayals of old people as 'vulnerable', 'sexless' and constantly in need of care. Contrast this with the emergence of the American 'teenager' in the 1950s, famously depicted by Hollywood stars like James Dean. From a Marxist perspective you can argue that the capitalist system constructs categories, like 'child' or 'teenager' in order to create markets and consumers for toys, clothes, records/CDs, and so on.

How do sociologists categorise the ages?

Before the 19th century children were considered a part of the livelihood of the family and took part in domestic and agricultural chores (note compulsory education for children in England and Wales did not take place until 1870!). Post-structuralists argue 'discourses' about childhood were created in the 19th century with the emergence of new sciences, e.g. psychology with its emphasis on childhood in personality formation.

Grouped into categories by government departments and social scientists, concepts such as 'childhood', 'youths', 'adulthood', 'middle age' and 'old age' create broad generalisations about lifestyles and age. For example, the demand for state and private provision of public services (e.g. education and heath care) will vary according to these different age groupings.

Age, class, ethnicity and gender

What we eat varies immensely depending on our class background. In general, the diet of the middle classes tends to be healthier than that of the working classes. This in turn impacts on the elderly in both classes. Better housing and diet earlier on in life is likely to mean less demand for health care when old. A state pension alone will not provide for the kind of life style that many middle-class families have come to expect as the 'norm'. While many middle-class families will have private pensions and savings, in most cases, it is the working-class pensioners' only source of income.

The experience of being young, middle-aged or old also varies according to ethnicity and gender. David Gillborn (1990) argues education, employment and job promotion opportunities vary depending on ethnicity. Feminists argue that women earn less (and get promoted less) but live longer than men making them the larger of the two pension groups. Lower wages means that their pension is significantly less than males because they have contributed less over the years that they have worked.

Conclusion

Lower birth rates and longer life expectancy mean the generation of 'elderly' people living in Britain today, themselves the teenagers of the 'swinging sixties', will be fitter, healthier and more economically independent than their parents had been. Governments earn less money in the form of taxation and national insurance to fund pensions which in turn could mean no state pension for those who retire in generations to come.

On the other hand 'grey' identities in the future are likely to be very different to what they once were. Whereas the 20th century characterised the elderly as a burden, the 21st century might see travel agents, fashion houses, universities and perhaps even the sex industry increasingly targeting this growing market niche. Politicians are also aware that while in the past they have paid lip service to the needs of the elderly, in the future their own political futures might well rest on capturing the 'grey vote'.

For consideration:

1 What key government policies can you think of (e.g. 'New Deal') that target specific age groups?
2 How might these policies have to change in the future?

❋ Key Idea

Post-structuralists argue that 'discourses' are created by bodies of knowledge (e.g. medicine with its own body of experts, authority, specialist knowledge and language) that determine and restrict how we see the world. We 'internalise' (take for granted) the discourse and are incapable of seeing the world in a different way. Western medical discourses about 'care' and 'preventative medicine' in the UK mean that it is difficult to perceive elderly people in a positive light despite their being today fitter, economically more independent and increasingly marketed as 'sexually desirable' e.g. Sean Connery, Harrison Ford, Joan Collins.

✍ Coursework Suggestion

Explore the social construction of age by carrying out six in-depth interviews with three separate generations (one male and one female for each generation) exploring what it means/meant to be a teenager. From an interpretive perspective you can explore and examine the perceptions of your sample and then seek to account for the differences by applying different theories to your interview data.

3.13 What role does 'globalisation' play in the formation of national identities?

High street shopping around the world – how different an experience is it from one country to the next?

66 99 Key Definitions

- Anthony Giddens (1990) argues that the general term for the increasing interdependence of world society is **globalisation**. For him, globalisation is where the world has become a single social system as a result of growing ties of interdependence which now affect virtually everyone. These social, political and economic connections cross cut borders between countries and change the fate of those living within them.

- **Nation state'** – this concept means an organised political community under one government. However, this concept can be problematic for sociologists because it seems to imply the existence of one homogenous or single type of people who share similar cultural values or even a single national identity. We only have to look at the diversity of cultures in England to realise that such concepts have to be questioned very carefully by sociologists.

What does this mean?

Take a close look at the clothes you or your friends wear. How easy is it to identify a person's culture from the clothes they wear? The chances are it is quite tricky. Has this always been the case? Does the food that we eat or the television programmes that we watch make it any easier? The term '**globalisation**' is used to describe the processes involved that make the world increasingly interconnected. You can eat at MacDonald's in Manchester or Calcutta. You can eat curry in Delhi and New York. In all four places you could be watching an episode of 'Friends' while you eat. What does that tell us about national identities?

Different sociologists have different ideas about how this affects national identities. 'National identity' refers to the way in which the identity of a group of people is connected linguistically, culturally, historically, geographically and politically.

Is there such a thing as a national identity?

It may seem surprising that the concept of a national identity is a comparatively recent one and is also what sociologists refer to as a social construction (a concept that we learn from our culture and that we help construct but also one that shapes how we perceive, feel and think). Surprisingly, it has only been since the 16th century that most societies began to become single '**nation states**' and that we started to talk about national identities. Germany and Italy only became nation states in 1871 and the state of Israel was 'created' in 1947.

How are national identities formed?

Andy Green (1997) argues that education helps form national identities by giving us one national curriculum where we are socialised into one national culture through a common language and the teaching of a national history, literature and religion.

However, to what extent does a British national identity exist? The British may well be a mix of social groups who call themselves 'British' but this identity is a social construction. This involves the inventing of traditions (the Sunday roast), symbols (the Union Jack) and mythologies (Robin Hood and King Arthur) to bring about a sense of national unity and identification helped along by a mass media that focuses on national institutions such as the Royal family. How does this then relate to the different ethnicities, religions, sexual persuasions, etc, that exist in Britain?

How might globalisation affect our national identity?

- Taking into account the speed at which people can now fly from London to Beijing or New York, or the speed at which a business deal can be concluded electronically, David Harvey (1989) argues that compression of time and space affects national identities. People in London and New York watching the same live-to-air TV report of a volcano in one part of the world are in effect experiencing, if only temporarily, the same space and time. The media brings into our homes music, fashion, style and even religion from other parts of the world (think of the impact that MTV, MacDonald's and more recently the Asian cultural explosion has had on the 'British way of life'). See also section 17.

- Harvey also emphasises the effects of the revolution in global finance since 1970, with the emergence of global markets in stocks, commodities and currencies. These markets are able to operate instantaneously around the world. This means that if there is a crash in markets in one part of the world, this can have disastrous effects on the national economies of countries in another. If a Japanese car company goes bust in Japan it can affect employment patterns in a northern town in England if, as a result, the factory has to close down.

- The growth of 'supranational' organisations such as the European Union confuses any description based around a single national identity: are we British or European or both? Finally, with the growth of the Internet and the speed with which people can communicate, does it really seem likely that single national identities can remain unchanged by this process?

Conclusion

So where does this leave us? Globalisation could on the one hand mean that national cultures may decline leading to a 'hybridity' of new cultures and identities through inter-marriage, with subsequent generations of all ethnic groups subscribing to values and norms from both their inherited and adopted cultures. This view is challenged by Marxists who see the process as one in which a single homogeneous, commercialised global culture reflecting American, Western capitalist ideas may well come to dominate all societies.

☞ Who is this Person?
World famous sociologist Anthony Giddens was born in 1938 and studied at the University of Hull and the London School of Economics before taking up a post as lecturer at Leicester University. Since then he has held several academic posts and has been a major influence behind the thinking of Tony Blair and New Labour. His theory of 'structuration' successfully combines macro and micro sociology.

✳ Key Ideas
Anthony Giddens' *Structuration Theory* is an attempt to combine macro or structural sociology with micro or interpretive sociology. He argues that people 'interpret' the world around them, deciding how they will act. But the choices that people make are constrained, determined or shaped by the structures in society that individuals have helped to form. Some of these structures *constrain*, for example rules and regulations, but others *enable*, i.e. without the structure of language we would not be able to communicate with each other.

For consideration:

1   How many words in your own language on closer examination stem from other languages?
2   Look at what you wear – identify where each garment has been manufactured. Can what we wear tell us about national identities?

3.14 How is identity shaped by community and locality?

✓ Top Exam Hint

Examiners love it when you identify an idea from one sociological theory and then draw out similarities with another. This shows real sociological sophistication. One way of doing this is by comparing Tonnies' (1955) *Gesselschaft* and *Gemeinschaft* (see page 133) with Durkheim's (1886) *Mechanistic Relationships* and *Organic Relationships*. Mechanistic relationships are rural, face-to-face and with clearly defined roles and group identity. Organic relationships are urban, anonymous, roles are less clear and identity is more individual. You will be rewarded highly for these comparisons.

◆ What, When and Why?

Urbanisation refers to the many processes that take place as a result of the movement of people from the countryside into the cities. In 19th-century Britain this major source of social change led many writers to comment on the implications for housing, transport, employment and health and safety. For many politicians, urbanisation was seen in an extremely positive light and was an indication of 'civilised' or 'modern' societies. For many social scientists, including Durkheim and Weber, urbanisation was to be viewed extremely critically.

What does this mean?

While the concept 'community' may appear to have a geographical meaning in that people identify (positively or negatively) with people from a particular area or country, for sociologists this is not always the case. The assumption is that there is a set of shared norms and values or an 'identity' within any particular community. However, the word becomes more complicated when we refer to the Muslim community, the European Community or even a cyber-community. Locality, on the other hand, describes the geographical area such as a country, where different social and psychological characteristics are found to be identified in the people living there.

How classical sociological theories help us understand community and locality

1   Emile Durkheim (1886) was essentially pessimistic about the urbanisation process. While certainly more people came into more contact with each other through this process, these relationships were superficial and, he argued, lacked any real moral dimension. However, functionalists argued that communities exerted social control over the individuals who lived in them by establishing 'moral order' and by the high degree of 'surveillance'. Individualism is discouraged.

2   Concerned with what he described as the 'disenchantment' of modern communities, Weber (1905) argued that medieval cities, while bureaucratic, were more communal than the modern communities that emerged during industrialisation.

3   Marx (1867) was quite critical about rural life, arguing that the traditional ideas that passed from one generation to another restricted working-class revolutionary hopes. While urban areas were indeed dreadful places at times (lacking in sanitation), they were also localities of changing ideas, changing identities and a place where revolutionary consciousness could be woken.

How recent sociological theories help us understand community and locality

- From a feminist perspective, women are both exploited and respected within communities. Power relations within communities invariably reflect patriarchal structures. However, very often it is women who are responsible for maintaining local community ties.

- Interpretive or interactionist sociologists look at the mechanisms that operate within communities and how these create or maintain particular identities within the community, e.g. via gossiping and surveillance and the way that these either pull in or exclude people.

- Utilitarian theories argue that communities and the individuals that live in them are out to gain the best from each other by mutually beneficial exchanges.

- Postmodernists, with their concern over the dissolving of boundaries and the impact of technology, argue that localities are mere constructions in the minds of individuals (e.g. the perception that people living on the north side of the Thames are different from those on the south side). They also point to the 'hyperreality' of shopping centres where it's possible to encounter Chinese/Indian/Mexican 'boundaries' within 50 metres.

- Anderson (1983), a neo-Marxist, argues that the nation state is an 'imagined political community'. By this he means that 'community' appears to give the impression that people know each other – something which is impossible if we are talking about the whole population of a country. A variety of methods help create this 'community' including the development of the printed word in a common language and the construction of legends (e.g. Robin Hood), which help us to believe in a common shared past and a 'national anthem'.

Conclusion

Postmodernists would also accept that cyber-communities and the identities that result, are as 'real' as any geographical community. With the advent of increasingly advanced mobile communications technology (i.e. video messaging, surround sound, integrated cameras etc.), who can predict what new communities and identities will emerge?

For consideration:

1 Make a list of as many different types of communities that you can think of and then apply the words 'consensus' or 'conflict' to each example.
2 Which theory could you now apply to those communities that have either the words 'consensus' or 'conflict' next to them?

✳ Key Ideas

- Georg Simmel (1858–1918) remains one of the most influential classical sociologists of his era and as with all good theorists his ideas can be used when looking at communities and localities. He contrasted rural with urban ways of life. Rural communities were vibrant, personal, traditional and (using Weberian language) 'enchanting'. However, urban lives were money-orientated, rational, bureaucratic (again Weberian language here) and obsessed with 'sophistication'. As a result, distinctly different identities are produced in the different localities.

- Ferdinand Tonnies (1955) coined two terms used today by sociologists. **Gemeinschaft** refers to close and long-lasting relationships where people are mutually involved with each other. **Gesellschaft** refers to relationships that are on a larger scale, more impersonal, superficial and based on the desire to further individual need. While these terms were not necessarily used to describe 'rural versus urban' identities, the concepts are useful to you in order to describe the development of identities in communities in the exam.

3.15 How does the workplace act as an agent of socialisation?

◆ What, When and Why?

Since the 1970s, two factors have changed sociologists' thinking about 'job security' in Britain.

1 Multinational companies have been investing more money in Asia and the USSR rather than Western economies as before.

2 Since the 1970s the power of trade unions in the UK to represent workers' rights has been weakened by government policies. This means they no longer have the same ability to act for the interests of workers.

Some sociologists (generally Marxist sociologists) fear that working conditions are worsening as a result of the two factors above.

✳ Key Ideas

- 'Alienation' is a Marxist term used to describe how people are increasingly removed from the creative side of work. The products they produce are sold to others for profit which does not go back to the workers. Repetitive work under these conditions reduces work satisfaction and can produce feelings of anxiety, frustration and powerlessness.

- Neo-Marxist Braverman's (1974) *Labour Process Theory* looked at how 'alienation' at work covered more and more sectors of the working world in the latter half of the twentieth century. He used the word 'proletarianisation' to describe how workers were being affected by the pressure to accept lower incomes, fewer hours of work, reduced job security, degraded job conditions and less opportunity for career development.

What does this mean?

Sociologists have always focused on the workplace in an attempt to see how the conditions of work affect our identities. Sociologists refer to these processes as 'professional socialisation'. Changing arrangements in the way we work has meant that the formation of identities needs to be re-examined by sociologists.

- The amount of time that people spend in the workplace is far greater than that spent with families, loved ones and even our time spent within education. Most people work full time from their early twenties until their mid-sixties. It is therefore not surprising that this must in some way affect our identities.
- Paid work has been one of the central defining experiences for many people throughout the 19th and 20th centuries. In other words, people would describe themselves (their identities) in terms of the work they did.
- The very nature of paid employment until recently has meant that the socialisation processes traditionally affected more men than women. However, over the last twenty years more women have entered the labour market because of gaining better qualifications, changes in technology (which has reduced the need for physical labour traditionally carried out by men) and a booming service sector.

The nature of work

It was Henry Ford's motor company that was to transform modern production techniques in the early half of the 20th century. Workers for the first time worked on production lines and specialised in one particular activity.

In the years after the Second World War, such methods of production became associated with a boom period in most western economies. It also became associated with job-security and rising living standards, particularly those of the working classes. 'You've never had it so good' was the catchphrase aimed at the working classes.

However, such production line work was also tedious and repetitive. The Marxist notion of job alienation was easily identifiable here. Nevertheless until the late 20th century people's identities were tied up with the type of work they did and the work-based communities they lived in.

The modern workplace

Many sociologists argue that by the end of the 20th century, the nature of work had changed and could be described as 'post-Fordist'. Whereas in the past, work places were hierarchical and bureaucratic and workers had a limited variety of skills, in today's economies workers need to be 'multi-skilled'. People no longer expect a job for life and must continuously update their education and training. The change from 'Fordist' to 'post-Fordist' economies has also been accompanied by a change in all aspects of our lives, including gender roles, education, family life, political affiliation and leisure.

Men at work

Throughout most of the 20th century men defined their adult identity in terms of what they did for a living. They were expected to work most of their adult life from the age of sixteen until they had usually retired aged sixty-five. What they 'did' (their 'professional identity') defined how other people saw them and in many cases the life styles they 'took up'.

However, in modern economies the structure of the workforce has grown more diverse and insecure. It can be divided into two broad components: the 'core' made up of secure workers with good rates of pay and promotion and the 'periphery' made up of part-time temporary workers on short-term contracts. This uncertainty about the duration of particular jobs and the variety of skills needed makes defining somebody's identity by the work they do extremely problematic.

Conclusion

Historically, men have defined and dominated the 'public' world while women's work and identity was traditionally 'private', unpaid and took place in the home. However, the entry of large numbers of women into the labour markets has changed this situation. Female employment rates are growing (although for many this still means lower paid part-time work).

The Confederation of British Industry has even recommended that its top one hundred companies should be run by women if the British economy is to outperform its rivals. Their reasons rest in women's greater ability to work in teams, to be good managers and most importantly being able to 'multi-task', i.e. concentrate on more than one thing at a time. Nevertheless, women are still generally paid less than men, have fewer managerial positions and are confronted by prejudice because of their sex. So how does work affect women's identities?

For consideration:

1 Why are some jobs described as being done by 'professionals' and others not?
2 How might the post-structuralist idea of discourse (e.g. the discourses of 'competition' or 'managerialism') help us when discussing changing identities at work?

● **Synoptic Link**

By using the term 'post-Fordism' a link can be made to stratification and work by focusing on the changing pattern of work and how it is increasingly difficult to define a 'working' class when production techniques and rising living standards complicate traditional definitions based around class.

✳ **Key Ideas**

In post-Fordist economies modern work techniques include redesigning work processes, globalising production and using new technologies (including more intensive use of information technology). There is also movement away from a manufacturing work force to service industries (i.e. banking, insurance and tourism). We are changing the basic shape that work once took from manual activity towards more information-based work and/or more service provision.

✍ **Coursework Suggestion**

Choose a particular group of 'professionals' and interview them to find out if their 'identities' have changed during the time they have been working. You can then use different theories to account for this change.

3.16 How does the mass media act as an agent of socialisation?

What does this mean?

In the last twenty-five years we have witnessed a media 'explosion' as new forms of technology bombard us with sensory experiences unimaginable a century before. Videos, CDs, computer games, the Internet, video conferencing – all have the possibility to stimulate, activate and even socialise minds and bodies.

For some, this has meant a more informed population with increased choice and diversity (pluralists and some postmodernists). They point to the diversity in newspapers, the range of documentaries available on satellite and cable and the opportunities of distance learning through organisations such as the Open University. For others (neo-Marxists), the picture is less rosy, referring to this new form of 'mass culture' as 'Americanisation' in which the masses are fed a 'diet of trivia' made up of identical mass-produced goods.

So what has changed?

* Many writers argue the postmodern media is different from that of modernity. Pluralists argue that the media was like a 'mirror' reflecting the world as it actually was. It did not seek to influence, change or 'ideologically corrupt' its audiences but rather provide a 'true' picture that also met the variety of different needs and tastes that existed.

* Some of this media was 'high culture' made up of the ballet, classical music and the broadsheet newspapers, produced and consumed by elite society. Some of it was 'low culture' composed of pop-music, television 'soaps' and football. Either way, the media reflected and met the needs of these distinctly different cultural realms.

* Such views about the media during the modern era were strongly challenged by Marxists and feminists. Marxists argued that the media ideologically influenced its audiences to reflect the needs of the capitalist society and those who profited most within it – the ruling elite – creating a false conciousness. Feminists argued that the media (itself, dominated by males) was ideologically influencing audiences that patriarchy was the 'normal' order of things.

◆ What, When and Why?

Many writers argue that the period of 'modernity' started in the 18th century and continued until the 1970s. During this time, many traditional ideas were challenged by the new disciplines of the 'natural sciences' (chemistry, physics, astronomy, and so on). These challenged traditional structures that placed religion as the central organising principle of any society. However, many postmodernists argue that this belief in science as a 'way forward' for 'mankind' started to be criticised in the late 20th century with the use of science as a tool of war (e.g. the holocaust, Vietnam, and so on) and its role in the many environmental concerns that people share today.

- Those who believe that we are living in a postmodern era argue that things are very different. For pluralists, the increased choice of cultural product in turn (they argue) means that the working classes have the ability to 'broaden their horizons'. Pointing to the Internet explosion, they argue that political and social awareness is enhanced as knowledge is more widely distributed and not simply held by those in power.

- However, some postmodernists disagree with this positive view of the media. Not everybody has access to the above technology. They also argue that much of what we see has little to do with 'reality' but rather, as Baudrillard (1995) argues, a 'hyperreality' where the stories of soap opera stars become headline news in our daily newspapers. 'Hyperreal' products and the choice and diversity that Baudrillard writes about can be seen in the music we listen to – a digitally mixed version of tracks by one artist, mixed with the music of another. This patchwork of styles is typical of the postmodern media with which our identities are bombarded and affected on a daily basis. See also section 17.

How does this impact on culture and identity?

Writing from a neo-Marxist perspective, Bourdieu (1993) argues that cultural goods (the newspapers we read, the music we buy, the sports we watch and in some cases the food that we eat) are an indicator of class. By this he means that particular tastes and lifestyles are associated with specific occupational and class groups. Swingewood (1977) took a more positive view arguing that 'consumer capitalism' can generate different levels of taste and different audiences, resulting in a culture and identities that are varied.

Neo-Marxists disagree, arguing that dominant '**hegemonic**' values of the elite will always dictate what is considered to be 'culturally superior' and what is not. The Centre for Contemporary Cultural Studies (CCCS) argues that while some elements of the working classes resist middle-class dominant values, institutions have the ability to adapt to this resistance and commercialise their culture at considerable profit. One example is the way that the restaurant business has marketed 'bangers and mash' as 'rustic', selling such traditional working-class food at highly inflated prices.

For consideration:

1. Looking at the media products available to you (e.g. television programmes, magazines, CDs, radio shows, newspapers and magazines), list which ones are an indicator of class. For example, which class might watch 'Big Brother' and why?
2. Which of these 'cultural' products do you respect and which do you not? Give reasons for your answers.

66 99 **Key Definition**

Hegemony – this concept stems from Marx and is developed by Antonio Gramsci. Writing about 'cultural hegemony', Gramsci argues that this is the way that the working classes are manipulated and exploited by the media through production of ways of 'thinking and seeing' which rule out other (better?) ways of 'thinking and seeing'. Think about the way in which, by reading the media, many people are 'persuaded' to support war against others whom they have never met but who, in many cases, may be working-class people like themselves. The media plays a decisive role in this process of socialisation promoting 'false consciousness', which convinces everybody that capitalism is a natural process and the only acceptable way that societies can work.

☞ **Who is this Person?**

Antonio Gramsci (1891–1937) died in an Italian jail at the age of 46 having been leader of the Italian Communist Party. What we know about his ideas comes from his Prison Notebooks, written during his time in jail. First a journalist, then a political activist and finally a politician he was brought up in poverty and attended (though did not graduate from) university. His background formed the ideas he was later to be so critical about – namely fascism, Italian history, the role of the media in the creation of ideology, education and cultural hegemony.

3.17 What do postmodernists say about identity?

What does this mean?

Until the 1970s discussions about identity focused around issues to do with class and occupation. These explanations argued that identities were 'fixed' or unchangeable. Identity formation was also discussed within a debate that on one side stressed the importance of nature and on the other, the importance of nurture. Women's identities were often ignored by sociologists particularly as far as statistical data was concerned. Postmodernists have attempted to challenge these and other traditional debates.

Identities in the period known as 'modernity'

Postmodernists argue that in the period known as modernity, 'metanarratives' (big stories) were part of any discussion about identity. Metanarratives are any sets of theories that claim to offer 'truths' attempting to offer explanations of the world e.g. scientific theories and religions. Postmodernists argue that metanarratives, e.g. 'Christianity' or 'biology' helped form the norms and values that helped create (and name) our identities in the past.

Unlike today, identities in one part of the world were also less likely to be affected by rapid change in other parts of the world. Imagine life over one hundred years ago, without television, radio or the Internet! Imagine how difficult and time-consuming it was to travel from one part of the world to another. It is easy to see that under these circumstances our identities would be less likely to be influenced by distant events – traditions would last longer and our identities could remain fixed. (See section 13.)

Identities in the period referred to as 'postmodernity'

- Postmodernist Lyotard (1993) argues that there are no truths and therefore metanarratives or theories do not help explanations about identity. One theory can be seen to be 'relative' (or different) to another but cannot claim to offer explanations of how things actually are. Any theory about identity, e.g. one based around 'class', while interesting, cannot claim to offer a true picture of what identity is. (See section 9.)

British sociologist Stuart Hall is one of the world's foremost authorities on issues surrounding identity.

✳ Key Ideas

Traditional views of identity, e.g. Marxist and functionalist approaches, stress the importance of social structures in shaping people's identities. Stuart Hall (1996) argues these old identities, e.g. class and religion, which helped us make sense of the social world for so long are in decline. Describing this as a 'crisis of identity', he argues that in a rapidly changing world the loss of these central structures weakens the frameworks in society that make people feel secure.

- Postmodernists argue that we don't just have one identity that is fixed but rather that we posses multiple identities. Like a small child in front of a pic'n'mix sweet section, postmodernists argue that people can construct their own identity by dipping their 'selves' into gender, ethnicity, religion, sexuality, family patterns, work, music, fashion, the arts – creating, changing or exaggerating whatever identity they chose.
- Postmodernists argue that consumerism defines individual identity in a way that class, gender and ethnicity used to in the modern world. As consumers we are influenced by popular culture and its obsession with image. '**Hyperreal**' images of actors or pop-stars in turn become part of our identities as we choose what we like or detest. On the streets of San Diego, or in the deserts of Rajasthan, how we look may well be more influenced by MTV than by our class, ethnicity, gender or sexuality.
- Whereas travel and communications in the 'modern world' involved time and expense, in the 21st century we can watch in our own sitting rooms events from around the world – instantly. Through technology our identities are open to images of war, religion, theatre, art, politics, sex and many other types of social interaction in a way never previously possible. Postmodernists argue that this 'collapse in time and space' means that identities are now far more likely to be influenced or socialised by the variety of images made available.

Criticising postmodernist approaches to identity

- One popular criticism about postmodernism is that surely it too is a metanarrative, which is offering itself as an alternative to existing theories!
- Postmodernists claim that the media helps define our identities, but whose identity are they talking about? Are some cultures, ages and genders more 'exposed' to media than others?
- Postmodernism is deterministic, claiming that identities are shaped or influenced by the hyperreal images present in the media.
- The postmodernist attack on theories centred around class, gender or ethnicity seem empty when considering the differences in educational attainment for both these categories.
- Anthony Giddens (1990) argues that we are in 'late modernity' and not 'post-modernity'. However, he *does* describe identity markers such as 'class' or 'ethnicity' as problematic and that these need to be re-examined in light of the rapidly changing world we live in.

For consideration:

1 Describe your own identity by using the following words: class; ethnicity; gender; sexuality; age; fashion; musical taste; and region.
2 Which 'indicator' is most important to you when discussing your identity?

66 99 Key Definition

'**Hyperreality**' – this term is used to describe the difference between that reality lived by individuals and the one portrayed by the media. Baudrillard (1995) says that in postmodernity these two realities have become 'blurred' to the point that individuals/social actors cannot tell what is real or 'hyperreal'. How 'real' is the world of reality TV series such as 'Big Brother' – and yet the front pages of newspapers are dominated by news of these characters, with whom we are encouraged to relate.

Coursework Suggestion

Carry out in-depth interviews with a sample of people from a mixture of working and middle-class backgrounds (make sure you operationalise what you mean by 'working' and 'middle' class). By interviewing these people see if you can either agree with or challenge postmodernists by identifying what they believe to be the most significant elements to their identities. Do they define themselves along class lines or by some of the other variables discussed in this section?

3.18 What does post-structuralism say about identity?

What does this mean?

Post-structuralism is a theory that looks at how writing, language and 'discourses' construct and determine social interaction. It can be used as a theory to examine how identities – whether they be individual or national – are shaped by 'institutions' such as the church, the state, sport and education.

It is also a theory that allows sociologists to study how certain groups or individuals may suffer oppression as a result of the 'taken-for-granted' labelling in operation in different institutions.

What do we mean by 'discourses'?

Discourses are patterns of thoughts or language that, post-structuralists argue, organise the way we think, feel and interact. Michel Foucault (1977) argued that discourses determine how power circulates within a society. One example of this is the very simplistic ways that we classify groups in society. For example we use words like 'young' and 'old'; 'straight' and 'gay'; 'fit' and 'unfit', or 'slim and 'fat'. Post-structuralists would argue that these very simplistic 'discursive tools' have the hidden yet powerful effect of shaping how we view the world.

By having these categorisations we tend to view others around us according to them and assume 'norms' and values' where perhaps no such norm or value exists. For example, the classifications of 'slim' and 'fat' completely deny the fact that most of us are in between, or claim that there is some measurable point at which we are either 'slim' or 'fat'. As a result many people will look at themselves and consider they are overweight when in fact they are normal. This is an example of discourses at work.

Trapped in a discursive web

Post-structuralists argue that we are not just involved in one discourse but many discourses, all with competing power/knowledge components. Your identity may be part of an educational discourse but also a parental one. You may be subject to the discourses of medicine and employment and your own (or others') religion. Foucault argues that our sense of identity

● Synoptic Link

Synopticity examines the themes of social differentiation, power and stratification. We can combine power with the concept deviance. Remember that deviance is a socially constructed definition meaning deviating from the norm. By 'deviance' sociologists mean that what may be considered deviant today may not be deviant tomorrow, e.g. women in Afghanistan prior to the war following the events of '9/11' were considered deviant if they did not wear a veil or if they attended university. Deviance can be looked at from a post-structuralist perspective if we accept that elite discourses are sometimes used as the official definitions of deviance, thereby punishing those so defined. Power, in this case, is used by elites to define those who are deviant and those who are not.

comes from the way that we respond (or 'position' ourselves) to the effect that these discourses have on us.

The discourse of psychiatry has the ability to determine some patterns of behaviour as 'sane' and some as 'insane' with the outcome that some people will be hospitalised and some not. 'West' and 'East', 'developed' and 'underdeveloped' and 'First' and 'Third' world are discourses that Stuart Hall (1996) describes as those of cultural superiority – the need by some nations to express what they believe is their economic and political domination. Both individual and national identities are affected by such discourses.

Post-structuralism, education and identity

One institution that many post-structuralists write about is that of education. Post-structuralist Stephen Ball (1994) writes about the discourse of 'performativity' that is shaping the educational system. Sharon Gewirtz (1997) uses the word 'managerialism'. In both cases they refer to the element of competition that exists within the educational system, something we have become completely used to (or, to use post-structural language, we have internalised). We take for granted league tables, streaming, setting, and different types of schools regardless of the effects (both positive and negative) they have on children.

Conclusion

By internalising the fact that competition is normal, we completely ignore the fact that some groups in society consistently do badly. Many children with backgrounds from both the working class and ethnic minorities suffer in a system that is meant to be meritocratic. As such their identities are shaped by the discourses that circle within one of many institutions. Foucault argues that such discourses are so powerful that they prevent us looking for alternative solutions to the problems we encounter.

For consideration:

1 How many discourses can you think of that you are involved in?
2 Which ones have the most significant effect on you and why?

✍ **Coursework Suggestion**

Combine your knowledge of the concept of discourse, with your knowledge of the sociology of media and the human body. Carry out coursework that explores the recent increase in anorexia and bulimia in males. Try and establish a pattern that correlates (is similar to) the increase in male magazines targeting fashion. Remember that this is a highly sensitive subject area. You could carry out content analysis or semiotics (see section 13) to show how the output of magazines has corresponded to the increase in the illnesses.

3.19 Is identity macro, micro or both?

What does this mean?

We have seen how macro theories argue that structural forces beyond our control are responsible for the shaping of individual, institutional and national identities. Micro theories, on the other hand, claim that individuals can exert control over these forces and thus individuals can 'determine' their own identities.

Other sociologists, most notably, Anthony Giddens (1990) and Derek Layder (1993) argue that we should combine both approaches to analysing all sociological phenomena, including that of the construction of identities.

Macro sociological approaches

- Whether adopting a 'consensus' approach (e.g. functionalism) or a 'conflict' approach (Marxism, neo-Marxism and the feminisms), macro sociological approaches argue that identities are 'determined' or shaped by structures (e.g. the economy, religion and patriarchy).

- Functionalists argue that within a 'meritocratic' society the norms and values we learn shape our identities in a way that, like organs in the human body, serve to meet the needs of society as a whole. The structures vary from institutions like the family to nation states and the global economy. Male and female identities develop to meet the needs of the system as a whole.

- In many cases Marxists agree with functionalists; however, they are critical about the nature of the structures that determine our identities. They argue that the conflict that these structures produce means that identities are oppressive and create a false consciousness. The majority of people do not realise that they are confined by a capitalist system that works against their interests.

- Also challenging the consensual notion of society are the variety of feminists' views which argue that female identity is oppressed and shaped to meet the needs of a patriarchal system that exploits women. They argue that the institutions that exist (e.g. religion, education, the family) have been culturally shaped in a way that subordinates women in structures that are dominated by male power and authority.

✳ Key Ideas

The debate surrounding structure and agency (macro sociology versus micro sociology) in relation to identity remains an important problem for sociological enquiry. However, it is far from new. Classical sociologist Max Weber alternated between a micro and macro approach to sociology when looking at how capitalism developed in certain countries. The micro side of his research focused on the values that people shared when believing in a certain religion (he concentrated on Calvinism a Protestant branch of Christianity). However, his macro approach to sociology showed how these 'values' were responsible for the rapid growth of capitalism in certain countries.

❝❞ Key Definition

Bourdieu (1993) describes how cultural capital, i.e. the shared tastes and values of a particular class can link the culture of a society with that of the individual. Those who possess a certain cultural capital that corresponds with those of a particular institution (e.g. education or the legal system) are more likely to do well in that system. This explanation can be used to show how certain class, religious, ethnic and gender identities may (or may not) achieve within an institutional framework (for example, culturally biased IQ tests that are written by middle-class professionals using ideas that many working-class children will not have come across, e.g. word games involving classical musical composers' names).

Micro sociological approaches

- Interpretive sociologists are not overly concerned with the structures that have been mentioned (see Top Exam Hint). They are far more interested in the processes of action, reaction and the construction of meanings that all individuals go through when social interaction takes place. Society is both a 'construction of meanings' and a 'creation of its members'.

- Individuals construct their identities through interactions with others. These constructions take place in a world of signs and symbols and the job of the sociologist is to examine how people create or maintain particular identities (e.g. by observing how certain students get 'labelled' in the classroom.)

The structuration theory of Anthony Giddens

Anthony Giddens has attempted to combine both macro and micro approaches to sociology. In his structuration theory instead of talking of macro and micro, he uses the phrase 'social practices' arguing that the social practices which we are involved in on a daily basis both produce, and are produced by, social structures. These social structures are made up of 'rules' and 'resources' that we produce in the process.

Giddens (1990) argues that individuals (agents) create and recreate the class structures that exist. Parents play a key role in the way their children speak, dress and behave in public (rules), which in turn can determine their later employment prospects (resources). For Giddens this means that individuals recreate the very structures that determine their life chances in the first place.

Conclusion

So where does that leave the sociology student? Kathy Woodward (2000) argues that while the concept of identity may encompass some notion of individual action (agency), there are also structures that exist in which both material and social factors can limit the degree of agency that individuals may have. Structuration theory is one way of explaining how both can and do affect identity.

> **For consideration:**
>
> 1 How might you apply Giddens' idea of structuration to the construction of identities within the education system?
> 2 What are the similarities and differences in the way that Giddens and Weber theorise?

✔ **Top Exam Hint**

A-level sociology has traditionally taught the subject as macro versus micro. However, in the exam try not to be black and white when evaluating these approaches. In reality most sociologists use both sides of the argument to help them draw upon ideas and ways of carrying out research. The difficulty is trying to create a theory that allows you to do both at the same time. Mention this in the exam and the examiners will reward you for your sophisticated sociological imagination.

3.20 What is the connection between power, the individual and identity?

What does this mean?

The concept of 'power' is far more complicated to unpack than it first appears. In general, however, it refers to the ability of one person or a group to impose their will on others whether or not they resist. Any discussion surrounding power and the individual has to be informed by the variety of theories available – some of which are represented below.

What are power resources?

Marshall (1998) argues that it is not just enough to consider the concept of power but it is also necessary to recognise the various resources available to those that wield it. These include wealth, control over jobs, the ability to create structures in organisations, competence and expert knowledge, control of information, occupation of certain social positions and control of instruments of force (e.g. the Army). As you read the views of the theories below, think about each of these resources and how they could be used (and by whom).

How can structural theories help your understanding?

- Using the notion of 'consensus', many functionalists argue that power is something that many of us accept as something we either do or do not have. Using the idea of 'authority', we allow others to hold power in the belief that they have the authority to do so. In the eyes of functionalists, some are more able to do this than others. Those that can, hold power – those that cannot, do not!

- As conflict theorists, Marxists challenge this consensual notion of power arguing that in the hands of the wrong people power can be used as an ideological tool to manipulate and exploit the working classes. The most obvious example of this was the way that Hitler manipulated the media in Nazi Germany to gain and maintain support for the Nazi Party.

- Neo-Marxist Antonio Gramsci (1935) argued that through 'cultural hegemony' those in power can make people ignore the failings that exist in society by making them believe that the capitalist system works well most of the time, for most of the people.

- Influenced by Marx and Engels, Max Weber (1905) argued class, status and party were of fundamental concern when considering the nature of power. An individual's class background and their identity

● Synoptic Link

At the heart of stratification 'power' is one of the central concepts in sociology connected to every theme you will encounter as a sociologist – indeed some would argue that it is what sociology is about. As a synoptic link power can be used to show how any group (e.g. based around age, gender, class, ethnicity or sexuality) can hold power over others or be exploited by others because of its status. By thinking about who has power as a sociologist you are automatically thinking synoptically.

✓ Top Exam Hint

Both post-structuralism and social action theories accept that the individual is not always constrained by structures. Score high evaluation marks by drawing out differences between these two theories and the structural theories described in this section. Like social action approaches (or interpretivist theories) post-structuralists argue that power (working through various discourses) can push people into responding in ways that challenge certain discourses and those in authority, e.g. students challenging teachers and the education system and workers going on strike.

was a direct result of their economic power (or lack of it). Status was concerned with the amount of power held by an individual in a particular social group. Parties were groups active in the political sphere chasing political goals. Either way, Weber argued that power was unequally distributed throughout society and that your 'life chances' depended on the degree of power you held.

- While it is impossible to talk of any one feminist strand (feminisms consist of, for example, black, liberal, Marxist and radical), most would argue that patriarchal structures in society represent those where power is located in predominantly male hands.
- In public life what feminists refer to as a 'glass ceiling' (an unacknowledged discriminatory barrier) tells us that while women are dominating men within most levels and areas of education, men still hold the majority of powerful and influential positions in companies. Privately, while laws change, and liberal attitudes become more fashionable, most women still do 'triple-shifts' of paid worker, emotional carer and domestic servant.

How can post-structural theories help answer this question?

Although post-structuralist Michel Foucault was strongly influenced by many of the structural approaches to sociological theory, he challenged the idea that power is something that a class, bureaucracy, gender or culture can wield over somebody or groups of bodies.

Foucault challenged Marxists and feminists over their claims that power can be identified in any one particular area by arguing that it operates through 'discourses', which are systems of language or bodies of knowledge. Involvement in these discourses creates a power relationship that excludes others who have no access to such a discourse. Education is composed of lots of discourses, one of which is the particular 'discursive' relationship between students and teachers.

This discursive power relationship is one in which students internalise and take for granted the fact that the teacher has knowledge and power over them (even, if in some cases that may not be true). The same situation applies in the doctor/patient relationship, where the discourse of medicine excludes all those who have not studied to become doctors. This means that we automatically assume (or assumed – now alternative/complementary medicine is 'empowering us') that the doctor knows best.

Michel Foucault (1926–1984)

☞ Who is this Person?

Highly controversial and enormously influential post-structuralist, Michel Foucault (1926–1984) worked in a psychiatric hospital and taught at the University of Uppsala in Sweden. He was made Professor of Systems of Thought at the Collège de France in 1970. He has written about madness, medicine, prisons and sexuality. Like philosopher of science Thomas Kuhn (1970), he challenged the very nature of knowledge by showing how 'regimes' of truth order our knowledge, affect the way we categorise things, shape our beliefs and what we actually do.

For consideration:

1 How might the different theories describe the relationship between the individual and each of Marshall's power resources?
2 How might you use the idea of 'discourse' to explain the power relationships that many women and men have in their private lives?

3.21 What does it mean to be a member of a youth subculture?

✳ Key Idea

Hebdige (1989) uses the concept 'ideological incorporation' to describe the way that the capitalist system, through the media, can quickly 'incorporate' or 'trivialise' what is originally a strong anti-system statement. One example of this was the way that Swampy, the teenage environmental campaigner in the 1990s was quickly turned into a character of fun and ridicule by the media despite the fact that his group of campaigners were dealing with serious environmental concerns. By doing this, the serious concerns he raised about government economic and environmental policy were quickly ignored.

✓ Top Exam Hint

Remember to use a cross-cultural perspective when evaluating youth subcultures in the exam. By this we mean that textbook explanations of functionalism assume that the journey from youth to adult is the same experience wherever you are. But, the nationality, region, religion and ethnicity you possess as well as the country you are living in will make your experience as a teenager very different. Comment on this in the exam and you will be awarded high evaluation marks.

❝❞ Key Definition

'Criminal', 'delinquent' and 'deviant', are all controversial terms. Classical sociologists use 'deviant' to describe people who differ from the norm, i.e. dress differently. 'Delinquent' often refers to young people who break rules but who don't commit criminal acts, i.e. by insulting people in the street or spraying graffiti. 'Criminals' are people committing crimes where a criminal record is a likely outcome, i.e. robbing the local corner shop. The problem however is, depending on class background, these terms are often used differently.

What does this mean?

Taking drugs, **criminal** and anti-social behaviour are 'popular' conceptions of what youth subcultures are all about. However, does this really convey the reality of this fascinating branch of sociology? In the affluence of the 1950s and 1960s early theories argued that young people had too much time and money with little responsibility and that this, along with a new and thriving teenage industry was responsible for youth subcultural groups such as 'Teddy Boys'. Since then, the growth of subcultures (e.g. 'crews') has been matched by the variety of theories to explain their existence.

Youth culture as a social construct

'Youth' as a concept is one that really emerged during the 1950s with the teenager being identified on American television for the first time. It is a social construct as the meaning varies from one culture to the next. The existence of 'juvenile offenders' (young offenders, often convicted of stealing mobile phones, drug offences and anti-social crimes) is linked to fears of recession, globalisation, youth unemployment and the breakdown of the welfare state. Quite often teenagers are useful scapegoats. However, many of these stereotypical views are constructions, i.e. not necessarily true but based on statistical assumptions and media reports which themselves represent the prejudices of other people.

What is 'deviance amplification'?

For Stanley Cohen (1980), a moral panic is often an exaggerated (or 'amplified') concern over **deviant** behaviour of a particular youth subculture. Political problems can effectively be swept under the carpet by 'blaming' a particular subculture. A group is 'labelled' or stereotyped as being a threat to social order. Press reports will demonise or create 'folk devils', e.g. sufferers of AIDS, illegal immigrants, extreme Islamic fundamentalists and even social workers. Governments can be 'seen' to be bringing in legal changes in response to popular concern (changes they had wanted to establish all along!).

How do theories help the understanding of youth subcultures?

- From a functionalist perspective, membership of youth subcultures helps teenagers deal with the stress associated with the need to achieve and acquire status in a highly competitive society. A lack of identity and status in families can also be addressed by joining a subculture. Functionalists argue that the breakdown of the family and the loss of respect for traditional values accounts for the **delinquent** behaviour of some subcultures.

- Those on the New Right blame today's 'youth problem' on the erosion of the traditional patriarchal role of the father which allowed 'everyone to know their place'. In turn they blame young single mothers for bringing up children without what they consider to be 'correct' moral values.
- Marxist explanations blame the bad behaviour associated with some youth subcultures on high levels of youth unemployment and the breakdown of the welfare state.
- Neo-Marxist explanations argue that hegemonic capitalist values (i.e. the cultural values of the ruling classes) are challenged by some youth subcultures in their dress styles and musical tastes which in some cases reject the capitalist value system (e.g. 1970s punk and 1990s grunge).
- Postmodernists challenge the assumption above by arguing that many youth cultural industries rob the styles and tastes of their cultural and political meaning and turn them into superficial fashion statements.
- Symbolic interactionists use labelling theory (see section 8) to show how powerful groups such as religious organisations or the media shape social attitudes to deviance by making the rules for powerless groups such as the young. Once subcultures are labelled as being deviant young people may see themselves as deviant – a self-fulfilling prophesy.

Boy gangs and girl gangs

Mac an Ghaill (1994) suggests that as the work force is becoming more feminised and traditional job opportunities for young men are declining, men may experience a crisis of masculinity. This creates anxiety, which can be resolved by joining anti-school subcultures or by involvement in violence and crime. Campbell (1981) argues that the growth of girl gangs can be explained by the need to compensate for their low status in their families and communities and as an alternative to taking on low-skilled, tedious, low-paid jobs.

Conclusion

The Vision Research Survey (1999) showed that most teenagers are, like their parents, committed to family life, ambitious, desire education and are anti-crime.

For consideration:

1 Using the Internet, find out what the Contemporary Centre for Cultural Studies (CCCS) have written about youth subcultures in the UK.
2 How do these ideas contribute to Marxist explanations about the existence of youth subcultures?

◆ **What, When and Why?**

The Centre for Contemporary Cultural Studies (CCCS) is based at Birmingham University. Over the last thirty years, this highly influential and critical research department has focused on producing research literature exploring the representation of ethnicity in what it considers to be a 'pro-capitalist' media. One example of the work carried out by the CCCS is Stuart Hall's (1978) *Policing the Crisis* where he suggests that ethnic groups are frequently 'defined' in the British media as 'problems'. Although now dated, Hall's research can be usefully applied to the gun law debate and the British government's attack on 'black rap music' in early 2003.

Does the media treat this 'youth subculture' in the same way it does others?

✎ **Coursework Suggestion**

By combining content analysis (the quantitative approach to analysing the media) and semiotics (a qualitative approach where the researcher explores the deeper and often hidden meanings behind particular words, phrases or pictures), look for stories in the press that cover incidents involving teenagers. Try to identify if the language used in the stories varies depending on the class background of the culprit (e.g. do the drunken brawls of Cambridge students get written about in the same way as football hooliganism?).

3.22 How can we connect identity to debates about crime and deviance?

● **Synoptic Link**

Use the synoptic concept of 'identity' with education to show how education can lead to social stratification. Cohen (1980) argues that working-class boys commit crime because parents do not give them the needed skills to succeed in education. He finds that these 'deviant' identities form subcultures, whose members are rewarded with a higher status that they did not receive when they were in the school system.

✳ **Key Idea**

Whyte argues that deterioration in the lifestyles and life chances of working-class young people has created the conditions for increasing social unrest and, at a personal level, identity crisis. Struggling daily economically (lack of money) and socially (lack of employment leading to isolation) is bound to affect the identities of young people and as such produce a variety of responses, some criminal and some deviant.

What does this mean?

Both crime and deviance are what sociologists refer to as 'social constructions', i.e. what may be defined as a 'crime' or 'deviant' in one part of the world, may or may not be considered a crime in another part. Synoptically speaking this means that some groups are socially differentiated depending on who has power and how that power may be used. It also means that particular 'identities' may be labelled 'deviant' by those who possess power in any one society, at any one point in history.

Where psychology meets sociology

Discussions around criminology and identity form that grey area where it is difficult to tell the difference between psychology and sociology. Many argue that certain identities are inherently different from those of 'normal' people claiming that people with those identities are born that way. Biological or physiological theories claim there is a deficiency that 'makes' that person act the way they do.

Psychological or social psychological theories also claim that criminal or deviant people are inherently different from 'normal' people. They argue that their mental processes have become damaged perhaps during birth or from some sort of accident. However, discussions around identity from a sociological perspective tend to look more at the social processes that may create, change or give the impression that an identity has been classified by society as 'deviant'.

The social construction of 'crime' and 'deviance'

A deviant is somebody who 'deviates' from the norms and values associated with a particular culture. Sociologists use the word 'culture' to mean the sets of shared values, norms and beliefs of a society or group of people. Any one *dominant culture* is the culture whose norms and values are seen to be the most powerful and generally accepted.

The problem with this is that people see the world in very different ways and if a particular identity happens not to possess those very norms and values, the individual in question may be classified as 'deviant' or 'criminal' depending on how the legal system treats such deviancy. For sociologists, this means that both crime and deviance are what are referred to as socially constructed definitions.

Merton's strain theory

Functionalist Merton's (1968) strain theory is a way of starting to identify types of identity which result from trying to succeed in the societies we live in. One can refer to identities that:

- *Conform* – such identities conform to day-to-day norms and values of society that aim to receive material rewards (e.g. money, a place to live).
- *Innovate* – such identities, fearing that 'success' cannot be obtained, will commit acts of deviancy or crime in an attempt to gain the rewards that 'success' brings, i.e. a nice house, car, and so on.
- *Ritualise* – such identities neither expect nor truly desire material rewards to the extent that the first two do, but slavishly carry out day-to-day tasks.
- *Retreat* – such identities struggle with the ambitions, hopes and desires that modern societies require – and 'retreat', often by drug or alcohol abuse.
- *Rebellion* – such identities reject the values of society wishing a complete change and the adoption of a new value system, probably through radical forms of political action including terrorism.

Strangely, although a functionalist idea, Merton's theory can be applied to the approach of Paul Gilroy (1993), a post-structuralist, who argues that crime committed by black people is a political act. It reflects anger at the way that white society has historically treated black people. In this light, acts of crime can be considered acts of 'rebellion'.

Self-fullfilling prophesies

Symbolic interactionists use labelling theory to show how institutions such as the police, schools, religious organisations and the media shape social attitudes to crime and deviance. Once a particular group (or subculture) is labelled as being either criminal or deviant, the theory argues that young people may see themselves as such – hence the self-fulfilling prophesy.

Studies by Matza (1990) on policing argue that working-class young people or, in particular, members of black ethnic minorities are negatively labelled as deviant or criminal by police, resulting in disproportionate 'stop and searches' leading to higher arrests than other class groups. Any self-fulfilling prophesy in this sense can be used in the exam to argue that a change in identity has come about as a result of the institutional labelling that takes place.

> ### For consideration:
>
> 1. How could you combine Durkheim's concept of **Anomie** with Merton's strain theory to come up with explanations for deviant or criminal identities?
> 2. To what extent do you think institutions should take responsibility for crime and deviance?

✓ Top Exam Hint

Remember that crime and deviance can be looked at from a post-structuralist perspective by arguing that 'elite' discourses are sometimes used as the official definitions of crime and deviance, thereby punishing those so defined. Most recently you can refer to the rapidly changing views in England on the smoking of cannabis and the application of the laws in Lambeth in London. The laws were relaxed regarding the punishment of the smoking of cannabis in this borough, raising the question: who decides when this same act is considered either legal or illegal and why?

✍ Coursework Suggestion

Contact the Law Society and attempt to e-mail or write to as many members of the legal profession as you can – preferably judges and barristers – and ask them if you can interview them. Ask them to what extent Merton's strain theory is, in their eyes, an acceptable explanation for deviancy. Use their answers either to agree or challenge the theory or to assess to what extent the legal profession is itself a conservative institution and therefore responsible for the labelling and self-fulfilling prophesies that interpretive theorists write about.

66 99 Key Definition

Anomie – is a term associated with Durkheim's functionalist theory. It refers to the feeling of 'normlessness' that some people experience when they feel unable to fit into the society in which they live. Durkheim argues that in many cases economic changes in societies happen faster than changes in moral values and this has a negative effect on some people. In extreme cases feelings of anomie can lead certain people, according to Durkheim, to commit suicide.

3.23 Examination advice

What does the exam ask me to do?

This exam will be 60 minutes and will be composed of one structured question from a paper of two questions. In both questions there will be an item of information that you must read followed by four questions.

Part a) (worth 8 marks) will always refer directly to the data given. You will be asked to 'Identify and briefly explain…' two features within the data. This is testing your skills of interpretation and analysis which means you don't necessarily have to include studies, concepts or theories. Identify each feature clearly – use two separate paragraphs.

Part b) (worth 8 marks) will ask you to 'Identify and briefly explain…' two specific aspects of sociology, without referring to the item. This question is testing your knowledge and understanding, and you are expected to include relevant concepts and/or studies. Identify each aspect clearly – use two separate paragraphs.

Part c) (worth 18 marks) will ask you to 'Outline and briefly evaluate…' two specific issues. Most of the marks are available for knowledge and understanding, and therefore there should be reference to concepts and studies and/or theories here. You are also asked to make a brief evaluation if you are to score full marks. Using link words, such as 'however,' can lead you to be evaluative. Make sure you address the two issues, and evaluate each one.

Part d) (worth 26 marks) will ask you to 'Discuss…' a view. Treat this as a short essay. There should be concepts, studies and/or theories, and/or contemporary examples in your answer. You are being tested on your knowledge and understanding, interpretation and analysis and evaluation. In order to discuss a view you must evaluate (using another view), and you can use both positive and negative comments.

How can I best achieve maximum marks?

The following bullet points should help you in your final stages of preparation for the exam.

- Make sure that you read the questions first before reading the item. That way you will, without realising it, automatically focus on key issues within the item of the exam.

- Make sure that you read the item twice to fully understand and use it in your answers.

- Make sure that you have learnt all the key terms and concepts in this chapter (e.g. 'subculture'; 'locality').

✓ **Top Exam Hint**

Now that you have come to the end of the unit, examine your folder. In what sort of state are your notes on this unit? Have you divided them into the various topics looked at in this chapter? Can you *clearly* see your class notes, handouts, homework exercises and marked work returned from your teachers? Have you placed all of these in *separate* transparent wallets or are they all bunched into a handful of such wallets making it difficult to actually know what you have in your folder in the first place? When reading through your notes do you highlight the important bits so that you don't have to re-read it all again when you revise at a later stage? Get your notes in shape and you will find revision so much easier in the weeks leading up to the summer.

✎ **Coursework Suggestion**

Carry out coursework that explores the many identities expressed in music videos, e.g. rap. Interview (qualitative research) young people to see to what extent the characters portrayed in videos actually represent identities that they themselves experience. You might also carry out quantitative research using questionnaires. Remember that when deciding what questions to pose you will have to be extremely clear about the definitions you deploy, the sample you use and the theoretical framework you will adopt. You will also need to bear in mind that when evaluating your work you can revisit these issues and discuss them as methodological problems.

- Make sure that you have looked at all the 'top exam hint' boxes in the margins of this chapter and have built them into your exam revision programme.

- Memorise all the 'key ideas' and use them in the exam to show your high level of understanding of this subject area.

- Make revision cards with all the case studies you have come across in this chapter and memorise them for the exam.

- Be clear about the problems that this area of sociology poses for methodology (e.g. to what extent is quantitative data useful/not useful when exploring this topic?).

- Make sure that you are fully aware how postmodernism challenges traditional theories about the individual, culture and identity.

- Make sure you are clear about the difference in meaning between 'production' and 'consumption' and the implication this has for concepts such as class, i.e. remember that Marx argued that your class position was determined by who owned the means of production.

- Make sure you fully understand what 'globalisation' means and its implications for this unit.

- Memorise the ten sociological variables of: age; class; cross-cultural perspectives; ethnicity; gender; globalisation; historical perspectives; religion; region; and sexuality. Use these to evaluate concepts and claims made by sociologists and their theories.

Key points to remember

- Be absolutely clear about the type of question that you are facing in the exam. Ask your teacher to show you as many past exam questions as possible.

- Sociological studies are the key to your success in the exam. Memorise them and be clear about which particular theory they relate to, and use this as evidence in the exam answers you write.

- Identities and the agencies of socialisation.

● Synoptic Link

The synoptic module will examine whether you can make connections with this unit and other areas of the specification. This can be done by referring to methodology and social inequality and connecting these two with this unit. However, there are a variety of other concepts that will enable you to make links with the synoptic module and all other areas of the specification. These concepts include 'power', 'locality', 'social control', 'identity' and, of course, 'class', 'gender' and 'ethnicity'. Make sure that your folder has got these links highlighted before you start year two. Show your folder to your teachers and get them to check that these synoptic links are correct.

3.24 Pushing your grades up higher

What do I need to do to get a good grade?

1 Remember to always back up whatever point you are making with evidence. That evidence may be in the form of a study by a sociologist, a concept, a theory or an example from contemporary society.

2 Examiners will love the fact that you can identify the period that the research was carried out in. Of course you are not taking a history exam but the high-achieving student should be able tell the examiner which decade the research took place in and, ideally which half of the decade (e.g. 'Willis' study carried out in the mid-1970s . . .').

3 Try to identify the case study with a particular theoretical framework, don't just say 'Paul Willis' study . . .' but rather 'Marxist Paul Willis' carried out a study . . .'

4 When discussing the findings of the case study you refer to, you can then gain extra critical evaluation marks by mentioning whether the research was 'quantitative' or 'qualitative'. By doing this, you can then link one particular study to another to build up your argument.

5 Look at the style of writing you use. How do your sentences start? If they just start with 'Marxist writer Paul Willis . . .' you are losing valuable evaluation marks. Much better to use evaluative phrases, e.g. 'in addition to this Marxist writer Paul Willis argues . . .' or 'in contrast to the above Marxist writer Paul Willis . . .'. See the difference?

6 When an exam question asks you to discuss the 'contribution' that a particular sociologist has made to an issue, it is important to realise that 'contributions' can be both positive and negative. Remember this, as it will then allow you to fully evaluate the work of the sociologist in question.

7 Always remember the concepts of 'validity', 'reliability' and 'representativeness'. By applying these terms you will show the examiners that you are extremely critical.

8 This unit tends to be based on concepts and studies (empirical evidence) more than theories, but students can use theory when discussing a question. In this unit treat them as 'friends' to be called upon when you feel you cannot write any more. Ask yourself 'how might a feminist or a postmodernist analyse this particular issue?'

Key points to remember

- You must offer evidence in support of whatever argument you are making. Without it, the examiners will not reward your argument with marks.

- Try to use 'sophisticated' language when evaluating the theory, case study or concept. Make sure you start sentences or paragraphs with those key evaluative phrases.

Frequently asked questions

Q. Is 'identity' the same as 'personality'?

A. No! Although both terms are interpreted in a variety of different and often conflicting ways. 'Personality' is a concept that tends to be explored more within the world of psychology rather than sociology. It assumes that we have a number of characteristics that we possess over a long period of time and which can be externally evaluated. 'Identity' is generally explored by sociologists as a social construction, i.e. something that is created through a variety of socialisation processes.

Q. What do 'discourses' actually mean?

A. A concept that is associated with post-structuralism, 'discourses' can refer to structures of generally accepted ways of thinking that restrict people in seeing alternative forms of action. For example, if I believe that discourses in education involve 'competition', 'large classes', 'league tables' and 'assessment', I might not question that perhaps there might be alternative and better ways to teach young people in school.

Q. What does 'hegemony' really mean?

A. A term originally associated with Marxism, 'hegemony' has come to mean any set of overriding and dominating ideas or ideologies (e.g. American hegemony; patriarchal hegemony). Developing the ideas of Marx, Antonio Gramsci argued that hegemony was something to be found in the 'private' and non-state levels of society (i.e. it had nothing to do with the use of force by the state). By 'manufacturing consent', you and I might believe that the capitalist society we live in is generally a fair one. For Gramsci such beliefs would be created by cultural hegemony, i.e. the production of ways of thinking and seeing through newspapers, films and literature (see section 16). Marxists therefore argue that hegemony must be confronted at every level.

Chapter 4

Family

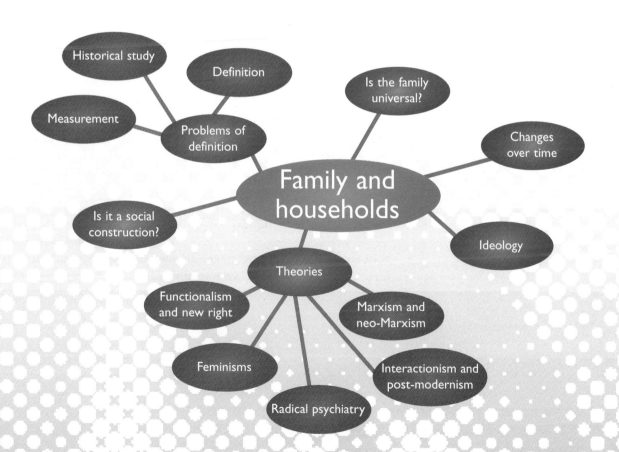

 CD-ROM 4.1

Key issues in family sociology

Why are sociologists interested in the family?

Sociologists are interested in the family since it is seen to be central to how society works. Families offer:

- socialisation of the norms and values of society
- an opportunity to develop self-identity
- an environment in which babies and young children can be protected and cared for.

Families are central to society, and therefore, they are central to sociology. Many issues that sociologists are interested in stem from or link to the family in different ways. For example:

- gender roles
- crime and violence
- inequality
- social control.

All these issues can link to the family; therefore this makes the family an important topic to think about. It is also the case that other aspects of society link to the family.

- Education might be affected in a positive or negative way by the family you live in.
- Your identity might be affected by how you are brought up.
- Crime might link to the family. Some families might expose children and young people to crime and criminal values more than others.
- Your family will be affected by the class you have – and your class will be initially given to you by your family!
- Your health will likewise be affected by your family's habits and their attitudes to money. Again, this is perhaps a product of class.

As we can see, therefore, most aspects of society can link to each other, yet the family is particularly central to these links.

What are the key debates in family sociology?

In terms of family sociology, the key debates we need to think about are:

- What problems do we have in defining the family?
- What does the media say about the family?
- What do politicians think about families?
- How have families changed over time?
- What are the problems with looking at the family in history?
- What do functionalists think about the family?
- What do Marxists think about the family?
- What do feminists think about the family?
- What do interpretive sociologists think about the family?
- Why is the family important for socialisation and social stability?
- What are the changing patterns of marriage and divorce today?
- Do families need fathers?
- Do we have family diversity?
- Will diversity lead to the breakdown of society?
- Does the family have a dark side?
- Do we have postmodern families?
- What might the future of the family be?
- Is childhood a social construction?

What are the key ideas and concepts in family sociology?

Sociologists are interested in how families have changed over time, and in how they affect those who live within them. They are also interested in what families do for society: how do families 'fit in' to the overall structure of society? What does 'the family' as an aspect of society do, and does the family do the same thing across all societies?

✓ **Top Exam Hint**

Try to show how the family fits into wider society. Show the links between the family and other aspects of sociology and society that you are studying. This way you can start to get depth in your answers.

● **Synoptic link**

If you can spell out the ways in which the family links with other aspects of society, then you are actually being 'synoptic'. You are demonstrating how different bits of society all join up and interrelate to each other.

✎ **Coursework Suggestion**

Many students choose family sociology as the basis for their coursework, either at AS or at A2. Don't forget that if you do choose family sociology then you should try and link what you do to other aspects of sociological study.

4.2 What do we need to find out about family sociology?

✓ **Top Exam Hint**

Use these bullet points as headings to help you to organise your notes and your revision.

✎ **Coursework Suggestion**

You could study the roles in the home, or between different ethnic groups as your A2 coursework project.

What does the specification say about the family?

We can break down the specification into the following ideas, which this chapter will look at.

- Changes in family life over time and the patterns of living they lead to

- Ways of thinking about different family types: ways of 'classifying' families to make comparisons and contrasts

- Family diversity

- Power and roles in the family

- What families do – for the individual and for the wider society.

How will you be examined in this topic area?

The family topic area is to be located in section 2: 'Culture and socialisation'. The focus of this module is to locate issues of culture and identity to real-life, lived experience. You will have an hour and 30 minutes examination and will have two structured questions to answer. These could both be from the family topic, or from the family topic and another option if you have been prepared for one by your teachers.

How well does this topic relate to coursework?

The family is a very popular topic for coursework. This is probably because as an AS exam subject it is one of the first pieces of sociology you will actually get to grips with, but secondly, since we all have families it gives us something real to focus upon. Remember, however, because we all have one, it might be very difficult to be detached when doing research – a real problem for all sociologists looking into this area.

How well does this topic help with synopticity?

In a sense, the family as a topic in sociology has the aspect of synopticity already built in. This is because, as mentioned in the previous section, the family is seen to play a central role in society, and therefore, also in sociology. We all have a family of one sort or another (depending upon the definition you might be using), and we are all able to recognise the importance of families in society. We all think about and maybe talk about our 'family' on a regular if not daily basis. The relationships we build with those in our family are vital, and they affect how we live our lives. Since we all go back home to our family each night, the family has a massive impact on our lives, and therefore has a massive impact upon all else that we do. In other words it is very synoptic.

What is important to try to remember is that the synoptic links that sociology encourages you to make can all be seen to impact from or impact on the family. In other words, the family can cause things to happen and to change in society, or can be influenced by society in the ways in which it is structured or made up.

- **Culture** – families give us our culture, yet their structure and 'type' is a product of our culture or sub-culture.

- **Socialisation** – families give us the most important socialisation of all, primary or early socialisation, yet in turn, we are socialised by society (and by the family) to believe that the family is the 'right' way to live!

- **Identity** – our 'identity', in other words, who we think we are is the product to a large extent of how we have been brought up, yet at the same time how we have been brought up will shape the sorts of relationships we make, and maybe even the sorts of family structures and patterns of living that we ourselves create when we have the chance to, later in life.

Whatever we do, the family is always there – behind the scenes, shaping our life, patterning society. Therefore, it is very important that we study it in sociology.

Key points to remember

- The family is a popular topic for coursework because it appears 'familiar' to us.

- The family is a really useful synoptic tool.

- Studying the family requires us to try very hard to give up our common-sense assumptions.

66 99 Key Definition

- **Socialisation** means learning the norms and values of society.

- **Identity** is used in sociology to simply mean knowing who you are. The family is important in this process

● Synoptic link

Try to use these concepts in your family exam for added depth.

How can we find out about the family?

As with all areas of sociological investigation, studying the family poses some general and some quite specific problems.

1   **General problems** – sociologists will need to make a very careful decision about what research method to choose, and what sample to create and this is true for all research. The sociologist will also need to make a decision about what type of data to produce, to create either quantitative or qualitative data, or maybe to somehow combine the two.

2   **Specific problems** – first, gaining access to families might be an issue. After all, if you think about it, most of our time spent in families is 'behind closed doors'. How can we gain access to this most private of all aspects of society? Another quite important problem is the fact that since family lives are very personal (if not the most personal) things in our life, we might not actually welcome sociologists questioning us about them. After all, how would you feel? This is an important point to remember when doing coursework if you have the opportunity. Do we as sociologists really have the right to know? Do we really have the right to pry?

As you can see, in some senses studying the family is simple – they are everywhere! Look out the windows of your house, go to the supermarket or the park; you will see families going about their lives and living their routines. But, at the same time, they are also very secret and very private.

How have sociologists tried to measure the family?

Through this chapter you will come to see that different sociologists have attempted either quantitative or qualitative measurements of the family and the sorts of things that families do.

*   **Quantitative family studies** – these often look at size or structure, and they often try to measure how family and marriage might change over time. There are, however, huge problems with historical records about the family. In the past, having children outside marriage was a serious act of deviance, and so records are often incorrect as families often covered such things up. Equally, although divorce has been legal for a long time, arguably, it is more socially acceptable today than before. Some families could therefore be considered 'empty-shell' families, that is, the family members stay together, but without a warm or close relationship.

✓**Top Exam Hints**

*   Try to think about methods in relation to studies on the family. It is actually very difficult to study the family since it is so private. Give a sense of this in the exam for added evaluation marks.

*   Always try if you can to question the reliability and validity of quantitative secondary data. How do we know these 'facts' are true?

- **Qualitative family studies** – these often look at the feelings and emotions of those in family relationships. What does it mean to have the role of 'father' or 'mother'? How might different ethnicities and classes have very different experiences of family life? These studies try and achieve what we call '*verstehen*' i.e. they try and 'see the world through the eyes of those involved'.

What methods do sociologists tend to use to study the family?

Some methods are probably more appropriate than others when it comes to the family.

1   Covert (hidden or undercover) methods would be very difficult to use unless you were to study your own family. And, if you did that, you probably wouldn't be detached anyway – not a good idea for a sociologist.

2   Questionnaires could be used, but, as with all studies that produce quantitative data, these would not tell us much about what it would feel like to be a family member. Quite often, however, questionnaires are very useful if we want to study family size, or even to look at issues such as housework, i.e. issues that involve adding things up, or measuring time spent doing things.

3   In order to understand the feelings of belonging to a family, many sociologists use the interview method. However, it is important that such interviews are conducted with great sensitivity and care.

What problems with definition are encountered in family sociology?

The fact of the matter is that the family is not actually a single, clearly identifiable thing. We all have one, we can all recognise them when we see them, but they are very different from one another – and certainly very different from the sorts of families we might see on TV or advertisements. This is because there is such a wide variety of family types; we call this 'diversity'. It is very difficult to measure and study something that can't be easily defined. But, what is interesting is that this is only clear when you try and think about it. Before this, if someone said you to 'I don't know what a family is', you would probably think them silly. But now?

Key points to remember

- Like any topic, studying the family poses some specific problems for research.

- It is very difficult to clearly define the idea of a 'family'.

- Quantitative and qualitative studies of the family are very different.

What problems do we have in defining the family?

Why are there so many different types of family?

What does this mean?

Families are central to all that we do. From when you wake up to when you go to bed, you will probably have seen your family, or maybe tried hard not to see them, spoken about them or thought about them. Even if you haven't done this with your own family, you almost certainly will have seen someone else's, if not in real life, then maybe on TV. Go to the bus stop or the park and you will see families. Walk down an average road, and behind all the closed doors will be whole families or parts of families, people who are family to each other and to others living elsewhere. They are an essential part of life – an essential part of living.

But what are they? This is a difficult question, since it asks us to really try as sociologists to take a step back, and to think about possibly the most obvious feature of social life in a fresh light. Think about the following questions:

- Are all families the same?

- Do families do the same things as each other?

- Do we all feel the same way about our roles and positions in our family?

- Does everyone like their family?

It is probably more useful to think about the family as a symbol, rather than as a real thing. It is obviously true that families are 'real' – you can see them after all! However, what you can actually see are people, and the reality of this thing called 'family' is in our and their heads: it is a symbol for a set of relationships and a series of interactions. It is a product of culture.

Is the family 'natural'?

This is a very important sociological argument, and one that causes great academic debate. Are humans the products of their upbringing, their culture, or are they the product of natural genetic pre-programmed chemical responses?

1 Sociologists in the main feel that that what humans do is down to 'nurture', that is, we are the products of the environment we live in and of the culture into which we have been born. At its most extreme, this view sees humans almost as 'blank sheets of paper' upon which our culture (and in particular our language) writes. We are not born who

we are, we are born with the potential to become whatever we are brought up to be. When applied to the family this viewpoint argues that families are created by culture, and this is why there are so many different types, and also why different cultures around the globe 'do' family life in a wide variety of ways.

2   The opposite view to the nurture view is that of **sociobiology** which holds that it is not nurture that shapes us but 'nature'. When applied to the family this view asserts that it is natural to want to live in the thing we call 'family'. Sociobiologists Tiger and Fox (1972) suggest that humans are pre-programmed to form family relationships; there is something within our natural make-up that directs us towards certain patterns and ways of living. TV documentary-maker Desmond Morris (1968) also argued in his book and TV series 'The Naked Ape' that humans create cultures based upon the natural responses and urges they have. There might be cultural diversity in the ways in which we live, but the needs and desires we have are all located in our genetic make-up, directing the path our lives take as a species. We are basically apes without fur – naked apes, that can create and develop new ways of living, but these are always locked into or based upon natural patterns of biological need.

What is the family?

If we think about the family as a 'symbol', then it might help to see the family as an '**imagined community**'. This means that it is a set of abstract relationships that we learn through socialisation and that take on meaning for us as we develop the skills to understand and use language to describe our surroundings and our thoughts. It is an imagined set of feelings. All our families are different, but we can all use the word to refer to what is familiar about the relationships we have with certain significant people. In this view, a very 'interpretive' one, we are taught what families are by socialisation and so they are not natural.

Conclusion

Zygmunt Bauman (1990) describes the family as an 'insider group': which is a way for us to tell who we are or are not. It is a way of developing an identity and of giving security. Again, however, this is what they are in the abstract. It is very difficult to generalise about what families are, what they are like and what they do. For many people, families are not a source of security – quite the opposite. They can be very damaging, causing great physical and mental harm. As sociologists, we must remember that people are different, and therefore so too are their families.

For consideration:

1   Do you think families are natural or cultural and why?
2   Why and how might we be able to claim that families are 'not real'?

✓ Top Exam Hint

It is always good practice to start the longer mark questions by defining and explaining the words in the title of the question. In the case of the family exam, your introduction to these answers could focus on how it is difficult to define the concept, making it hard to get sociologists to agree how to measure it.

◆ What, When and Why?

The ideas of **sociobiology** go back to those of Charles Darwin on the process of evolution. These ideas have been very influential in the 'nature vs nurture' argument, although many sociologists reject such claims and instead take an alternatively extreme position know as cultural relativism. This is the idea that as humans we are nothing except that which our culture makes us.

※ Key Ideas

•   The phrase '**imagined community**' is the idea that the relationships we have with people and the bonds that tie us together are essentially abstract symbols that we make real by acting as if they are real. By doing this we come to know who we are, and where we belong.

•   Perhaps the best way to think about the family is to think about other words that the word 'family' is like. It is like the word familiar, and in fact, both come from the same Latin original source: *familia*. This means that the family is something 'familiar', something that is part of ordinary life, something that we take for granted. A habit, almost.

4.5 What types of family structure do we have?

Is this still a typical family today?

✳ Key Idea

Feminist sociologist Diana Gittins (1993) has described the family in the following way:

'There is no clear, unambiguous definition of what a family is – indeed, it has been argued that the family is little more than an ideology that influences and informs the ways in which people interact and co-reside with one another.' (1993, p.155)

✓ Top Exam Hint

Feminists accuse the New Right of having an ideological image of the family, as you shall see later in this chapter. This is a good piece of evaluation to remember for the exam.

What does this mean?

The term 'structure' refers to how something is patterned or how it might be made up or constructed. How are different families constructed differently? This is an important question as we must understand that not all families are the same.

Can we define the term family?

Diana Gittins (1993) suggests that the family is an idea rather than a physically real thing, and in fact that the reality of family life is very different from the idea. We all speak of 'the family' as if it is a single, common object, but in reality it is a wide variety of different practices. It has different sizes, different roles and different relationships within. When we talk about the family in ordinary language ('common-sense thought'), we often miss this important point.

What is the ideology of the family?

Some sociologists like Gittins, talk about the 'ideology of the family', which is sometimes referred to using Ann Oakley's term 'cereal packet family' since it is the view we might have gained about family life from the media's representation of the family. In particular, think about breakfast cereal adverts, that is, two parents, children, around a table, happily sharing the family breakfast. How true is this really?

What types of family exist?

As sociologists, we use a great variety of terms to describe the family.

1 Traditional extended family – three generations or more in the same house.
2 Peter Willmott (1986) has added to the idea of a traditional extended family with the following three further distinctions:
    • Local extended family – separate nuclear families who are related, and see each other often since they live in close proximity to each other.
    • Dispersed extended family – nuclear families that are related and who see each other quite frequently but do not live together.
    • Attenuated extended family – nuclear families that are related and see each other or have some sort of contact infrequently.

3   Nuclear family – the sort of family type we often see on TV, that is, two generations living together. This is the image of the family in common-sense thought.
4   Reconstituted family – reconstituted means making something more out of previous pieces. In other words, families that have step relationships.
5   Lone parent/single parent family
6   Symmetrical family – Young and Willmott (1975) use this term to describe families that have joint roles between the partners in terms of the duties and chores they perform.
7   Dual-worker families – families where both partners contribute to the family income. This would certainly make the type of family life different from families where only one partner works, in terms of childcare and disposable income amongst others.
8   Cohabitation families – where partners live together without being married.
9   Same-sex families – families based upon lesbian or homosexual relationships.

What are households?

As we can see, families might be different from one another for reasons such as size, roles, number of generations, marital status or number of partners.

There is also a very important distinction to make between:
*   family – symbolic shared practices
*   households – where you live, the dwelling you live in, and its size and structure
*   roles – the relationships between the people who live together
*   kinship – feelings of belonging with others; feelings of being part of the same family as others.

Conclusion

Households and families are not necessarily the same thing, and this further confuses the picture of what family life is like. For example, we might not be related to the people we share a house with; think of student halls of residence, for example, or people sharing a flat. Equally, if households are close by, this might actually change the type of family life you have. You might live in a cohabitation family, a nuclear family or a single parent family, but have other kin living so close by you see them often. If this is the case, what sort of family do you really have? Equally, families change with time; you might be a member of lots of different types of family structures in your lifetime.

For consideration:

1   Why do you think there are so many family types?
2   What implications might such family variety have for social research?

✓ **Top Exam Hint**

Revise these words for types of family structure – they often come up in the very early shorter questions in the exam.

◆ **What, When and Why?**

Neo-conventional family – this idea, associated with Robert Chester (1985) suggests that although we might construct nuclear families in different ways (through maybe divorce and re-marriage or through cohabitation) it is still a nuclear-type structure that most people try to strive for most of the time. This is the 'new-norm', or the new convention.

4.6 What is the ideology of the family?

✳ Key Idea

An **Ideology** is a way of seeing society. Many sociologists think that the powerful use ideologies to control how the powerless think about society.

✓ Top Exam Hint

Learn these two quotes off by heart. You can use them in a number of ways in a number of different topics – in fact, anywhere and everywhere that you talk about ideology and power; these concepts are the essence of sociology!

What does this mean?

An **ideology** is a word associated with more 'critical' or 'radical' theories such as Marxism and feminism. It means ideas that are used to justify how things are. Or, sometimes, it can be seen as a way of thinking about society that encourages us not to see power inequality.

Marxists and feminists argue that those who have power in society are able to control how society thinks about itself. In order to do so, they present social ideologies (ways of thinking) that hide or cover up inequality and the fact that those in power run society for their own benefit. This idea is summed up in the classic Marxist phrase,

> 'The ruling ideas are, in every historical epoch, the ideas of the ruling class.'

In other words, those who rule society continue their rule by shaping the ideas of the population. Michel Foucault (1977, 1979) has said a similar thing. He says that,

> 'Things are not powerful because they are true, but they are true because they are powerful.'

Sociologists such as Abbott and Wallace (1997) and Diana Gittins (1993) talk about an ideology of the family which can be seen in the views of politicians, doctors and religious leaders. They also argue that this ideology about the family is present in the media. An ideological view of the family is one which is believed by people to be 'common-sense' so it is simply accepted and not questioned. In fact, its so-called 'truth' may be very different from the reality. For example, we might use the term 'cereal packet family' to refer to how the media tends to suggest that nuclear families are the norm, whereas in fact what exists in society is wide family diversity.

Why is the ideology of the family a problem?

Feminists and Marxists argue that the ideology of the family that exists in modern UK society is damaging, controlling and limiting. It hides the true nature of family life. This is often to protect traditions and assumptions that themselves might affect how people think about the society they live in. For example, many tabloid newspapers regularly criticise single-parent families, and many politicians blame such families for so-called rises in criminal behaviour (not that we can know for sure that crime is on the increase since it tends to be hidden).

Barrett and McIntosh (1991) have argued that in common-sense thought, we tend to see single parents as 'bad' and the nuclear family as 'good'. They refer to the nuclear family as an '**anti-social family**' as the ideology (the common-sense view) makes other types of families seem worse, and the nuclear family as the best sort. But is it really? We need to look at the sociological evidence before we make our minds up.

What ideological assumptions exist in society?

This ideology of the family (seen in the media amongst other places) makes a number of assumptions about family life which people in society take for granted and might not question. These assumptions become seen as fact, but they are really untested.

The ideology of the family says:

- families are natural

- family life is normal

- families should have opposite sex parents

- women should care for children

- the nuclear family is best

- too many single-parent families will lead to a crisis in society.

How often do people believe these statements do you think? How often are they questioned? How often do you see these views in the media? As sociologists we must ask ourselves how true these statements really are. And how can we tell? Where is the evidence?

Conclusion

Interestingly, some sociological and political ideas, as we shall see throughout this chapter, share this ideological image. In particular, the New Right, the New Left and the functionalist view can be attacked by feminists as having an ideological image. In this view the nuclear family is seen as the best family of all, the perfect way to build a stable and functioning society. Is this really true? Many feel that the family has a 'dark side' – a massive set of negative consequences.

For consideration:

1 Do you think an ideology of the family exists in modern society?
2 How can you tell?

☀ Key Idea

Barrett and McIntosh have described the nuclear family as being '**anti-social**'. They do not mean by this that those in a nuclear family behave in an anti-social fashion, but rather, that the ideology of the nuclear family is such that it makes us believe in the so-called 'common-sense' idea that the nuclear family is the 'best sort', thus making other family types seem inferior and not as good for society – quite untrue!

✏ Coursework Suggestion

You could investigate how the media has an ideological image of the family for A2 coursework. Study adverts on the TV using the methods of semiology and content analysis.

4.7 What do politicians think about the family?

What does this mean?

Many sociologists – quite often from the Marxist or feminist traditions – have criticised political views on the family as being 'ideological', that is, based upon false, untested assumptions.

In recent years we have seen both Conservative and New Labour governments openly state that single parents are damaging for society and that this crisis in the family (and in 'traditional values and morality' in general) will lead to a crisis in society due to a lack of stability.

In the Conservative, or the New Right view in sociology, the family is a basic building block of society. It is at the heart of society, ensuring that people learn the 'right' values to ensure stability. Marxists would attack this, suggesting that this is ideology – a way of controlling what people think in order to maintain an unequal society.

Many feminists such as Gittins see family diversity as a really positive feature of society since it will allow freedom of choice. In this view the ideas of politicians limit choice, since they proclaim that some types of family are 'better' than others.

What do politicians say about the family?

Politicians tend to share the idea that society is changing, but that the family should remain the same to protect us from these changes. In this way, society will make sense to us, and we are able to build a smooth-running society.

Anthony Giddens (1994) notes that many politicians, as shown above, often talk about 'traditional family values'. Giddens notes that this claim is very unrealistic. We know today that families are not always a source of comfort for everyone and, equally, that in the past women and children were often treated badly in the family, lacking power, decision-making ability and often the victims of physical abuse. Such abuse also continues today, irrespective of the sort of family structure that might exist. It is therefore very difficult to say that a certain type of family is better than another or that we should return back to an age when the family was 'perfect': it simply never was.

The ideas of Giddens and the work of Janet Finch (1989) would both suggest that this type of thinking, is little more than what is known as a 'golden age'. There are assumptions made about the past and the present state of families, but without any real hard evidence.

✳ Key Idea

Gittins (1993) says,

'Family households are a vital and integral part of any society in some shape or form. Family ideology is not. There is no ideal family. When politicians articulate a fear that there is a crisis in the family, they are not worried about divorce or rape or incest as such, but rather that the ideology is being challenged.' (1993, p. 168)

The New Labour government of Tony Blair said in the 1997 election that families were the building blocks for society. What does this mean?

- The past is seen as an age of strong morality. Strong roles were in place and the family is seen to have functioned to maintain moral standards through the socialisation of norms and values. (This is similar to the functionalist argument in sociology as we shall see later in this chapter.)
- In this way of thinking, the present is seen as having reached a crisis point. Strong morality does not exist and society is collapsing since the family is unable to perform the functions it once did.

This is a 'golden age' since it is a completely unrealistic image of the past as some perfect time that we should return to.

Giddens suggests the opposite. He claims that individuals (and in particular women and children) have more freedom than ever before, freedom to decide who they are and how they wish to live their lives. This is referred to as a 'plastic identity'. Who we think we are is mouldable. We are able to take control of our lives, our lifestyles and, unlike ever before, the sort of family choices we wish to make. He refers to society as being post-traditional, unlike those on the New Right in the Conservative Party, who wish to return to traditions that are assumed to have existed, but which might not have been as 'perfect' as we might think. This raises some serious questions about our knowledge of the past development of the family. How can we really tell anything about the lives of those before us?

Conclusion

Often politicians are responsible, along with the media, for creating what we call '**moral panics**' about the family: an exaggerated sense of fear about a largely fictitious threat. Modern-day family moral panics have included:

- concern about 'absent fathers'
- concern about homosexual families
- concern about single parent families
- concern about a lack of discipline among the young due to a break down in family socialisation
- concern about a change in the gender roles in the family
- increased sexual abuse of children

For consideration:

1 Why do you think we have so many moral panics about family life?
2 Why do you think some people see the past as being much better than it might actually have been?

◆ **What, When and Why?**

Consider these examples:

- In 1997 the Conservative Party election manifesto said: *'The family is the most important institution in our lives. It offers security and stability in a fast-changing world.'*
- In the same election, New Labour said: *'Families, in all their forms, are a basic building block of society. But the nature of families is changing. This has brought about new stresses which must be addressed.'*
- And, from the Liberal Party: *'We will uphold family life as the most secure means of bringing up our children. Families are the core of our society.'*

66 99 Key Definition

Moral panic – an unrealistic or hyped fear

Folk devil – the largely exaggerated or even fictitious group we have moral panics about

Key Idea

Joan Smith (1997) sees these moral panics as further evidence of the existence of what feminists have termed 'patriarchy' in society – male dominance and the control of women. These panics serve to increase the control of women by labelling some women and men as 'dangerous' and as 'deviant'. The feminist view in general argues that the New Right views on the family are especially patriarchal since they advocate that women and men should return to 'traditional' roles, otherwise society will collapse.

How have families changed over time?

What does this mean?

In order to study what families do and how and why they do it, many sociologists are interested in looking at how the family has changed over time. Like any aspect of society it is important to see the family as in flux, that is changing, not fixed or static. Society is constantly changing, and so too are the ways in which people live their lives.

What is the theory of transition?

This view is associated with the ideas of functionalist thinkers Talcott Parsons (1955) and Ronald Fletcher (1966). This view sees the family as changing to meet the needs of the society that it serves. Like a view often expressed by politicians, the family in this functionalist image is seen to be at the heart of both society and social stability. Parsons and Fletcher suggest that as society becomes more complex and industrial, the family loses functions. Other institutions take functions away from the family (such as education and health care, now provided by the state), allowing the family to better perform the essential functions that it is left with, that is, socialisation and stabilisation. This process of the loss of functions and the specialisation of others is known as 'structural differentiation'.

William Goode (1963), another functionalist thinker, has suggested that the process of 'transition' is a global trend. The extended family is being replaced by the nuclear family as the better and more suitable type. Many feminists attack this idea claiming that it is little more than an ideological view of the family.

How has the family changed due to industrialisation?

1   A key debate involved in the issue of how families might change and develop over time is that of the role that industrialisation might have played in changing the family. The classical functionalist view is that industrialisation caused the decline of the extended family, and the creation of the nuclear family. This is because workers moved into the newly created towns, leaving their extended families behind them. In recent years, this view has increasingly come under attack.

2   Starkey, and others such as Peter Laslett (1965) and Michael Anderson (1971), suggest that rather than creating the nuclear family, industrialisation actually increased the likelihood of the extended family. This is because as people moved to newly created towns, they moved in with relatives in order to find comfort and security. We see

✳ Key Idea

Transition means changing or 'evolving' over time; adapting.

✔ Top Exam Hint

Try to show that what sociologists often say is actually a product of the times they were writing in.

◆ What, When and Why?

David Starkey at a sociology conference in 1995 described this classical functionalist view as 'nonsense, sentimentalism and not founded in historical fact'. He is referring to the idea that this view represents a rather generalised view of history, with little attention paid to actual historical data.

this today with patterns of migration around the globe. People often move near to, and even move in with, people they know before they establish themselves in a new place. Starkey goes further and argues that due to the crowded living conditions in the newly created towns, the time of industrialisation was probably the only period in the UK when the extended family was in high numbers.

3   Extended families are, however, often seen to be related to the class of the families themselves. It is important to remember that factors such as age, class, ethnicity and location will all increase the likelihood of family diversity. In a study of Bethnal Green in East London, Young and Willmott (1962) argued that kinship patterns in working-class communities tended to be based more upon extended style family structures than isolated nuclear structures, which in turn are more associated with middle class or affluent families.

4   Finally, Young and Willmott (1975) also suggested that as the nuclear family develops, we will see a changing of the roles between the partners within the family. They describe what they call a 'symmetrical family', which can be seen as very similar to the functionalist view of 'transition', as follows:

- Stage 1: Pre-industrial families – families worked together as a unit of production

- Stage 2: Early industrial families – the extended family is broken down by geographical mobility due to the rise of towns and urban areas. Traditional gender roles develop as men become 'breadwinners' in the home.

- Stage 3: Symmetrical families – as time develops, life in the nuclear family becomes more 'home-centred' and the roles become increasing shared, hence the term symmetrical.

Conclusion

As we can see, the history of sociological debates on the family is based upon the idea that industrialisation had a massive impact on how we lived our lives, and on the types of families we created for ourselves. However, we often have to question the reliability of the historical picture we are painting.

For consideration:

1   Why do you think sociologists tend to focus upon the industrialisation era in history when discussing the family?
2   How easy or hard do you think it might be to study historical changes in the family?

✓ Top Exam Hint

In the near future we might be able to see another rise in the extended family. A number of sociologists have noted that many ethnic minority groups in the UK favour extended family structures over the traditional nuclear family. Again, this can be explained partly because of the different traditions that different cultures might have, and also because migration tends to increase the likelihood that people of a similar ethnicity will live together, creating new communities over time in new societies.

4.9

What are the problems with looking at the family in history?

What does this mean?

Studies of the family and how it might change over time are often only as good as the historical evidence and data the researcher has at their disposal. Such data is often patchy and incomplete, or at least, quite open to interpretation.

What problems exist with historical data?

* **Problems about size** – it is difficult to tell exactly how big families were in the past. Since divorce was illegal until this century, and not easy to obtain until changes in the law in 1971, many families stayed together but in name only. Equally, illegal abortions often occurred when children were conceived outside of marriage, or illegitimate children were given to work houses or orphanages. Occasionally, these children were taken into the family under the guise of being the offspring of the married couple, who were in fact really the grandparents. Such changes do not easily show up, if at all, in historical data.
* **Problems about relationships and roles** – while we might learn from parish records details about births, deaths, marriages and therefore the size of families, this tells us little about what life was like within the families themselves. Historically, we might be able to use life documents and other secondary sources to complete this picture, and to give us more qualitative historical information. For example, we might be able to use paintings, diaries, love letters, etc.
* **Problems about measurement of structure** – even if we can find out in a reliable fashion how big households were, it still doesn't tell us about the inter-relationships between households. For example, a road might look as if it has 20 nuclear families living in it. Yet, some of these households might have kin in other houses in the same or nearby streets. What might look like a nuclear family might actually be a modified extended family instead, but how would quantitative data tell us this?

How have families changed over time? What is a typical family today, and how can we really know what happened in families in the past?

✓ Top Exam Hint

Try to show in the exam if possible that you understand the problems of historical data on the family. This is good evaluation.

What can we tell about the past?

Using parish records in England from 1564 – 1821, Laslett (1965) has been able to identify the existence of only about 10 per cent of families that were not nuclear in structure. These results are very different from the previous ideas of Parsons.

1 Anderson (1971) obtained census data from 1851 on Preston, and has noted that extended kinship was strengthened and not weakened with the process of industrialisation.

2 In a similar study to that of Anderson, Liz Stanley (1992) looked at Rochdale in the 1980s and found that the 1980s mirrored the 1880s. There was high female unemployment and wide-ranging family diversity.

3 American sociologist Litwak looked at nuclear families in the 1960s and still found that in 52 per cent of cases such families still had regular contact with wider kin – including at least weekly contact with other family members. This again suggests that what might look like a 'nuclear' family, and what might actually be a nuclear family are very different, but this is difficult to tell from the size of the family alone.

4 In 1993 Finch and Mason conducted a detailed survey in the Greater Manchester area, looking at how families took on and divided up the responsibilities of care and support for ill kin. After interviews with 978 people and a further 88 questionnaires, they found that in over 90 per cent of cases, assistance and mutual support between kin was widespread. Many in the sample had offered or received financial support from kin, or had helped out with childcare or the care of ill relatives. This again indicates that although we might have nuclear families, we still have a great deal of modified extended support networks.

What about now?

It is possible to point to a number of changes that the family seems to be going through in modern times:

- divorce is on the increase
- marriages are taking place much later in life
- those that get divorced are more likely to get remarried than people getting married for the first time.
- there is an increase in cohabitation relationships
- there is an increase in births outside of marriage and in single parenthood
- family members are living much longer today than ever before
- family size is decreasing – we are having fewer children
- increasing numbers of women are having children later in life
- step relationships are increasing.

Brigitte and Peter Berger (1983) maintain that although in recent years society has accepted that the nuclear family has a considerable dark side (which is more frequently discussed and revealed than ever before) we still have not found a real alternative.

For consideration:

1 What methods do you think are best to get at the reality of family lives?

2 What changes do you think the family will go through next?

✓ **Top Exam Hint**

As part of your revision put all the names from this chapter onto revision cards and then every time you practise a past exam question try to see which names would link and why – this way you will be able to use these ideas in a unique fashion, rather than assuming they can only be used in the way that we have presented them to you here.

✍ **Coursework Suggestion**

You could, for A2 coursework, study people's attitudes to the future of the family. Try to find out what their anxieties about the family consist of.

✳ **Key Idea**

Robert Chester (1985) has suggested that such changes only serve to indicate that we have a new norm. We have a new form of the nuclear family, but one more flexible than before, based on cohabitation and maybe re-marriage and step relations, rather than nuclear in the tradition sense. Humans still, after all, enter into relationships and partnerships with each other, and will always continue to do so.

What do functionalists think about the family?

What does this mean?

Functionalism is a theory in sociology associated with the views of founder Emile Durkheim (who died in 1917), and with sociologists such as Talcott Parsons (1955) and Ronald Fletcher (1966), who both wrote in the 1960s. Functionalism was a very popular 'macro' sociological theory during the 1960s, but is often seen to have been replaced in the history of sociological ideas by neo-Marxism and feminism in the 1970s and 1980s. Having said this, the ideas on the family held by functionalists are important to the sociology of the family as a whole, and although they are rather old ideas, they are reflected in many modern-day views held by the New Right, the New Left and by many politicians.

What is functionalism?

- The starting point for all functionalist analysis is to ask 'how does this aspect of society function?' They start with the assumption that things that exist in society exist for a reason and contribute to the whole, or the larger pattern in some way.
- At the heart of how functionalists see society in general is a notion called the 'organic analogy'. This idea helps functionalists to focus on how the parts of the society all inter-relate together and combine in various ways. They argue that society can be seen as a living, growing and evolving entity, like a body. The parts of the body contribute something to how the whole thing works and each has a function to perform.
- This is an example of what we call a 'consensus theory'. The basic functionalist starting point is that society's normal state is one of balance, of harmony between the parts that make up the whole.
- The family is seen as a key institution in society to help keep society in balance.

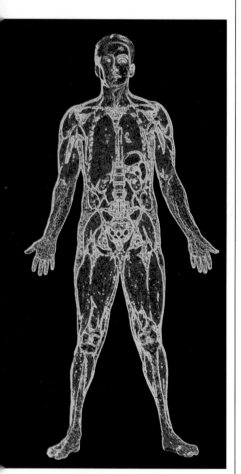
Functionalists compare society to a living body; all the parts connect to make up the whole

What functions does the family perform?

1   George Murdock (1949) – In a cross-cultural study of 250 societies, Murdock identified what he claimed to be four universal functions of the family for every society:
   - sexual – the family provides new members to allow society to continue
   - reproductive – the family allows sexual expression to be stable, by regulating and creating laws and guidelines about who we can enter into sexual relationships with and when

- economic – the family provides for its members
- educational – the family teaches new members the values of society, allowing for balance to be maintained over time.

In this view, the family is universal. Every society needs the structure of a family since every society needs the above four functions to occur in order to stay 'healthy' and in balance.

2   Talcott Parsons (1955) – After Murdock, Parsons has suggested that modern-day families have lost some functions, but have specialised in those they have retained. Parsons suggests there are two essential functions families now perform, but again, like Murdock, these functions are seen to be vital for continuing social stability:
- primary socialisation of children
- the stabilisation of the adult personality

For Parsons if these two functions are not adequately met, then we will have a dysfunctional society. Functionalists refer to this situation as 'anomie' meaning normlessness. This is like sickness in the human body, if we continue the idea of the organic analogy.

Parsons has argued that the nuclear family is the most functional family type of all in modern society since it is most ably suited to perform these two basic and 'irreducible functions' needed to ensure **social order**. Many see this claim as a product of its times (the 1960s) and as a highly ideological view of the family.

3   Ronald Fletcher (1966) has suggested, like Parsons, that the family has lost functions, noting that the non-essential secondary functions families once performed are now largely performed for society by the state instead – functions such as health care provision, education etc.

criticism

The family is left with three essential functions that it now performs:
- stable satisfaction of sexuality
- production and rearing of children
- home provision.

Conclusion

In this functionalist view, families are essential. They maintain balance and order. They teach us the values and norms of our culture. Without families, society would collapse.

For consideration:

1   What do you think of the functionalist view? Are families like this?
2   How might families cause dysfunctions in society?

Social order – functionalists think social order is vital. Without it we would have instability and society would be 'sick' and dysfunctional.

What do Marxists think about the family?

What does this mean?

The sociological theory of Marxism comes from the ideas of Karl Marx (died 1883), his writing companion Fredrick Engels and their modern-day followers, many of whom might describe themselves as neo-Marxists since there have been considerable changes and up-dates to the traditional macro Marxist view as sociology has developed.

The Marxist view is often seen as the opposite to the consensus-based theory of Durkheim and the functionalists. Marxism itself is often described as a radical or conflict theory since it sees society as based upon power inequalities due to the existence of a class hierarchy.

Having said this, however, there are many similarities between these two so-called opposites.

- Both are macro theories, i.e. they look at how society is patterned as a whole.
- Both are interested to look at how and why people follow the rules of society.
- Both believe that there is strong social control and order in society.

Where they differ is that whereas for functionalists social control is largely positive, creating a balanced and orderly world to live in, Marxists see social control as the ability of a ruling powerful group to control the rest of society, creating inequality.

What do Marxists think about society?

- Marx starts with the general observation that society is divided in terms of class, since it is what he refers to as a 'capitalist' society. By this he means that in modern society there are two main groups that have a conflicting relationship with each other – the ruling class and the working class.
- Society is therefore seen as unequal and as exploitative. Those in power keep the rewards of society for themselves, controlling the actions of those below them in the structure of society.
- Like functionalists, Marxists believe that society has order, but that this order hides the true nature of society. Order is really about the control over those who have no power in society, allowing such an exploitative society to continue over time.

What do Marxists think about the family?

1 Early Marxist views on the family come not so much from Marx, surprisingly enough, but from Engels. Engels (1972) argued that the

> **66 99 Key Definition**
>
> Class is defined in the traditional Marxist view as the relationship one has to the means of production, i.e. everything needed in society to make an end product, to produce the goods of society. For Marx, there are only two possible relationships: either you own the means of production and therefore have power, or you don't, and you work for those that do.

family is shaped by the economic structure of the society in which it exists. This is a classic Marxist idea called **economic determinism**: those who hold and own the means of production can control all else in society, and can control how features of society are shaped. Engels suggests, in a view that actually crosses over with early feminist writings, that the family as we know it was 'invented' at the same time in history as private property and the state. Monogamy (one man married to one woman at one time) was invented to control women in order to establish legitimate lines of inheritance for private property. The reasoning behind this idea was that fathers needed a stable sense of who their offspring actually were in order to ensure that property was passed on to their own kin. This also invented patriarchy – the notion that men dominate women in the family and in society.

2   Eli Zaretsky (1976) suggests that the family serves an unequal society by providing emotional support for ordinary people who are exploited in such a society. It is what is known as a safety valve. It allows for comfort and security, making people feel that society is fine and permitting their exploitation and powerlessness to continue. In this way, it contributes to '**false consciousness**' – it makes society seem better than it really might be.

3   Neo-Marxist Louis Althusser (1971) makes an important distinction between:

   *   repression – controlling people physically or with the threat of force
   *   ideology – controlling people by affecting how they think about society

He suggests that the family appears to be a private institution, but is really the subject of much state control. Within the family, ideologies are socialised into each new generation, making them accept how society is.

4   Jacques Donzelot (1985) argues that the family is not as 'private' as it might seem! Although we might feel safe from the problems of society behind the closed doors of our family lives, the family is actually in the middle of a complex series of power relationships including the regulation and monitoring by the state, doctors, the police, teachers, social workers, etc.

Conclusion

In the Marxist view, the family is a source of social control, unlike the functionalist view which sees it as the building block of society and more like social cement.

For consideration:

1   Which approach do you find more realistic – Marxism or functionalism?
2   How can the family teach us to be uncritical of the society we live in?

※ **Key Ideas**

*   Economic determinism – this idea can be used to describe most Marxist views on how the whole of society operates. It simply means that the class system, and the inequalities that it produces are the most important features of all society – and that class allows some to shape the whole of society in their interests.

*   Marxists make a distinction between false and true consciousness: **false consciousness** means you are a victim of ideological control and do not really see the 'truth' – you do not see how those in power make society unequal.

*   Marxists in general also look at the role played by the family in the reproduction of capitalist and ruling values over time. They argue that families do teach values to the next generation, as functionalists also do. However, these values are termed, 'ideologies'. They justify the way things are in society, and stop us from questioning how society really is.

4.12 What is the interpretive view of the family?

What does this mean?

Interpretive sociology goes by many other names. We might call this 'micro sociology' or sometimes interactionism. This sort of sociology is the other side of the coin to the more structural approach of theories such as Marxism and functionalism.

The interpretive approach, as the name suggests:

- looks at roles and relationships between people
- looks on a small-scale level at how people act and interact with each other
- tries to understand how people understand or 'interpret' the world around them and their place in it
- looks at the meanings and motives people have for the actions they undertake
- asks how the world make sense for those in it, or how those in it make it make sense?

As we can see, with its emphasis upon looking at why people do what they do, and how people form relationships and roles, it is a very useful tool for us to use to think about the nature of family life.

What does interpretive sociology say about the family?

- For Berger and Luckmann (1967), what we regard as 'real' in society is the product of '**social constructions**'. In other words, what we consider to be real is what our culture tells us is real. What we consider to be 'normal' is shaped and moulded by the norms of the culture that we are brought up in and socialised by. When applied to the family, we can see that in this view, our common-sense dominant image of the family is itself a cultural creation – this is a very different view to that held by sociobiology which argues that the family is a product of natural instincts.
- Erving Goffman (1969) has advocated the adoption of what he refers to as a '**dramaturgical approach**' in micro-sociology. He suggests that a useful analogy to use when describing the world is the term 'theatre'. We have roles, we take on parts, we follow scripts depending upon the roles we have. Again, when applied to the family, it is interesting to see how we 'act out' family life, how being in a family gives us many different scripts or roles to follow: father, mother, stepfather, sister, son etc. Each role comes 'ready-made' with a meaning attached to it, but we have to live out or act out the role in order to

make it come alive – to make it 'mean' something in our lives and in the lives of those whom we act and interact with.

How does the interpretive approach see marriage?

Due to its emphasis upon looking at what people do and how they act and create and share meaning with those around them, the interpretive approach is a useful way of thinking about what the relationships within the family are like.

- Berger and Kellner (1964) have suggested that the roles learned and adopted in the family are '**ongoing constructions**'. When we first enter into these relationships the roles are not clear, and they need to be learned, and then practised just like learning any script. The relationships we build in the family are very fragile, they need to be negotiated, renegotiated and constructed again and again. They have to be built by those involved.
- David Clark (1991) looks at how we can think about the differences in the reality of how people create married relationships. He asks how married life makes sense to those in the process of acting it out. What does it feel like to be married, and does it feel the same to everyone? As we can see, these are very 'micro' concerns – they look at what people think and how they make sense of what they do. For Clark, like all interaction and like all roles we might take on, marriage is something we need to practise – it is something we 'do', rather than simply 'have'.

How can we study power in the family?

David Morgan (1996) argues that food and how it is used in the family can give us an insight into common-sense assumptions about power. It can symbolically represent power inequality in the family.

For example: someone has to shop, decide what to eat, unpack the shopping, to cook, decide on the meal time and someone has to wash up.

Who is it that does all these things? How is it organised? Is there power inequality in this action?

Conclusion

The micro approach when looking at the family is useful since it allows us to think about the nature of the relationships within the family. It allows us to see families not as fixed or static 'things', but as livings sets of interactions. People make families real by 'doing them'.

For consideration:

1 How useful do you think the interpretive approach is when looking at family life?
2 What does it mean to say that families are not 'things' but are 'practices'?

4.13 What do feminists think about the family?

In what ways is the family a source of control for women?

What does this mean?

First, it is important to note that there is no such thing as a single feminist sociology. Instead, there are many varieties of feminist theory. However, as noted by Barrie Thorne (1982) they all share in common the following ideas about the family:

- society is male dominated – it is patriarchal
- the psychological experience of being in a family is different for men and for women
- the family is a source for the control of women
- families socialise us with gender roles that themselves reflect and continue patriarchal ideologies
- families are not 'private' – they are controlled by the state, and women in particular are the subjects of massive social control
- there is no biological need for the family – it is a product of culture rather of nature

What do feminists think about society?

In general, the starting point for most feminist analysis of **society** is to see society as being made up of unequal structures of power between men and women. We call this **patriarchy**, which literally means 'rule of the father', but in general usage this term is used to refer to the ways in which society is male-dominated. This is seen to be a product of culture – it is not natural. This is very different from the sociobiological view that would argue that the family is a biological product of our natural needs.

What do feminists think about the family?

Beechey (1986) notes that in common-sense thought in society, the family is often taken for granted as natural, without any real questioning of this, and is also thought about in a gendered fashion: families seem to require different things from men and from women. We are seen to need and to want to live in families, they are seen as the best way to bring up children, and women are seen to have the main role in this childcare. This is an ideological view of the family as far as Beechey and other feminists are concerned. It is untested and it allows male dominance to continue. Men are seen to benefit from the family more than women.

Feminists point out the following 'dark side' of the modern-day family:

1   The family contains a large amount of psychological harm for women

2 Women do the majority of housework, even today
3 Women do the majority of emotional work
4 There are lots of instances of sexual and domestic abuse of women in the family context

- **Marxist-feminism** – this view, held by writers such as Barrett and McIntosh (1982), claims that the family serves the needs of capitalism; patriarchy in the home allows capitalism to continue in wider society. The exploitation of women and the care women provide men in the home allows feelings of alienation and exploitation from work to be reduced, allowing society to go unquestioned. Equally, women are needed by capitalism to raise the next generation of workers.
- **Radical feminism** – this view held by Shulamith Firestone (1979) argues that male power is based upon natural biological physical strength. Family life serves to benefit men as it is designed to allow men to benefit from the care work provided by women. This inequality is underpinned by the use or the threat of male violence against women.
- **Black feminism** – the writers Amos and Parmar (1984) are keen to point out that ethnicity has a massive effect upon the nature of family life, and therefore on women's experience of the family.
- **Post-feminism** – this view suggests that women's lives are freer than ever before. It claims that the need for feminism is over, since patriarchy in the family has been massively reduced. Women can now choose what they want.

Conclusion

The ideas of Sylvia Walby (1990) and the approach sometimes called 'triple systems feminism' are of great use when thinking about how the family links with patriarchy in society as a whole. Walby identifies six main ways in which patriarchy works in society:

1 domestic labour serves men
2 paid work – women are still bounded by 'traditional values'
3 the state – promotes an ideological image of the family and marriage which is patriarchal
4 physical violence by men often occurs in the home
5 women's and girls' sexuality are limited and controlled by the family more than men's
6 the media also presents a highly ideological image of women's family roles.

For consideration:

1 What do you think is the most valuable insight about the family made by feminism?

◆ **What, When and Why?**

According to the 1996 British Crime Survey, it is estimated that 6.6 million people in the UK have experienced some sort of domestic violence, including threats of violence as well as actual physical harm. Interestingly in this study, 23 per cent of women claimed to have been physically harmed by a partner, but so too did 15 per cent of men in the sample of 11,000 people nationwide.

✓ **Top Exam Hints**

- Make sure you show, for added depth, that you understand that there is a whole variety of feminist approaches in sociology.

- The ideas of post-feminism have some things in common with the ideas of Giddens and also with the theory of postmodernism. They all see that there is increased freedom of choice in society. Try to show comparisons like this in the exam where possible.

What are conjugal roles?

What does this mean?

The term 'conjugal roles' refers to the roles shared by the partners in the family. The term conjugal itself means the specific relationship between two people who are married. We use this term in sociology to refer to the ways in which housework, childcare, etc. are divided up and distributed, and whether this is done on a 'fair' basis or not. Another way of expressing this is to talk about the 'division of domestic labour'.

How are roles in the home divided?

The feminist view tends to argue that segregated roles are much more widespread than joint roles. In the majority of cases for example, it is women who provide housework, and not men.

Many contemporary feminists talk of a 'triple shift' in the experience of women's lives. Many women go out to work yet many women still perform the majority of housework. Also, many women provide emotional work for the family, caring for relatives when they are sick, etc.

In this view, women's lives are three times harder and paid work outside the home has not 'liberated' women in the ways we might think.

Why do we have inequality over domestic tasks?

According to the functionalist Talcott Parsons (1955), there are segregated roles in the family because these are 'natural'.

Men have '**instrumental roles**', bringing in resources from the public world of work, and women have '**expressive roles**' based on emotional support and childcare.

This is a highly sociobiological argument, and is reflected in many of the ideas held by the New Right on the family today. Parsons argues that men and women simply have naturally different roles and that both are needed for the family to run in a smooth fashion. This is also similar to the ideas of New Left thinkers Dennis and Erdos (1992) who have suggested that families need fathers. The father's role as an authority figure is needed in order to maintain standards of discipline and control throughout society as a whole.

The New Right have suggested that single parent families are 'damaging' for society since they lack adequate socialisation. The traditional nuclear family, with a traditional gender role division, is seen in this view as 'most suited' to society.

What do feminists think?

Hannah Gavron (1966) describes women as being 'captive wives'. She suggests, as many other feminists have done since, that the psychological

✳ Key Idea

One of the earliest descriptions of conjugal roles comes from Elizabeth Bott (1957) who suggested that there are two main types of roles that couples in the family might adopt:

- **Segregated roles** – based upon a traditional gendered separation; the male is the breadwinner, doing DIY etc., the woman tends to the home and provides emotional support and child care

- **Joint roles** – based on an equal sharing of decision-making and tasks and responsibilities between the couple.

◆ What, When and Why?

According to the 2001 Labour Market Trends survey, there are 12.5 million women in paid work in the UK – this is roughly 73 per cent of women aged 16–59. However, this survey also shows that the factor that influences women's paid work the most is the presence of dependent children in the family home, suggesting that women still put childcare before paid employment. However, there is a significant increase in 'working mums' than ten years ago.

experience of being in a marriage is different for women and men. Women have high expectations of marriage, and there is a great deal of pressure and expectations put on the relationship by women and men. The interviews in Gavron's research revealed that women had a high expectation of freedom, yet were then even more affected by the reality of the unequal division of domestic labour. This led to feelings of being 'captive'; of marriage feeling like a prison, confining the women and determining who they were by the traditional roles they took on.

- A classic feminist study on housework and housewives, comes from Ann Oakley (1974). She takes a critical stance against the claim made by Young and Willmott that families are becoming increasingly 'symmetrical' as time goes on. For Young and Willmott, roles between the partners are increasingly likely to become shared and to be based upon joint decisions and a sharing of tasks and responsibilities. Oakley's research shows this not to be the case. She identified the existence of strong segregated roles, and that women did the overwhelming majority of housework.
- There is an assumption that families are more likely to be 'symmetrical' if they are middle-class. The research of Stephen Edgell (1980) suggests that this is still not the case. Even middle-class families are likely to have segregated relationships.
- Mary Boulton (1983) goes further and argues that large-scale quantitative surveys, if anything, are more likely to exaggerate and increase the amount of housework men do. Questions about who does what often do not take into consideration time spent, and they certainly do not show the psychological experience of being in a relationship where the woman takes responsibility for caring, nurturing and developing children for the whole of their lives. This is a very difficult relationship and 'burden' to show, by simply asking who does what tasks in the home.

Conclusion

The overwhelming evidence seems to suggest that families are no longer symmetrical, but that women are working in paid work more than ever before, and that there is increased democracy for women.

The rise of modified extended families, especially amongst some ethnic groups in the modern UK, also raises questions about the idea of conjugal roles. It could be the case that the roles and responsibilities performed by family members are not solely confined to the married couple anymore.

For consideration:

1. Do you think traditional conjugal roles still exist in the majority of families? Explain your view.
2. Do you think families will ever be 'symmetrical'? Explain your view.

✳ Key Ideas

- A recent study by Ermisch and Francesconi suggests that if women work in full-time paid employment while bringing up children there might be an effect on the education of the child. This is a longitudinal survey of people born in the 1970s, based upon a sample of 1,263. Using data from the British Household Panel Survey, these authors have argued that where mothers work full time, children are less likely to gain A Level qualifications, more likely to be unemployed later in life and more likely to suffer from psychological disorders associated with stress. (This research was published by the Joseph Rowntree Foundation in 2000.)

- Many feminists have argued that government welfare policies encourage a very patriarchal view of the family. They encourage marriage, a traditional nuclear family, and work on the assumption that women will do the majority of childcare. For example, there are presently tax credits for those who are married rather than cohabitating together. Plus, with family allowances and tax credits the assumption is that women are encouraged to stay at home with children rather than go to work. In fact, even the TV advert for this scheme shows traditional nuclear family structures, and shows the man as the breadwinner. A very patriarchal view.

- Giddens (1992) provides a different interpretation of family life. He suggests that, unlike ever before, there is an increased 'democracy' in the family, and that women's roles and lives are freer now than at any other point in history. He sees increased opportunity for women to take control of their lives, and increased freedom to make choices.

4.15 What are the changing patterns of marriage and divorce today?

What does this mean?

Patterns of marriage vary considerably – across the globe, between classes and regions, and within the same society over time. At a common-sense level you might be aware that many people today are not getting married, but what does this really mean? What does the evidence really say? Many politicians fear the 'death of marriage' and discuss this as a new family crisis. Is this true, or a moral panic?

What types of marriage exist across the globe?

There is great diversity across the world, although the common-sense ideology of the family in Western thoughts tends to tell us that **monogamy** is 'natural'. Often family types and marriage diversity vary according to ethnicity and religion. For example, many people have arranged or even enforced marriage in the UK today, because of their ethnic traditions.

Polygyny is more common than **polyandry**. Sometimes societies use polyandry as a form of birth control since it limits the number of children born to the husbands. For example, traditionally in some parts of Nepal, young women marry more than one man, all of whom are brothers – insuring that there are lots of 'family members' available to look after children.

Do we have a crisis with marriage?

The New Right, the media and politicians in general tend to wish to protect marriage as a way of making society stable. Feminists refer to this as an ideological view of the family. Divorce certainly is on the increase, and family diversity is also increasing, but this does not mean to say we have a crisis.

A particularly dramatic rise in divorce has occurred since the 1971 Divorce Law Reform Act, which arguably made divorce easier and more acceptable. There are a number of possible reasons why divorce might be on the increase.

1 Divorce is more acceptable.
2 People who marry young might grow apart or regret the decision.
3 Young people might have high expectations of marriage which are not fulfilled.

What will the future of marriage be in society?

66 99 Key Definition

We can make a distinction between:

- Monogamy – one man married to one woman. In recent years, due to the rise of divorce and re-marriage, we have a situation of serial-monogamy in the West, i.e. we have different partners in a lifetime, but not at the same time.

- Polygamy – one person marrying more than one person at the same time (illegal in many western countries). There are two types of this:

  polygyny – men marry more than one woman at the same time; and

  polyandry – women marry more than one man at the same time.

184   Sociology AS for OCR

4   Increased freedom and rights for women to take control over their lives.
5   Increased social condemnation of domestic violence.
6   Longer life expectancy means couple have more chance to grow apart.
7   The rise of the nuclear family might mean that some people are increasingly isolated from wider kin and this might increase the psychological pressure on married relationships.

Many sociologists are now claiming that divorce is the norm.

- Robert Chester (1985) has said that the nuclear family will not die out as such; it will change its form and accommodate new ways of living, but will still be based around the two-partner model – such as step families or people living together.

- David Morgan (1996) suggests that divorce is commonplace, and that this change has occurred in just 20 years. It is another stage for many along the life course. However, divorce offers freedom for some, but poses interesting problems and diversity for our family relationships and for our individual identity and the roles we might take on. The more divorce and re-marriage increase, the more we find ourselves part of many different families at the same time, and the more we accommodate different roles and ways of acting which shape who we might think we are.

- Anthony Giddens (1991) suggests that divorce poses challenges and opportunities. It can cause great psychological harm, yet can also offer new opportunities and freedoms. It certainly offers many people the chance to re-assess who they think they are. Giddens refers to this as 'ontological insecurity' – concern over who we think we are; concern over knowing our own identity. Giddens says that divorce and its increase has fundamentally changed the nature of modern-day family life. It is both a reflection of, and a further influence on increasing post-traditionalism, the decline of old ways of living. Giddens refers to this identity which people are given the opportunity to rebuild as a 'plastic identity' since it can be shaped and moulded.

Key Idea
Cockett and Tripp (1984) suggest that family break-down, and family break-up, or separating is a new norm.

Conclusion

As we have seen, there are great changes taking place in marriage in recent years. We are possibly yet to see their full impact on society and on our daily lives, but many feel that society will no longer be the same. This is very realistic as all human actions change over time, and often change gradually; it is often the case that we don't see or understand the changes until they appear dramatic or overwhelming. Maybe this is why so many people in society are worried about the future or the 'death' of the family?

For consideration:

1   What do you think is the main reason for divorce?
2   How might widespread divorce dramatically change society?

4.16 Do families need fathers?

What does this mean?

Many politicians and New Right sociologists claim that we are witnessing a death of the family: the rise of single-parent families will lead to a massive change in how society operates, and the loss of important social stability. How can we investigate this claim?

Why do we need fathers?

Functionalist Talcott Parsons (1955) suggested that both the traditional gender roles of the parents are vital for the well-being of the family, and this early view is often still reflected today in the ideas of politicians on both the New Right and on the New Left. Parsons argues that due to biology, men and women offer different things to the family, and to the children they bring up. As we can see, this idea reflects the influence of sociobiological thinking on sociological views. For Parsons, men have an 'instrumental role' based upon provision for the family, whereas women have an 'expressive role', based upon providing care and emotional support. This has brought Parsons under attack from many feminist sociologists who see this argument as highly patriarchal.

Do families need fathers? Do families need mothers?

✓ **Top Exam Hint**

Try to link the ideas of functionalism to the ideas of sociobiology, and then you can attack functionalism with feminism. This is how you can build up evaluation in your answers, by 'bouncing' theories and ideas off each other.

Muncie and Wetherell (1995) note that such traditional images of male and female parenting roles have existed in the UK state's view on the family for a very long time. For example, the welfare state, created in 1942, assumed that marriage was the goal for all adults and that women would support the family. Even today, on adverts for state benefit we see very traditional parenting roles represented – the mother staying at home, the father as the main provider.

Interestingly, many families in the modern UK have women as the strong discipline figure, not the man as would be traditionally expected. Barrow (1982) for example, has documented well the fact that amongst some ethnicities (such as UK West Indian families) the mother is traditionally the strong family figure. Many West Indian families are what are known as 'mother households' – two generations of women plus children living together.

We can also question the extent to which 'house-husbands' might exist in UK society. Research in 1999 by the Joseph Rowntree Foundation indicated that the father role has changed, but the idea of the male as the breadwinner for the family remains very strong. Instead, fathers are having to become 'super-dads' doing much more than ever before. They are keeping the traditional father roles, but are adding to this an increased expectation from children and wives to become more 'involved' in the upbringing of children, as well as providing for the family.

For the New Right, however, the traditional male father figure remains an important feature for a stable society. The New Right view on the family is also, like Parsons' view in the 1950s and 1960s, a product of the time it developed in – the late 1980s. Many from the New Right and the New Left claim that we have a death of the family, and 'absent fathers' were seen to be to blame, as well as young women choosing single parenthood as a means to receive welfare – a situation quite exaggerated and impossible to prove.

Conclusion

New Left thinkers Dennis and Erdos (1992) have argued that lone parenthood has a considerable effect on the rise of deviance and crime: the absence of an authority figure causes young children to lack proper respect for the rules of society.

This is a controversial claim, but certainly one that echoes the ideas of Parsons some 45 years ago. We are certainly seeing the rise of government policies that seek to put more responsibility on families for bad behaviour in schools, truanting and delinquency.

For consideration:

1 Do you think the father and mother gender roles are natural? Why?
2 Do you agree that absent fathers lead to social breakdown?

◆ **What, When and Why?**

Hilary Land (1995), not a New Right sociologist, describes the changes that were taking place in society when this view became popular:

- By 1987 14 per cent of families with children were lone parents in the UK
- In 1989, 644,000 lone parents received state welfare
- By 1989, 27 per cent of births took place outside marriage

✳ **Key Idea**

State overload – The New Right uses this idea to refer to the crisis point welfare spending has reached (if this is true) because of the fact that some people are taking money from the state. In this view, the state should not provide welfare, and this would force people to 'help themselves'.

4.17 Do we have family diversity?

What does this mean?

Diversity means variety – lots of different types. When applied to the family and to households, we can offer lots of different ways of thinking about how families might be different from each other:

Rhona and Robert Rapoport (1982) identify five different ways in which we can think about diversity:

1 Organisational diversity – families might have different structures and different roles within them.
2 Cultural diversity – ethnicity and religion might make some people have different types of families and ways of living from others.
3 Class diversity – the income that the family has and the '**cultural capital**' of the class background of a family may dramatically affect the lifestyle of the family members.
4 Life course diversity – where different families are along the stages of their life will also affect what sort of family they have, for example, if they are young couples, middle-aged with children, or elderly where children have young families of their own.
5 Cohort diversity – those born at the same time represent a 'cohort': a group of people who have common experiences of the world as they have lived through common historical events. This affects, among other things, your family life. If you lived through the second world war in London, for example, you may have been evacuated away from your family to the countryside for the duration of the war, giving you and your cohort a similar experience of family life.

How might geographical location affect family diversity?

Eversley and Bonnerjea (1982) illustrate that where you live in the country will affect the sort of family you are more likely to have:

• Affluent south of England – mobile two-parent families, children leave at an early age to seek employment or to go to university or to boarding school.
• Coastal areas of England and Wales – retired couples and elderly widowers often move to these areas to 'retirement homes'.

✓ **Top Exam Hint**

Think about the synoptic ideas of class, gender, ethnicity, location and age as ways in which to think about the diversity of families.

❝❞ Key Definition

Cultural capital – this means the ways in which your class background benefits you and allows you to increase your provision of the rewards of society. For example, your accent, language codes and values are part of your culture, and may advantage or disadvantage you and your family.

- Industrial areas and inner cities – old working class traditional communities with extended family-type structures and large support networks.
- Recently declining ex-industrial areas in the Midlands and the North of England – large-scale unemployment will put massive pressure on family life.
- Inner cities – wide turnover of population; many people arrive and live in these areas for a short period of time; large differences between very poor and very wealthy; lone parents; single person households and large numbers of multi-adult households.

How can we understand cultural diversity?

The modern UK includes many different ethnic groups, religious groups and therefore many different types of family practices.

Ballard (1982) looked at South Asian families in the UK. Across the generations these families had very different expectations of family life, the older generations being more traditional than the younger ones. The influences of Western culture and traditional family culture increase diversity since they lead to new mixed ways of family living, or might further increase tradition as a response to racism, or feelings of a loss of identity. These types of families made great use of extended family style structures.

Ann Oakley (1982) studied Cypriot families in the UK. As discovered in the findings of Ballard above, such families often used the extended family network as a means to establish community ties and support networks, much needed after migration. These families also tended to fulfil an economic function together, perhaps working alongside each other in family businesses.

Conclusion

Rhona Rapoport (1989) suggests that family diversity is a European experience, not simply a UK experience. However, for Katja Boh (1989) it makes little sense to use the term 'diversity' because we are all being diverse in the ways that we are mixing and combining different family structures and traditions together. Therefore, we may as well talk about 'convergence' – we are all moving towards a new normal, mixed set of family relationships.

For consideration:

1 Why do you think family diversity is important for the sociologist trying to understand the modern-day family?
2 What sort of diversity do you think would have the most impact on making families different? Why?

◆ **What, When and Why?**

The average number of people in households is on the decline in the UK from 3.1 in the 1960s, through to 2.4 in 1999. The latter figure was once the average number of children per family, but now is the average number of all persons in all households – a very different picture. The fastest growing type of household is the single male household.

4.18 Does the family have a dark side?

✓ Top Exam Hint

Use the ideas in this section to make evaluative criticisms of the functionalist and New Right views of the family in the exam.

What does this mean?

Sociologists use the term 'the dark side' to refer to a negative feature of an aspect of society that is hidden, misunderstood or unspoken about. The ideology of the family paints a picture of 'happy families' caring for each other, but how true is this really? What goes on behind the closed doors of the family?

Often this dark side of family life consists of the fact that some family relationships, as we would expect given how many there are, are dysfunctional. They might be based upon violence, control, inequality and psychological harm.

How does the family control and affect its members?

*   First, the family is not the safe haven that the ideology says it is. Both domestic violence and child abuse take place in some families. In fact, it is probably the case that we know less about this sort of crime than we think because it often goes unreported and undiscovered.

*   Sociologists Dobash and Dobash (1979) conducted interviews with women who had been victims of violent assault within the family. They point out that when women are the victims of rape, murder or assault, it is usually a family member that is the criminal, and more often than not the husband. The family is the most likely source for such crimes, rather than society as a whole, as is more generally feared.

*   Jan Pahl (1980) notes that male physical control of women in the family is usually combined with more economic control. Women are often not able to leave the situation if they wish to, for fear of having no way to supprt themselves.

*   Radical feminist Brownmiller (1976) goes one stage further and argues from a 'separatist' position that all men are rapists. She says that men are biologically violent, and that the act of heterosexual sex is actually an act of violation and domination of men over women.

*   Smart (1976) and Heidenshon (1996) have both noted that women and teenage girls are more likely to be controlled by the family than men and boys. They are more likely to have their freedom limited especially in terms of going out at night and in terms of sexuality.

- Another way we can think about the negativity of families is to think about the inequality in household roles that takes place in many families. Feminists such as Anne Oakley (1974) and Hannah Gavron (1966) illustrate that men do many fewer of the household chores than women do. Traditional gender roles thus oppress women more, making them 'captive' in the home.

- A further way in which we can think about the family is offered by radical psychiatrist R D Laing. He claims that the family is an 'emotional pressure cooker'. Because many people do not have wider kin to turn to on a regular basis the relationships in the family can get very strained. He thinks that such pressure in the family leads to the increase of mental illness in society, in particular the rise of schizophrenia, since family members feel under pressure not to be who they might want to be.

Conclusion

Not all families have the problems outlined above, but some do. This is enough to enable sociologists to reject common-sense and ideological views of the family as always a 'perfect' way to live.

For consideration:

1 Why do you think that in common-sense thought we often ignore the dark side of the family?
2 Why do you think the mass media might exaggerate this dark side?

✍ **Coursework Suggestion**

For A2 coursework you could look at how families treat male and female children differently. If you looked at families from different classes, ethnicities, and with parents of different ages, you might be able to make some interesting comparisons.

4.19 Do we have postmodern families?

What does this mean?

The postmodern view is a relatively recent addition to sociology. This theory claims that a massive and irreversible change has taken place in society in the past 20 years, making the world a very different place from what it once was. Such is the impact of this change, we are 'beyond the modern'. We have raced into fast forward, experiencing rapid change in all that we know – change at both macro and micro levels. Change that makes us question the nature of our very selves.

What are the features of a postmodern society?

- According to French sociologist Lyotard (1984) the 'postmodern condition' is about the rise of the relativity of truth. What this means is that things we used to believe in, or things that used to be true, are now uncertain. We now question the values, ideas and traditions of the recent past; certainty is becoming uncertain. We used to believe in science, for example, but many are now worried about the effects of science, and feel that we can't really believe what scientists tell us any more.

- In this postmodern view, Baudrillard (1988) claims that the previously stable knowledge we had of the world – the way we saw society and our place in it – has 'decomposed': it has all come crashing down.

- Although he is not a postmodernist, Giddens' ideas are reflected in the view above (1991) with his concept of 'manufactured uncertainty'. Giddens claims that we are increasingly aware of our place in the globe and of the ways in which there are many risks to daily living, many of which humans themselves have caused in the first place. This makes us anxious about what the world is really like and it makes us uncertain what our future might be like.

What are postmodern families?

The central change we have witnessed in terms of the family in recent years is the rapid increase in diversity and choice. This increase results in new ways of living and relating to others, and in turn the withering of older, more traditional values concerning how we should live our lives. Many sociologists agree that this change has occurred, and this certainly seems to match some of the ideas of the postmodern view above.

Postmodern families are 'undecided', 'uncertain' and they are always changing.

Postmodern families:

- allow for more choice

- are not 'fixed' by past traditions

- offer new ways of living and relating to each other

- might offer more freedom to think about who we are and what we want

- might offer increased anxiety – we might decide we no longer know who we are, or what we want; there might be too many choices to make and the world might feel too uncertain.

Conclusion

When looking at the family, we can see two different possible consequences of this post-modernisation process, if it is true.

- The postmodern optimistic view – claims that increased diversity will lead to further choice and increased freedom

- The postmodern pessimistic view – claims that increased choice might lead to less certainty and therefore more anxiety about our world, our lives and our selves.

For consideration:

1 Do you feel the world is undergoing great change? How can you tell?
2 Do you feel families are uncertain?

4.20 What might the future of the family be?

What does this mean?

Sociologists have spent a great deal of time looking at the family in the past, and how it has changed. Some have tried to go one stage further to think about what it might be heading towards. What most sociologists agree on is that it is always changing.

What can we say about the changing family?

We can identify the following trends in the sociological treatment of the family, as seen in this chapter:

*   the family feels private – but it might actually be open to quite a lot of public scrutiny

*   we have wide family diversity

*   many politicians might feel diversity in the family is damaging for society

*   many sociologists can identify a clear ideology of the family that exists in society

*   historical records on the family are often open to question

*   common sense tells us that the family is natural – but how do we know for sure?

*   the reality of family life is complex

*   families are not things, but they are **practices** – they are ways of thinking about how we act with some people and what our roles mean.

Where does this leave us?

*   For the New Right and the New Left the family is to be protected at all costs – the future of the society we live in depends upon it.

*   The feminist approach, however, embraces family diversity. They feel that diversity best matches the reality of the modern family in the UK, although many feminists point out that the family is still a massive source of the control of women in society. Diversity might be a way of challenging this, however, since it means that women might have more options than ever before.

✔ **Top Exam Hint**

Use these bullet points as a way of making evaluative conclusions in appropriate exam questions.

✳ **Key Idea**

David Cheal uses the term 'family practices' rather than just 'family' to try to make the point that families are not 'things', but rather they are 'doings' or '**practices**'.

- For Giddens the family is more democratic and equal than ever before. We have witnessed massive social change in our personal life and in our personal relationships with others and these changes have increased the opportunities and the challenges open to us. This could be a source of anxiety, or it could be a source for personal liberation and identity formation.

- The postmodern view on the future of the family would be to argue that present-day diversity is both a consequence of and a contribution to the increased post-modernisation of society in general, and of our personal lives, emotions and identities in particular. We are living through a world under rapid change.

Do we have 'brave new families'?

Ulrich Beck and Elisabeth Beck-Gernsheim (1995) argue that in our modern world the family is under question unlike ever before. Clearly the family always changes, but for Beck and for Giddens (1991, 1992) we are now able to think about and reflect upon these changes. We are aware of the changes while they are happening – this makes us uncertain about the future of the family as individuals and as a society.

Postmodern thinker Judith Stacey (1990) suggests that the time we are living in is 'contested' – we are uncertain what will happen. Beck's response to this is to say that we will always have some sort of family as it is, after all, the best symbol we have to describe those closest to us. Quite what it will be, however, only time will tell.

Conclusion

Berger (1963) noted a long time ago that the family is central to who we are. He refered to this as the 'sphere of the intimate'. This means that the family and the relationships we build help us to create our own personal biography, i.e. how we see who we are and the experiences we have had through our life course to date. If the future of the family is uncertain, then who we are is uncertain and who we might end up becoming.

For consideration:
1 What do you think the future of the family will be?
2 Do you think we are living through a period of change? Why?

✓ **Top Exam Hint**

It is interesting to note that in this chapter we have come across a few sociologists who make observations about the family whilst working with their own family members who are also sociologists. There are in fact three examples in this book so far. What might this tell us about our need as humans to understand our own family life?

4.21 Is childhood a social construction?

What does this mean?

The 'family' is a social construction since, as we have shown, it is a symbol that we think of as real, that we use in our minds and with others to describe the feelings we have and the relationships we have with those close to us.

Equally, as with other social constructions, the concept of age in general and of 'old age' and of 'childhood' in particular link to our understandings of roles within the family. In this view, childhood does not exist in terms of real biological ages, but rather, the reality of childhood lies in the value and interpretation that our culture places upon it.

What is age?

We often use the idea of a 'life course' to describe the ways in which time, age and the family all relate to each other. We can locate certain key points for our culture along the course of our life:

- birth
- early infancy
- childhood
- teenage years
- early adulthood
- middle age
- old age.

Different cultures however, interpret the roles and 'scripts' associated with these stages in different ways. Equally, within societies over history, these roles change. Today, we are all too familiar with the idea of a 'stroppy teenager' – like the character of 'Kevin' played by comedian Harry Enfield. However, many sociologists agree that the idea of a 'teenager' was a product of the post-second world war era, with the creation of extended schooling and the rise of youth culture due to the creation of a music industry. Before the second world war, 'teenagers' as we understand them today simply did not exist. Instead, boys, for example, wore shorts at school, and then at fourteen left school, took up a trade if they were working class, started to wear long trousers and become an adult. No difficult transition – no hormones. This therefore suggests that age is a cultural creation if its characteristics can change throughout history.

What is childhood?

The role played by children in the family, and the notion today of what we call 'childhood', is again an interesting social construction, as is the notion of old age.

Is childhood and teenagehood 'real'?

- Childhood is seen as a biological given, yet it is the object of great public concern. The media and politicians frequently discuss how best to deal with deviant children and how best to protect our children from deviant adults. We have massive moral panics about child pornography, yet at the same time have young girls modelling for fashion houses in provocative dress. Archard (1993) notes that in our common-sense thought, childhood is based upon notions of 'separateness' from adulthood. Children are not adults, they are separate from adults, and need to grow up to be able to join the adult world. Children need to be protected from the adult world, yet at the same time taught how best to fit into it.
- This is very different from the Victorian time in the UK when children were 'seen but not heard'. Today we have what various writers describe as 'child-centredness' where many families put the wishes and desires of the children before their own. Brigitte and Peter Berger (1983) have noted that since the general decrease in infant mortality in the nineteenth century, children have become ever-present in the household. This has changed their role in the family quite considerably, from being able to offer an economic contribution, to the present dependence upon family members for the first sixteen years of their life.
- Phillipe Aries (1973) has argued that the idea of children as vulnerable to a harmful adult world is a recent cultural creation. For example, in the Middle Ages, children over five were actually considered to be adults and as such had economic and sexual roles in society – the latter a notion found abhorrent today.

Conclusion

Robert Bocock (1993) has suggested that over the past century we have seen the rise of a consumption role for children, and also in particular for that age we describe as 'teenagehood'. Capitalism needs people to buy the things it produces, in order to keep profits flowing. Children today, unlike ever before, are part of this process. Many products are aimed directly at them, effectively 'creating' or 'constructing' their identity as children – from toys to sweets, from clothes to the singles charts. All of this spending on, by and for children links directly to the ways in which the family is now often centred directly on children. Previously, before the creation of capitalism, children contributed to the family, rather than the family providing for them.

✳ Key Idea

Neil Postman (1985) suggests that childhood is disappearing in modern society; it is being decomposed. Due to the rise of the mass media, children are able to experience things that previously were only available to adults. As such they are growing up more quickly and in time this means our notions of age and of childhood will need to be changed once more.

For consideration:

1 Why do you think notions of childhood might change?
2 Can you see anything contradictory about how our society presently thinks about children, and their roles in the family?

4.22 Is old age a social construction?

Thinking like a Sociologist

The idea of a calendar age and time is not universal. Elias says that in the West, we know our birth date, our age and we use the time to measure our day. We use the notion of a birthday to categorise and classify people: they tell us who we are, and are used by the state to recognise us, for example on passports, by banks etc. Yet, in many cultures calendar time is not measured by clock time.

● Synoptic link

Age is a really good – and very underused – synoptic link. The elderly, for instance, are often disadvantaged in society. Age is also a good way to think about family diversity. Try to use this in the exam.

What does this mean?

Age, and time for that matter, are both cultural creations. Clearly age does exist in a physical sense since our bodies get older, and eventually we will die. Yet, the meaning of age, and the social roles and expectations associated with different ages are the products of the culture you come from. Again, this is further confused by the fact that as we get older there are some things our bodies can no longer do.

How do we think about age?

- Sociologist and historian Norbert Elias (1992) has shown us that the very ideas of time and age vary quite considerably across the globe. In the West we think about a measurable, calendar age, related to the centrality of time for our cultures. Marxists add to this that capitalism needs a strong concept of time in order to be successful – the economic production process needs people to be able to measure time in a common way. Workers need to have a common sense of time in order to make sure they all arrive for work at the same point!
- In many cultures time might be measured by reference to the passing of historical events, or the passing of natural events such as floods or monsoons. There are many people around the globe who do not know their 'age' in the Western sense that they would know their birthday, the number of years lived, and the calendar age they had reached. This is something that in the West we would find almost incomprehensible, such is the dominance of clock time and calendar time in our culture.
- Time is everywhere, as are watches. Age gives roles to people; it allows people to think about themselves and allows others to think about them.

What is old age?

- In terms of old age, people are living longer today than ever before. This has fundamentally changed our experience of the family. We have more families today who have reached the end of the life course. Their children have moved away, creating the idea of a 'retired family'. Retirement, however, and the way that this affects the family, varies according to the class of the people involved. Retirement for an elderly couple with savings and a private pension will be very different and will offer more choices than it does for a couple with neither.
- Since people are living longer, old age becomes something society ends up thinking about and noticing more. Some suggest that we are facing a future of an 'aged society' where the number of elderly

people dependent upon the state for welfare will outnumber the number of people in full-time work. This is, rather stereotypically, sometimes referred to as the 'greying of society'.

- How society 'treats' the elderly, how ordinary people 'see' those who are old and interact with them, varies. In many cultures the elderly are treated with respect – they are seen as sources of great wisdom, as heads of the household. Many Marxists have pointed out that in modern-day capitalist societies the elderly are often defined as not useful. This is because they do not work and they often cannot buy very much, thus, they do not really make a contribution to the continuation of the capitalist economy. This is why the elderly, like children, are seen as a 'problem' for society, rather than as a rich source of knowledge and status. They are seen as a problem since they are really a problem for capitalism.
- Marxist Chris Phillipson (1982) suggests that the elderly are often defined in capitalist societies in the West as people whose usefulness to society has passed. They are ex-workers, retired from making a financial contribution to society. They are seen as a drain on the financial resources of the state.
- Giddens (1986) notes that in modern society the longer life expectancy of family members has had a massive effect on the nature of family life. Since people are living longer, we are increasingly exposed to a wider variety of relationships within the family. We have the increased likelihood of building relationships with grandparents and even great-grandparents, relationships that previously would never have existed since people would have died before it was possible to build them.

Conclusion

Many postmodern authors in sociology have also argued that as a society our attitude to the elderly is under considerable re-assessment in recent years.

- The elderly are beginning to develop an economic role of consumption – there are more things associated with old age for the elderly to buy.
- There is an increased recognition that the elderly can do things we would never have thought possible, e.g. exercise, wear fashionable clothes, etc. Our notions of old age are undergoing great change.
- There is the development of medical industries aimed at keeping the elderly younger, for example, hormone replacement therapy, plastic surgery and the invention of Viagra.

Meyrowitz (1984) has suggested that age is undergoing a reversal. Children are growing up and are becoming more adult-like, whereas adults are becoming more child-like; they are stopping their ageing process.

✳ Key Ideas

- Giddens also argues, as does Elias, that due to the increase in old age, as a society our attitude to death is also under great change. Death is now much more hidden than it once was. As Elias says, *'Never before have people died as noiselessly and hygienically as today'* (p.85). As people are living longer, death is becoming more invisible.

- Featherstone and Hepworth (1991) suggest that we are experiencing the rise of a 'mask of aging' brought about by medical and scientific development. We can change and mask the age we are, we can challenge unlike before how others think of us.

For consideration:

1 How do you think notions of old age have changed in society?
2 How does increased life expectancy affect the family?

4.23 Examination advice

In order to do the best you possibly can, follow the advice given over the next two sections of this chapter. You might also wish to think about the advice given at the end of every chapter (even if you don't actually study the topic, there still might be some good general advice you can follow).

You will answer two questions on this paper. Each of the questions you answer has two parts. You can answer both questions on the same topic, or on different topic areas.

In each question:

Part a) is worth 15 marks, and you should spend no longer than 15 minutes answering it. It will ask you to 'Identify and explain...' two specific features of the question area. It tests your knowledge and understanding, so you need to include studies, concepts and theories wherever you can. Make sure you clearly differentiate between the two points you make – use bullets or numbers.

Part b) is worth 30 marks and you should spend no longer than 30 minutes answering it. It will ask you to 'Outline and discuss...' a view. You are being tested on your knowledge and understanding, interpretation and analysis and evaluation so you should include studies, concepts and theories. Try to make specific evaluative comments throughout, but also ensure that you look at other views on the question. If you do this you will be juxtaposing your views, and you will be rewarded evaluation marks.

- Know the time limits of the exam. Before the exam, practise past papers to the timing of the exam: time yourself so that you can devote the right amount of time for the right sort of questions.

- Do the right sort of revision: it might help to think about revision as taking things out of your head – rather than as putting things in. It actually doesn't matter how much you know (or rather, 'remember') if you cannot actually get it out of your head onto paper – which, after all, is what the exam is asking you to do!

- There is more to 'learning sociology' than simply being able to remember things. Make sure that you also practise evaluation skills. They are much more important next year, but are still important this year. Think about what studies and theories agree and disagree with each other. Make lists of these agreements and disagreements as part of your revision, this should help with the longer mark questions in the exam.

- Make sure that you see the connections between the concepts and the studies or the named examples. One way of revising this would be to

● Synoptic link

Try to show in the exam that the family influences and in turn is also influenced by other aspects of society such as class, ethnicity, culture, education etc. This is a good way of exploring interesting ideas and of getting depth. You will also be practising important synoptic skills.

✍ Coursework Suggestion

The family is a very popular A2 coursework topic. it is an aspect of society that we are all familiar with after all. You could look at family diversity – how different classes or ethnicities structure their family relationships in different ways. Equally, you could look at roles around the home – who does what, and how does this link to the sociological literature?

✓ Top Exam Hint

Try to explore (but only if relevant) the fact that the family topic area is the victim of a series of massive methodological problems – problems with measuring, defining and gaining access in order to be able to do social research. This will help your answer have both depth and evaluation.

keep a vocabulary book throughout the year, and when it comes to revision make sure that you learn each concept and what it means, and for every concept make sure you have a named example that would agree and a named example that would disagree.

- Theory is an easy way of getting depth. Make sure that in your answers for the longer mark questions you are able to show a sense of the theory (the background) to the specific named example you are using. This is a way of putting the study or even the concept into a wider and more detailed context.

- You might think about the problems of historical context in the family exam. Is it the case that what a particular sociologist thinks about the family is the product of the time period they were writing in? It probably would have some influence on their views after all.

- Try to see if you can work issues of methods into your exam. It is actually very difficult to really know what goes on in families; they are, after all, 'behind closed doors'.

Key points to remember

1   Try to practise timed past papers as part of your revision.

2   Try to explore issues of methods in the exam.

3   Practise your evaluation skills.

4.24 Pushing your grades up higher

If you can try to follow the advice below, then hopefully you will be able to push your grades up as high as possible. None of the following tips are, however, a substitute for good revision, but they will help if combined with good revision.

1   When it comes to answering questions on the family, make sure you can show that there are many problems regarding the measurement and definition of what families are and of what they do. These problems will have a huge effect on how sociologists see the family, and therefore the theories they have about the family. Try to spell out this important evaluation point if you can.

2   A major theme that runs throughout the whole of family sociology is the idea of an ideology of the family. This idea is relevant to a wide range of debates, exam questions and theories. It is also an excellent way to develop important evaluation skills – by questioning what we hold to be 'common-sense' and to be able to illustrate that these ideas might be open to question by sociological analysis.

3   Try to give a sense of the centrality of family life for the whole of society, and as a product of this, the centrality of family sociology to the whole of the subject. In a sense, the topic has in-built 'synoptic skills' since most things can be or are believed to be, related to the family.

4   Make sure that you read a good quality newspaper throughout your sociology course – there are often stories about family welfare policies and family legal changes. Keeping up-to-date with these changes will really help you to be able to apply recent legislation to the ideas and theories that you have learned, in particular the ideas of the New Right and the New Left.

5   The feminist view in the sociology of the family is an excellent tool to be used for evaluation. In a sense this theory has evaluation built into it, since it is highly critical of the common-sense view of the family and highly critical of the ideology of the family that it sees as being present within New Right thinking and the views of politicians.

6   Although it wouldn't be recommended that you do this very often, brief reference to how the media might portray the family and how this might have changed might also help you to build a picture where you can discuss the ideology of the family in some detail. You might be able to refer to a TV advert you have seen in order to discuss modern-day views on housework, etc.

Key points to remember

- Try to demonstrate the problems we have with measurement of the family

- Brief reference to the media and to current newspaper articles on the family might help you build depth

- Try to use the idea of an ideology of the family where possible in order to be able to demonstrate the critical nature of sociology

4.25 Frequently asked questions

Q. Why are sociologists so worried about the family?

A. It is certainly true to say that sociologists are worried about the family; almost every sociology course you could imagine tends to deal with the sociology of the family at some point, and often quite early on in the course. The reason for this is that for many sociologists, the family is seen to be at the centre of society, therefore, it ends up at the centre of sociology as well. The family is a source of socialisation – it is our point of first contact with the world, and it provides our upbringing in this world. It is therefore very central to our thinking about our lives, our identities and our futures.

Q. Are there 'better' types of families than others?

A. No. Although the media, politicians and many on the New Right might try to claim that some families are better than others, sociologists tend to take a very different view. We hear a lot in the media about 'dysfunctional families' which are often associated with single parents, homosexual partnered families and families receiving welfare support, but this is a massive generalisation. In fact, many sociologists would go further than this and say that this type of thinking is an 'ideology' – a way of re-enforcing traditional values in society, values that tend to end up oppressing women.

Q. Why can't sociologists agree on the definition of the word 'family'?

A. The simple reason is that since there is so much family diversity, it is very difficult to say what exactly the family is – there are so many different types! Even to say what families do is difficult, since the different types might actually do different things from each other.

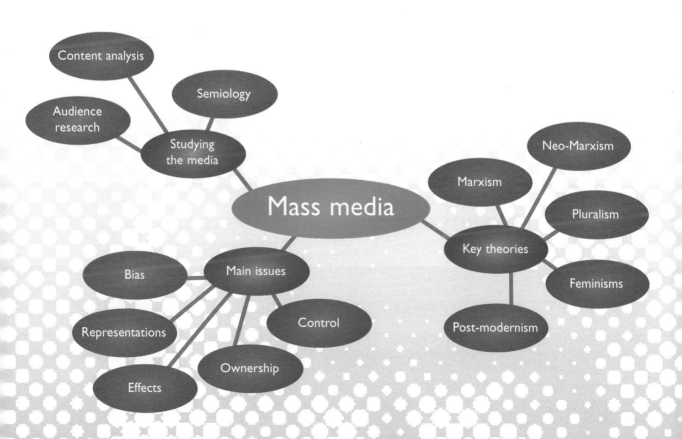

Chapter 5

Mass media

 CD-ROM 5.1

Key issues in media sociology

Why are sociologists interested in the sociology of the media?

Sociologists are interested in the mass media because of the enormous power it seems to have over our lives. Sociologists have wanted to address questions such as: How does the media influence the world of politics and how can politics influence the media? How does the media influence our private lives and identities? How important is it that most of our knowledge of the world comes from the mass media?

What are the key debates in the sociology of the media?

The questions above have led to several key debates in the sociology of the mass media.

- Do the media just present the views of powerful social groups, or do all views get a fair hearing in the media? There is debate on this between Marxists and pluralists (see sections 5 and 6).

- Is our behaviour and our sense of a personal identity determined by the mass media, or do we have the ability to select and shape our own destiny? If so, to what extent and how can we be sure of this?

- Is the knowledge and information we gain from the media both objective (true, factual, uninfluenced by emotions) and balanced? Some sociologists argue that influences by powerful social groups and the fact that society is stratified (divided into social levels) may lead to systematic biases in the information that is broadcast by the media. To say that the media reflects systematic biases means that people in the media select what should be shown according to their own personal tastes and prejudices, and that this occurs in a patterned way. For example, a white news editor may think that news items about race are not important, and so may regularly ignore such items.

What are the key ideas and concepts in the sociology of the media?

There are several key concepts that we should start with.

- Firstly, consider the term 'mass media' itself. This refers to any form of communication with a mass audience, e.g. books, newspapers, radio, television, the Internet. Sociologists argue that these media can have important effects on society due to their mass audiences.

- Another important, but debated, concept is **ideology**. Ideologies produce distorted views of reality. Some sociologists believe that the media produces and broadcasts ideologies, and that these work as a form of social control, maintaining social order.

- Lastly, related to these previous concepts, the idea of media effects suggests that the mass media can influence our behaviour in many ways.

What are the key problems in the sociology of the media?

Some of the key problems that arise in studying the mass media are methodological and theoretical. Methodological problems arise from the way in which concepts are defined and studied. Theoretical problems are concerned with the general assumptions that researchers may have, such as whether society is characterised by conflict or cooperation, or in the case of the media, whether audiences are active or passive.

- Many of the concepts we use are hard to define and measure. For example, when looking at whether people's behaviour is influenced by violent or sexual programmes, we have to decide how we define 'violence' or 'sexual'. Sociologists refer to this as **operationalisation** (for an example, see section 15).

- It is hard to disentangle causes and effects. If a person acts violently (whatever that may mean), can we be sure that the media caused the behaviour? It might be only one element in a complex set of causes.

- A key theoretical problem is whether audiences are active or passive. This relates to the different types of theories in sociology: action theories and structural theories (see Introduction). Sociologists have very different views as to whether we can act as we wish or whether our actions are constrained by social structures.

66 99 Key Definitions

- **Ideology** – a set of beliefs that forms the basis of a political or other system, which reflects the social needs and aspirations of an individual or group.

- **Operationalisation** – this refers to the way that sociologists define concepts. If we are trying to measure 'violence' in the media, we need to be able to show how we define it. Does it include things like verbal aggression? This can sometimes be as traumatic as physical violence. Having made a definition, sociologists need to select an indicator. For example, an indicator of class is occupational title. There is often debate about how a concept is defined and whether the indicators chosen are valid.

✍ Coursework Suggestion

If you are doing your coursework on the media it's very important to discuss how you have operationalised and measured key concepts in your project. Discuss why you defined and measured the concepts in the way you did, and why that was better than some of the alternatives you could have used.

✓ Top Exam Hint

You can always use methodological concepts to evaluate theories and findings in sociology. Operationalisation is a really good term to use for this. However, lots of students fail to make the most of it, thinking it's enough just to write the word down. Make sure you explain what it means (with an example) and show how it might lead to a completely different way of interpreting a piece of research and often a rejection of the researcher's conclusion.

● Synoptic Link

It's vital to make the connections between key sociological issues, such as the methodological points on operationalisation and the theoretical debates on structure and action. This is because these will influence the answers that sociologists reach and you therefore need to show that you understand how and why researchers come up with different answers. So if you do this, it will show that you are trying – and succeeding – in thinking sociologically.

5.2 What do we need to know about media sociology?

What does the specification say about the media?

The OCR specification identifies three main aspects of the media for students to investigate: media institutions; content and representation in the mass media; and the effects of the mass media.

This covers issues such as: how sociologists explain the relationship between ownership and control; the influence of owners, how media content is selected and represented; the role of media professionals in selection; media stereotypes; theories of media content (pluralism, Marxism and postmodernism, see sections 5, 6 and 20); and the effects of the media on audiences.

It's a good idea to take the opportunity to show your understanding of the issues discussed in Module 2532, 'The Individual and Society', and its focus on the creation of gender, ethnic, national and class identities, as well as sociological concepts relating to socialisation and the relationship between the individual and society. The media can be seen as playing a big role in socialisation, and you will impress examiners if you are able to discuss the relationship and role of the media in this process in a relevant way. It will also be good to demonstrate the links between media and key concepts like stratification and power.

How will I be examined in this topic?

If you are studying this option you will have to answer one 2-part structured question on the mass media. Part A is worth 15 marks and Part B worth 30 marks.

You will have 45 minutes to answer this question.

How well does this topic relate to coursework?

There is lots of scope for coursework in this topic. Content analysis is a relatively easy research method, and most people have access to the mass media. As gender, race and class identities (as well as issues such as age and disability) are hotly debated now, there is a wide choice of topics to investigate. Also don't forget that these issues can be studied in relation to the Internet, and this itself also raises new questions about technology, media, and identity.

How well does this topic help with synopticity?

There are lots of links between the media and other topics.

Family How are our views of social policy and social problems formed by the media? Consider media portrayal of different social groups, e.g. underclass, teenage mothers, single parent families (see sections 9, 10, 11, 12, 18).

Education There have been moral panics (for key definition, see section 18) about various educational issues in recent years. These include debates about standards in education, as well as concerns with discipline, and fears about drug use and sexual abuse.

Crime and deviance How does the media influence our view of crime and deviance (see sections 15, 16, 18)?

Sociological theory Our understanding of the media has to be related to several key theoretical debates, such as: the structure/action debate (agency, active/passive audience), and debates about globalisation (for key definition, see section 21) and postmodernism (for key definition, see section 20). See also sections 14, 15, 17, 18, 19, 22.

Methodology This topic involves some important general methodological problems in sociology, in particular the problem of operationalisation and measurement. Examples from this topic can be used to illustrate your understanding of this key methodological concept. You can also use your understanding of the links between the media and violence, and the wider issue of media effects to highlight the problems in trying to identify the causes of social action (see sections 14, 15, 17, 19).

Key points to remember

- Check your specification, and get copies of past papers and mark schemes.

- Find out how this topic is related to other parts of your sociology course.

- Think about how this topic relates to general sociological concepts (especially theory and method) and remember to use the course themes.

66 99 Key Definition

Synopticity – this refers to the links between different topic areas you have studied in sociology. This is clearly important for examination purposes, but it is also good sociology. Sociologists can only explain social phenomena (things that happen in society) by exploring the links between different aspects of society. You cannot fully understand the media without a good understanding of theory and methods. Similarly, sociologists would say that you cannot fully understand how we think about crime and deviance in our society without also understanding how views about crime are shaped by the media.

How can we find out about the mass media?

How have sociologists tried to measure media effects?

Sociologists use the whole range of research methods available when studying the mass media. Which method they use will depend to a considerable extent on what they are trying to find out. Research on the media tends to fall into two groups.

1 Projects investigating media effects and audiences' response to the media.
2 Studies focusing on investigating media messages and representations.

The former may use well-known research methods such as interviews, questionnaires, focus groups, or experiments. The latter tend to use less common methods like content analysis and semiology (explained below).

The strengths and weaknesses of the research methods used in the first group mentioned above are well known (see Chapter 2, Sociological research skills and methods). Sociologists also have to pay particular attention to issues of operationalisation and validity (does the study give a true picture of reality?) when using these methods to study the media. Content analysis and semiology, although they are very appropriate in studying the media, are less well-known methods, so they will be the main focus here.

What methods do sociologists tend to use to study the mass media?

Content analysis is a quantitative method, which allows sociologists to analyse and measure the content of the media. Observers can, for example, examine and measure the extent of bias in news reports, identify how much time the media spends on certain issues, or see whether characters in adverts or soap operas are stereotyped (e.g. on grounds of race, class, gender, age, and so on).

Researchers select certain programmes or types of programmes to view (using **sampling techniques**), and then analyse the content using a coding scheme. A coding scheme allows the content of the media to be placed into a category. For example, researchers watching prime-time viewing on British television channels could record a category of 'violent characters contained in programme', by noting every time they saw a 'violent' character in a programme. At the end of a programme the researcher would be able to quantify the number of 'violent' characters seen in the programme. Other coding categories in the scheme might allow the recording of further information, e.g. whether the perpetrator of violence was male, their age, race, and so on.

✓ Top Exam Hint

Comments on methodological issues such as the strengths and weaknesses of a particular method, or comments on validity, reliability, or the operationalisation of a concept, are a good way to evaluate and analyse the accuracy of research findings and theories.

66 99 Key Definition

Sampling Techniques – sociologists can use various sampling techniques in order to gain a representative sample of media output. They can use a sampling frame, such as a newspaper list of all the programmes being broadcast. They could then pick every 10th programme, for example to gain a systematic random sample. Alternatively they could, by entering all the programmes onto a database, use a computer to pick a number of programmes entirely at random (making the sample truly random).

Semiology is the scientific study of signs and symbols, developed by French thinkers such as Ferdinand de Saussure (1974) and Roland Barthes (1973). Semiologists argue that all societies have a shared understanding of language, including signs and symbols. This means that we can examine the media and analyse the meanings of the language and signs that are used. For example, images of a national flag could signify nationalism, and images of pretty women could signify and reinforce patriarchal ideals of femininity and the female role.

What problems with definition are encountered in studying the media?

The main problem with content analysis is that it can be very hard to ensure that coding schemes are reliable, and interpretation of the coding scheme can become very subjective (see Chapter 2, Sociological research skills and methods). This is a problem with definition. In the previous example for instance, different researchers (and media audiences) may have widely differing views as to whether a character or indeed a programme is 'violent'. This can mean that the research lacks reliability, and it also means that the quantitative data produced by content analysis may not give a true reflection of how a message or representation is received by an audience. Therefore content analysis may lack validity. This means that it may not be giving a true picture of reality because it is highly dependent on the way researchers select and categorise the data. It may also lack reliability because different researchers may reach different decisions, and so they may collect and be interpreting different information.

As for semiology, critics have argued that signs are always interpreted from various social positions, and that audiences may interpret signs in widely varying ways. As some critics of semiology put it, meanings (for our purposes much the same as 'definitions') are not fixed; they are polysemic (open to many different interpretations).

Conclusion

Content analysis and semiology assume that the media audience is passive and that media content will inevitably have powerful effects. They seem to neglect the possibility that people will challenge media representations. These methods also involve considerable difficulties in defining the representations and concepts that sociologists are studying. This does not mean we should not use these methods, but we should be aware of the pitfalls.

Key points to remember

- Content analysis depends on coding schemes – and these are open to interpretation.
- Semiology works on the assumption that there are shared views about the meaning of signs – but others argue that signs are polysemic.
- Understanding media content and its effects can only be achieved by looking at the meaning media content has in its social context – and this may be contested.

☞ **Who are these People?**

Ferdinand de Saussure (1857–1913) and Roland Barthes (1915–80) were both important French academics. Both were interested in the way in which symbols are used socially to create meanings and the social effects that such symbolic use has.

● **Synoptic Link**

Remember that you can use this topic to answer synoptic questions about methodology. However, it is always a good principle to demonstrate sociological understanding by showing how theory, methods, and substantive topic areas have to be interrelated for a full understanding.

What have Marxists said about control of the mass media?

5.4

✳ Key Idea

Marx's own work best illustrates what could be called **'traditional Marxism'**. Some 20th-century Marxists can also be described in this way, though they vary in their detailed assessments of Marx. Traditional Marxists argue that all aspects of society can be explained in terms of their relationship to the economy. The fact that there are owners and workers, and that these two classes exist in conflict, shapes (or determines) everything else in society.

❝❞ Key Definition

False class-consciousness – this Marxist concept assumes that the proletariat fail to recognise that they are exploited and oppressed. This has been strongly debated, with critics claiming that it is illogical – is it only Marxist sociologists who can correctly identify the existence of exploitation?

☞ Who is this Person?

Karl Marx (1818–1883) was a prolific thinker and writer. Born in Germany, he is famous for writing *The Communist Manifesto* and for being the inventor of communism. He studied philosophy before becoming a journalist and political activist. His political activities made him unwelcome in Germany and France, and he settled in London in 1849. He is important for his writing on the nature of capitalist society.

What does this mean?

Marxist theory has traditionally seen the mass media as a form of social control, as a way in which dominant social classes perpetuate their own dominant ideas. Marxists claim that the media simply transmits the dominant ideology. Dominant ideologies are the ideas that are most powerful, and Marxists argue that these are always the ideas of the capitalist ruling class. This is said to make the working class have a **false class-consciousness**. This means that they have a false understanding of their true position in capitalist society. Marxists would argue that watching a diet of soap operas and game shows on television dupes the majority of the working class into a passive (unquestioning) acceptance of the capitalist system and their own exploitation within that system. This view is known as the manipulative or instrumentalist approach and makes several key claims.

- The capitalist owners of the mass media deliberately aim to popularise ideas that will be to the direct benefit of capitalism and the capitalist class (of which they are members).

- The owners of the mass media have direct control over the ideas communicated through the mass media.

- The mass media is an instrument that allows them to ensure that their ideas and interests are the ones that gain most attention.

- The owners manipulate the mass media in the interests of the capitalist class by controlling the material that their editors and journalists publish. This means that they can and will intervene in the day-to-day running of the mass media, promoting the publication of particular items or news that they feel strongly about, and suppressing others.

- The mass media audience are seen as passive consumers of the distorted and partial accounts of news, and the cheap distracting entertainment, which the media provides them with. The mass audience uncritically accepts what is given to them and so public opinion is easily manipulated by the mass media.

Why have neo-Marxists been so critical of traditional Marxist views?

In the 20th century neo-Marxists, such as Gramsci, were keen to rectify what they saw as the mistakes of traditional Marxism. Neo-Marxists argue that empirical evidence contradicts the idea that the owners of the media always directly control and manipulate the content of the media. Far more important, they argue, is the fact that the majority of managers, editors and journalists share a similar social background (class, race and gender); the media is still dominated by white, middle-class males. They also believe that with the wide variety of media outlets now available, even views critical of capitalism find their way into print and onto the airwaves and the Internet.

These points seem to suggest that the Marxist view is wrong. However, neo-Marxists say that it just means that Marxism has to be modified to take into account the changed circumstances of contemporary society. They argue that ideological dominance works in a more subtle way than traditional Marxism assumed. Ruling-class ideas are dominant in the media because those who run the media have a shared set of assumptions and social backgrounds. Neo-Marxists use the concept of hegemony, which means dominance or leadership. The dominant ideology is seen as being one of many sets of competing ideas, and its dominance or leadership is never complete. Alternative ideas always exist and can challenge it. Manipulative media owners do not suppress alternative and critical views. According to neo-Marxists these views are more effectively marginalised if they are permitted to exist. This has the advantage of reinforcing the legitimacy and fairness of the dominant ideas, since all ideas appear to have had a fair hearing. At the same time, alternative viewpoints can often be easily made to appear to be naïve or lacking in common sense.

Conclusion

Like many theories, Marxism has been adapted to changed circumstances. However, whilst neo-Marxism may seem subtler than traditional Marxist accounts, it is worth remembering that many non-Marxist sociologists would agree that the content of the media is indeed manipulated by owners and others, at various times for many different reasons.

☞ Who is this Person?

Antonio Gramsci was an Italian Marxist and member of the Italian Communist Party in the 1920s. He was imprisoned by Mussolini and eventually died in prison. Gramsci worked as a journalist and political activist. His political experiences led him to reflect on the importance of cultural factors and ideology in preventing the development of revolutionary ideas, and this led him to develop an influential critique of traditional Marxism.

✳ Key Idea

Neo-Marxism was very influential in Britain in the 1970s and 1980s. It seemed to be a good way of dealing with the obvious weaknesses of traditional Marxism, by providing a more sophisticated picture of the relationship between the state, capitalism and the ruling classes. It demonstrated that culture was an important aspect of capitalist society, by showing that the norms or values about race or gender were the result of cultural beliefs and were not caused by economic factors.

✓ Top Exam Hint

You will impress examiners if you show that there are different schools of thought within Marxism. A key difference is that between traditional Marxism and neo-Marxism.

● Synoptic Link

Relate your general theoretical knowledge and understanding to this topic. You could discuss how recently Marxists have dealt with the problem of economic reductionism (seeing everything as being caused by economic factors, e.g. neglects cultural beliefs like religion). You could also gain a lot of credit by relating this to the structure/action debate. Marxism leans heavily towards the structure side in this debate. Say how big a problem you think this is and whether there are any points Marxists can make in reply.

For consideration:

1 Is Marxist analysis still relevant?
2. Does the neo-Marxist approach underestimate the power of those who own the mass media?

5.5 What do pluralists say about control of the media?

✻ Key Idea

Pluralism

Pluralists believe that power is spread widely throughout society, and that all groups can obtain power if they really want it. They also see society as consisting of lots of different groups competing for power. These groups have to cooperate and negotiate and no single group monopolises power. The pluralist approach to the study of the media is linked to functionalist approaches, and developed particularly strongly in 1960s America. Its popularity should be seen in its historical context. Highly critical of the radical views of the Frankfurt School (see section 14), pluralism reflected the belief that American and Western societies were democratic and free, in contrast to the totalitarian regime of the Soviet Union.

Robert Maxwell (1923–1991) succeeded in building a publishing empire that spanned the world.

What does this mean?

Pluralists such as James Whale (1997) argue that the Marxist case neglects important empirical (observed) facts, exaggerates the power of the media, is not based on an accurate idea of the way audiences respond to the mass media, and uses unhelpful concepts such as 'ruling class ideology'. This means that the picture of the role of the mass media in contemporary society presented by Marxists lacks validity.

Pluralists make several key claims.

- They claim that society consists of many competing interest groups. None of these groups inevitably gets their own way in the mass media, and views are continually being contested. Large and powerful interest groups are often challenged and criticised, and sometimes these challenges may be successful.

- Pluralists claim that access to the media is now easy for all to gain. It is in the interests of the media to cater to the needs of minority interest groups; they can after all be another source of profit for media organisations.

- Pluralists also argue that not all media owners try to control media content. In fact owners who attempt to exert day-to-day control of the content of the media (as did media tycoon Robert Maxwell) are the exception rather than the rule. Pluralists taking this approach can also point to the many cases where top newspaper editors become involved in disputes with owners over control of editorial content.

- Pluralists also argue that media owners and professionals cannot afford to ignore the views and interests of the public, since if the public dislike a newspaper or television/radio station, they will stop buying it or watching/listening to it and this will mean the end of business for that organisation.

- Finally pluralists argue that the concept of a ruling class ideology provides an unconvincing model of how people act (human agency). People are not stupid, they have consciousness and the ability to think for themselves, and they use the mass media in an active way. Mass audiences pick and choose what they listen to, read, and watch, and they are also capable of knowing when they are being lied to. Audiences should be seen as '**active audiences**'.

What criticisms can be made in response to the pluralist case?

Several criticisms can be made of the pluralist view.

1 Marxists would argue that there is not equal access to the media. Minority interest groups can easily publish a newsletter or run a website, but they will find it difficult to equal the sales revenues of large media corporations, which is important if they wish to maintain a publication or media outlet for a long period of time to gather and build support.

2 Media owners can try to control the content of the media if they choose. Owners are not always successful in doing this, but they still have more power to do this than most other groups in society.

3 Governments do attempt to manage the media. They are not always successful, but it seems unlikely that they always fail. The pressure to provide what the public wants can lead to a reduction rather than an increase in choice, as it may well become uneconomical to publicise minority views.

4 Finally, the mass media is still dominated by white, male, middle-class professionals, and this influences the content of the mass media.

Conclusion

Pluralists argue that the ownership and control of the mass media do not inevitably lead to bias. However, the pluralist approach is founded upon the highly contested view that all members of society, and all interest groups, have equal power to gain access to the media, and indeed to the truth.

For consideration:

1 How could people's freedom to choose and interpret media representations and images be constrained? How could this influence your assessment of the pluralist view?
2 Has the expansion in the number of television channels led to a significantly wider range of views, opinions and representations in the media?

66 99 Key Definition

Active audience theories argue that media effects are always limited because the audience have to be seen as having the ability to choose and interpret media representations and messages. This assumes that people's behaviour is not completely determined by structures – they have agency.

✓ Top Exam Hint

In evaluating and analysing the pluralist view, it's worth noting that you cannot reach conclusions simply by viewing one sort of evidence. Empirical evidence (this means evidence gained from research) is of course helpful, but its significance has to be interpreted, and this can only be done by using sociological theories. Remember in sociology, theory and method always go together.

● Synoptic Link

It is important to link your understanding and knowledge of theoretical debates about power, structure and agency to this issue.

5.6   Who owns the media?

Rupert Murdoch, though Australian-born and a US citizen, has a strong grip on the UK media sector as well as the American and Australian media.

What does this mean?

Media ownership is increasingly complex. Ownership of the mass media tends to be increasingly dominated by a small number of large corporations. For example, in the USA currently about ten corporations dominate the media, whilst in Britain four companies produce around 85 per cent of national and Sunday newspapers. New patterns of ownership mean that one individual very rarely owns these corporations, and this raises questions as to how such complex corporations can control media content.

Marxist views – ownership equals control

Traditional or classical Marxism argues that there is a direct relationship between the ownership of the media, and control of media content. Owners are, in other words, able to ensure that only views that they approve of are published in the media. The media is therefore seen to act in ways that reinforce capitalism and the interests of capitalists.

Neo-Marxists claim that this view no longer accurately reflects media ownership and control. Because there are very few examples of media corporations that are entirely run and owned by one person, neo-Marxist theorists argue that the influence of ownership will be more complex and there will be a more indirect form of control. Neo-Marxists argue that media owners may vary in the degree to which they control media products. Far more important, neo-Marxists argue, is the fact that the media reflects the assumptions and ideas of the dominant social groups. It is the worldview of this elite, which is predominantly white, male, middle-class and middle-aged, which is reinforced by the media. Media ownership is important then, even though ownership is less concentrated in the hands of a few individuals. This means that capitalist influence is even subtler and more powerful than the classical Marxist tradition assumes. Neo-marxists would also be highly critical of the idea that more competition leads to diversity in the media, arguing that instead it leads to conformity and the marginalisation of minority views.

Pluralist views– the public gets what the public wants

Pluralists argue that Marxist views are highly exaggerated and make a number of criticisms of the Marxist approach.

1   Pluralists point out that the public exercise choice in the media products they use. If the media does not provide what the public wants, then they will stop buying newspapers and television licences, satellite television, and so on. Thus ownership does not matter,

because the owners are not all powerful – they have to satisfy public demand.

2 Moreover, pluralists would argue that the power of the media is democratically controlled and accountable, since governments regulate the media and there are anti-monopoly laws in most countries that prevent one owner having too much power.

3 Pluralists can point to the government policy of deregulation, and argue that competition in a free market does indeed allow the public to choose which media providers they wish to use. Deregulation means that the government has decided that it is best to have a free market approach to the media. The government imposes a minimum of controls on the media and media ownership and encourages competition between media providers. This enables consumers to choose what they read, listen to and watch.

4 Pluralists would point to the many examples of journalists and editors who act against the wishes of media owners and who work hard to hold the 'powerful' (e.g. politicians, public officials and top business leaders) to account. If ownership really did mean control of media content, then surely this sort of high quality journalism would never get published at all?

5 Lastly, pluralists argue that Marxist approaches mistake the nature of the audience. Audiences are not passive and uniform; they are diverse and critically engage with media output from many different perspectives, and do not simply believe everything they read or hear.

Conclusion

It seems clear that media ownership is increasingly concentrated in the hands of a small number of large corporations. Pluralists are right to point out that new technology means that almost anyone can publicise a particular view or interest that they have. However, this does not mean that all views can gain an equal amount of attention. The crucial aspect of this issue is then the effects of restricted media ownership. All sides in this debate make useful points on this matter. Ultimately, though, the evidence has to be interpreted in terms of a theoretical perspective. One of the key differences between Marxists and pluralists is their view of power and it is this that leads them to reach very diverse views about the importance of new patterns of media ownership.

◆ **What, When and Why?**

Sociological and public debate on the ownership and control of the media reflects the concerns of a particular time. Issues of ownership have not always been so controversial, for example in the earlier part of the 20th century. In recent years though, the growth of cross-media and transnational ownership, and the domination of the media by figures such as Rupert Murdoch, has led to increased debate and concern on the issue.

✓ **Top Exam Hint**

In assessing the importance of ownership and its influence on editorial control, remember to use the theoretical perspectives to interpret and analyse empirical findings.

For consideration:

1 Has the expansion in the number of media outlets in recent years (digital and cable TV, the Internet, commercial radio) led to a broadening of ownership?
2 Do media owners take sufficient notice of viewers' opinions? What factors encourage owners to listen to public feedback?

5.7 Who decides what counts as news and how is it selected?

Princess Diana and Mother Teresa died within five days of each other in 1997, yet Princess Diana's death received vast amounts of media coverage compared to Mother Teresa's. What does this tell us about the selection of news?

What does this mean?

Many people would probably agree that what we read in the newspapers or see on the television is called 'the news' precisely because it is novel, unpredictable and exciting to us. It is, in short, new.

However, sociologists have argued that the process by which journalists create the news is a manufacturing process and its production processes are quite predictable.

Philip Schlesinger's (1978) study of news production showed how journalists use a 'news diary' to make their job easier by creating a daily routine. The 'news diary' consists of important national events, such as key political events (Budget Day for example), around which editors can start to plan coverage. This means that articles can be prepared months, weeks or days in advance of an event. Planning which 'stories' will be covered, and having some advance notice, is vital for journalists who usually have to work to very tight deadlines.

However, journalists do not just randomly pick out what seem to them to be interesting items. They are guided by 'news values' – shared norms and values about what is of importance and interest to the audience. Research by Galtung and Ruge (1981) shows that there are two key sets of factors involved in determining journalists' news values: bureaucratic and cultural.

Bureaucratic factors refer to the routines of journalism and the form that these impose on news items:

- News items must be immediate, and refer to current affairs, not to historical or dated issues or events.
- News has to be brief.
- News has to be simple.

News is also defined by cultural factors and has to be:

- Novel, exciting and different, e.g. disasters.
- It must focus on elite decision-makers, and on personalities rather than issues.
- It is ethnocentric – people are interested in news that they see as most relevant to their life. Ethnocentric means centred on one particular ethnic or cultural group.

Do the media set an agenda for society?

Sociologists would say that since journalists (influenced by news values) manufacture the 'news', the whole process of making the news is socially constructed. Most sociologists who have studied the mass media have drawn the conclusion that since this is true, it follows that media professionals have the power to present agendas (lists of issues) as to what key issues society should be concerning itself with at any particular time. This happens in several ways.

- Stuart Hall (1982) argues that the elite groups of decision-makers and public figures who are regularly featured in the media become the 'primary definers' of public affairs and debates.
- Studies by McQuail (1972), and McCombs and Shaw (1973), say that the media act as 'agenda setters'. What this means is that as media professionals select what is newsworthy, they are in a position to shape the way public debate is conducted, to influence what issues are seen as being most important and worthy of debate, and of what issues are seen as being unimportant.
- Herbert Gans (1974) suggests that key figures, such as editors, act as 'gatekeepers'. They are able to make decisions as to which news items are of most significance and thus which should gain access to media space.

This gives the media tremendous power to influence public debate, and this is why government advisers ('spin doctors') are so keen to control the media and get it on their side. It is also why various interest groups and pressure groups employ press officers to liaise with and attempt to influence the media.

The Glasgow University Media Group (GUMG) has become famous for their research in this area. They have shown not only how the media are selective in their choice of what issues deserve reporting, but also in the presentation of the news. In their study 'Bad News' (1976), the GUMG show how television news has routinely been biased in its portrayal of industrial disputes, through for example, asking biased questions and focusing on particular issues such as strikes and disputes in large companies (see section 8).

Conclusion

Sociological studies show that what we think of as a spontaneous and unbiased recording of 'news' is in fact socially constructed. Journalists' shared notions of 'news values' guide their activities. Moreover, their ability to **set agendas** and to control access to the media through '**gatekeeping**', means that the media can have a considerable influence on public debate.

For consideration:

1 Does the media set the agenda for public debate, and does it matter if it does?
2 Are media professionals still recruited from a narrow range of social groups?

66 99 Key Definition

The terms '**gatekeeper**' and '**agenda setting**' refer to the way in which senior editors are able to control access to the media, and thus determine which stories and information are broadcast or published. By selecting only certain information and news items, the media help to form an 'agenda' for debate. An agenda is a list of issues that will be discussed at a meeting.

✓ Top Exam Hint

If a question asks you to evaluate the role of the media in the selection and presentation of the news, it's a very good idea to use the theoretical views discussed in previous sections to help you do this (see sections 4, 5, 6).

● Synoptic Link

The ideas of 'news values' and 'agenda setting' are seen as an important influence in the social construction of crime and deviance (see section 16).

Is the media biased?

Is the media biased?

Key Definition

Bias – this means that a view is one-sided or distorted. A biased view does not give a true reflection of reality.

What does this mean?

'**Bias**' means prejudice or distortion. Many sociologists have argued that the media is often biased in its representation of social groups and in its presentation of social issues. For example, many news programmes have been seen as giving only one side of the story, or as neglecting some stories as being of no interest to the audience. One of the most famous groups of sociologists who have studied bias in the media is the Glasgow University Media Group (GUMG).

How do organisational factors cause bias?

Sociologists point out that the way the media is organised is itself a cause of bias. In terms of news for example, the media as we have seen, have to package and present news material within certain restraints, e.g. time, amount of space and news values. In addition, media editors and owners are in a powerful position to influence the coverage of the media through agenda setting, gatekeeping, and norm setting. However, these factors also apply to other branches of the media, whether it is light entertainment or highbrow documentary programmes. Media producers are in a position where they can, and in fact have to select the content that they believe their viewers, listeners or readers will want.

What other factors might cause bias?

The media is also influenced by political constraints that limit what can and cannot be printed or broadcast, and this can led to various biases. For example, the government operates what is known as the 'D notice' system, which enables it to prevent the disclosure of military and defence-related information. The media are also required to adhere to guidelines imposed by the Press Complaints Commission and the Independent Television Commission, although critics argue that these are lightweight regulatory bodies with relatively little power.

In addition to these factors, sociologists would also argue that the media can be biased by ideological and structural factors. In terms of ideological factors, sociologists would refer to the dominant ideas within a society, and argue that these can lead to systematic bias in what or how particular issues are reflected in a society. For example, the long tradition of the 'page three' topless woman in *The Sun* newspaper reflects the patriarchal values of British society. This example can also be seen as reflecting the structural factors that lead to bias – a key one in this case being the need for profit. Marxist-influenced sociologists would argue that the need to make a profit leads to bias in the media. This is because media editors and owners have to publish and present material that meets the demands of the audience. Moreover, the media also have to be sensitive to the needs of those businesses that buy advertising space. Articles that bring attention to, for example, the dangers of smoking, or the exploitative employment practices of a large multinational corporation, could clearly have a negative effect on a business. Businesses can therefore exert pressure upon the media, since the media depend not just on their audience, but also on advertisers.

The work of the GUMG in the 1970s found evidence of considerable bias in the coverage of industrial relations disputes. In the 1960s and 1970s relations between workers and employers in the UK were characterised by mistrust and conflict, and strikes were common. The political situation, with trade unions seen to be questioning the right of the government to govern, meant that strikes were very newsworthy. In this climate, claims of biased reporting became quite common (on both sides) and so it was an obvious area for sociologists to investigate.

Conclusion

In the light of the evidence considered here it seems indisputable that the media is biased. In theoretical terms, many sociological viewpoints would concur (see the frequently asked questions at the end of this chapter) with the idea that the media is inevitably biased. However, this does not necessarily mean that we have to be completely despairing of the media. Sociological research shows us why we need to view the media more cautiously, and indeed by showing us the techniques media professionals use, it teaches us how to be more critical. Also criticism from academics has forced media professionals to think more carefully about their editorial decisions.

For consideration:

1 What effects can bias in the media have and how important are these effects?
2 Is it possible for the media to be unbiased?

◆ What, When and Why?

The Glasgow University Media Group (GUMG) has been researching the media since the1970s. They found that coverage of industrial relations was routinely biased in various ways. Trade unionists were usually filmed protesting outside factories, and this made them look like mob leaders. Managers, on the other hand, were filmed in their offices, looking calm and professional.

✓ Top Exam Hint

In discussing and evaluating to what extent the media is biased you will show a greater understanding of the issue if you can relate it to other concepts and perspectives studied in the topic. Pluralist, Marxist and neo-Marxist perspectives on the media would be very different with regard to the extent of bias here and whether it should be considered a problem. These different views are the result of the different view of power that each perspective adopts.

Is the media sexist?

THE OTHER WAY TO YOUR MAN'S HEART IS DOWN THE M6 AND OFF AT JUNCTION 4

A recent advertisement for the 2002 Motor Show, which caused much debate. Does it support the view that the media is sexist?

✳ Key Ideas

- Gender
Remember that sex and gender are two distinct things. Gender, or sexual identity, refers to the way ideas about the sexes are socially constructed and learnt. The media is an important source of reinforcing or even creating certain gender roles and stereotypes.

- Masculinity
Sean Nixon argues that media images helped to create new views of masculinity in the 1980s. Nixon studied the way men's fashions were represented in men's magazines like *Loaded*, as well as looking at advertising. He argues that media representations did contribute to a changed cultural climate, where it was more acceptable for men to act in ways previously considered feminine, for example wearing an earring, and using a range of perfumes (aftershave, deodorants, and so on).

What does this mean?

Sexism is discrimination against individuals or groups on the basis of their sex.

Many sociologists have claimed that media representations or images discriminate against one sex or the other by portraying them in a narrow and **stereotypical** manner.

How are men and women portrayed in the media?

There is a great deal of research showing that media representations of men dominate the media and are more positive (but nevertheless still stereotypical) than those of women. Representations of women tend to reflect negative stereotypes.

- Since the 1970s, for instance, various studies (e.g. Dominick and Rauch (1972), Brelt and Cantor (1988), Cumberbatch (1990)) have shown that images of men are predominant in adverts, usually in more authoritative roles or in higher status occupations. The majority of voice-overs in adverts use male voices.

- Studies such as Marjorie Ferguson's *Forever Feminine* (1983) and Dee Meehan's *Ladies of the Evening* (1983) argue that media representations promote and reinforce powerful norms of femininity. Women in the media thus tend to be portrayed in roles submissive to men. They are, for example, sex objects, housewives and mothers; roles that are emotional and passive rather than physical and assertive.

- Feminist sociologists such as Gaye Tuchman (1978) have therefore concluded that women are symbolically annihilated (symbolically destroyed) and marginalised in media representations. Men have tended to be represented in the opposite way to that of women as detailed above, usually being portrayed as strong, independent, resourceful, and authoritative. Some male and female characters may fail to meet the norms, but the obvious implication in such media representations is that these characters are not 'proper' men or women.

Do media representations of gender matter?

To some extent we probably all dislike being stereotyped, but sociologists have been interested in whether negative media representations can have harmful effects on us. For example, feminists such as Andrea Dworkin (1981) have argued that the negative portrayal of women may reinforce male violence and aggression. Susie Orbach, counsellor and author of *Fat is a Feminist Issue* (1986), has argued that the dominant images of 'supermodels' play an important part in causing some young women to develop eating disorders (anorexia and bulimia). This is not just something which affects women; increasingly we may see images of the male body as an object of desire in the media, as research into men's magazines and fashion by Sean Nixon (1996), and Tim Edwards (1997) has shown.

However, not all sociologists would agree that media representations are necessarily harmful. Sociologists who emphasise the ability of people to construct their own identity may suggest that the audience can actively use media representations – positive or negative – to help them do this. In other words, people may reject some representations, and react against them, and accept other representations and perhaps try to emulate them. The sociologist Sherry Turkle (1996) takes this approach in her study of women and computers. The women Turkle studied were able to use the fact that the world of computers appeared unfeminine and closed off to them, to construct a version of femininity that made a virtue of the fact that women were not assumed to be conversant with computer technology. In this version of femininity, women asserted their superiority to the technology-dominated world of computing.

Conclusion

In assessing how important media representations of gender are, we have to take into account sociological ideas about power. Many models of media effects, including some of the ideas discussed here, assume that the audience is a passive consumer of media representations. This may not necessarily be the case. We also need to remember that masculinity and femininity are not fixed categories. They change over time and so do media representations of them.

For consideration:

1 How can women use media representations as a source of identity and meaning?
2 Are men now being represented as objects of sexual desire in the media? If so, is this a good thing? What does it tell us about how masculine identities are changing in contemporary societies?

✓ Top Exam Hint

If you have to evaluate the relationship between media representations and gender, remember to link the material in this section with different theories of the media (sections 4, 5, 20, 22) and with the material on how audiences respond to the media (section 14).

● Synoptic Link

Remember that gender is an aspect of stratification, so you can draw on material in this section in answering synoptic questions on stratification in the A2 Sociology exam. This section has examined different views about how media representations of gender can influence gender identities and thus how these might reinforce one aspect of social stratification.

5.10 Is the media racist?

What does this mean?

When sociologists make the claim that the media is racist they are making a claim about the way that the media represents ethnic minority groups. Sociologists might also want to claim that the media operates racist employment procedures – just as many other employers may do. But sociologists' main focus of attention has been on the question of whether media representations are racist. However, we are still left with the issue of what is meant by 'racist' media representations. The term '**racism**' is often used rather loosely in everyday language, and many people associate it with deliberate prejudice and discrimination. Sociologists use the term rather differently to refer to systematic stereotyping and bias in the portrayal and representation of members of ethnic minority groups – this is a form of **institutional racism**. Racism in the media may not necessarily be intended to cause offence, but it may nevertheless exist.

How are ethnic minorities represented in the media?

A number of sociological studies over a long period of time indicate that media representations do reflect a biased and stereotyped image of members of ethnic minorities. In the 1970s, Stuart Hall (1978) argued that media representations helped to construct the 'myth of black criminality'; while Hartmann and Husband (1974) found that the media played a key role in reinforcing racist views amongst the media audience.

More recently, studies by Alvarado (1987) and by Van Dijk (1991) have demonstrated that media representations of ethnic minorities are overwhelmingly presented in terms of various negative stereotypes. Van Dijk, for example, conducted an extensive content analysis of newspapers and found that ethnic minorities were presented in terms of a severely limited number of negative stereotypes. Thus, black people were portrayed as criminals, as abnormal or alien, as presenting a threat to 'normal society' (e.g. being thought to be illegal immigrants or terrorists), as dependants (illegal immigrants, victims of famine or natural disasters, incapable of being independent) in need of help or aid, and lastly were often marginalised through being portrayed as unimportant in comparison to issues affecting the white majority.

Are media representations changing?

These findings may not reflect our own experience of the media. This may be because of our own social position or identity (see section 14), but it may also be because media representations have changed since the 1970s and are continuing to change. For example, you may have seen what are often considered to be more positive stereotypes, such as movie directors like Spike Lee, or actors like Halle Berry and Denzel Washington winning an Oscar. There are also the examples of television programmes like *Goodness Gracious Me*, *The Kumars at Number 42* or *Smart Guy*, and the more assertive black identity presented by rap artists, to support the idea that representations of race are changing. However, Jhally and Lewis (1992) point out that television programmes such as *The Cosby Show* (a popular black sitcom in the late 1980s/early 1990s featuring a successful middle-class black man) are highly unrepresentative of the situation of the black population in the USA, and it might be argued that stereotyping blacks as athletes and musicians still traps them within a limited framework of stereotypes.

Black people are still less likely to be shown in other successful roles, e.g. medicine, law or business. One way of explaining these complex media representations comes from Manuel Castells (1997). Castells argues that ethnicity, as well as being a source of oppression, can also be a source of identity and meaning. Thus some black Americans have been able to gain access to the mass media and create new ethnic identities and challenge old identities. However, this does not mean that oppression and discrimination do not exist. Instead Castells argues that we are living in a much more complex situation, since ethnic groups have fragmented on the basis of class and other divisions.

In a landmark win for black actors, Halle Berry and Denzel Washington take home Oscars for best actress and best actor at the 2002 Academy Awards. But why is this still considered a landmark?

Conclusion

The implication of recent research by sociologists like Manuel Castells implies that in evaluating how media representations portray ethnic groups, we have to acknowledge the different social positions (including class, gender and religious positions) that can divide what may seem to be a single ethnic group. Evaluating this argument means thinking carefully about the nature of social stratification. As stratification systems in contemporary societies and attitudes to race and ethnicity are changing, so too are the ways in which the media represent race.

For consideration:

1 Do media representations cause or merely reflect racism?
2 How important are media representations?

✓ **Top Exam Hint**

If you are evaluating media representations of race, remember that a lot of the studies mentioned here are based on content analysis. This means that they will, of course, reflect the weaknesses of that method. A common criticism of content analysis is that the categories used in analysis lack validity and reliability. The findings of such studies are therefore open to question.

● **Synoptic Link**

Remember that race and ethnicity are aspects of stratification, so information in this section can be used in synoptic questions about stratification in the A2 exam. Issues about race are also relevant to perceptions of crime and deviance (see sections 16 and 18).

5.11 Is the media ageist?

What does this mean?

Many people believe that characteristics such as race, gender and age are natural categories. Sociologists, however, are keen to point out that all of these categories are socially constructed. In the case of age, sociologists are interested in examining how age is represented in the media because this can tell us something about the dominant ideas about age in our culture. Studying the media and age also allows us to see how these representations are created, how audiences respond to them, and the social effects that they have.

How is age represented in the media?

Some studies, such as that by Signorelli (1989), have found that there is an under-representation of the very old and the very young in television programmes, but a content analysis by Lambert (1984) found that over a period of two weeks 50 per cent of programmes depicted people over the age of sixty. Significantly though, the people involved tended to be predominantly male and were often 'experts' or in positions of authority, such as that of a news presenter. A more recent content analysis study by Simon Biggs (1993) found that middle-aged and older characters dominated UK soap operas, and in situation comedies the portrayal of older characters was largely negative. A more sophisticated case study of one magazine (*Retirement Choice*) by Featherstone and Hepworth (1995) found that positive images of older people could be found, but these images emphasised how youthful older people could be. In summary then, representations of old age do tend to portray it as a social problem, and the evidence here provides some justification for describing the media as '**ageist**'. However, representations of age can reflect the seniority and high status conferred by the wider society to men, as opposed to women.

At the other end of the spectrum, youth too, tends to be represented as a social problem, in need of firm control, as sociologist Stan Cohen's ground-breaking research indicated (see section 18). However, there are alternative representations available within contemporary culture. As James and Prout (1990) argue, the dominant images of the young in our culture portray them as dependent innocents in need of the protection of caring adults. The media are therefore quick to spot the newsworthiness of stories about the destruction of childhood innocence (e.g. by cases of child abuse, abduction, and so on). Above all though, these representations portray age and the ageing process as something natural and unchangeable, not as a social construction.

How do audiences interpret representations of age?

Sociological views about how audiences interpret the various representations of age in the media reflect the theoretical models discussed later on in this chapter (see section 14). Many contemporary sociologists take the view that audiences do not automatically agree with the way a social group is represented by the media, and social forces such as class, race and gender, as well as the culture of a particular society, will structure the way in which audiences respond.

Conclusion

Sociologists disagree in their views as to the effects of these media representations of age. Those taking a more structural view, such as Dick Hebdige (1979) for example, would argue that the media reinforces the idea that age differences are natural biological categories, and that they have the effect of justifying (or legitimising) the way our society deals with the young and the old, and the ageing process itself. Those taking a Marxist perspective will see this in the context of the needs of capitalism for a trained, obedient, and efficient workforce. Others, influenced by action theories, or more recently postmodernism, would argue that people can use media representations more creatively, accepting or rejecting particular elements to create their own identity. However, these views can be criticised for exaggerating the amount of freedom people have, and neglecting the influence of factors such as class, race and gender in terms of economic and cultural differences.

For consideration:

1 What factors could limit (or structure) the way audiences respond to media representations of age and how could they do this?

2 Would media representations of age be altered if the media employed more people over the age of sixty, or if children (under sixteen) had a greater influence on programming decisions?

✓ Top Exam Hint

It's worth remembering here our previous points about the problems with content analysis. How are categories operationalised and measured (e.g. what counts as 'very old' or 'very young')?

● Synoptic Link

The issue of how audiences interpret representations of age and the effects of these representations provides a good demonstration of the structure/action debate in sociology.

⚖ Thinking like a Sociologist

Three evaluations to use in the exam are:

1 Remember, age is not the only aspect of stratification.

2 If a media representation is portraying a particular stereotype of age, it will also be important to consider how that representation is related to other aspects of stratification, such as class, race or gender.

3 Age is not such a stigma for men, and studies have shown that there are a greater proportion of older men, in comparison to older women, represented in the media.

5.12 How is disability represented in the media?

✳ Key Idea

Disability

The idea of 'disability' may seem natural, but is in fact socially constructed. Tom Shakespeare (1994) takes the view that 'disability' is simply one difference that society treats as being a significant aspect of a group or category of people. Shakespeare also argues that the term disability has such negative connotations that we should instead refer to 'impairment'. All of us have bodies that are 'impaired' – or not perfect – in some way, or will become so eventually.

🔔 Thinking like a Sociologist

Three evaluations to use in the exam are:

1 Sociologists need to be sensitive to history, and not assume that all the phenomena they observe are new.
2 Michael Oliver (1990), a sociologist who has researched disability, reminds us that media representations of disability go back to Long John Silver and Captain Hook (evil), Sir Clifford in *Lady Chatterley's Lover* (pathetic), and Douglas Bader the one-legged fighter pilot in the Battle of Britain, as depicted in the film, *Reach for the Sky* (heroic).
3 The protests of those who are impaired and others is support for the idea that people do not respond passively to media representations.

What does this mean?

Sociologists are interested in the way disability is represented by the mass media for the same reasons that they are also interested in the representation of other social differences, such as class, race, gender and age. In examining these differences, sociologists will want to answer several key questions. First, are the disabled involved in media production and what images of disability are created? Second, how frequently is disability portrayed in the media and in what ways? Lastly, sociologists want to know how audiences interpret these representations and what effects they have.

How is disability represented in the media?

The first question above is hard to answer with precision, but it would seem that most media professionals are 'able-bodied'. It is much easier to discover what images of disability are created. Research conducted by sociologists indicates that the media do present stereotypical and stigmatised representations of disabled people. Cumberbatch and Negrine's research (1992) found that the disabled were predominantly seen as figures we should pity. Other research (Longmore 1987), found that the disabled were seen as dependent, maladjusted or even evil. There could, however, be interesting variations on this theme, for example when the disabled were turned into heroic figures coping courageously with their fate. However, it is also important to note that the disabled do not appear in the media very often. The 1999 Broadcasting Standards Commission survey found that the disabled only appeared in 7 per cent of programmes in their sample. It seems that the disabled are a social group the media would prefer not to publicise; there is a denial of their existence.

How do audiences interpret these representations?

Cumberbatch and Negrine (1992) found that how audiences respond to these representations depends upon their own experience of disability. Those who had some experience of disability were more likely to reject stereotypical or stigmatising representations of disability. This reminds us of some general points about media effects and audience interpretation. Audiences are reflexive, and they can 'read' media messages in alternative ways.

Conclusion

The effects of media representations always have to be seen in the social context in which they are constructed and interpreted. As Cumberbatch and Negrine's study indicates, audiences can reject stereotypical representations of disability. Equally though, those who have no experience of disability (either individually or within their family or friendship groups) may well be confirmed in their view that disability is to be defined as a social problem. Part of the wider social context in which we have to examine disability, then, is in terms of a culture that portrays disability in a negative light.

Sociologist Tom Shakespeare has researched and written a great deal on the sociology of disability, and he argues that contemporary culture is one where the role for disabled people is as what he calls 'dustbins for **disavowal**'. What he means by this is simply that society tries to ignore the fact that disability occurs and, very importantly, tries to avoid the fear and anxiety that disability not surprisingly gives rise to. The sort of approach that Shakespeare takes would be very similar to the cultural effects approach we examine later (see section 14). However, we have to evaluate that model of media effects with care, and as we have noted here, audiences are varied and can read media representations in a variety of ways. The effect of media representations of disability can therefore also be varied. Perhaps most important is the finding that disability is largely disavowed by the media.

Dr Tom Shakespeare is Director of Outreach at the Policy, Ethics and Life Sciences Research Institute, Newcastle-upon-Tyne

☞ Who is this Person?

Tom Shakespeare is a sociologist involved in studying disability, health and genetics. He is himself achondroplasic (he is what is commonly called a 'dwarf'). Clearly this may help us understand his interests in disability and encourage us to reflect upon whether sociologists really can be entirely value-free in their choice of research topics.

❝❞ Key Definition

Disavowal – this means that we deny knowledge or responsibility for or about something. In the case of disability, Shakespeare is arguing that society refuses to accept its reality, and that this works as a way of diffusing the anxiety which disability arouses, since we could all become victims of it, either ourselves (e.g. through an accident) or for example, through our own children or other relatives.

For consideration:

1 Do you think that media representations of the disabled would become more positive if greater numbers of disabled people worked in the media?
2 In what ways does the media contribute to the social construction of disability?

5.13 How does the media represent class?

Did the BBC show bias in its coverage of the 1970s miners' strike?

What does this mean?

Many sociologists interested in the media have been influenced by Marxist approaches to the media. Sociologists from this tradition, such as Stuart Hall or the Glasgow University Media Group (GUMG) for example, have been very interested in examining how the media portrays classes and class relations, and how it transmits ideologies that legitimise class inequality. If it does all these things, then the media is an important means of social control in capitalist societies.

What evidence is there for biased and stereotyped representations of class?

The work of the GUMG suggests that the media present biased and stereotypical representations of class. The GUMG (1976) has shown how the news coverage of industrial relations by the BBC in the 1970s was biased against workers and strikers, and tended to portray the arguments of management in a more favourable light. Workers were all too easily portrayed as rowdy and ill-informed troublemakers. Representations such as these could be conveyed by interviewing managers in neat and tidy offices, whilst workers were filmed huddling around a fire outside the factory gates, trying to keep warm and preventing lorries entering or leaving.

Studies by Glennon and Butsch (1982) and Jhally and Lewis (1992) also support the view that television entertainment programmes tend to feature more middle-class than working-class figures, and that middle-class figures are more likely to be represented positively than working-class characters. Glennon and Butsch, for example, found that in the US only 4 per cent out of 218 family sit-coms were set in a family where a blue-collar (manual) worker was the head of household, whereas such families actually constituted about 36 per cent of the US population at that time. In the US study by Jhally and Lewis it was found that the percentage of working-class characters in television programmes actually fell between 1971 and 1989 (from 4 per cent to 1 per cent). Whether research on British programmes would today yield the same results is unclear. Certainly though, it could be argued that working-class characters in British soap-operas and comedies are represented in a stereotyped way – as either honest but poor or as lovable rogues, but further research is needed to ascertain the empirical accuracy of this hypothesis.

What effects does the representation of class have?

Sociologists influenced by Marxism, such as Stuart Hall and Raymond Williams, would claim that the media has helped to legitimise (justify) class inequalities and has reinforced strong class identities. Positive representations of the middle and upper classes have made them seem to be society's natural leaders, whilst negative representations of the working class portray them as naturally inferior. Hall and Williams would see the media as a means of social control. Creating strong class identities leads to a strong 'them and us' feeling and so perpetuates a class hierarchy. Hall has studied the history of the BBC and has argued that it enabled the ruling classes to promote their culture as the dominant culture, trying to promote a shared national culture, and aiming to bring the masses what it considered to be the best in culture in order to 'educate, entertain, and inform'. It even tried to establish the RP (Received Pronunciation) accent as the preferred way of speaking.

Critics of the Marxist approach (pluralists and postmodernists) argue that such views exaggerate the force of social structures and underestimate the freedom people have (agency). Stuart Hall, though, is more influenced by neo-Marxist or Gramscian views (see section 4), and would claim that ruling class cultural domination is never total or complete. In fact it is strengthened by challenges to its authority, since these help to make it appear more negotiated and open than it really is, thus justifying it as a tolerant and liberal regime. This view of media effects can be challenged though, and other sociologists (see section 14) would argue that people (and audiences) are not passive and are much more able to interpret and reject media representations than neo-Marxists assume.

Conclusion

Whilst there have been some very clear examples of biased media representations of class, many sociologists would now recognise that this is a very complex issue.

David Morley's research (1980) (see section 14) offers a particularly useful way of drawing some conclusions on this matter. Morley's study, *The Nationwide Audience*, study makes several important points that are relevant here. First, Morley suggests that the audience negotiates media representations. This means that how audiences interpret or respond to a media representation will depend on their own position in the social structure. Second, Morley notes that social structure does not just mean class, but also race, gender, age and culture. Moreover, these different factors can be mixed in quite complex ways. This means that media representations of class do matter and do have effects, but that they are worked out in many different and complex ways, depending upon the other structural factors influencing the various social groups that go to make up an 'audience'.

For consideration:

1 Does the media continue to transmit representations of social differences in terms of social class or are postmodernists right to say that identity is now constructed around consumption categories?

2 Do you think that different social classes are more likely to watch particular TV channels? Do the different TV channels appear to target particular social classes and if so, how do they do this?

✓ **Top Exam Hint**

Media representations of class can be important sources of identity but some sociologists argue that people do not accept them unquestioningly. Remember that class is only one element of stratification. We don't all consider class to be the most significant aspect of our identity. For some people other elements, such as race or gender, may be considered more important. This matters, because it means that media representations of class may not be as important as some sociologists imply.

● **Synoptic Link**

If you go on to study Social inequality for A2 Sociology, remember that both topics are interrelated and you will need to show you understand this in synoptic questions. This section has shown that some sociologists argue that media representations can play an important role in forming class identities.

✎ **Coursework Suggestion**

Given that many sociologists argue that class has fragmented and the lack of British-based research in the account here, it would be very topical to conduct a content analysis of class identities in the mass media. Are there still strong class stereotypes in the British media?

5.14 How do audiences respond to the mass media?

What does this mean?

A famous radio broadcast of H.G Wells' story, *The War of the Worlds*, in the 1930s led hundreds of American listeners to be panicked into believing that aliens from outer space were invading the earth. Throughout the 20th century, political leaders like Adolf Hitler have been able to use the mass media as a powerful means of propaganda. In more recent times, public debate has focused on the possibility that violence and other criminal behaviour is simply learnt and copied from the media. Are we really so easily led?

☞ Who are these People?

The Frankfurt School of sociologists included a number of academics, including Theodore Adorno, Max Horkheimer, and Herbert Marcuse. These academics were all German Jews and they left Germany in the 1930s, fleeing to the USA to escape persecution by the Nazis. All of the Frankfurt School were interested in the way in which mass societies as different as Nazi Germany, the communist Soviet Union and capitalist America, used the mass media as a way, in their view, of indoctrinating a population.

What have sociologists said about audience response?

There have been four main models or approaches that sociologists have proposed to explain how audiences are affected by the mass media. The first approach to be developed suggested that the mass media could have a direct and dramatic influence on human behaviour, acting much like an injection of a lethal drug. This led to the approach being termed the '*hypodermic model*'. This model assumes that the audience is helpless to resist the seductive power of the mass media. This approach was used by psychologist Albert Bandura (see section 15). It was mainly developed though by the so-called 'Frankfurt School' of sociologists.

A slightly more sophisticated approach argued that the influence of the media was not so direct. The '*two-step flow*' theory, developed by Lazarsfeld (1944) in the 1940s, claimed that individuals were influenced by a significant figure such as a teacher, a parent, or employer. It was suggested that the media first influenced opinion at these levels, before being fed down the chain as it were, to street level. Later this theory was challenged by the '*uses and gratifications*' model, developed by various sociologists, including Trenaman and McQuail (1961) and Rosegren and Windahl (1972), which suggested that people were in fact much more active in their use of the media. Rather than just believing each and every media message they were fed, people actively used the media for their own purposes. The media could not, therefore, control them as if they were mindless puppets. More recently several theories, which can be collectively called '*cultural effects theory*', suggested that media effects were a background influence – some likened the effect to a dripping tap – and that constant exposure to the media gradually came to have a pervasive influence on behaviour.

How can we evaluate these different approaches?

To evaluate these theories we can first of all examine the theoretical assumptions that they involve, and then assess what empirical evidence is available or would be needed to confirm them.

- Most of the above theories assume that the audience is passive, and this is a common criticism. The hypodermic model also assumes that the audience is homogeneous and reacts in the same way to media messages. This seems unlikely since we know that 'the audience' is highly differentiated (e.g. by class, race, gender, age, religion, nationality, and so on). Surely the diversity of social characteristics means that a range of different reactions is more probable?
- The two-step flow theory does not assume that all of the audience is passive, but it is unclear why only some individuals have the ability to influence others – can't individuals think for themselves? Additionally, it is not at all clear why there should be only two steps to influence – why not three or four, or more? There seems no clear reason why the media cannot exert influence through numerous individuals or social positions.
- In contrast, the pluralist-influenced uses and gratifications model suggests that media audiences are more active than the other models imply, and are able to selectively choose what to watch. However, it neglects differences amongst the audience and the view that media organisations determine what choices viewers have.
- Morley's influential research *The Nationwide Audience* (1980), reflecting an approach very similar to the 'cultural effects theory', found that the way an audience responded to media messages depended on social position, e.g. class, race or gender (see section 13). The benefit of this model was that media effects are seen as only being comprehensible by looking at the social situation of the audience. However, it may be that the cultural effects model exaggerates the audience's power and neglects the important limitations to audience choice imposed by limited ownership and control.

Conclusion

In terms of empirical data, a key issue is whether studies based on the models discussed can demonstrate that any effects or changes in behaviour are due to the media and not some other cause, for example, socialisation or the social background of an individual. Examples in other sections will examine this issue in detail. For the moment we only need to make a general methodological point that perhaps sociological research cannot control the many variables influencing human behaviour sufficiently to offer conclusive evidence on this matter.

✓ Top Exam Hint

When evaluating these models it's a good idea to apply key sociological concepts like power. The hypodermic and cultural effects models reflect broadly Marxist views, whilst the others reflect a pluralist approach. You can therefore apply the criticisms made of each view (see sections 4 and 5). It's also worth pointing out that the question of whether the audience is active or passive echoes the theoretical debates about structure and action and the problems of free will and determinism (the opposite of free will – all our actions are caused by social structures).

● Synoptic Link

This topic has lots of important links to other topics in sociology. There are important links to theory and method, about whether we should see the audience as passive or active, and how we can study media effects and distinguish them from the effects of socialisation. It also links to crime and deviance, politics and stratification, to name just a few.

✍ Coursework Suggestion

If your coursework uses or proposes the use of content analysis, it's a good idea to point out that a weakness of this method is that it tends to assume that audiences are passive and will be influenced by media content. This section indicates that there are many views about how audiences respond to media representations.

For consideration:

1 Is there one 'audience' for the mass media?
2 Are media messages intended to influence the behaviour of the audience?

5.15 Can the media cause violence?

In 1993, 10 year-olds Robert Thompson and Jon Venables were caught on CCTV camera and convicted of the abduction and murder of 2 year-old James Bulger. Judge Mr Justice Morland stated that he suspected exposure to violent films to be an explanation for their actions. But, can the effects of violent images on young children be conclusive?

☞ Who is this Person?

William Belson is an American media researcher. He was funded by the American media organisation CBS to conduct his research on violence and television. This raises questions about the relationship between researchers, funders, and the outcome of research. Some would suggest that there may be serious conflicts of interest, and such research may reach conclusions that support the prejudices of the funder.

What does this mean?

It is probably a common assumption that the saturation of our lives with images of violence must invariably de-sensitize us to violence, and may therefore lead some of us to be more likely to copy what we see in the media. The frequency of moral panics about violence (see section 18) seems to support this view. Also the hypodermic model we examined in section 14 suggested that the media could have direct effects on social behaviour. Sociologists have therefore wanted to find out whether the media really can cause violent behaviour. If the media can be found to be an important cause of violent behaviour, the implications for social policies regulating the media would be clear. We could simply ban the portrayal of violence and expect to see a rapid decline in violent behaviour.

What research has been conducted and what have been the findings?

As indicated, there has been a huge amount of research on this issue from psychologists and sociologists. One of the problems with the research though is that it is not conclusive – different researchers reach differing conclusions and the findings are contested. Three key studies usefully summarise this body of research.

The psychologist Albert Bandura carried out laboratory experiments in the early 1960s, and claimed that exposure to aggression and violence in the media would indeed lead to violent behaviour. Bandura explained these findings in terms of modelling and what he called 'social learning theory'. Bandura claimed that our behaviour is learned in an imitative sort of way, as we learn to model our behaviour on that of others. The media, as a key influence in young children's environment, was also liable to act as an influence, as young children could imitate things they saw in the media.

Another influential piece of research was that conducted in the 1970s by William Belson (1978). He carried out detailed interviews with a large sample of young boys and claimed that his results indicated that exposure to high levels of violence on television led to a higher level of involvement in violent behaviour.

In contrast to these pieces of research, however, the findings of the 1994 PSI (Hagell and Newburn, Policy Studies Institute) research into the influence of media violence was far more ambiguous. This research investigated two sample groups; one consisting of 78 juvenile offenders who were interviewed; the other consisting of the views of 538 children (non-offenders), gathered using a questionnaire. The research found no significant differences in terms of the amount of television watched, and both groups had very similar favourite programmes and videos/films. This research concluded that as young offenders appeared to be watching no more violence than other children, it seemed extremely unlikely that there is a 'direct **causal connection**' between watching violence and behaving violently.

How can we evaluate this research?

Given these contradictory conclusions, we have to evaluate the findings very carefully. Why do some studies show clear evidence of media effects, while others are more ambiguous? To answer this question it is vital to look at how the research was done.

Bandura's research can be criticised for its artificiality. Sociologists often avoid the use of laboratory experiments because they do not allow the observation of participants in a natural setting. This can mean that participants alter their behaviour because they are being watched, a phenomenon very similar to interviewer effect. This means that the research may lack validity.

Belson's research has been criticised because of the way in which he operationalised violence in the media. Belson examined the viewing habits of boys and then rated the programmes for their relative violence. However, Belson used adults to judge which programmes were violent and to what extent, and they may have had very different views from those of the young boys. Belson also used self-reporting to find out how much violent behaviour the boys exhibited, and he then categorised this himself. At each of these steps, validity may have been affected and so we cannot have confidence in Belson's findings and conclusions.

Conclusion

Both of the studies examined above have been based on the hypodermic theory of media effects. However, the criticisms detailed, in conjunction with the findings of the PSI survey, seem to indicate that there are good methodological reasons for doubting that the mass media can have such direct effects.

For consideration:

1 Would levels of violence fall if the media showed less violent behaviour?
2 Would violence decline if the media mounted a major advertising campaign discouraging violence?

66 99 Key Definition

Causal connections. A causal connection or relationship exists when one factor can clearly be seen to have caused another.

✓ Top Exam Hint

Make sure you use methodological concepts when evaluating complex debates such as the one discussed here. You need to use terms like 'indicator', 'operationalisation', 'representative' and 'validity'. Show that you understand them and show why they are relevant to the question.

Thinking like a Sociologist

Three evaluations to use in the exam are:

1 It is important for sociologists to interpret statistical data with great care.
2 In the case of Belson's study, many sociologists would point out that 'correlation does not equal causation'. This means that just because there are high levels of violence in the media, correlating with a high level of violence in society, we cannot assume that one factor has caused the other.
3 We need to remember that there may be other factors at work.

5.16 How does the media represent crime?

What does this mean?

Several sociological studies indicate that the media does not in fact present a true picture of crime. Research by Philip Schlesinger and Howard Tumber (1993), for example, suggested that the BBC programme 'Crimewatch UK' did indeed tend to focus on atypical and violent crime (although the BBC dispute this claim). Research by Williams and Dickinson (1993) found that about 12 per cent of current affairs reporting focused on crime, and that over 60 per cent of the space taken by crime reporting was concerned with cases involving violence. This finding has to be put into context – such crimes constituted only 5 per cent of all crimes recorded by the police at the time of their research. Other crimes appear to be relatively neglected by the media, such as domestic violence, pollution, corporate crime or breaches of health and safety rules in the workplace. All of these can involve injury or death and could be considered just as serious as violent crime.

Why does the media seem to be so obsessed by crime?

Steve Chibnall is one sociologist who has argued that the media are indeed obsessed by certain types of crime. In his study *Law and Order News* (1977) he suggests that the reasons for this are related to news values and the 'newsworthiness' of certain types of events. The media are concerned to get as many readers (or viewers/listeners) as possible, since this means that they gain more income. This in turn means that the media has to provide stories or news that will interest or excite their audience; the news media are therefore always seeking something out of the ordinary or dramatic.

Chibnall claims that newsworthiness involves about five key factors. A good news story must be highly visible and spectacular; it must have sexual or political implications; it must lend itself to graphic presentation (e.g. exciting, dramatic, pictures); it must involve individual pathology (an unusual, abnormal or sick individual); and it must involve some element of deterrence and repression. The last point means that good news stories allow society and journalists to blame and repress those who have broken social rules, and that these stories thus help to serve as reminders to deter others from doing the same. The more a particular event reflects these factors, the more newsworthy it is. Certain types of crime thus become a key source of good stories for the mass media, and this explains the media fascination with a particular type of crime reporting. It is also true that certain types of victim become more newsworthy than others, for example, attractive young women and frail elderly women.

What are the social consequences of the media's representation of crime?

Stuart Hall (1982) has argued that the media gets a lot of information about crime from the '**primary definers**' of crime. The media therefore reinforces dominant views about crime and contributes to the social construction of crime and an agenda-setting process. As Steve Chibnall (1977) points out, the media is always selecting and presenting 'news' about crime in the light of various dominant views, and these will usually reflect the priorities of the institutions responsible for law and order. We cannot treat news reports on crime as simple representations of fact; they are always selected and perceived as more newsworthy than another story. Sociologists are interested in how and why these decisions are made. Sociologists also argue that the media reporting of crime can in fact 'amplify' or increase the amount of crime being committed. The media may also create 'moral panics', which simply mean a high degree of social unrest about crimes. These issues are discussed in more detail in section 18.

Conclusion

The way that the media represents crime can have far-reaching consequences, influencing both public opinion and social policy. The fear of crime, for example, may be influenced by the nature of the media's crime reporting. Powerful social groups and politicians will shape their views as to what types of crime need urgent action at least partly on the basis of what they learn from the media. Of course, all this begs the question of whether the users of the media actually believe what the media tells them. We also need to remember that institutions and groups can be reflexive, and can use the media for their own purposes, as the use of the media by the police has recently shown.

For consideration:

1 How can the 'primary definers' of crime use the media to promote their own institutional interests?
2 What sort of person is most commonly represented by the media as criminal and how can this be explained?

---

66 99 Key Definition

Primary definers – this refers to the idea that some institutions have the most influence in defining crime. Hall (1982) sees this power as lying with the criminal justice system – essentially the police, the courts, and the Home Office (the government department which deals with law and order issues).

✳ Key Idea

Reflexive/reflexivity

This term is used by Anthony Giddens (1990) to refer to people's capacity for reflection and action. The idea suggests that far from acting passively, human beings have lots of knowledge about how society works, and they use this knowledge in their everyday lives. In this context, the idea implies that people are sometimes able to use the media for their own purposes. Giddens refers to the idea of 'plastic identities'. By this he just means that our identities are mouldable, and the media is a resource we can use to give us ideas about the specific identity we want to create, by copying other people, fashions or media personalities. This links up to the idea of the 'uses and gratifications' model of media effects (see section 14).

✓ Top Exam Hint

You can use Marxism and pluralism to evaluate the idea that media representations of crime are biased against certain social groups and do not give a valid picture of the nature of crime.

● Synoptic Link

Remember that this aspect of the media is highly relevant to crime and deviance at A2. You will be asked to demonstrate your understanding of the way this topic is related to broader issues in crime and deviance. In this section we have focused particularly on how our perceptions of crime and criminals may be highly influenced by media representations.

5.17 How does the media influence politics?

What does this mean?

Sociologists are interested in the ways in which politicians can use the media to **legitimise** their activities, to influence public opinion, and to influence the voting process. All of these issues raise important questions about democratic politics and decision-making. Sociologists want to know whether politics in contemporary societies really are as democratic as is often claimed.

Does the media influence voting behaviour?

Early studies of the media, such as the work of Lazarsfeld (1944), were directed towards the question of how the media could influence voting behaviour. Contemporary sociologists, though, are now generally critical of models such as the two-step flow model or the hypodermic model, and see the media as having a more complex influence on politics. In recent years in the UK, voting has been far more volatile, with voters switching allegiance more readily than in the past.

Recent studies in the UK (Curtice and Semetko 1994, Ivor Crewe 1992) have suggested that voters are not easily swayed by media opinion. Crewe's research indeed suggests that voters use information from the media to make their judgements, but they can be critical. Particularly interesting was that in a time of increased volatility, voters would use media information to help inform tactical voting. This seems to be evidence favouring a theory of media effects that acknowledges people's capacity to think and act reflexively.

The media may not determine voting behaviour in a direct way, but one contemporary sociologist thinks that the influence of the media is now greater than ever.

How else does the media influence politics?

Manuel Castells (1997) argues that the influence of the media on contemporary politics is considerable, and he identifies a number of changes leading to the current situation of what he calls 'informational politics'.

Castells argues that electronic media (e.g. television, the Internet) have now become the key source of information in modern society. This means that politicians have to use the media to get the attention of

Manuel Castells, Professor of Sociology at the University of California, Berkeley

☞ Who is this Person?

Manuel Castells is a Spanish sociologist, and he is currently Professor of Sociology at the University of California. He was an outspoken critic of the Spanish dictator Franco (1939–1975), and had to leave Spain to continue his education. Castells started his academic career as a Marxist, and though he has tried to apply Marxist concepts to contemporary society, he has modified his views. His current work focuses on the importance of technological changes in the media, and the way these are creating what he calls a 'network economy' and the 'information age'.

voters. To do this, however, politicians increasingly have to follow the logic of the media. This has several important consequences for political debate and presentation in the media.

First, political issues have to be simplified, and they have to focus on events, personalities and conflict, and have to present action rather than lengthy explanations. In other words, politicians' messages have to match the news values of media organisations (see section 7), if they are to gain coverage. As Castells notes, this is because politicians are competing to gain media space. Most of the other competitors are entertainers of one sort or another, and Castells is arguing that politics can only compete by being portrayed in terms of drama, personalities and conflicts. One result of this is that it is mainly 'bad news' that attracts the attention of the media and of the public.

Second, Castells makes the claim that this new form of informational politics is what has led to a greater focus on political scandal or what has been called 'sleaze' in the UK. Castells even says that this will now be a key political tactic, something that he sees as an inevitable consequence of the way politics has been dramatised and reduced to debate about personalities rather than issues.

Conclusion

It is these factors that have helped bring about the current marketing of politics in our society, and they help to explain the increase in the number of government media advisers ('spin doctors'). Castells does not claim that the media determines public opinion, but he does argue that the logic of the media helps to shape politicians' and political parties' actions. What is new about this, though, is the scope of new media technologies, which enable political parties and governments to respond to changes in public opinion very quickly. All of these, however, restrict and shape political life, and make it rather self-obsessed, with even media statements about politics becoming political events. Society and the media are becoming increasingly reflexive.

Bill Clinton and Kevin Spacey show support for Tony Blair at the 2002 Labour Party conference in Blackpool.

✱ Key Idea

The idea of informational politics suggests that politics is now dominated by the control of flows of information, rather than by substantial differences in ideology. This idea is also used by French postmodernist Lyotard (see section 20), although note that Lyotard has a more sceptical view about the nature of the so-called 'information' than Manuel Castells.

✓ Top Exam Hint

Use the new material here to evaluate Marxist and pluralist accounts of the role of the media. Both Marxist and pluralist views are now dated, and the views of Manuel Castells can be used to provide a more up-to-date assessment of the role of the media in what he calls 'the information age'.

> **For consideration:**
> 1 Will the Internet lead to more political participation by the electorate and political interest groups?
> 2 Does the new media technology (e.g. Internet, digital TV, and so on) cause political change or are political changes simply harnessing the power of new technology?

5.18 Can the media create moral panics?

66 99 Key Definition

Moral panic – this occurs when an incident, an individual or a group are seen as presenting a threat to society and the dominant social values. This response involves demands for action to solve the problem.

Professor Stan Cohen is Professor of Sociology at the London School of Economics

🖙 Who is this Person?

Stan Cohen came to the UK from South Africa, and worked as a social worker in London, before going on to do research into deviance for a higher degree at the London School of Economics. His view of sociology above all reflects a concern for the underdog, something that is also reflected by his interest in human rights.

✳ Key Idea

The idea of the 'deviance amplification spiral' suggests that far from eradicating perceived social problems, moral panics see those 'problems' increase. The targeting by the media and law and order agencies of a particular problem leads to the identification of further perpetrators, and creates a cycle of action and reaction.

What does this mean?

The sociologist Stan Cohen created the term '**moral panic**' in the early 1970s (1973). What he was trying to say was that just as individuals can have panic attacks when some stressful or unusual event shocks them, so too can societies. However, in the case of societies, these panics usually arise over what we can broadly call 'moral issues'. This means issues over which social groups have sharply differing opinions about what is right and what is wrong. Examples of the sort of issues Cohen means would be crime, hooliganism, abortion, AIDS and homosexuality. If you examine any society carefully for a while, you will find that big debates about these and other moral issues arise quite frequently. The effect of a moral panic, though, is that a certain group of people is stigmatised and negatively labelled, and become seen as presenting a threat to society.

How are moral panics created?

Cohen argues that the media play a key role in creating moral panics. Moral panics start when some behaviour or events are identified as a problem. Cohen famously used the example of gang fighting at seaside resorts in the 1960s to illustrate his point. The reporting of these minor disturbances in the local press alerted the police and other public officials to the problem. This led to a sequence of events whereby the police were ready to seek out more examples of this sort of offence, the courts were concerned to deter others from copying the behaviour by giving harsher sentences, and the media reported all this activity in order to maximise sales and readership. Cohen argues that the result was that the deviant activity was in fact amplified (increased), causing what he termed a 'deviance amplification spiral'. The sequence develops because the initial police activity appears to be justified by further outbreaks of trouble. Cohen argues that the initial 'problem' is heavily exaggerated and the group identified as causing the trouble are 'demonised' and scapegoated, and are portrayed as a threat to society.

How useful is this concept?

Although the idea of 'moral panic' has been very influential in sociology, it does need to be evaluated carefully. One criticism is that the idea is too deterministic. It therefore makes deviance amplification seem inevitable. Cohen acknowledges that amplification may not occur, but nevertheless he argues that once a moral panic is underway, it does indeed follow a logic that is determined by what he terms 'recurrent processes of news manufacture', or the inability of the media to put down a good story. However, we may want to consider whether this neglects the fact that many different institutions and groups are involved in creating a moral panic, and that some of these groups have the power to reject media representations. Sociologist Anthony Giddens' idea of reflexivity suggests that as people learn about ideas such as 'moral panics' they can change their behaviour.

Conclusion

Sarah Thornton has argued that the type of moral panic that Cohen identified is outdated (1995). The concept never really involved a sophisticated view of the audience, implying that they would simply accept media symbolisations (see section 14). Thornton argues that contemporary society is fragmented and very diversified, and so it no longer makes sense to talk as Cohen did of a 'societal reaction'. In contemporary society it is more likely that there will be many different reactions. Some groups labelled as 'folk devils' for example, may, as Thornton argues, fight back with their own alternative symbolizations.

In July 2000, 8 year-old Sarah Payne was abducted and murdered. Her death sparked nationwide outrage, supported by the *News of the World's* campaign to 'name and shame' sex offenders and implement 'Sarah's Law'.

● Synoptic Link

Don't forget to use the concept of moral panic if you go on to study crime and deviance at A2 level. Sociologists such as Steve Chibnall argue that 'crime waves' are in fact simply moral panics and do not necessarily reflect real changes in the rate of crime. Just like crime itself, crime waves are social constructions.

For consideration:

1 Does the concept of moral panic assume that there is some degree of consensus about key social values?
2 Do you agree with Thornton's view that some groups now actively seek to be scapegoated as 'deviant', since it gives their sub-culture 'authenticity'? How can sub-cultures use moral panics for their own purposes?

5.19 Does advertising really influence people?

Coursework Suggestion

Advertising would be a good topic to study for a coursework project. You could usefully relate advertising to changing definitions of gender identities. How does advertising appeal to differing conceptions of either masculinity or femininity? Does it determine gender identities or can people use advertising to create their own sense of gender identity? See also section 9.

Synoptic Link

Advertising is a pervasive aspect of our lives and it links with many other topics in sociology. Advertising can be related to: families and households; gender and sexuality; how advertising influences how we live and what we see as normal; politics and power (can it shape our political views?); health (are health campaigns effective?)

Top Exam Hint

Asking questions about advertising and searching for empirical evidence to answer those questions can help us review our theoretical ideas about the role of the media in capitalist society. So don't forget to apply the ideas from previous sections (see particularly 4, 5 and 14) to this section and to any questions on advertising.

What does this mean?

Studying advertising forces us to reconsider some important theoretical questions that have occurred up throughout this chapter, such as:

*   Are we the passive victims of media messages?

*   If advertising is influential, what implication does this have for Marxist and pluralist theories of the media (sections 4, 5, and 6)? Initially it would seem to imply that the Marxist view is more accurate, and thus imply that we are all the victims of powerful capitalist interests.

*   If advertising is influential it also has important implications for our evaluation of theories of media effects (section 14).

How do advertisements work?

Advertisements can work in many ways. Earlier in the 20th century advertisers made assumptions similar to those in the hypodermic model examined previously (see section 14). Now though, advertising can be very sophisticated, and advertisers may aim to tap into the audience's consumerist aspirations (in terms of desire for high status goods), or by appealing to a target audience's perceived social identity and desire for status. Marxist-influenced sociologists would suggest that we have a limited ability to resist these messages, whereas pluralists or postmodernists would emphasise the ability of audiences to select and use those messages most in tune with their own beliefs, values and desired identity. Businesses presumably do believe that advertising works, given the sums of money they are prepared to spend on it. At the very least they are not willing to risk losing trade by opting out of the advertising market.

What does empirical research tell us about the effects of advertising?

David Buckingham (1993) is one sociologist who has researched this question. He found that children appeared to be quite knowledgeable about advertising. They were able to resist advertising and could be very critical of television adverts. However, criticisms can be made of Buckingham's methods. He used small discussion groups (focus groups). These can be seen as lacking in representativeness, allowing the interviewer to influence responses, thus threatening validity.

Does advertising influence the content of the media?

It has been suggested that advertising does not just influence audiences, but that it can also have important effects on the content of the media. Peter Curran (1996) points out that advertising is a big source of income for many media organisations, and this puts pressure on them to attract a large audience/readership. This in turn pressurises media organisations to adapt their content to suit the mass market, and this may involve 'dumbing down', and avoiding controversial issues (including critical questioning of business practices of companies who also provide the media with lots of advertising income). However, these are not the only outcomes, and it can be very difficult for sociologists to find conclusive evidence that media organisations have been influenced in these ways by advertisers.

Conclusion

Reaching firm conclusions about the effects of advertising is not easy. In the case of advertising's effects on both audiences and media organisations, evidence can be hard to come by, and when it is available it has to be interpreted through competing theoretical perspectives. Perhaps it is less debatable though, to claim that while advertising does not work according to the hypodermic model, it certainly reflects the norms and values, and aspirations, of the culture it is situated in. This means, though, that the effects of advertising will not be simple. Advertising acts upon different social groups in different ways, and whilst people can resist the pressures of advertisements, they may not always do so. So understanding the effects of advertising will always have to involve understanding the nature of power and social stratification.

Thinking like a Sociologist

Three evaluations to use in the exam are:

1 Remember to mention that when sociologists are evaluating complex research findings and theoretical arguments, they may often draw upon and synthesise differing views.
2 This means that they will reject some aspects of each theory, but draw together a few elements to create a new theory.
3 This new synthesis modifies the views of those theories it is constructed from.

For consideration:

1 What sociological concepts help explain why people cannot always effectively resist the pressures of advertisements?
2 What theoretical explanation of media effects best matches the conclusion reached in this section?

5.20 Is contemporary society dominated by the media?

Jean Baudrillard, French social theorist

☞ Who is this Person?

Jean Baudrillard (born 1929) is a French writer. At the beginning of his academic career he was strongly influenced by Marxism, and wrote on consumerism and consumer society. From this he moved on to study gift giving and other forms of exchange, and this eventually led him to reject Marxist views of the importance of economic factors, and instead to take the view that meanings are created and negotiated through interaction. This led him to the study of signs, symbols, and media.

66 99 Key Definition

Postmodernity – this refers to the idea that we are living in a very different historical period from modernity. A key part of this idea is that society is fragmenting, and differences such as class, race, and gender are no longer socially significant. Identity is instead formed through consumption. The media plays a key role in this new form of society, creating and transmitting the images through which identities can be created.

What does this mean?

The claim that the media dominates contemporary society is one that has been made by postmodernist writers such as Jean-Francois Lyotard (1983) and Jean Baudrillard (1985). They argue that we are living in a new and distinctive period in history, which is dominated by the media. By this they mean that our knowledge of the world comes predominantly from the mass media, and that our identities are formed in terms of images that come from the media. They argue that this makes contemporary society (i.e. now) very different from modern society (i.e. anything from the 18th century onwards).

What is postmodernity?

Writers like Lyotard and Baudrillard argue that we are living in a period of time that they call **postmodernity**. They make a distinction between modern society and postmodern society, arguing that various social, political, economic and cultural changes have occurred. For our current purposes there are three important characteristics of this period that postmodernists identify.

- Postmodernists argue that consumption (what we spend our money on) is now more important than class position (what we do to earn our money) and class identity.

- Economically there has been a shift to produce goods, services and products (including media, e.g. television programmes, magazines, mobile phones, computers) for small niche markets.

- In terms of culture there is a blurring of the boundaries between so-called high culture (this means cultural or artistic forms like classical music or ballet which are mainly watched and enjoyed by elite social groups) and mass culture (the cultural or artistic forms, like television or pop music, used by the mass of people).

The upshot of all this, postmodernists say, is that we are able to construct our own identities in postmodernity, and we are not constrained by structures of class, race and gender, as people were in modern society.

How has the media changed in postmodernity?

Baudrillard claims that we now live in a society that is 'media saturated', meaning that it is now impossible for us to escape the influence of the mass media. Media images have become part of our way of seeing the world. Baudrillard claims that the media creates a view of reality that is distorted and exaggerated, and he terms this 'hyperreality'. Baudrillard is suggesting that the media is constantly trying to produce images that are so accurate and realistic that they are in a sense, 'more real than reality'. Baudrillard argues that they are not at all realistic, but since so much of our knowledge comes from the media, we are no longer in a position to be able to tell the difference. The media presents us with 'simulacra' – artificial images or reproductions (copies) of events.

Lastly, the media has tended to reduce differences between cultures. News and other material and images transmitted by the media have tended to make all cultures more similar to each other. An example of this would be the way we can see Hollywood films or Australian soap operas all over the world. This is very closely related to the idea of globalisation, which is explained in the next section.

Raymond Williams (1990) would add a note of caution to these radical views. Writing in the 1980s, Williams also talked of the way that we live in 'media saturated society'. However, Williams points out that it is a very sweeping generalisation to suggest that it is the media that has changed society. On the contrary, Williams argues that the nature of contemporary television is shaped by contemporary society. In his view it not that our world is being transformed by television, rather, it is the rapid social changes we are experiencing which are changing television and the media.

Conclusion

One of the big problems with postmodernity and the views it has about the role of the media in contemporary society is that it is very hard to find evidence to support it. The claims outlined above are all very hard to measure and study empirically. Postmodernism and postmodernity are primarily theoretical ideas, and whilst they may be convincing in some ways, they are very hard to test. Some sociologists are therefore highly sceptical of postmodernist views. Whilst they are provocative, a key weakness is their lack of empirical evidence and rigour.

For consideration:

1 Are postmodernists right to say that we live in a media-saturated world? What evidence is there for this view?
2 What implications would postmodernism have for theories of media effects?

✳ Key Idea

Hyperreality
Hyperreality is the view of reality that we get from the media – the media constructs our idea of what reality is. There is no way to tell whether this view is in fact the 'truth' or not.

✓ Top Exam Hint

When evaluating postmodernist views of the media several key issues ought to be addressed. You need to highlight the issue of whether there is any empirical evidence for postmodernity, and also the theoretical criticisms that can be made of postmodernism (e.g. its relativism). Relativism is the view that there is no single or objective truth, just different opinions which are all equally valid.

Has the media created a global culture?

What does this mean?

Postmodernist sociologists have been particularly influential in arguing that the media is reducing cultural differences and that cultural products from Hollywood and Western societies are increasingly available all over the world. Bollywood films can now also be seen world-wide. Postmodernists would say that this means that Asian culture is becoming more and more like a part of Western culture. These supposed trends are examples of what sociologists call **globalisation**. Globalisation can be seen in terms of cultural, economic and political change, but when studying the media we are interested in the cultural aspects of globalisation.

What effects is globalisation supposed to have had on the media and society?

The idea of cultural globalisation implies that the mass media has become a global phenomenon. For example, we can travel around the world and see Western media products everywhere, such as Hollywood films, American TV programmes, and computer games from California. There is now a global market-place for films, television programmes and other mass media.

Sociologists who believe in globalisation say that this is having the effect of creating an increasingly global culture. By this they mean that more and more people all over the world share the same beliefs and values, and traditional local cultures are in decline. Media globalisation thus leads to cultural globalisation. Because so much of our knowledge and shared social meanings are now transmitted through the media, the same cultural values and meanings are generated across the globe. This is called 'cultural homogenisation'. An example of this might be how American cultural values are spread across the globe through the selling of television programmes like 'Friends'.

Anthony Giddens is one sociologist who has developed the idea of globalisation (1990). Giddens argues that globalisation has the effect of spreading a cosmopolitan lifestyle and culture, but that it does not necessarily lead to a homogenous culture. This is because there is often resistance to the pressures of globalisation, as people reject what they see as cultural values which threaten their traditional way of life.

Ali G, Sacha Baron Cohen's ethnically blurred comic creation – an example of media cultural globalisation?

What empirical evidence is there for this idea?

There is evidence both for and against the view that cultural globalisation is occurring. Evidence supporting claims of globalisation comes from the quantitative research showing, for example, that in the 1980s 44% of programmes on European TV had been imported, and that over 40 per cent came from the USA (Varis 1984). Another researcher calculated that five large Western news agencies were responsible for 80 per cent of the world's news items (Masmoudi 1979). These examples support the theory because they suggest that the production of media content is heavily biased towards one main source.

Against this evidence, Colin Sparks (1998) has argued that while there has been an expansion of cable and satellite television – for instance – in the UK one-third of households now have these services, the audiences of anything that could be termed 'global' media such as satellite television are minute. By and large, most of the population in the UK watch British terrestrial television channels and read the British press. Most of the population do not appear to be interested in using 'global' media.

Conclusion

Sociologists disagree as to whether cultural globalisation has occurred. Cultural globalisation in terms of ownership is at least a growing trend, but it seems clear that there is often resistance to globalisation from local cultures. In an age when the mass media seems to be becoming increasingly globalised, which culture, and whose culture the mass media transmits is, however, becoming an increasingly contested issue.

For consideration:

1 Is cultural globalisation mainly the result of changes in technology?
2 What effects can cultural globalisation have on cultural identities?

● **Synoptic Link**

Globalisation is an issue that relates to a wide range of topics. It can be useful to demonstrate the links between the OCR topic of individual and society, where there is a section on the formation of culture and identities as well as social inequality in the A2 year, and themes of power, socialisation and social differentiation.

✓ **Top Exam Hint**

You can use the idea of globalisation to update your evaluation of other theories and concepts in the mass media topic. For example, applying the concept of globalisation to the Marxist/Pluralist debate puts that debate into a completely new perspective (see section 22 for more tips on this).

5.22 How has the media changed and how has it changed us?

66 99 Key Definition

Public sphere. The idea of the public sphere suggests that public opinion and debate is a phenomenon of modern society and did not exist in the same way in traditional societies, which were much more dominated by elite groups

☞ Who is this Person?

Jurgen Habermas is a philosopher whose work has been important to sociology. Habermas grew up in Nazi Germany, and in many ways he shared the optimism of a post-war generation seeking a new and democratic way of life. After completing his PhD, he worked for two years as a journalist, and this may have led him to develop his interests in communication and the role of the media in contemporary society, and the possibilities of democracy.

◆ What, When and Why?

Postmodernist views have recently challenged many of our ideas about the media. Thinkers such as Lyotard (1924–1998) and Baudrillard (1929–) have suggested that all of our knowledge of the world comes from the mass media, and indeed that we can no longer tell the difference between reality and the media representation of it. However, one critical comment on this would be that postmodernist views themselves are a response to the chaos caused by the rapid social change we have witnessed in recent years. It may be that it is not the media which has changed us, but that it is we ourselves who have changed the media.

What does this mean?

The mass media is the product of modern societies, and by 'modern' we usually mean from around the mid-late 18th century onwards. Sociologists believe that this was an important period of change leading to very different forms of communication from those used by individuals in traditional society. The German philosopher Jurgen Habermas (1989) has argued that the invention of the modern mass media led to the creation of a '**public sphere**' – a separate area for the debate of political and social issues. This meant that public opinion became important in the politics of modern societies. Habermas, though, argues that this has not led to greater democracy, as public opinion is managed and controlled by dominant social groups, and the media becomes a means of cultural transmission for these groups.

How has the media changed?

In recent years there has been great change in the world of the mass media. We have witnessed enormous technical change, including the development of digital, satellite, and cable television, DVDs, the Internet and the World Wide Web. There have also been tremendous changes in the concentration of ownership in the mass media and in the content of the media.

American media writer Marshall McLuhan (1963) has suggested that the type of mass media technology a society has is important; in an age of electronic media the nature of mass media has led to significant developments. For example, media information can now be transmitted much more quickly than previous technologies allowed, and over greater distances. Many sociologists see these changes in the relationship between time and space as important characteristics of globalisation.

How has the media changed us?

Sociologists maintain that these changes in the media have had important social effects, and that in fact they have changed our social world. For example, the boundaries between our public and private lives are now blurred, since the media now intrudes into areas of people's lives which were previously private or closed off to some social groups. There are no longer separate social spaces where the media does not intrude, and privacy is hard to maintain. This is very clear to us from the many examples of how those in public life may fall foul of media scrutiny and lose their jobs. It also affects people's everyday lives, influencing the way that identities are socially constructed, and our perceptions of gender relationships, or class or race, for example. Postmodernists claim that these changes open up a wide range of choice for us in terms of our personal identity.

The Marxist and pluralist perspectives we examined earlier are also still important. Some sociologists argue that the expansion of the mass media, through technologies such as the Internet, provides more space for alternative views. Others take the view that this will only lead to a stronger cultural hegemony and to a new social division between those with access to new technology, and those who don't have this access (**information rich** and **information poor**).

Sociologists are highly aware of the need to consider how social and technological change has influenced the media. We can now have even more *apparent* control over how we use the media. For instance, digital television opens up the possibility of a huge range of channels. Interactive television lets us choose the views, images, and sounds we see and even interact with the programmes. Some satellite TV allows us to 'freeze frame' particular images. All of these changes would seem to give more fuel to pluralist arguments. However, conflict and Marxist inspired views suggest that we need to be aware that the role of powerful owners and social elites may remain a key issue.

Conclusion

So the media has changed a lot, but as we have seen, the effects of the media are experienced through the influence of social structures, and people do have the capacity to interpret the representations of the world provided by the media. Nevertheless, our identities and our self-image as modern individuals are things that are themselves in part the product of the mass media.

✳ Key Idea

Information rich/information poor. This term refers to new types of inequality in contemporary society. Information rich refers to those who have access to information, usually through ownership of their own computer, whilst those who cannot afford such technology are 'information poor'. As computer technology becomes more pervasive, and used for activities such as applying for jobs, and communicating with government agencies, for example, it seems clear that not having access to, or ownership of a computer will put many people at a disadvantage.

● Synoptic Link

The division between information rich and information poor can be related to stratification. This, is a new dimension of inequality and it can have important social effects.

For consideration:

1   Does our bombardment by increasing numbers of media signs and symbols mean that we now have a limitless ability to construct our identities in contemporary society?
2   Does the development of the Internet mean that public debate will be more democratic?

5.23 Examination advice

What are the examiners looking for?

The examiners want to see what you know about the sociology of the media and test your understanding by seeing what you can do with that knowledge.

In each question:

Part a) is worth 15 marks, and you should spend no longer than 15 minutes answering it. It will ask you to 'Identify and explain…' two specific features of the question area. It tests your knowledge and understanding, so you need to include studies, concepts and theories wherever you can. Make sure you clearly differentiate between the two points you make – use bullets or numbers.

Part b) is worth 30 marks and you should spend no longer than 30 minutes answering it. It will ask you to 'Outline and discuss…' a view. You are being tested on your knowledge and understanding, interpretation and analysis and evaluation so you should include studies, concepts and theories. Try to make specific evaluative comments throughout, but also ensure that you look at other views on the question. If you do this you will be juxtaposing your views, and you will be rewarded evaluation marks.

What do I need to know?

Make sure that you have covered all the ground in this topic. Go back and look carefully at section 2, but also look at a copy of your exam specification. This will familiarise you with the language and terms used by the exam board.

You need to make sure that you have a thorough knowledge of the following.

* The main theories of the media, theoretical debates, and key concepts, as discussed in this chapter.

* The key studies discussed in this chapter.

* Key methodological and theoretical concepts in sociology in general. Don't forget the AS course themes – socialisation, culture and identity, and social differentiation, power, and stratification. If you use these words (concepts) carefully you can show the examiners that you have a sociological imagination.

How do I remember everything?

Try to use different techniques to make revision easier.

- Mind maps, spider diagrams, checklists (key points, key studies), and mnemonics, are all useful methods.

- Test yourself regularly (in addition to tests set by your teacher) – make your revision active. Tape record some of your lists of key points and listen to them on a personal stereo.

- Get hold of past papers and work through the short answers with a friend. For longer answers, making essay plans is a very good way of thinking through ways of applying your knowledge.

- Lastly, try to make your revision sessions frequent (a bit every day), and sharply focused. Avoid making them too long; about an hour is probably most effective.

Key points to remember

- You need a strong knowledge of key studies, concepts and theories, but you also need to show that you can identify, analyse, interpret and evaluate sociological studies, theories and concepts.

- Remember to use general sociological concepts and theories.

- Make your revision sessions frequent, focused and active.

✓ Top Exam Hint

To show the examiner that you are evaluating, analysing and interpreting sociological material, use these words in your answers, e.g. 'In evaluating the Marxist approach to the media, sociologists need to address the criticism that this theory is economically deterministic'. A good answer would then continue to explain what this means, and whether and why it is an important criticism.

● Synoptic Link

You will not be asked to make synoptic links in the AS exam for the mass media topic. However, if you are taking the A2 exam next year, you can use knowledge from this topic to answer the synoptic questions on either crime and deviance or stratification.

✍ Coursework Suggestion

If you find an exam question which relates to coursework that you have done you can relate this material to the exam question. However, use this sort of material sparingly and with great care – you do not want to give the impression that it's the only thing you can remember about the topic.

5.24 Pushing your grades up higher

What do I need to do to get a good grade?

Students often have a number of mistaken views about the skills required for successful exam performance; some remarkably optimistic, such as the belief that 'you can cram it all in at the last minute', and the more pessimistic 'you've either got it or you haven't'. Both are far from the truth. The following points should convince you that the key to success lies in your own hands.

1   **Time management**
    You must apportion your time in a logical manner. You should never spend more time on a question worth 6 marks than you do on a question worth 8 marks. It is only 2 marks difference, but if you follow this principle through you will come unstuck and will not do as well as you could have done. Generally you can make a rough formula of around 1 minute for each mark, and around 15 minutes reading and planning time for all the questions.

2   **Answer all questions**
    This does not mean that you should attempt all questions on the exam paper! It means that you must answer the correct number of questions. This is vital. Even if you are not doing your best work, if you attempt all parts of a question you will collect a few marks and these can make a significant difference. Grade boundaries in most exams are pretty narrow.

3   **Lay out your answers in a clear and logical manner. Write as neatly as you can.**
    The shorter style questions in the AS exam (often, for example, requiring you to 'identify and explain two advantages or disadvantages') require careful presentation of answers if you are to avoid losing marks. Many students seem to be skilled at making the same point twice, or missing out part of the instruction, e.g. not bothering to 'explain' both points in the above example. If you present each part of the answer clearly by, for example, leaving a line between each part, it is easier for both yourself and the examiner to clearly see what your points and explanations are.

4   **Demonstrate your sociological knowledge**
    There is no point in waffling on about how 'sociological studies show that . . .', or 'some sociologists argue that . . .'. Be specific. In a sociology exam it is a reasonable expectation that you will be able to show that you know about a range of relevant studies, concepts and

theories. Use the language of sociology and show that you understand what it means.

5   **Use the skills explicitly**
Both the AQA and OCR specifications place a big emphasis on skills of identification, analysis, interpretation and evaluation. Examiners do not want to see how many studies you have learnt parrot-fashion (though they do expect knowledge of studies). They want to see how much you understand, and this is demonstrated through AO2 skills. Make this explicit by recycling the skill words, e.g. 'it is useful to evaluate this study in terms of its methodology, since positivists would claim it lacks representativeness'. You would then need to develop the point in detail.

6   **Practise planning and writing balanced, logical and coherent arguments**
Longer questions at AS level require an argued answer in response, not a narrative or description of lots of studies or theories. Get hold of past papers/practice questions, and practice planning out answers, working out how you would evaluate different sociological approaches.

7   **Develop your points in an extended manner**
Do not assume that readers will understand your point if you make a brief, unelaborated point, e.g. 'Marxism is often criticised for being an economically reductionist theory'. This is the start of some evaluation – it needs to be developed in full.

8   **Express ideas in your own words**
Avoid learning quotations to use in the exam. Make sure that any notes you make in revision have been put into your own words.

Key points to remember

*   Manage your time carefully and answer all the questions.

*   Develop your command of English and your ability to write a coherent and sustained argument.

*   Make sure that you have a good knowledge and understanding of key studies, concepts and theories, and the skills of analysis required to use your knowledge.

Frequently asked questions

Q. Is bias in the media inevitable?

A. Yes. Bias is about power, and as the French thinker Michel Foucault reminds us, it is impossible to escape from power relations. Therefore there will always be bias in the media. However, this shouldn't prevent us from challenging and fighting bias, and it shouldn't prevent us from trying to make the media a truly public forum for debate.

Q. Is more choice of TV channels a good thing?

A. Your answer will depend on which sociological perspective you find most convincing. Those influenced by Marxism will be sceptical that having more channels actually does create more choice, simply providing more of the same and 'dumbing down' standards. Pluralists might take the view that more channels mean more opportunities for minority interest groups to air their views.

Q. Why can't sociologists agree about the effects of the mass media?

A. First, the methodological issues around operationalisation mean that researchers disagree about how and what to measure, and can generate very different results. Second, the structure/action debate shows us that sociologists have very different ideas about how much freedom people have in their lives. Whichever view you think is best, make sure you can support it theoretically and empirically.

Chapter 6

Religion

- Can religion change society?
- Does religion hold society together?
- How do we measure religion?
- Religious control
- New movements
- Problems of definition
- How popular is religion

Religion

- Classical sociology
- Functionalism
- Marxism and neo-Marxism
- Feminism
- Theories
- Post-modernism
- Symbolic interactionsim
- Weberianism
- What is the impact of religion?
- Class
- Age
- Gender
- Sexuality
- Ethnicity

Key issues in the sociology of religion

◆ What, When and Why?

Remember that the founders of sociology (e.g. Auguste Comte, Emile Durkheim, Karl Marx and Max Weber) were writing in Europe during the 19th century – a Europe that was by and large Christian and therefore many of their ideas used Christianity as a focus for their research questions. They were not interested in the 'truth' of different religions but the connection between religion and how people were socialised.

● Synoptic Links

The sociology of religion can be linked synoptically to both the concept of power and methodology. The concept of power can allow sociologists of religion to examine how religion might be a source of 'power' for some groups and not others; examine why this might be the case and finally explore the effects of that power on different classes, ethnicities, genders, ages and sexualities.

Methodological problems exist when researchers are unclear about definitions. This is particularly difficult with religion because of its personal nature. Religion means different things to different people. This can make researching religion an extremely sensitive area and can create further difficulties when talking about the validity, reliability or representativeness of sociological research.

✓ Top Exam Hint

Make sure that by the end of this chapter you can clearly write one sentence about each debate using the following theories: functionalism, Marxism, neo-Marxism, feminisms, Weberianism, symbolic interactionism and postmodernism. Make your revision even easier by turning these sentences either into a revision table or creating cards that you can then use to revise from (each card should include the name of the sociologist, date and aim of the research along with the findings and one criticism).

Why are sociologists interested in religion?

The sociology of religion manages to grab the attention of all types of sociologists – whatever their theoretical background. The founders of sociological theory, e.g. Durkheim, Marx and Weber, were fascinated by the role that religion played and we have inherited this interest from them. For some sociologists, religion acts as a way of integrating (and socialising) people into the norms (accepted ways of behaving) and values that are seen to be of importance for a particular society. However, for others, religion is a source of conflict particularly when issues surrounding gender, class, ethnicity, age and, increasingly, sexuality are put under the sociologists' microscope.

What are the key debates in religion?

You need to be aware of *four* key debates that examiners are keen to explore when setting exam questions:

1   Secularisation (to what extent is religion more or less popular than it once might/might not have been and how it has changed over time).

2   Whether religion is (or can be) a means of socially controlling people.

3   Whether religion can (or should) act as a means to cement or 'integrate' people into society.

4   Whether religion is a 'conservative' force (i.e. to what extent religions stop the processes of social change).

What are the key ideas and concepts in religion?

- You need to be aware of the views about religion from the point of view of the classical sociologists, functionalists, Marxists, Max Weber, neo-Marxists, interpretive sociologists and feminists.

- You also need to be know about the different ways that we classify religions – the most popular being 'church', 'sect', 'cult', 'denomination' and 'new religious movements'.

- Finally, you need know what role religion might play in any future society. Postmodernist writers offer an exciting discussion about this when they examine the variety of religions that are on offer today and how these might impact on society tomorrow.

What are the key problems in the sociology of religion?

When discussing to what extent research may be *reliable*, *valid* or *representative*, sociologists have to face two specific problems when examining religions. By 'representative', sociologists mean that the research carried out represents the population or group from which the sample was taken.

1 'Operationalising' (or 'defining') what we mean by religion.

2 Measuring any particular aspect relating to religious belief or practice.

In order to debate the sociology of religion, it helps to have a shared understanding of what we mean by 'religion'. A methodological problem is that there is no one shared understanding of this complex concept. For some it's magic; for some, it's a belief in a god or gods; while for others, it may well be that a rock or animal is considered 'sacred'.

The second methodological problem faces sociologists when they are attempting to 'quantify' or measure any aspect related to religious practice. How do you know if somebody is 'religious'? Is it if they attend a church or mosque regularly? Is it if they are seen to be kneeling in worship? Is it simply if they are seen to be wearing a particular item of jewellery or clothing (e.g. the Sikh scimitar)? And what about those aspects of religion that perhaps we don't see – the silent prayer, confession or simply a 'thank you' to whoever may be listening. Who is to argue which type of behaviour is more religious?

These two methodological problems make sociological research very difficult when trying to make historical or cross-cultural comparisons about the purpose or impact of different religious traditions.

✳ Key Idea

Social action theories see the major focus of sociology to be that of the individual. They focus on the meaning and interpretation of human action and how other humans perceive such actions. Social action theories include Weberianism, symbolic interactionism, phenomenology and ethnomethodology.

✍ Coursework Suggestion

Carry out an exploratory study based on interviews with people who believe in 'new age religions'. You will need to decide which particular religions are of interest to you. Explore whether there is a connection between either class, gender or ethnicity and the particular religion that you are focusing on. Explore what the 'function' of this particular religion might be for the respondents involved in your study.

What do we need to know about the sociology of religion?

✓ **Top Exam Hints**

- Remember that in the exam it is not important to go into enormous detail about each religion – that is *not* what the examiners are looking for. Be clear what *sociologists* have to say about the different religions and their effects on individuals and society as a whole. Do this by making sure you fully understand the different theories that you will come across in this chapter.

- The AS exam will ask you to evaluate. Evaluation in the exam means that you could question how data was gathered and when. You question to what extent the empirical data can be 'verified' for its accuracy. You analyse the argument to see if it holds together logically (i.e. no wild claims are being made). Finally, you identify to what extent the theory, study or claim is 'comprehensive', i.e. that it can be used to explain other situations in a different culture, time or place.

✎ **Coursework Suggestion**

Religion can be examined to see the role it plays in the creation of nation states. You don't have to be a Max Weber to do this. By adopting semiology or content analysis it might be fun to explore the words of politicians in news coverage, newspapers, or magazine articles to see how many times religious words, symbols or leaders are associated with particular national movements, wars or uprisings (e.g. Bush and Blair's use of the word 'crusade' after the 9/11 bombings!) In this way you can identify how religion might be a tool used by governments to create a sense of national identity. Semiology is an interpretive method of research for examining the contents of the media. It explores the hidden messages behind words, pictures or phrases.

What does the specification say about the sociology of religion?

The OCR specification that you will be expected to know about:

- *Classifications of religious groups* – i.e. church, denomination, sect, cults and new religious movements. You will need to explain their relationship to each other and to society by focusing on the sociological variables of class, age, gender and ethnicity.
- *How does religion affect what people do and how society is?* – i.e. the secularisation debate; religious fundamentalism; religion and control (in connection with ethnicity, gender and sexuality).
- *The founders, religion and sociological theory* – i.e. Marxism and what it has to say about religion, ideology and conflict; functionalism and what it has to say about religion, stability and consensus; Weberianism and what it has to say about religion, social action and social change.

How will I be examined in this topic area?

The exam for this unit will be 90 minutes and will be composed of two 2-part structured essay questions, chosen from the same or different options (i.e. religion, family, mass media and youth and culture.

As with all of the OCR units you will have to show competency or ability in the assessment objectives of AO1 (*knowledge & understanding* and *presentation & communication*) and AO2 (*interpretation & analysis* and *evaluation*). For AO1 you need to show *knowledge and understanding* of: the names of sociologists and their case studies; the relevant theories; the key concepts (e.g. 'secularisation'); evidence to support the claims that sociologists make (e.g. figures showing the decline in church attendance); and show a keen awareness of the research methodologies used by sociologists of religion.

For AO2 you need to show how you can actually *interpret and apply* this knowledge when putting forward a particular argument and *evaluate* continuously throughout any answer you are writing. For example, this might mean that you draw on the ideas of a theory or case study that was carried out thirty years ago and see how it might (or might not!) be relevant to an area of religion today. You might also identify trends from the past and see to what extent these trends still exist today.

How well does this topic relate to coursework?

One of the advantages of living in a multi-cultural country like Britain is that it gives the sociology student the possibility to explore the diverse range of religions associated with the many ethnic minorities living in the UK. By focusing on issues of class, ethnicity, gender and age, a variety of aims and objectives for coursework can be generated.

Traditional and 'new age' (e.g. feng shui) religions can be compared and contrasted in an attempt to explain the 'role' or 'function' they play for the class, gender, ethnic minority or age group. Religious ceremonies themselves can be examined (try interviewing religious community leaders) for the purpose and impact they may (or may not have) on the inhabitants of particular communities.

How well does this topic help with synopticity?

By focusing on the concept of power religion can also be used in association with stratification to show how many religions have helped maintain particular stratified societies (e.g. the feudal and caste systems where there was a strong division between serfs and land owners, and in India the divide between Brahmans and Untouchables). Sociology students can make some easy connections with social differentiation and the breaking away from the 'norms and values' that some religions enforce or encourage.

You can also highlight methodological issues that occur when studying sensitive areas such as people's religious beliefs. Debates as to whether quantitative or qualitative methods of research are best can be applied to areas such as secularisation or the functions that religions play in particular societies.

Key points to remember

- The sociology of religion raises a variety of synoptic possibilities with social differentiation, power and stratification.
- This topic makes for an exciting option in coursework due to the availability of different cultures in the UK and the research opportunities that that provides.
- Identify, practise and perfect the skills required for AO1 and AO2 described above (the many examples in this chapter will help you do this).

● **Synoptic Link**
By applying a 'historical perspective', i.e. identifying how things might/might not have changed over time, it is possible to identify how many religions have created socially unacceptable (deviant) groups (e.g. through wars; through the labelling of women as witches; through causes such as the anti-abortion movement). Religion and the concept of 'power' can also be used to analyse gender relationships both historically (the lack of women actively involved in professional religious organisations) and privately (the way that some religions justify the exploitation of women in the home).

How can we find out about the sociology of religion?

Politicians are often keen to refer back to a 'golden age of certainty' where the norms, values and everyday actions were said to be more fixed and predictable. These 'certain' times are described in a positive light and are said to have existed until the early 1960s. This 'golden age' is quite often contrasted with what is sometimes referred to as a period of 'uncertainty' that many writers argue exists today. You can question the validity of both claims, i.e. that the past was 'certain' and 'good' and the present is 'uncertain' and 'bad'.

❝❞ Key Definition

By 'quantitative' sociologists refer to any research method or data that attempts to explain its findings using generalisations, statistics, tables, charts and diagrams. Quite often questionnaires and structured interviews are used to gather such data. 'Qualitative' research (i.e. data generated from more unstructured interviews, letters, diaries and observations) tends to be richer or 'valid' (i.e. 'in-depth'). Interpretive sociologists prefer this form of data gathering because it represents the 'interpretation' of the respondent's view of the world rather than any 'social reality' that positivist socialists believe exists.

✳ Key Idea

Glock and Stark (1965, 1968) argue for mixing quantitative and qualitative approaches to investigate the sociology of religion, by studying:

- the level of belief of the individuals and group.
- the personal involvement in religious acts of prayer and celebration.
- individual and group *feelings* of supernatural, sacred and spiritual experience.
- the knowledge individuals possess about their own religions.
- to what extent all of the above influences the day-to-day lives of the researched individuals.

How have sociologists tried to measure 'religion'?

Whether we view 'religion' as an individual activity carried out in private or analyse it from the point of view of a belief system, this area of sociology provides huge possibilities for you to show off your knowledge of sociological methodology. Sociologists choose their methodology as a result of a number of issues that include:

- *The nature of the research problem* (e.g. are you researching documents or people; is the research 'covert' (carried out 'under cover') or 'overt' (carried out with the full knowledge of all concerned) or is the researcher looking back over time and comparing past with present)?
- *The traditional research strategies, methods and data sources* thought to be appropriate for a particular problem (e.g. using church statistics when analysing the popularity of religion).
- *How available or accessible is the data* that the sociologist requires (e.g. how might the lack of written sources of data in some cultures restrict sociologists in determining what religious practices exist or have existed)?
- *The resources at the researchers' disposal* (e.g. funding, time, equipment and assistance).

Values also determine how a particular sociologist approaches the sociology of religion. Are they a Marxist, or feminist or symbolic interactionist, or indeed a Jew, Catholic or Muslim? In all cases the aim or particular focus of their research will reflect the theoretical interest of the sociologist carrying out the research.

Such values will also determine whether or not the researcher is gathering **quantitative** data or **qualitative** data and this might depend on whether they consider themselves to be 'positivist' (i.e. 'scientific') or 'interpretive' in their approach to the sociology of religion.

What methods do sociologists tend to use to study religion?

Sociologists have a wide variety of methods they can use but quite often the nature of the subject being studied will dictate what kind of method can/should be used. Questionnaires are a useful form of data gathering when making broad generalisations although they are not particularly personal – something that religion almost always is. Sociologists also analyse historical documents. However, can we really trust the statistics or the conclusions drawn from them? Here are three sociologists who have used a variety of methods to study 'religion'.

- Feminist C. Butler (1995) carried out interviews with second generation Muslim women in England in order to challenge some of the stereotypical media images associated with women and the Islamic religion.
- Bryan Wilson (1985) used a quantitative approach to religion by analysing church attendance figures to prove that religious thought and practice are in decline.
- Eileen Barker (1984) used participant observation, in-depth interviews and questionnaires in an attempt to explain how and why people joined the 'Moonies' and to discover what kind of people they were.

What problems with definition are encountered in studying 'religion'?

- Remember that whatever definition we use to start our research will then affect what we look for and what we uncover as a result.
- If religion is defined as an organised group of individuals that share a system of beliefs, then how do we include Christians, Muslims and Buddhists under one similar category? The latter is so very different from the first two (both of which are 'Abrahamic' religions). How do we explain differences between Catholics and Protestant forms of Christianity or Sunni and Shi'ite Islamic beliefs?
- Discussions surrounding the 'secularisation debate' (the idea that societies may or may not be as religious as they once were) are confusing if 'being religious' is defined by mosque or church attendance. How do we know that people went or go to church for religious reasons? How many children are 'made' to go to church by their parents?

Key points to remember

- There are a variety of reasons why sociologists choose the methods they do – learn these for the exam.
- Memorise not only the key names associated with the sociology of religion but also the method of research they adopted.
- The importance of 'definition' or 'operationalisation' when discussing any research that takes place – evaluating somebody else's research is impossible unless we know what they mean.

☞ **Who is this Person?**

Eileen Barker – a professor of sociology at the London School of Economics (LSE) – was born in Edinburgh and gained her first degree in sociology in 1970. Her PhD thesis was published as 'The Making of a Moonie: Brainwashing or Choice'. Her research focused on the process of recruitment used by the 'Moonies' (members of the unification church, a new religious movement that was founded in 1954 and attempted to mix Western and Eastern culture in order to bring about a 'physical kingdom of God'). She was interested in what kind of person would get involved with such a movement.

❊ **Key Ideas**

- Barker's work was inspirational because she rejected the divide between positivist ('scientific' sociological explanations that seek to offer 'cause and effect' explanations) and interpretive methodological approaches ('anti-positivist' approaches that look at with how people interpret their 'social reality') that had characterised debates within sociology for much of 20th century. She argued that to achieve a true understanding of how society worked, sociologists must use a variety of methods. This is known as 'methodological pluralism' or 'triangulation'. In Barker's case she produced both quantitative and qualitative research data.

- The term 'Abrahamic' is quite often used to describe the religions of Islam, Christianity and Judaism, which all take as their starting point the religious figure of Abraham. This means that far from these three religions being considered extremely different from each other, they share very strong similarities – something that is quite often overlooked by journalists, politicians and in some cases the religious believers of these three faiths.

✓ **Top Exam Hint**

Durkheim's (1912) classic study of religion can be criticised as being 'Eurocentric' i.e. it is viewed from the perspective that European culture is superior to any other culture being discussed or studied. Such a perspective can 'distort' research by producing culturally-biased aims, objectives, hypotheses, analysis, findings and conclusions.

6.4 Why is it difficult to define the concept 'religion'?

What does this mean?

Interactionist Berger (1990) argues that 'definitions cannot, by their very nature, be either "true" or "false", only more useful or less so. For this reason it makes relatively little sense to argue over definitions'. Sociologists analyse the relationship between religion and society by studying the role that it plays in people's lives. The problem, however, is that everybody (including sociologists) has a different idea as to what religion is and this can create a variety of different theoretical perspectives and research findings.

Difficulties in defining 'religion'

There is no singular definition as to what religion is other than a generalized agreement that they are a set of **belief systems**. This makes the job of deciding the 'function' of religion very difficult because this will change depending on what religion we are talking about and where the religion might be taking place. Living as a Christian in an area of famine in Africa and being a Christian in New York will provide two very different 'religious' experiences.

Any discussion about whether religion is in decline or growing (sociologists call this the 'secularisation debate') will depend on what religion we are talking about or indeed how we define religion in the first place. Some sociologists refer to religions as 'ideologies' meaning that they are sets of ideas about the world that embody morals and values.

Useful concepts when attempting to define religion

Animism/Totemism – the belief that natural phenomena (e.g. trees, stones, and rivers) are made up of spirits or souls which can affect society.
Atheism – the belief that no one god (or gods) exists.
Agnosticism – neither a belief in, nor a denial of, one god but happy to believe that a god may exist if enough evidence is produced.
Magic – the belief that by a force of human will, the gods can be made to follow your will.
Monotheism – the belief in one singular god.
Polytheism – the belief in more than one god.
Superstition – the belief that one can be protected from evil events (or bring about positive ones) by a set of certain actions (e.g. the crossing of fingers).

66 99 Key Definition

Polyani (1958) says that any **belief system** contains three components.

- A *'circularity' of ideas* – Where each idea within the system is explained referring to another idea (e.g. Mohammed's connection to Abraham in the Islamic religion).
- *Explanations for difficult situations* – If a particular idea cannot be seen to work there will be religious 'reason' for this (quite often this is put down to 'faith').
- *Other belief systems are unacceptable* – A devout Christian will find it impossible to accept a Buddhist interpretation of 'spirituality'.

❊ Key Idea

Polyani (1958) tells us that belief systems are the ideas which we believe to be right and that offer guidelines on behaviour along with justifications for that behaviour. This means that disciplines like politics and science are also 'belief systems'. In other words, belief systems contain norms and values that inform how social interaction can and should take place.

Supernatural – the belief that science and modern common sense cannot explain all events that take place.

Durkheim offers two helpful concepts in attempting to define religion. The first is 'sacred', by which he refers to aspects of life having to do with the supernatural that inspire awe, reverence, deep respect and sometimes even fear. His second concept is 'profane', by which he refers to aspects of society supposedly not concerned with religion but instead are part of the ordinary aspects of everyday life.

Of course, what may be 'ordinary' in one part of the world may not be in another. For example, it is quite ordinary in Sumatra, Indonesia when serving customers in restaurants to stop, go the corner of the restaurant and offer flowers to a mini-altar. Is this everyday act 'sacred' or 'profane'?

Hammond (1985) argues that it is wrong to only associate religion with the 'sacred'. While religion may well be sacred in modern societies, so too are beliefs of nationalism, science and technology, where the passions for all three can be as strong as any commitment to a 'god' or 'gods'.

The danger of ethnocentricism

Another problem when attempting to discuss and define what we mean by religion is the possibility of placing religions in a hierarchy and implying that some are better than others. Adapting an evolutionary approach that was fashionable at the end of the 19th century, Tylor (1891) charted the course of religious development from 'primitive fantasies' to more 'sophisticated' beliefs in modern times. However, sociologists need to be careful when defining religions that they do not make value judgements about whether some religions are 'higher up' the evolutionary ladder than others, e.g. comparing animism with Christianity or Judaism and implying one is more primitive than another.

Conclusion

When attempting to define religions the classical sociologists were concerned with macro grand theories by which they focused on whole societies and analysed large historical periods in time. Thomas Luckman is one of many sociologists who, from the 1960s onwards, have tended to adopt a more micro level on analysis by looking at new age beliefs, the decline in church attendance in some cultures, and the growth in denominations, sects and cults. This is sometimes referred to as 'The New Sociology of Religion'.

✳ Key Idea

Something can be considered to be 'ethnocentric' if it places importance on one cultural set of values over and above others. For example many textbooks may be written from a white, often male and European perspective which implies that other parts of the world are less sophisticated. This would be the worst example of 'ethnocentric' writing. This idea can be applied to different theoretical views on different religions.

✓ Top Exam Hint

Remember, while you may discover many definitions about religion in this chapter you do not have to know the details of the religions, just the definitions of them. What you must be able to do is evaluate them by 'seeing them in the eyes of other definitions'. If you can do this you will be able to draw out the strengths and weaknesses easily and in a sophisticated way which will impress the examiners.

For consideration:

1   Using the concepts of 'sacred' and 'profane' what other examples of religion could you argue fit into these categories?
2   How might your answers to the above point be helpful in building a case for a postmodern approach to religion?

Why is it difficult to measure the popularity of religion?

What does this mean?

One of the big debates that dominates the sociology of religion is the 'secularisation' debate and we will explore this more fully in the chapter. There is a lot of evidence to show that in Western societies the popularity of the mainstream religions is decreasing although interestingly the popularity of other forms of spirituality (e.g. feng shui and astrology) is growing. Church membership figures for the 'Trinitarian churches' (Roman Catholic, Anglican, Presbyterian, Methodist, Baptist, Orthodox and other free churches) showed a drop from 9.1 million members to 6.4 million members from 1970 to 1995 (Social Trends 27: 224).

However, the term 'popularity' is problematic because we need to be able to look back and see how popular something was at an earlier stage in history. And here lies the difficulty. The evidence that does exist may, on closer examination, not tell us anything about how popular religion was, but perhaps about other roles that religion played in societies.

Finally, the very concept 'religion' means different things to different people. If two sociologists have two different definitions (another word sociologists use is 'operationalisations') for religion, then any research they carry out is going to have different results because of the way they have 'operationalised' the concept of religion.

Why do/did people attend spiritual rituals?

In Europe many people argue that there are fewer people attending church ceremonies now than in the 19th century. While this almost certainly is the case, it does lead to the question 'why do/did they attend in the first place?' Was it ever for purely 'religious' reasons? Herberg (1956) suggested that church attendance in the US was evidence of commitment to the *local community* rather than an indication of religiousness.

Examine why many people publicly celebrate their religion. There is, for example, evidence that shows that as we get older, we attend more religious ceremonies. Is this out of fear of getting old and perhaps the acknowledgement of an after-life? Could it also be that as we get older it becomes increasingly difficult to meet new people and therefore the local religious organisation (church, mosque, temple or other) can offer a social network that we can belong to?

Does attendance at religious ceremonies tell us anything about the popularity of religion?

✳ Key Idea

Greeley (1992) refers to the 'myth of the golden age' in which he challenges the idea that older, traditional worlds were safer, more religious places and modern/postmodern worlds are not. Bruce (1996), studying English historical documents, shows how it was quite normal for peasants to be playing cards and firing shotguns in churches during the 18th and 19th centuries. Fink and Stark (1992) point to the American towns of Dodge City and Tombestone as being famous for 'lawlessness, vice and violence' rather than places associated with religious virtue.

Other reasons for attendance at religious ceremonies are to do with social acceptance within the community generally. One hundred years ago in the UK, it was considered socially unacceptable if you did not attend 'church'. As a result this could mean you were looked down upon within the community you lived in. The same is true for many communities today.

In addition to this, in the past many people would attend ceremonies if they were about to get married in a church (even if they did not actually believe in the religion). There was also far greater emphasis on religious ceremonies for children (e.g. Roman Catholic first communion and confirmation and Jewish Bar Mitsvah) than exists today. More women attend ceremonies as they get older than men. In many cases this is to do with the fact that women live longer than men. Religious organisations can offer many of these women the care and support and social network they desire having lost their partners.

Religion and nationalism

Nationalism refers to the feelings of loyalty that people may have to a particular nation or people. Although the word has a variety of different meanings, in many cases national or ethnic identities of a particular group are bound up with a particular religion.

We can see this in Northern Ireland with the conflict between the Catholics and Protestants still taking place. But we can also see this in the way that the 'West versus Iraq' situation is wrongly being portrayed as a Christian West versus an Islamic East. At such times religious enthusiasm can actually exaggerate the popularity of a religion – particularly if it is considered to be unpatriotic not to celebrate the religion concerned.

Conclusion

In addition to the reasons listed above, war brings about the loss of loved ones and the need for solace and comfort that many religions provide. As a result, during times of war, many religions experience an increase in popularity. This makes the work of the sociologist harder when trying to establish long-term trends in the popularity of any religion.

For consideration:

1 What other reasons, apart from those mentioned in this section, can you think of that make religions popular at particular times or with particular people?
2 Why is it more difficult to answer this question when we go back hundreds or thousands of years?

● **Synoptic Link**

You can link religion to social differentiation – it was (and is, in some societies) considered 'deviant' not to attend or be part of a religious organisation. Some religions are 'demonised' by politicians and the media. Islam has faced much negative labelling at the hands of politicians and the media. This tells how 'deviancy' is both a culturally and historically changing concept. Mention this as a sophisticated way of telling the examiner you are aware of the variety of interpretations such terms can have.

✓ **Top Exam Hint**

One problem that you will encounter in the sociology of religion is the domination of ideas from a 'Christian' perspective. A lot of sociological research has been gathered from Christian organisations. This can be a problem when making generalisations about other religions. As a sociology student, you should mention this point early on in the exam – perhaps in the introduction – and also be prepared to apply some of the ideas to the mosque, temple or other religious place of worship.

✍ **Coursework Suggestion**

Read this chapter carefully but always with a notebook at your side. Every time you come across a reason for why people attend ceremonies, or believe in a particular religion, write it down. By the end of the chapter your reasons can be turned into questions and thus you will have a questionnaire. Carry out research on a cross-section of twelve people using this questionnaire in order to find out the reasons for their religious belief. Compare your findings with the writings of other sociologists.

What did the classical sociologists think about religion?

What does this mean?

At the time the early sociologists were writing, 19th-century religious values were considered to be extremely important in every day life. Children received their education in many cases from priests; family life revolved around religious customs and the head of the Protestant Church in the UK was the king or queen of England (and still is today). The very structures, constraints and in some cases freedoms that religion offered people were a matter of interest to the emerging discipline of sociology.

Writers such as Comte, Weber, Marx and Durkheim, the latter two both from Jewish backgrounds, stated that rather than 'godly creations,' traditions were the creations of 'men' and as such were suitable subjects for sociological inquiry. The enormous wealth of some of the religions (e.g. that of the Vatican) also brought into question issues of power and exploitation.

Auguste Comte (1798–1857)

The classical sociologists were interested in the relationship between types of religious beliefs and types of society. Comte divided the history of society into three stages.

- *Theological society* – knowledge is based on a belief in magic, superstition and religion. The emphasis is on blood ties, and the belief in intuition (the ability to 'feel' if something is 'OK' or not).
- *Metaphysical society* – moving away from a belief in a variety of gods (polytheism) to a belief in one god (monotheism).
- *Final 'positive' society* – a 'secular' society where subjects like sociology offer 'scientific' answers to the questions formerly addressed by the religions.

Emile Durkheim (1858–1917)

Durkheim stressed the role of religion as a way of forging common values and a **conscience collective** in society (see section 7). The 'profane' world is a world of 'empirical knowledge', i.e. knowledge gathered through the senses. However, for Durkheim there was also a 'sacred' world that inspired 'awe' and 'reverence' and that was considered above the profane.

His work on the 'totem' as used by the Arunta tribe in Australia shows how a sacred (and profane) symbol can symbolise both god and society.

✓ **Top Exam Hint**

Point out the similarities between Marx and Comte. Both theorists argue that there is a 'historical' or 'evolutionary' pattern to society. Comte talks about the three types of society (see this section) and Marx talks about the five stages of history (primitive communism, slavery, feudalism, capitalism and communism). Both view history as a set of 'stages' that societies move through.

✳ **Key Idea**

Comte hoped for a 'priesthood' of sociologists in what would become the new 'secular religion'. Comte developed the enlightenment tradition of going beyond common-sense or tradition as explanations for the commonplace. His sociology was one that was to be rooted in evidence.

In this way he argues that religious ceremonies encourage a sense of common purpose that unites people beyond their own selfish interests. Religion is a force that binds the individual to society.

Karl Marx (1818–1883)

Marx is often described as a 'materialist', meaning that he did not believe in the supernatural. To him religion was an ideology that helped create and maintain the 'false consciousness' that people lived under – this, Marx believed hid the 'evils' of the capitalist society. By 'false consciousness' he meant that religion stopped workers seeing that they were, in reality, being 'exploited' by their 'bosses' – the middle classes.

The social order that Marx was so critical about was maintained with the help of religion. By promising a life hereafter and teaching honour and respect for those above, religion helps keep the capitalist system alive. Religion was, for Marx, the ideological tool of the ruling classes.

Max Weber (1864–1920)

Whereas Durkheim and Marx both argued that religion helped maintain the status quo, Weber argued that religion was a force for social change. Calvinism (a form of Christianity) for example, believed that by demonstrating self-reliance and hard work, divine approval would be automatic.

By looking at China, India and Europe he argued that it was the religious beliefs held by Calvinists that hastened the arrival of a capitalist system in Europe. Many of the Eastern religions were 'anti-materialist', i.e. they did not value the possession of goods – essential for the survival of capitalism.

However, this view can be criticised by arguing that it was the other way around. Protestantism developed in countries where capitalism was already starting to develop. In addition to this, other highly capitalistic countries such as Japan do not have a Protestant tradition.

Conclusion

The theories of Comte and Durkheim are referred to as 'teleological', i.e. they explain norms, values and customs by referring to the particular end they serve. Functionalists, for example, explain the existence of social customs by explaining the purpose that they serve, i.e. to maintain society as a whole. These theories can therefore be criticised for assuming that all human action is purposeful, which others might argue is not.

For consideration:

1 According to all four writers, what is the social function of religion?
2 In what ways are the classical theories expressed above both similar, and different, to the contemporary sociological theories?

66 99 Key Definition

The 'conscience collective' was for Durkheim, the existence of one social and moral order, i.e. a shared set of beliefs and values of the individuals making up traditional societies. He argued that it could act as a force on the individual that in turn produced a consensual society. The problem for Durkheim, however, was that as societies modernised, this 'conscience collective' was weakened.

● Synoptic Link

Use Marx's views on religion to provide a synoptic link between religion and stratification – more specifically – class. Remember that Marx viewed religion as an ideology that created a false picture of what reality was, according to him, really about – the exploitation of the proletariat by the bourgeoisie. Religion helped maintain a system where the stratification of the classes existed and prevented the working classes from realizing that revolution was the way to end an unjust capitalist system.

✳ Key Idea

By taking Weber's idea that there is something 'religious' in the everyday act of work, it is possible to make links with both the New Right and New Left government approach to policy. Both views stress the 'moral' aspect to living life on a day-to-day basis, of 'hard work' and 'sensible' investment. These components were, according to Weber, a vital component within the Calvinist tradition – a tradition that Weber argued was responsible for the success of capitalism.

6.7 What is the functionalist view on religion?

What does this mean?

Durkheim was convinced that religion played a crucial role in how societies worked. Remember that Durkheim was a consensual sociologist who believed that shared norms and values were essential in 'functional' societies ('consensual' meaning that societies and individuals in general were *not* in conflict). Since 1912, other functionalists have adapted and developed his ideas to examine the role that religion plays as one of society's biggest institutions.

What functions does religion fulfill?

1   Durkheim (1912) argues that religion demonstrates the moral superiority of society over the individual.
2   Functionalist Malinowski (1954) argues that the function of religion is to bond the community together at times of stress or danger.
3   American sociologist Talcott Parsons (1977) argues that religions provide 'core' values which in turn produce social solidarity. Parsons' version of functionalism in the 1950s was referred to as 'structural functionalism'.

How does Durkheim argue these functions are fulfilled?

Durkheim argued that religion was a social construction. He said that religion reinforced the 'collective conscience' by providing regular opportunities to establish and reinforce shared values and moral beliefs. Durkheim said that social life can be split into the 'sacred' (things to do with religion) and the 'profane' (things which are not). By bringing people together in the shared experience of religious ceremonies, the sacred affects the profane because people recognise the benefits of the social group (and society) and their dependence upon it. By doing this people automatically accept the importance that society has over them.

Durkheim argued that the symbols or '**totems**' that most religions use (e.g. statues, carvings, and pictures) help make the process of this continuous shared experience an easy one. Durkheim studied the Arunta an Australian Aboriginal tribe. He showed that totems were seen as sacred, i.e. considered religious by the clan, but also as profane by being clan emblems. This combination of both sacred and profane served to unite members of the tribe into a form of collective unity.

✳ Key Idea

Durkheim's concept of the 'conscience collective' is vital in any 'sociology of religion' exam (see also section 6). Durkheim argued that the collective conscience was far stronger before 'The Enlightenment' (see section 16) because people were controlled through various religious or traditional networks, whereas in the 'modern' world, the collective conscience is weaker because of the growth of individualism.

Aboriginals from Australia have their rituals – what 'rituals' do you have?

66 99 Key Definition

For Durkheim the most elementary form of religion is '**totemism**' – the belief that animals and plants have supernatural powers. In his study of the Arunta tribe he found that their totems were the lizard, caterpillar, rat, cockatoo and plum tree. The totem symbolised both 'God' and the 'clan' of Aborigines, i.e. being both 'sacred' and 'profane'. Talking about the totem Durkheim writes: 'if then, it is at once the symbol of god and of society, is this not because god and society are one and the same thing?' (Durkheim, 1912: in Stephens et al., 1998: p. 407).

How does Malinowski argue these functions are fulfilled?

While many functionalists argue that religion at all times helps to sustain social solidarity some argue that this only happens in times of transition and stress. Functionalist Malinowski shows this in his 1954 study of the Trobriand Islanders. These South Pacific fishermen had a number of prayer rituals they would perform before going out in the open sea. However, they would not perform these when sailing in the safety of the lagoon. Malinowski argued that the danger these fisherman faced by fishing in the open sea was a threat to the stability of the community, hence the prayer rituals.

How does Parsons argue these functions are fulfilled?

As a structural functionalist Parsons agrees with much that Durkheim said. Writing in 1950s America, he argued that religion provided core values and enhanced social solidarity. It also set up a framework for human action by which people's conduct could be judged. By combining concepts of the sacred and the profane the norms and values of the American political and social system were heavily informed by a framework that reflected Protestant values (e.g. 'God Bless America' is a chant quite often heard at the beginning of American baseball matches).

However, he also agreed with Malinowski that religion 'comforts' people in times of stress. For those who are close to death or who know people that have died it promises an after-life (or a chance of reincarnation). Religious places have served as important destinations to gather in times of war or threat to the community. In the former Soviet bloc countries, churches were quite often used as meeting places to discuss courses of action by those being oppressed. In London, during the Second World War, people would often gather in local churches during the blitz. Social solidarity in both these cases was strengthened as a result.

Conclusion

Drawing on the ideas of Durkheim some sociologists argue that the 'sacred' still exists today albeit in a wider form. Interpretivist Bellah (1967) and interactionist Luckman (1996) both argue that religion is being transformed rather than in decline. With the concept of 'transformation' they are able to argue that while 'public' forms of religion may well be in decline, personal belief and individual practice lives on in 'private' (whatever variety of forms that may take).

✓ Top Exam Hint

Score high evaluation by recognising that the word 'religion' can be interpreted in a number of ways. Interpretivist Bellah's (1970) concept of 'civil religion' shows the different interpretations of the word. His reference to 'Americanism' as a 'civil religion' with values rooted in the Protestant religion indicate that whatever 'godly' religion people believed, faith in the American way of life came above other beliefs they had. Refer to this in the conclusion as a thoughtful way of evaluating the concept 'religion'.

✻ Key Idea

Functionalist Robert Bocock (1985) refers to 'civic rituals' in which he argues that it is not just religion that provides us with ways to reinforce cultural values. If we are to take sporting events, theatre, cinema and even shopping, we can provide examples of how a 'sense of belonging' to society is culturally reproduced in non-religious ways. This idea can be used to criticise the importance that some sociologists place on religion as the main source for cultural values.

For consideration:

1   Functionalists argue that the rituals in religions reinforce cultural values and provide a sense of belonging. What other non-religious rituals do the same thing?
2   How might the American flag be argued to be both sacred and profane?

6.8   What is the Marxist view of religion?

Synoptic Link

Highlight the role that religion plays in maintaining the class system, something that most Marxists and neo-Marxists would agree with, e.g. Althusser. Marxists argue that religion not only acts as an ideological tool of the state but also allows people to live a false consciousness, i.e. to forget they are living in a class-ridden society. According to some Marxists, the promise of an 'after-life' can mean that people are prepared to 'suffer in silence' rather than change the nature of the society they live in.

❝❞ Key Definition

The Marxist term **'alienation'** refers to the idea that modern conditions at work, i.e. mechanisation results in repetitive tasks that are no longer satisfying to the worker but boring and breed resentment (see also chapter 3, section 15). The worker who lacks dignity makes no profit and only has their own worth to sell on an hourly, weekly or monthly basis. The worker is separated from what was once the 'skill' of the job, for example they are no longer a craftsman but a production line worker. For Marx it is the capitalist/ruling class that has placed the worker in this situation.

What does this mean?

Marxist sociologists concentrate on the ways in which religion reinforces the status quo. They argue that it acts as a conservative force, in that it upholds (or conserves) the ruling class and maintains the social and economic order through ideological control.

Why was Marx critical of religion as an institution?

Marx (1884) said that 'Man makes religion, religion does not make man . . . Religion is the sigh of the oppressed creature, the heart of the heartless world . . . It is the opium of the people'. You can use the quotation and apply the following points of evaluation in the exam.

- Marx argued that the capitalist system **alienates** and exploits people and that religion, rather than challenging the capitalist system, allows people to escape within their own beliefs.

- In most religions people are taught that if they suffer in this world their reward will come in the next – this view also stops people from challenging the capitalist system.

- By preaching words like 'honour', 'respect' and 'obey', religion can be seen as a method of social control whereby people accept rather than challenge the status quo.

How can religion challenge the idea of democracy?

Marxists argue that religion is an ideology, i.e. a system of thoughts and ideas that works in the interests of those in power. Until the enlightenment period of the 17th and 18th centuries, kings and queens in many western European countries reigned by 'divine right' (i.e. with God's consent). The acceptance of this ideology has been used by Marxists to show how religion legitimised both the oppression of the working classes and the privileges of the ruling classes. The automatic assumption that people are, by the right of God, allowed to rule over others is, for Marxists, a direct challenge to the meaning of democracy.

A distortion of real class relations

Marxists argue that an important ideological function of religion was to distort or hide the true nature of the division between the classes. The injustices of the capitalist system can be 'hidden' by the 'false consciousness' experienced when ruling and subject classes come under one roof in a place of worship. The illusion created is one in which there is a unity when, in fact, there is division based upon exploitation and alienation.

Even the tradition of the 'holy' institution of marriage is, for Marxists, a way to maintain property rights from one generation to another. By automatically accepting such traditions, Marxists argue that we fail to see an alternative where property might be shared communally.

A Marxist Utopia

Religion was, for Marx, an agent of social control in that by creating 'gods' and the belief in an after-life, people ceased to realize the exploitation that the capitalist system created. Any thoughts of rebelling against any state system could be threatened with 'eternal damnation'. Marx wanted a revolution that would change the nature of society as he saw it. He argued that the religious after-life that many religions wrote about where all humans could be treated fairly could be created today on earth once the capitalist system had been overthrown. He called this new society 'Utopia'.

Conclusion

Can religion alone bring about social change? If you are a Marxist then the answer to this question is 'no'! Marx argued that infrastructural change, i.e. changes in the economic structure of any society (most importantly, from one epoch to another) will carry with it superstructural change (family, legal system, educational system, religion, and so on). In other words, for Marx, profound social change always has an economic base and that the superstructure (e.g. religion) can only, at best, attempt to fit in with or reinforce the necessities of the economy.

> ### For consideration:
>
> 1   What recent events in the media have had a religious connection?
> 2   How might Marxists argue that these events have been used to maintain the capitalist system?

Princess Diana's funeral – religious mourning or a celebration of British nationalism?

What does Weber say about religion?

Can the ideas of classical sociologist Max Weber be applied to societies today?

66 99 Key Definition

For Weber, the 'spirit of capitalism' is the pursuit and renewal of profit together with the application of calculation and rational book-keeping. Such 'rationalism' was something he argued, that Calvinists have been extremely good at. Calvinism, a version of Christianity, stressed values of hard work along with a contempt for squandering money on trivial items. Therefore, as a large body of people, Calvinists were far more likely to become economically successful than other groups that did not possess such an everyday approach to life.

✳ Key Idea

Max Weber argued that as societies 'modernised', i.e. transformed from a mainly agrarian/farming way of life to the more industrialized way of living associated with cities, they became more 'rational'. 'Rationalisation' for Max Weber meant that societies increasingly use logic to solve problems whereas before traditional societies may have used religion and traditions to solve day-to-day problems. Weber used the German word 'zweckrational' to describe this process and this type of thinking.

What does this mean?

Max Weber saw religion as an agent for social change. In his book *The Protestant Ethic and the Spirit of Capitalism* published in 1905, Weber took the transition from the feudal system to the capitalist system as a case study to look at the importance of religion and ideology to the creation of major social change.

Why was Weber so interested in the Protestant religion?

Weber identifies all of the earliest capitalist countries as Protestant ones, rather than Roman Catholic, Islamic, Buddhist, or any other particular religion. He deduces from this that there must be something about Protestantism which makes it 'fit' capitalism and which encourages capitalist ways of looking at the world and acting within it (he calls this the '**spirit of capitalism**' and it is perhaps worth noting that even as a sociologist he was using words that reflected the highly religious influences of his time). Weber focuses on a particular type of Protestantism, Calvinism, because in countries which demonstrated Western capitalism the entrepreneurs and skilled workers were Calvinists.

How did this work?

Weber claimed that there are a number of factors within the Calvinist tradition that helped accelerate the processes of capitalism. The belief that hard work was rewarded by God was known as the 'work ethic'. The old expression '*the devil makes work for idle hands*' summed up the idea that hard work was rewarded by God and this meant that people worked efficiently and did not waste time. The Calvinist concept of vocation meant that work was a 'calling' and had to be done for the greater glory of God.

Calvinists also believed that they must work as hard as they can in this life to look for signs of God blessing them with (material) success. However, they also believed that it was wrong to spend money on frivolous objects and this meant that the money they earned was usually reinvested in ways that would generate more wealth later on, e.g. in land, machinery and tools. The belief that lending money at interest was not sinful combined with the relatively high literacy rates of Calvinists (Bible reading was considered essential to the religion) went hand-in-hand with the essential skills required for the entrepreneur.

What was Weber's methodoloby?

Weber was an historian who looked at the documentary evidence left from the past, but, as a structuralist sociologist, he attempted to find underlying patterns rather than simply deal with unique historical events. By using '*verstehen*' sociology Weber attempted to understand what it was like to be a typical Protestant and how this type of person would differ from somebody from a different religion. His 'ideal type' of Protestant was not any specific real religious group, but rather consisted of generalisations that included aspects of every different Protestant group. He intentionally created a 'model' to help analyse aspects of the Protestant way of looking at the world.

What do sociologists learn from Weber?

Weber's research shows that religious forces are important in their own right in creating very significant socio-economic change. It also shows how ideological factors shape economic and other behaviour. While Weber agreed with much of Marx's writings, he challenged a lot of the 'economic determinism' of Marx, i.e. the way that the economy shapes our institutions (e.g. the family, religion and the media) and our individual actions. However, it is not just the economy that shapes people's lives for Weber – his work has been taken to show that religion can influence social change.

Conclusion

In many societies today there is increased pressure on workers to work long hours as they fear being seen by bosses as shirking responsibilities if they arrive or leave on time. For Weber this type of uniform lifestyle is a characteristic of the standardized organization and reproduction of capitalism and its ever-continuing pursuit of profit.

For consideration:

1. In what other ways can religion be connected to the growth of capitalism in the 21st century?
2. How does Weberianism differ in its approach to religion compared to functionalism and Marxism?

66 99 Key Definition

The concept known as '*verstehen*' has always been associated with the work of Max Weber and is the attempt to understand the world from inside the head of someone else. The sociologist adopting this approach places the interpretation of the person they are studying at the centre of their own research.

✳ Key Idea

Do people of the same religion share the same religious experience (i.e. do all practicing Jews have similar thoughts, feelings and experiences of being 'Jewish'?) Max Weber challenged this idea with the notion of 'theodicies of privilege and non-privilege' ('theodicy' is a set of religious ideas which explain why people are in a certain social position). Religion is a set of ideas and beliefs that explain the existence of god/s. But the theodicy of the rich will be very different from the theodicy of the poor. While the rich have little to 'complain' about, the poor will see their religion as a way of justifying their unhappy existence.

● Synoptic Link

Use Max Weber's concept of 'theodicies of privilege and non-privilege' to make a synoptic link between religion and stratification. Some groups may develop a theodicy of disprivilege. For example, the Jews historically have seen themselves both as the 'chosen people' and subject to persecution. Quite often historically they have been placed in the lower strata of society (e.g. in ancient Egyptian times and more recently during the Nazi era). The poverty that they endured was made bearable by what they perceived was 'salvation' in the next life – such salvation was seen as compensation for the hardship they endured.

6.10 What is the neo-Marxist view on religion?

Friedrich Engels (1820–1895) – 'Co-founder' of Marxism and inspiration for many branches of modern feminism

☞ Who is this Person?

Friedrich Engels (1820–1895) was born into a wealthy family of mill owners in Germany. This influenced his critical outlook on life that was later to develop with the working relationship he had with Marx. In their many writing partnerships, some argue it is difficult to tell who wrote what. Involved in the European revolutions of 1848, they went into exile in England where Engels helped build the German socialist movement. An inspiration to feminists, Engels also wrote much on the subordination of women in modern societies.

✳ Key Idea

Turner (1991) was also interested in the ways religion controls sexuality and gender roles through inheritance of property and property rights through institutions such as marriage. Remember that until recently males (rather than females) in most societies inherited property. This meant that female gender roles were being socialised into norms and values that gave little or no material rights to women. The church sanctioned these extraordinary male powers with the words 'love, honour and obey' that the woman would have to repeat in the church marriage service.

What does this mean?

Marxist ideas argue that conflict exists between those who own the means of production and those who don't (and therefore have to sell their own labour to stay alive). Marx argued that the capitalist system is oppressive and class-based and religion helps people not to realise this. By 'neo-Marxism' sociologists refer to any theory or form of sociological analysis that takes and develops these ideas – the ideas of Karl Marx and Friedrich Engels.

Humanist and materialist forms of Marxism

When trying to classify different types of neo-Marxist writers it is helpful to recognise the different strands to Marx's writings, from which other writers have drawn their influences. Humanist Marxist approaches tend to focus on the importance of ideology and individual 'consciousness,' whereas materialist forms of Marxism are more concerned with universal laws that can be applied to all types of society. Both approaches are helpful when looking at the sociology of religion.

A dominant ideology?

Abercrombie and Turner (1978) question to what extent religion acted as a 'dominant' ideology controlling people in the interests of the ruling classes in the way that Marx (1845) had argued. They stress that economic and repressive control was far more effective than religion as a way of controlling the masses. Neo-Marxist Turner (1991) also argues that the nature of capitalism has changed. Whereas once it was possible to identify exploitation at the hands of individual members of the elite class, he argues that now business corporations dominate capital. Arguing that secularisation is taking place, he says that religion is no longer the social or moral force that it once was.

However, Turner also challenges many orthodox Marxist writers on the role that religion has actually played in the shaping of ideas. Taking Christianity in Europe as an example, from the period of the Middle Ages onwards, many peasants practised far older religions than the state-determined forms of Christianity (e.g. Catholicism and the Church of England). If that is the case, Turner argues that religion could not possibly have had the ideological effects that some Marxist writers claim.

Goods not Gods

Neo-Marxist Marcuse (1964) argues, like orthodox Marxists, that religion acts as a source of oppression on the working classes, stopping them from resisting the exploitative nature of the capitalist system. However, in an argument that supports the secularisation thesis, he argues that 'commodity fetishism' (the idea that we are obsessed with buying new products regardless of whether we really need them) will bring about a new 'god' that will replace the older religions – the god of 'consumerism'.

Marx argued that commodity fetishism is an inevitable capitalist process where goods take on a worth that is unrepresentative of the labour that went into it. For example, the price of a box of chocolates in one part of the world can be the same as an emergency trip to the doctor in another. Marcuse argued that as we become hungry for consumer goods, the older religions will cease to have meaning. Through institutions such as the media, this new religion will once again stop the working classes from realising the exploitative nature of capitalism.

Liberation theology

This is one example of where Marxist ideas have been developed alongside a religious set of beliefs. This blend of South American Catholicism with Marxism argues for social change. Christ is pictured as a 'revolutionary' who wished liberation for all people who were oppressed.

Attacking government corruption and exploitation, some of these Catholic revolutionaries supported the notorious rebel Sandinista movement against the government in Nicaragua in the late 1970s. Liberation theology is therefore one example of a religious movement committed to social change. A second example can be seen in Poland during the 1980s where the Catholic Church was often used as a meeting place for those wishing to bring down the communist government.

Conclusion

The ideas of Max Weber can be used to criticise both Marxists and neo-Marxists, who generally agree that religion does not bring about social change but rather is a force for conservatism. By looking at the development of capitalism in the aftermath of Protestantism (Calvinism) Weber argued that religion *can* bring about social change under the right conditions. By using the example of the liberation theology and pointing to leaders like Gandhi in India, and the events in Poland where the communist government was overthrown, neo-Marxist ideas can be criticised showing how religion can act as a powerful force for change.

For consideration:

1 To what extent do you believe that neo-Marxism is very different from orthodox Marxist approaches?
2 Think of as many religious leaders as you can. How many of these would have been described as 'revolutionaries' in their time?

◆ **What, When and Why?**

A Western movement of thought that generally started after the Second World War, Neo-Marxists developed the ideas of Marx and his followers in the 19th century. They started from analysing why the revolution that Marx predicted did not/has not yet taken place. Two strong branches of neo-Marxism are identifiable: those influenced by the Frankfurt School (a group of German Marxists who argued that the capitalist ruling class use the mass media and popular culture to shape society's thinking), who focus on the importance of 'culture' in maintaining middle-class hegemony; and structuralist ideas that focus on how 'structures' of language, thought or institutions maintain middle-class hegemony.

✳ **Key Idea**

Steve Chapman (2002) argues that the fact that liberation theology was disowned by the Catholic church is useful in lending support to the Marxist idea that the Church and mainstream religions in general can be ideological tools of capitalist states.

6.11 What is the interpretive view on religion?

What does this mean?

Structural (or 'macro') approaches to religion tend to argue that religion as an institution shapes or determines the way we are. However, interpretivist sociologists Berger and Luckmann (1967) argue that throughout human history religion has played a major role in how social actors (people) shape, determine and make sense of the universe around them.

Rather than seeing social actors (or humans) as being shaped, interpretivist sociologists focus on the meanings that religion has for its many different followers. In particular they focus on the meanings of certain symbols, rituals, beliefs and religious experiences. They are also interested in the sense of community provided by many religious organizations and the way that they contribute to a socially constructed reality.

The importance of symbols

Many religions use symbols, e.g. the cross (Christians); the crescent moon and star (Muslims); the Star of David (Jews). We have already seen how Durkheim stressed the importance of symbols to indicate what was to be considered sacred. Symbols are also used to separate the sacred from the profane. Daniel Bell (1973) argues that individuals *create* religious meaning because it meets fundamental and ever present emotional needs that all human beings possess. Philosophical questions such as 'What is mankind?' and 'Who am I?' are answered relatively easily if one has strong religious beliefs.

Berger and Luckman (1967) argue that individuals create, socially construct and develop reality by searching for meanings. For them, religion represents a means of constructing a social framework of meaning for people (i.e. a set of ideas and related values that allows them to make sense of the world). Interpretive sociologists argue that humans attach meanings to objects and events which they then use to communicate with others.

Interpretivists are particularly interested in the feelings of awe, reverence or hatred that such symbols evoke. We need to remember that many images, while worshipped by one group, can also symbolise the oppression of one religion by another (e.g. many Palestinians will not have the same feelings attached to the Star of David that most Israelis share). Either way, such images are a 'short hand' that convey shared knowledge about the customs and traditions of the religion, culture and identity of the person worshipping the particular symbol in question.

The importance of rituals

It is not only physical objects like the cross that can be described as symbols. Many religious rituals such as Jewish circumcision or kneeling in front of religious statues symbolise the feeling of reverence and respect for the deity in question. These rituals follow on from the particular beliefs of a religion that are often made up of values that are designed to show how people should lead their lives.

Remember that many interpretive sociologists argue that religion provides cultural meanings and a way for people to construct their identities (e.g. 'I am a Muslim'; 'I am a Sikh'). Interactionist Berger argues that a meaningful world is created for social actors by the use of mutually understandable symbols and rituals that create the sense of shared community found in many religions. By doing this, religions create order and meaning in people's existence.

A bleak outlook

Berger is however quite pessimistic about the role that religion plays in today's world. With the growth of technology, science and the media, traditional religion is plunged into a crisis of credibility, i.e. people no longer accept that religion offers answers to problems in the way that it once appeared to.

He goes on to argue that the loss in certainty and the fear of a loss in identity causes (and here he draws in the work of Durkheim) feelings of 'meaninglessness' or 'anomie'. He concludes that religion for so long a way of giving meaning to life, no longer has the power to do this.

For consideration:

1 Why do you think many churches are extremely tall with high ceilings?
2 How might a sociologist analyse the use of the word 'crusade' by American President George Bush after 11 September, 2001?

✓ **Top Exam Hint**

Remember to use the concepts 'reliability' and 'validity' (see chapter 2) when talking about interpretive sociological research. Because so much interpretive sociology is about individual, subjective meanings, it is very difficult for the sociologists who practice this to claim their work is 'reliable'; however, they may well wish to describe it as 'valid'. Students will gain evaluation marks for simply stating this in the exam. For a suitable conclusion mention these points there.

6.12 What is the feminist view on religion?

What does this mean?

Feminist sociology has two major concerns when focusing on religion.

1 What roles do women occupy within the various religious institutions?
2 What role does **patriarchy** play within religion?

Many feminists argue that religious institutions and beliefs help legitimise gender inequality. By studying these institutions and movements we can examine to what extent women's role and status is constructed by religion and to what extent religion oppresses women.

Women, witchcraft and medicine

The witch hunts were a 17th century phenomenon particularly strong in America where many women were tortured and burnt because they were believed to be witches. It seems strange that many women were burnt as witches for their ability to heal others. One argument for this is that the power women demonstrated threatened the newly emerging 'sciences' that were, at the time, dominated by men. Post-structuralist Michel Foucault (1974) argued that during the 19th and 20th centuries even women's bodies were, through the discourse of medicine, subject to male control (e.g. gynaecology) because the doctors were male. By 'discourse', Foucault meant the collection of related statements or events which define what we take for granted within a particular area of knowledge.

Women, Christianity and Islam

Grace Davie (1994) argues that not only do more women than men attend Christian services but they also view 'God' differently. Whereas men view their God in terms of power and control, women view God in terms of love, comfort and forgiveness. Many churches forbid the priesthood to women and Christian churches generally do not endorse either abortion or female homosexuality and bisexuality.

The popular (but very controversial!) conception of women within the Islamic religions is one of oppression due to the wearing of the veil, the tolerance of male to female violence (but not vice versa) and women's inferior legal status. However, such views are typically ethnocentric. Many Islamic feminists argue that the veil is liberating as it frees women from the predatory gaze of men. The wearing of traditional clothing is also seen as a cultural resistance to the effects of globalisation and/or Westernisation.

Fundamentalism and gender

Diversity and change can bring about fear and uncertainty and therefore, in some cases, a desire to return to traditional values. In rapidly changing times fundamentalists (e.g. Christian and Islamic) are attracted to (and find comfort in) the idea of women and men who have clearly defined norms, values and roles. The fear of change leads to a widening of the gender boundaries as a result.

A word of warning. While many writers argue that 'fundamentalism' (e.g. Christian and Islamic) has a negative effect on women (reducing many of the freedoms won by feminists during the course of the 20th century) good sociologists will appreciate that this view can be criticised for being ethnocentric. Such views are often held by white, middle-class academics and are therefore often biased. Many fundamentalists are themselves women who believe in the 'liberation' offered by the religious choices they have made.

Women and religious movements

Women have played a decisive, yet historically understated, role within the development of religious movements. Mary Wollstonecraft, one of the first feminists, wrote *A Vindication of the Rights of Women* in 1792. In the 19th century, it was Ellen White who set up the Seventh Day Adventists and Elizabeth Fry had enormous influence within the Quaker movement with her work on prison reform.

Writing about more recent 'New Age' movements, Bruce (1995) argues that there is a gender divide evident in the types of movement that women and men play a part in. He argues that women play a major role in complementary medicine (e.g. homeopathy) whereas men tend to be more involved in parapsychology (e.g. seeking causal explanations for poltergeists).

Conclusion

State-endorsed religious institutions (e.g. the Church of England) tend to emphasise the 'traditional' role of women within the family, for example by stressing the 'natural' maternal role of the woman (this reduces the opportunity for paid employment for women). We have also seen that many religions exclude women from key positions within their organisations, e.g. the Catholic priesthood. Finally, the emphasis on marriage and monogamy (having only one relationship) that most religions have, tends, historically, to be harder on women than men (i.e. women are judged more harshly than men if they have another relationship outside of marriage).

For consideration:

1   How does religion support the 'ideology' of family life?
2   How might religion support the notion of female obedience to their husbands?

✓ Top Exam Hint

Show the examiners excellent evaluation skills by applying the ideas of Anthony Giddens to the term 'fundamentalism'. 'Fundamentalism' is used to describe forms of religion that take literally the words of the scriptures (e.g. those of both Christians and Muslims). Christian and Islamic fundamentalists share a fear of change which often results in a non-acceptance of other viewpoints. Giddens argues that fundamentalist ideas are a way of rejecting modern society.

☞ Who is this Person?

Mary Wollstonecraft (1759-97) was an early champion of women's rights. A teacher, governess, translator and then literary advisor, she famously wrote the *Vindication of the Rights of Women*, which was a publication that argued for equality between the sexes. She was a strong supporter of the French Revolution and her ideas have been influential in the history of the liberal feminism movement.

What are churches, denominations, sects and cults?

What does this mean?

Sociologists differ in their views as to what 'churches', 'sects', 'cults' and 'denominations' are. However, providing you explain what you mean by these terms, the examiners will evaluate your work and award you marks according to your interpretation.

What is the difference between churches and denominations?

- Although definitions vary, most sociologists agree that by 'Church' we are referring to a large organisation quite often linked to the state, e.g. the Church of England. Members of churches tend to 'conform', i.e. go along with the norms and values of the society the church is in.

- Stark and Bainbridge (1985) describe denominations as 'diluted' churches. While denominations are separate from the state, they do not reject ideas held by the majority of society. However, while still highly bureaucratic and following many of the ideas of the established churches, they are open to new ideas and less inclined to follow the strict ceremonies associated with churches, e.g. the Methodists.

What are sects?

While often associated with a more deviant image, sects are generally what are called 'world-affirming' new religious movements, i.e. they do not challenge the way things are in the world. While often critical of other religious movements, nevertheless they tolerate their existence.

Some sects are described as being 'millenarian' movements which means that followers believe at some point the world will end (referred to as 'Armageddon') and that God will save them while not saving other groups of religious believers. Examples of these are the Jehovah's Witnesses. Other sects can be described as 'reformist', i.e. they want to reform or change society, but not in any radical or revolutionary way. One example of this type are the Quakers.

✓ Top Exam Hint

Examiners will offer high evaluation marks if they see that students are thinking about the data they write about. One very obvious weakness in much of the sociological literature is the fact that most of it is based around 'white' religious movements. This allows the sociology student in the exam to criticise the literature for being 'ethnocentric', i.e. written from a very 'white' perspective.

◆ What, When and Why?

One recent example of a sect that hit the newspapers was the Raelian Religious Sect in America. In December 2002 it announced that it had created a viable embryo from tissue samples from an unnamed American woman. The sect believes life on earth was created by aliens.

What are cults?

Cults are 'world-rejecting' religious movements or protest groups who are highly critical of the more established religions, churches and denominations. They tend to be quite small and elitist with highly committed members who often reject societies' norms and values. Members are usually asked to cut ties with family and friends. Like sects, some are described as being 'millenarian' movements. Examples include the American People's Temple where approximately 900 members took part in mass suicide in Guyana in 1978.

Some cults are 'manipulationist', i.e. they tend to be led by charismatic individuals that promise to 'unlock' spiritual powers, and, quite often through the use of meditation promise increased personal awareness and ability. The Scientologists are one example of this.

Why do sects and cults grow?

- Weber argued that those who felt marginalised (left out) in society could be drawn into either a cult or sect. The close-knit networks of support these organisations offer can provide marginalised individuals with a feeling of belonging (as well as offering food, comfort and in some cases shelter).

- Some individuals join either sects or cults because of the so-called 'exclusivity' they offer. If on joining individuals are made to feel they are special (some organisations require donations of money) then this feeling can quite often make up for the poor status that individual may have felt they had prior to joining the movement.

- The *Church–Sect cycle theory* can be applied to how some sects and cults are created. For churches to remain popular over long periods of time they have to make compromises (e.g. the growth of female Anglican priests over the last ten years). Such changes upset members of that particular church. Some members then decide to break away and form a new organisation. The new organisation (cult or sect) attracts recruits who come from economically poor backgrounds. This poverty is something that is seen in a highly positive light by the movement they join. The sect (or cult) grows in membership and the circle is completed when the sect takes on church-like characteristics. According to this theory the process will start again as new sects are formed as a result of some members leaving when disillusioned with the new organisation. The Methodist church has been described as a sect.

For consideration:

1 How easy is it to use Wallis' categories to describe all the different religious groups you can think of?
2 What does this tell you about using such categories?

Thinking like a Sociologist

Three evaluations you can use in the exam to describe religious groups come from the three classifications of Roy Wallis (1984).

1 *World-rejecting groups* whose members are hostile to the world around them.
2 *World-accommodating groups* whose members largely ignore the world around them.
3 *World-affirming groups* whose members largely accept the world but try to focus on making individuals feel better and more successful within the world they operate.

Key Idea

There are two possible problems that some sects or cults may face.

1 Reliance on a charismatic leader can mean that once that leader has died then so too does the organisation.
2 Those 'millenarian' organisations, which predict that the world will end, weaken their legitimacy if that prediction is believed to be unfounded.

What are new religious movements and why have they grown?

✓ Top Exam Hint

Introducing any question on new religious movements can be done by arguing that religious movements of one sort or another have tried to do one of two things. Either they try to offer a way of dealing with the way the world is or they try to transform the world into something completely different. By remembering these two very different solutions you can offer the examiner a number of evaluative similarities or differences throughout your answer.

● Synoptic Link

A theory associated with crime and deviance, Merton's (1938) Strain Theory offers five ways people respond to the 'strain' of living in modern societies. You might like to apply these to the religious movements you learn about:

- *Conformity* where no form of deviance takes place.
- *Innovation* where the failure to succeed in society draws individuals to commit criminal or deviant acts.
- *Ritualism* where people lose sight of the 'goal' of their existence but 'go through the motions' anyway.
- *Retreatism* where people drop out of society.
- *Rebellion* where people reject dominant norms and values and replace these with their own.

What does this mean?

The term 'New Religious Movements' is used by contemporary sociologists to recognise the enormous variety of religious organisations that have come into existence in recent decades. This has occurred at the same time that membership of much large-scale, mainstream religions has declined.

Indigenous and imported new religious movements

Roy Wallis (1984) describes *indigenous* new religious movements as those movements that drew on Judeo-Christianity, but developed into extremely enthusiastic and distinct versions of the original. One example being the 'Jesus People' popular with young people in the USA in the late 1960s. *Imported* new religious movements drew on distinctly different religious traditions quite often from Asian countries. One example popular in most Western cities are the familiar Hare Krishna devotees (usually dressed in white or orange and with shaven heads), followers of Krishna, who developed a form of Hinduism.

How were some new religious movements influenced by psychology?

Scientology, originally a form of self-help psychotherapy, has now finally been incorporated as a 'church' in America. Popular in the 1970s, scientologists received counselling, at a cost of several thousand pounds, in order to get back powers of spirituality that humans once possessed many centuries ago. Increased intelligence, the ability to function better at work and the reduction in psychological illness are the promised benefits of Scientology.

In a similar vein, Erhard Seminars Training (EST) drew on the ideas of Freud. Rather than emphasising collective ritual or worship it was designed as a way for an individual to achieve their full potential and promised 'to transform your ability to experience living'. Popular today with some of the 'Hollywood set', i.e. many Hollywood actors, directors and successful film makers, such movements are individualistic and are run more as multinational businesses rather than on traditional religious lines.

World rejecting and world accommodating new religious movements

Both Scientology and EST can be described as 'world affirming', i.e. they do not challenge the way the world actually works. Wallis offers two more ways of analysing new religious movements: 'world rejecting' and 'world accommodating'. By 'world rejecting' he refers to those new religious movements that reject the 'corrupt' world around them. As separate communities that believe in Christ, they anticipate some sort of spiritual revolution. One such group is 'the Children of God'.

By 'world accommodating', Wallis describes groups that do not wish to separate themselves from the rest of society but rather their religious practices allow them to carry on normal family and work life. Neo-Pentecostalists are one such group who are committed Christians who believe that the more orthodox religions (including mainstream Christianity) have become bureaucratized in modern times and have lost some of the vitality and spirituality that religion, in their eyes, should have.

Who joins new religious movements?

Norman Cohn's study *The Pursuit of the Millennium* (1970) argued that many religious movements were most likely to emerge during times of famine or war. Members were recruited from the 'dispossessed poor' and believed that their lives would change for the better as a result of joining the movement. Max Weber suggested that religion helped the underprivileged in a society cope with their situation by giving meaning to people's suffering. Weber termed this 'the theodicy of non-privilege'.

However, while popular opinion might suggest that new religious movements are made up of predominantly marginalised people, some research suggests otherwise. Eileen Barker's study of the Moonies and Wallis's study of Scientology for instance, both point out that the typical member of these new religious movements is middle-class, young, fairly well-educated, and often predominantly female.

Conclusion

In what Max Weber would refer to as a 'disenchanted world' modernity brings with it 'fragmentation'. By this he means that in more traditional societies the family would work *together* on the land in what were closer forms of community life. In today's competitive world fragmentation happens when children are separated from adults in schools and colleges and couples have separate professional careers. As a result some middle-class professionals search for their 'real selves' and join a new social movement to counteract their feelings of 'disenchantment'.

For consideration:

1　What are the differences in the functionalist concept of *anomie*, the Marxist concept of *alienation*, and the Weberian concept of *disenchantment*?
2　How could you apply these concepts when discussing why people join new religious movements?

A Moonie mass wedding. Eileen Barker explored reasons why people joined the sect known as The Moonies

◆ What, When and Why?

Sun Myung Moon's members of his 'Unification Church' (the 'Moonies') believed that it was down to the Moonies to bring about a 'physical kingdom of God'. A synthesis of Western and Eastern culture and founded in 1954, members would abandon homes, families and friends. Eileen Barker's (1984) study argued, however, that brainwashing did not occur. Those joining were individuals interested in religion and spirituality, often not needing much convincing to join. Membership rates indicated a rapid turnover of members, i.e. many people would be continuously joining and leaving the organisation.

✳ Key Idea

Stark and Bainbridge argue organised religion offers 'compensators' to those who do not achieve great health, wealth or happiness. People who are materially satisfied but who are relatively deprived (psychologically, spiritually), might need compensators to help them deal with this. When mainstream religions become more secular, people turn to other religious groups in order to gain the benefits of 'compensators'. New religious movements are able to fulfil this function, and it is the relatively deprived who are most likely to join such groups.

6.15 What is religious pluralism?

What does this mean?

Religious pluralism refers to the different forms of Christian and non-Christian beliefs along with all other types of religion that we have looked at in this chapter, e.g. Scientology, animism, and so on. Closely associated with the secularisation debate, the idea of 'religious pluralism' assumes that the mainstream religions (e.g. Christianity, Islam, Judaism) no longer appeal to all members of society. Instead what is in place is a 'market-place' of different religions where we are at liberty to pick and choose in the same way a consumer might do. This choice could be referred to as spiritual shopping.

Religious plurality or religious intolerance? Until the 1980s the turban stopped the employment of Sikh males in the police force.

Classical sociology on pluralism

Sociologists a hundred years ago did not predict the religious pluralism that exists today. While the opinions of the classical sociologists varied enormously about religions they generally agreed that as societies modernised and became more 'rational' and science offered more tangible reasons for why things took place, religions would eventually disappear.

However, with the growth of new religious movements and the expansion of older religions such as Mormonism and Pentecostalism, combined with the increasing fundamentalism that flourishes throughout the world, it is hard to disagree that religious pluralism is not a reality.

A plurality of beliefs and ideologies

Berger and Kellner (1981) argue that before the period of industrialisation religion provided societies with a 'fixed universe of meaning', i.e. one single set of core beliefs that people understood and felt secure in. Interactionist Berger (1990) used the word 'nomos' to describe the feeling of meaningfulness that religion helps bring about. Berger and Kellner argue that with the process of industrialisation values and ideas are subjected to a number of influences (e.g. the media, the workplace), which come into conflict with the traditional beliefs contained within most religions and which functionalists would argue brings about *anomie*, i.e. the feelings of meaninglessness and the opposite to nomos.

As a result this 'plurality of beliefs and ideologies', leads to what Berger and Kellner refer to as a 'collapse in certainties'. In other words, people start to question many of the claims that religions have made, leading them to question to what extent the traditional religions offer acceptable forms of knowledge and guidance. This leads to either the secularisation process, where some argue that a decline in religious belief is taking place or a move into one of the many new religious movements. Postmodernists ironically refer to this as 'shopping for God'.

Civic religions

It is not possible to answer any question on religious pluralism without talking about 'civic religion'. While the growth in most major religions (apart from Islam) has ceased, what does not seem to have stopped growing are the rituals that historically belonged to orthodox religion. If we think of the number of state ceremonies that can be watched on television, e.g. royal funerals, royal weddings and events like Remembrance Day, there is, according to some sociologists, a sacred element to these events. We can refer to 'civic religions' as those that celebrate the citizenship of the nation state. As such it forms part of the religious pluralism discussed in this section.

Conclusion

Living in multicultural Britain it is not difficult to see how, or why, at the beginning of the 21st century churches such as the Church of England or the Roman Catholic Church are struggling to maintain congregation numbers. With its multiethnic population, most parts of Britain have populations that celebrate a variety of faiths, e.g. the Islamic and Jewish communities, Hindus, Sikhs and West Indian Pentecostalists to name but a few.

However, while the idea of a 'market-place' where one can pick and choose whatever religion one desires may sound convincing, sociology students need to be highly critical of such thinking. With the storming of a mosque by police in early 2002 (a family of suspected illegal immigrants was arrested and deported to Germany) and again in January 2003 (this time in the fight against 'international terrorism'), the sacrilege laws that exist in the UK to defend the Christian churches do not protect believers of other faiths.

● Synoptic Link

Some religions 'socially stratify' and 'socially differentiate' certain individuals as deviant or 'untouchable'. The Hindu caste system is one example of religious stratification. The system does not allow people from different castes to marry.

✍ Coursework Suggestion

Carry out coursework that analyses secondary data (get permission first from your coursework tutor). Gather attendance statistics from one of the religious communities in your area. This might be difficult but you could try approaching religious leaders of local communities where such religions are practised. Gather statistics at two points in time, perhaps five years apart. By comparing the statistics over time you can apply some of the ideas looked at in this chapter to account for the changes in attendance that you have discovered.

For consideration:

1 To what extent do you think that the national curriculum subjects you have studied reflect the notion of 'religious pluralism'?
2 What type of evidence could you gather to show that many so-called 'minority' religions are actually growing in numbers?

What is secularisation and has it happened?

What does this mean?

Bryan Wilson (1966) argues that the process of secularisation is one in which religious thinking, practices and institutions are said to be in decline and losing their social significance. The 'secularisation debate' is one in which this process is hotly contested by some sociologists.

What has the Enlightenment got to do with secularisation?

Before the 17th century, traditional 'sacred' beliefs meant all explanations about the weather, love or war could be explained in terms of how 'God' or 'the gods' wished it to be so. In today's world, however, natural disasters are no longer explained in terms of the divine punishment of God but through scientific and rational explanations.

Classical sociologists like Marx, Durkheim and Weber were writing about the effects of this new 'modern world' (remember Weber's concept of 'disenchantment', i.e. the loss of 'magic' in the world). Associated with the Enlightenment has been the so-called 'modernity thesis', which maintained that as societies developed, the desire for religious beliefs would decrease.

What evidence is there to show that there is a decline in religion?

* The argument at first appears a strong one *if* we look at evidence based upon the Christian religions. There has been a decline in religious baptisms, confirmations and church marriages, traditionally major events in the lives of many Christians. Stephens et al (1998) state that 65 per cent of all babies in the UK were baptised into the Anglican Church in 1900. By 1993 this figure had dropped to 27 per cent.

* The traditional function of the church as a centre for community support, news and advice has declined in Western Europe with the growth of social services and the media.

* There has been a sharp drop in church attendance during the 20th century. At the beginning of the 20th century over a quarter of the adult population in the UK were regular church-goers. However by the late 1990s, only 1.5 per cent of the adult population attended

◆ What, When and Why?

The 'Enlightenment' refers to a period in European thought in the 17th and 18th centuries where, because of the developments in science, there was widespread disillusionment with religious and traditional explanations about the world. In particular the natural sciences (e.g. chemistry, physics and biology) could now offer explanations about how the world functioned. These beliefs severely challenged the authority of many religions. The Enlightenment referred to how these ideas were expressed through the arts, science, politics and philosophy.

✳ Key Idea

American functionalists Stark and Bainbridge (1985) talk of the 'reorientation rather than demise' of religion. By this they mean that the many religious movements that are springing up on both sides of the Atlantic are a direct response to a more secular society. The idea of secularisation is itself far too simplistic a term and fails to describe the complex sets of processes that take place: 'in the future, as in the past, religion will be shaped by secular forces but not destroyed. There will always be a need for gods'.

Church of England services and only one-third of Catholics in England and Wales went to church.

- Over the last decade it has been increasingly possible to shop and to buy alcohol on Sundays – something that was inconceivable in the 19th century. This development shows how the Church in England has lost much of its political power, although, as we shall see below, not all of it.

Is there evidence to show religion is not in decline?

- If, however, we look beyond the Christian religions then there is evidence to suggest that religion is growing. Many of the ethnic minorities in the UK have a variety of religions that members strictly follow.

- Hamilton argues that survey research in 1998 revealed that only 10 per cent of the population in Britain do not believe in god (although their definitions of 'god' varied from individual to individual).

- While the political power of the church may be said to be in decline (people cite the changes in the licensing laws as an example), the Queen is still head of the Church of England and the charter of the BBC still requires it to transmit religious programs albeit on a limited scale.

- The growth in alternative new age religions challenges the idea that we are an increasingly secular society. Robert Bellah (1970) argues that with the increasing disillusionment with traditional medical and religious doctrines/ideas comes renewed interest in astrology, the occult, oriental religions and more recently feng shui.

Conclusion

We should perhaps remember that while people may not be attending ceremonies, they may well be practising some sort of religion in the privacy of their own home. It is also hard to believe that religious beliefs are in decline with the growth of Christian fundamentalism in the USA and Islamic fundamentalism in many parts of the world today.

Whose house is this? Many churches today are being converted and sold off as luxury homes.

✍ Coursework Suggestion

Carry out a small number of in-depth interviews (five or six would be appropriate) with different religious leaders from the local community where you live, e.g. a Catholic priest, Jewish rabbi, and so on). Explore with them, in the interviews, the debate over secularisation, and see to what extent they believe the processes of secularisation are taking place within their communities. Compare and contrast your findings with existing sociological theories.

For consideration:

1 To what extent do people attend churches, mosques, temples or any other religious establishment for religious purposes, i.e. if they did not, would they be looked down upon within the community?

2 What activities could be considered to be replacing religion today?

6.17 How might secularisation be a problem for methods?

What does this mean?

Gather quantitative data (e.g. church attendance figures) and you might be forgiven for assuming that religion is in decline. Gather qualitative data (e.g. through in-depth interviews) and you might equally be forgiven for saying the opposite, i.e. that religion of all types are growing. However, as this chapter shows, such discussions are far more complicated and in this section we examine more closely some of the methodological problems researchers face when examining secularisation.

'PETS' as a form of evaluation

PETS stands for 'practical', 'ethical', 'theoretical' and 'sensitive' issues that must be considered when evaluating anything to do with methods or methodology. You can identify a number of problems associated with secularisation by applying these concepts. Here are just some examples of ways you can do this.

- *Practical problems* – To what extent can sociologists access reliable records from previous centuries that accurately tell us how popular religion was? Comparatively few people could read and write and therefore we have no real way of knowing to what extent they were 'religious' nor what they meant by the word.
- *Ethical problems* – Is it acceptable to question people about their own (often very private) spiritual beliefs? Is it then equally acceptable to publish the findings of research on the basis of what other people have told you about their beliefs?
- *Theoretical problems* – We know that quite often values of researchers drive the research in a particular direction e.g. feminists, Marxists and functionalists will be looking (and arguing) for different things when researching secularisation. Sampling strategies, research methods and operationalisations of concepts may all differ depending on the theoretical approach of the researcher.
- *Sensitivity* – Issues to do with secularisation must be handled carefully by sociologists. How representative, reliable or valid the research data is likely to be considered may well depend on how sensitive the researchers were when carrying out their studies.

Reliability, representativeness and validity

Good sociology (and therefore successful exam answers) means that any question to do with methods or methodology must be answered by referring to the following three concepts.

※ **Key Idea**

When discussing secularisation you must be able to apply and criticise the word 'religiosity'. A term coined by Gerhard Lenski, it was used by him to offer a way of comparing the degree of religious commitment in different types of political and economic societies/systems. Religiosity compared different degrees of belief (religious attendance at ceremonies), devotion (aspects of prayer) and communality (the extent that the religious group was part of the community/society). Use this term when evaluating what we mean by being more or less religious.

✓ **Top Exam Hint**

The issue surrounding 'sensitivity' needs to be considered when examining historical documents. Unless the researcher is aware of the meanings and customs of people living hundreds of years ago they may misinterpret secondary sources. Nobody today would be concerned if their neighbour was a woman practising herbal medicine – the same woman living four hundred years ago would probably have been burnt as a witch. Researchers must be sensitive to cultural/historical meanings otherwise they may well misinterpret the data. Mention this in the exam for extra evaluation marks.

1 *How reliable is the research data?* This refers to whether the same results could be achieved if the research were repeated at a later point in time, carried out by different researchers or using different methods and samples. Researching secularisation becomes problematic in this case because of the periods of time involved (we cannot interview people who lived over a hundred years ago); the way statistics are gathered, calculated, recorded, and interpreted differs greatly from one region to another; and the way that the concept of 'religion' culturally and historically changes.

2 *How representative is the data?* This concept is more associated with quantitative methodology rather than qualitative research and refers to the ability for generalisations to be made from the sample used in the study. Weber's research has been challenged on this issue because of the claims he has made about capitalism developing as a result of Protestant religious values. Looking at the highly successful capitalist economy of Japan, where no similar religious tradition exists, his work is criticised for not being representative of all capitalist economies.

3 *How valid is the data?* Despite many textbooks arguing that this concept is only associated with qualitative research, it actually refers to the ability of research data (both quantitative and qualitative) to reflect the true nature, attitudes, behaviour or characteristics of whatever the researcher claims is the case.

Remember at all times to question the methodology in any data that you are reading about using PETS and reliability, representativeness and validity. The following case shows how official statistics can be very deceptive. Most Germans pay a 'church tax' that is collected by the state and used to support many church organisations and the work that they do. While the tax itself is quite small, it does come out of the weekly or monthly pay cheque of German workers. Many Germans who attend church services will however *not* claim they are church attendees in order to avoid the tax. This means that if a sociologist is working from the tax figures in order to investigate church 'popularity', there will be fundamental flaws in the research.

Conclusion

As you can see, the secularisation debate throws up many difficulties for sociologists. Just because fewer people (in some religions) attend religious ceremonies now than in earlier times, this may not mean they are less religious. The reverse of this statement may well also be true.

Thinking like a Sociologist

Three evaluations you can use in the exam are the:

1 Empirical adequacy of the data on offer, i.e. is there sufficient and reliable data provided by the claim or theory?

2 Comprehensiveness of the theory or claim, i.e. can the theory or claim be used in all situations?

3 Logical cohesiveness of the theory, i.e. does the theory 'make sense' and fully explain the cause or effect of the situation being described?

Do packed churches mean a secular society? Functionalist Will Herberg argues that while 40 per cent of adult Americans attend church, they do this to express commitment to the community rather than for 'religious' reasons.

6.18 Can religion be a source of social control?

What does this mean?

All macro or deterministic theories would argue that to a certain extent we are socially controlled through the various institutions, e.g. the family, education, the media and of course religion. By 'social control', sociologists refer to the social processes by which the behaviour of individuals or groups is regulated.

However, while functionalist and New Right theories see elements of this control in a positive light, Marxist and feminist conflict theories are highly critical of the way in which religion determines people's lives.

Three ways religion can socially control people

1   *Ideological control* – the ability to shape ideas, values and attitudes through institutions such as the media, the family, education and religion.
2   *Repressive control* – the ability to force people to carry out actions both by physical and ideological means.
3   *Coercive control* – the ability to make others carry out actions against their will by threat of alternative action or fate.

What questions do sociologists ask when exploring issues of social control?

Gordon Marshall (1994) argues that there are four questions that all theories should address.

1   By whom is control exercised?
2   What techniques of control are used?
3   How far can individuals or groups resist processes of social control?
4   In whose interest does such control work?

By applying each of these questions to any theoretical approach, sociologists can evaluate to what extent religion can be used as a means of social control.

How can theories help?

*   *Functionalists* see social control as a vital element to the maintenance of social order. Religion and religious beliefs are a source of control in society because they give us our norms, morals and values (e.g. through the *Qur'an* and the *Bible*). People are united by a common set of beliefs which are often linked to national identity. For example, in Britain the Queen is the head of state and head of the Church of England. People have been executed in the past for breaking away from state religions – the act itself was considered treason.

- *Marxists* argue that women and men have created religion and then have allowed it to dominate them. It becomes a form of ideological control that stops people from realising they live in an exploitative society. It controls people by providing rules and examples of how to live life and promises an 'after-life' to anybody who follows the norms and values contained within that particular religion. As such it stops people from questioning all that may be wrong in any society they live in ('false consciousness').

- *Marxists* also recognise that religion has been imposed by conquering nations in times of empire building (e.g. the British and Spanish empires). The conquering nations used religion as a tool to keep people in their places by forbidding certain religions. The British often sent Christian missionaries out to developing countries during the Victorian era. By teaching English, building churches and schools, and establishing trade connections, such missionaries without realising it aided the colonialisation of many of these countries.

- *Feminists* also argue that religion can be seen as a mechanism of social control. The patriarchal structure in most religions (male mullahs, bishops, priests and rabbis) enforces the notion that women should remain in the home and not concentrate on professional careers – despite the fact that they often make up more of the congregation than men do. Many religions are also hypocritical in the punishments they offer men and women for love-affairs outside marriage, with women being judged more critically than men (e.g. the stoning to death of women in Nigeria).

- We can apply the post-structuralist ideas of Michel Foucault (1972) to the 'controlling' nature of religion. Through 'mechanisms of control' he argues that the human body is under continuous surveillance. By this he means that through institutions such as education, the legal system, medicine and, of course, religion individual identities are constrained. Applied to religion this means that humans will 'internalise' religious rules that dictate the actions of that individual – without the need for outside observers. Foucault refers to such processes as 'hidden forms of control'. In this sense humans police themselves through their beliefs in morals and the promise of a life hereafter.

Conclusion

All the above theories show how religion *can* be a source of social control; however, not all theories say that it *should* be. With the exception of functionalist theory the remaining theories are critical of the role that religion plays in controlling members of society.

For consideration:

1 To what extent does the institution of religion have more control over you than other institutions such as education or the legal system?

2 How might you argue that new religious movements socially control people?

✓ **Top Exam Hint**

Evaluate post-structuralism by drawing on its similarities to Marx' earlier work where he focused on consciousness and ideology (referred to as 'humanist' Marxism). This idea is similar to the 'internalisation' process that post-structuralists write about – they argue we create ideas such as 'competition' and 'success'. What we then do is internalise these ideas and allow them to shape how we think, act and react to those around us. In both cases, the theories say that we constrain or control ourselves. Mention this in a conclusion and be awarded high evaluation marks.

● **Synoptic Link**

By applying post-structuralist ideas a synoptic link can be made with religious power and state power. Religion acts as a control mechanism that changes our behaviour as a result of the 'internalisation' of religious rules, e.g. the Ten Commandments. In much the same way, the increased surveillance through CCTV and speed cameras changes our behaviour because we internalise the rules and regulations that these forms of surveillance are set up to govern. In this way both technology and religion act as powerful forms of social control without the need of external supervision.

6.19 Can religion be a source of social cement?

✳ Key Idea

Strongly associated with the New Right in America, the phrase 'WASP' stands for 'White Anglo-Saxon Protestant' and is used, sometimes in a negative sense, to describe white American Prostestant middle-class citizens. The phrase is significant for sociology students because it shows how a religion can be associated with a prescribed way of living. The New Right places great emphasis on individual freedom (presumably the freedom to choose whatever religious beliefs you desire) but also on Christian norms and values as the 'cement' that should bind societies together. This is a contradiction which you can highlight in the exam.

The Palestinian question: can Judaism and Islam 'cement' the state of Israel?

What does this mean?

This section asks you to examine to what extent religion acts as a unifying force on society, i.e. how (if at all) does it bring about 'social cohesion'? In fact the word religion comes from the Latin *religare* which means 'to bind'. However, as we also know, religion has been used as an excuse for conflict both in the past and sadly in the present. In the exam you must be able to offer a balanced argument that offers evidence on both sides.

How does theory help answer this?

- Functionalists argue that religion forms part of the social 'cement' that binds the structure of society together. The strong moral codes of behaviour that religions offer provide the norms and values of society through religious traditions and ceremonies. We develop a strong sense of social obligation around us through collective worship.

- When social cohesion is threatened, religion can be used to help bind societies in times of danger or insecurity. We know that from the work of functionalist Malinowski (1954) that the Trobriand Islanders used religious rituals before fishing in the dangerous open waters but did not do so in calm water.

- We can apply the ideas of Weber by arguing religion cements groups together by providing meaning to individuals through collective forms of practice and worship. Whether such forms of practice are shared through orthodox religions such as Christianity or Judaism or through 'civic religions' such as 'Americanism' is not important. Weber argued that the values of Calvinism provided the consensus needed for successful capitalist economies to work.

Karma and dharma

The Hindu religion offers an example of how religion cements society together. The highly stratified (and often criticised) Hindu system referred to as 'caste' means that the social position you are born into often becomes the one you remain in, through marriage, work and childbirth. The religious concepts of Karma and Dharma help explain how such a system remains unified.

Karma ('fate') is the acceptance that whatever existence you have is either reward or punishment for behaviour in a previous life. Dharma ('acceptance') is the belief that the more virtuous you are in this life, the better your next one will be. The belief in these two concepts cements this socially stratified system.

How do sociological variables help answer this debate?

If we take three such variables, namely class, gender and sexuality, then the issue of religion cementing society together becomes immediately more complicated.

- Marxists would certainly question to what extent working-class and aristocratic families 'worship' their religions in the same way. Does the church really 'cement' these groups together with the same sets of shared values that some functionalists claim exist?

- Feminists would question to what extent religion cemented men and women together. They would consider issues surrounding abortion, female sexuality and employment within religious organizations and freedom for women generally. Many feminists argue that most religions have been highly oppressive on these issues.

- Finally, to be gay or lesbian is still viewed by many religions as 'deviant'.

It would seem therefore that the social cement does not necessarily stick to all groups all of the time.

Conclusion

In some cases religion is used as an excuse by governments and people to engage in conflict. Some sociologists argue that we draw our sense of identity from the culture we live in. In some cases, where national identity is concerned, religion is a core part of that culture, e.g. being Irish can also mean being Catholic or Protestant or Yugoslavian can also mean being Muslim or Eastern Orthodox Christian. However, sometimes purely looking at religious reasons for conflict is far too simplistic (e.g. the Israeli/Palestinian conflict which is as much to do with conflict over land and resources as it is with religious beliefs).

For consideration:

1 What examples can you offer to back up the argument that religion does act as social cement?
2 What examples other than the ones in this section challenge this view?

◆ **What, When and Why?**

The division of Ireland into two separate jurisdictions took place at the beginning of the 20th century because of the differences between Protestant and especially non-conformist Protestant Irish (often of Scottish descent) largely grouped in the North, and the Roman Catholic majority mainly grouped in the South. This division has caused intense conflict between the two religions in Northern Ireland ever since.

✳ **Key Idea**

The idea that religion can be 'social cement' can be challenged by using the example of former Yugoslavia, a country torn apart by civil war during the 1990s, which was composed of Serbian, Croatian, Albanian and Bosnian ethnic groupings. These different religious traditions were a source of social conflict rather than 'cement'. Serb identity is mainly made up of Eastern Orthodox Christianity; Croatian from Roman Catholic Christianity; Albanian from the Islamic tradition; and Bosnian also from the Islamic tradition. Yugoslavia collapsed *partly* as a result of the conflict between these traditions.

6.20 How is religion a conservative force?

Has the attack on the New York World Trade Centre on the 11 September, 2001 forced social change or just strengthened and 'conserved' existing prejudices?

What does this mean?

Both functionalists and Marxists agree that religion can be seen as a set of beliefs that offer resistance to change. Both theories accept that religion is a conservative force that attempts to 'conserve' many of the existing structures in society. Certainly there is strong evidence to support the argument that religion helps maintain existing values rather than acting as a force for change.

The functionalist argument

Functionalists argue that religion is a conservative force that holds society together for the good of all. It also acts a force of social integration by reinforcing the norms and values of society.

By applying the ideas of Durkheim we can argue that religion exercises a 'regulation' role maintaining existing values and providing rules for common behaviour. Durkheimian approaches would see this in traditional societies, for example that of the Australian Aborigines where the totem is a focal point by which people can express collective respect for the values in that society.

In some cases religion can force the individual through coercion or persuasion into the acceptance of particular codes of moral behaviour (the threat of 'fire and eternal damnation' can be very persuasive!). Durkheim argues that once these values and norms have been internalised, habit takes over and these ideas become resistant to change.

The Marxist argument

Marxists argue that religion is only ever a conservative force that seeks to enforce the dominance of one class over another. They argue that religion is part of the ideological superstructure of any society and part of its purpose is to 'mystify' the real nature of the exploitative relationship between the classes.

As a conservative force we can see how the Church plays its part in this process when we look at how Church of England schools in the 19th century taught children from extremely poor backgrounds. At that time most of the clergy were members of the middle classes who helped reproduce the idea of a hierarchical social order by teaching respect and obedience to those 'above' them.

The feminist argument

Many feminists would also agree that religion acts as a force for conservatism in that it helps conserve the patriarchal systems found in many societies. The persecution of witches; the refusal of many religions to accept women as religious leaders; religious perceptions of the role of women within the family; and in some cases the particular forms of dress and segregation in some ceremonies – all of these point to a particular type of conservatism that wishes to conserve the subservient role of women that many religions endorse.

Conclusion

The idea that religion is a conservative force has been challenged. In Weber's *Protestant Ethic and the Spirit of Capitalism*, he argued that religion could act as a force for social change and that such ideas can change the course of history. Yinger also argues that 'religion cannot be understood simply as a force that blocks or retards change'; in other words, religion can *conserve* social stability or can be seen to challenge it.

One example of Weber's force for change is the way that some churches in other parts of the world have helped educate children to challenge many of the ideas pushed forward by the state, e.g. the role of Catholic schools in South Africa in contesting the apartheid system there.

A second example is that of liberation theology (see also section 10). This is a Latin American movement within the Roman Catholic church where progressive clergy (especially but not exclusively Jesuits) have become aligned with progressive and socialist movements, e.g. in Nicaragua where a Roman Catholic priest was a member of the revolutionary socialist Sandinista government.

For consideration:

1 Should religion act as a conservative force in society?
2 Do 'the ends justify the means' where religious conflict is concerned?

In South Africa between 1978 and 1985, Archbishop Tutu played a key role in the way Anglican and other Christian churches were involved, alongside communist and other radical groupings aligned to the African National Congress, in the liberation struggle against apartheid.

✓ Top Exam Hints

- Evaluate the argument that religion is a conservative force by criticising it. Offer examples to show that this is not the case and that in fact religion can be seen as a force for change. Apart from those examples offered in this section you can also use: Martin Luther King; Gandhi; the early Christians, and currently al-Qaeda.

- While the big changes described here brought about by religion challenge the argument that religion is a force of conservatism, Marxists would be critical of this. They argue that although religion might bring change in some countries, this is not significant compared to the economic shifts from one historic period to another, e.g. the huge economic change that took place as a result of the change from feudalism to capitalism.

6.21 How might secularisation be a feature of the postmodern world?

To what extent does the growth in Islam as a worldwide religion challenge postmodern claims of secularisation?

✳ Key Idea

Surely postmodernism is itself a theory that attempts to offer an explanation for current events. Are we therefore, as sociologists, to ignore this because its claims cannot be taken seriously? Remember postmodernists argue that all theories are just stories. Does this not equally make postmodernism a story? Use this in the exam as a way of evaluating postmodernist claims.

● Synoptic Link

Synopticity examines the themes of social differentiation, power and stratification. Apply these ideas synoptically to stratification. Postmodernists challenge traditional explanations of stratification based on class, gender and ethnicity. They argue that while these old-fashioned concepts belonged to an era where 'production' was what defined an identity (look at the professions), now it is what we consume that defines who we are – therefore these old labels are no longer appropriate.

What does this mean?

By 'modernity' most sociologists refer to the period of the 18th, 19th and early 20th centuries – a period after the so-called Enlightenment which was characterised by industrialisation and the widespread belief that science contained all the 'big' answers to some of the 'big' questions. Such questions included 'Why are we here?'; 'What is the purpose of human existence?'; or 'Can scientific theory (or any other type of theory) lead to an improvement in the human condition?' (See also section 16.)

Towards the end of the 20th century a number of writers have challenged many of the assumptions held during the period of modernity. Postmodernists writers like Jacques Derrida, Michel Foucault and Jacques Lacan have inspired many to believe that we are in another type of world altogether – a 'postmodern' world where none of the accepted theories or 'truths' or 'narratives' can be relied on. One really big narrative (postmodernists call these 'metanarratives') is that of religion.

What claims do postmodernists make?

- According to postmodernists the idea that science is a force for liberation is untrue. The mass extermination of Jews in the gas chambers, chemical warfare and increasing health scares prove that scientific theory has not 'liberated' the human condition.
- As a result no one theory, story or set of ideas can offer a reliable explanation for how the world (or 'afterworld') is.
- In a world where consumerism becomes much more important than production, what we consume becomes increasingly a part of our identity.
- Old explanations about identity – such as those built around class are meaningless in a world where we can 'pic'n'mix' clothes, music, food and even religion.
- Where once we believed in purpose and a sense of why we are here, postmodernists argue that we have become 'de-centred', i.e. a product of discourses, religious or otherwise.
- In what some postmodernists argue is 'hyperreality', the media has such a powerful influence on all our lives that fashions, beliefs,

debates and ideas come and go. In fact we can no longer really distinguish between media reality and fiction.

A pluralisation of life worlds

In pre-industrial societies religion tended to provide one set of ideas that explained the universe – a set of core beliefs centred around a particular religion. Referred to as lifeworld by interactionist Berger (1990), this particular lifeworld becomes 'lifeworlds' during the period of industrialisation as people increasingly become involved in a number of conflicting 'core beliefs', e.g. family values, work-place values, capitalistic values, religious and scientific values. This is referred to by Berger as a 'pluralisation of lifeworlds'.

Conclusion

- The dissatisfaction that many people are increasingly feeling towards so-called 'expert' opinion is having its effect on religions. Decreasing church attendance figures are evidence of this. People are becoming 'relativist' in their religious views, i.e. adopting the position that one claim may be as valid as another. This means that while somebody may call themselves Christian or Jew, they may also seek advice from astrological sources, medication from complementary medical practitioners or Chinese feng shui.
- Postmodernist claims that the media is increasingly significant in our lives make sense when we read stories such as the involvement of priests in the US in child-sex scandals, which has the effect of pushing people away and pulling them to other sources of religion. This 'push-pull' effect is met by the wide variety of religions that people can pic'n'mix' from. The growth in new religious movements is evidence for the diversity that postmodernists write about.
- Churches are trying to respond to decreasing numbers by marketing themselves in the community, e.g. hiring out church halls for public events; providing music at church ceremonies; and putting on local community events such as raffles and 'bring 'n' buys'. Meeting the needs of the consumer is yet more evidence that identity is no longer based on religion, class or any of the other significant variables – but rather, as postmodernists claim, the wishes and desires of a hungry consumer.

For consideration:

1 To what extent do you believe that postmodernists are guilty of over-generalisation?
2 If we are, as postmodernists claim, so dominated by the media, how do you explain the diversity of ideas, images and identities that exist?

✓ Top Exam Hint

When postmodernists claim diversity, choice and decreasing church numbers, point out that this depends on historical, cultural and regional circumstances. Where wars are being fought in the name of religion (e.g. Ireland, Israel and India), be highly critical of 'academic' explanations not taking into account the circumstances at the local level. Remember Weber's 'theodicy of non-privilege' argues that people experiencing poverty and hardship will have a different take on what their religion means to them.

6.22 What is the future of religion according to sociology?

Karl Popper, considered one of the greatest philosophers of science of the 20th century

☞ Who is this Person?

Karl Popper (1902–1994) was an Austrian philosopher who worked for most of his life at the London School of Economics. Professor of logic and scientific method, he was knighted in 1965. His contributions to the philosophy of science are enormous and you will probably study his work in your second year of sociology. For Popper, the job of the social scientist was to attempt to falsify concepts and theories rather than to prove them correct. Popper argued that for theory to be taken seriously then it must be open to falsification. Therefore any theory that makes predictions about the future (and therefore is not open to falsification) cannot be held to be scientific.

What does this mean?

First, to what extent can sociologists ask such a question based on their research and on the work of some of the writers looked at in this section? Second, what lessons can we learn (if any) and what predictions can be made? Most sophisticated conclusions will probably make reference to these issues.

The danger of predictions

There are dangers for sociologists when attempting to predict future events based on past events. It was Karl Popper who argued that so-called scientific claims about future events cannot be scientific if they are not open to being disproved (of course you may wish to debate about whether sociology should be considered 'scientific' in the first place).

Certainly, if, and only if, postmodernists are correct, there is widespread disillusionment with many traditional religions that offer so-called 'truths'. In addition to this, many interpretive sociologists would argue that religion along with science and all other 'disciplines' are all 'social constructions' and therefore religious claims are really just reflections on social experience.

Where does that leave sociologists?

*   Science and education have not stopped the human search for some of the 'big' questions. The discipline of philosophy shows us that human beings never stop asking: 'Why are we here?'; 'Is there an after-life?'; or 'Is there a god'? Religions in different ways provide possible answers to these questions and it is difficult to imagine human beings stopping their search for such answers.
*   Sociology cannot answer these questions above. Sociology cannot carry out objective tests to see if 'God' exists. Neither sociology nor the natural sciences can explain the purpose of life. Sociology can also not offer any proof of a life after death despite the claims made by many religions that this is the case. While many religions imply a moral superiority it is not the job of sociology to determine what is or what is not morally acceptable.
*   While sociology or any other discipline fails to come up with the answer to such questions, it seems likely that in future religions will grow, shrink, change form and multiply in much the same way as this chapter has attempted to portray. Sociology in the meantime will watch, analyse, discuss and debate all issues that concern power, culture and identity that go hand-in-hand with all the debates covered in this chapter.

Are we moving towards a secular world?

The secularisation debate looked at in this chapter provides many sociologists with enough evidence to show that the belief in religion is far from over. While many of the processes of industrialisation have been said to lead to secularisation, religion is still popular today.

Associated with the secularisation debate is the notion that we are moving within a period described as 'religious pluralism', i.e. the development of a culture characterised by widespread diversity of religious expressions. What sociologists can do is to continuously examine to what extent this is the case and help politicians create an environment that really is multi-cultural.

In changing times

One popular sociological issue, globalisation, must be taken into consideration when talking about any future direction for the religions. However we choose to define globalisation, we have to accept that many societies across the world are becoming increasingly inter-connected. Economic, political, technological or cultural connections must have an impact on any discussion that takes place over the future of religion.

Conclusion

This chapter has examined the way in which religion can act as both a conservative force and a force for change. For functionalists, religion 'cements' individuals together through dominant norms and values within a meritocracy. Both feminists and Marxists challenge the meritocratic idea arguing that religion helps maintain exploitative societies. Max Weber has argued that religion can act as a 'motor' of social change under specific circumstances. Postmodernists argue that the variety of different belief systems on offer is just evidence of the postmodern society they claim we all inhabit.

There have been many examples of all these ideas and sociologists will continue to examine what religion does and how it does it in the future – and to whom. However, what religion also does for some in troubled times is to offer support. Perhaps even sociologists need to remember that in their many theoretical discussions either praising or damning the role religion plays in human interaction.

● Synoptic Link

Synopticity examines the themes of social differentiation, power and stratification. By considering the future of religions in general this allows many synoptic links to be made with stratification. By taking class, gender, and ethnicity and placing a sentence in your conclusion about possible future developments, the examiners will recognise that you are interpreting, applying and evaluating concepts at a high level. Always remember to start your sentence with: 'Synoptically speaking. . . .'

For consideration:

1 Do you consider the history of religion to have been one that progresses in an historically straight line or are the new religious movements really just different versions of earlier religions?
2 What kind of developments can you predict for women in the next twenty years within the mainstream religions?

6.23 Examination advice

What does the exam ask me to do?

You will answer two questions on this paper. Each of the questions has two parts. You can answer both questions on the same topic, or on different topic areas.

In each question:

Part a) is worth 15 marks, and you should spend no longer than 15 minutes answering it. It will ask you to 'Identify and explain...' two specific features of the question area. It tests your knowledge and understanding, so you need to include studies, concepts and theories wherever you can. Make sure you clearly differentiate between the two points you make – use bullets or numbers.

Part b) is worth 30 marks and you should spend no longer than 30 minutes answering it. It will ask you to 'Outline and discuss...' a view. You are being tested on your knowledge and understanding, interpretation and analysis and evaluation so you should include studies, concepts and theories. Try to make specific evaluative comments throughout, but also ensure that you look at other views on the question. If you do this you will be juxtaposing your views, and you will be rewarded evaluation marks.

How best can I achieve maximum marks?

The following bullet points should help you in your final stages of preparation for the exam:

*   *Make sure* that you have learnt all the key terms and concepts in this chapter (e.g. 'church', 'sect', 'secularisation', and so on).

*   *Make sure* that you show that there is no singularly accepted definition of 'religion' – memorise the variety of definitions available in this chapter.

*   *Remember* that you cannot answer a question on whether or not religion is in decline unless first you are clear about how it is defined.

*   *Make sure* that you have looked at all the 'key ideas' in the margins of this chapter.

*   *Remember* that gender and religion are becoming increasingly popular topics for questions. Be absolutely clear about the positive and negative contributions that feminist theories have made to the sociology of religion.

✓ Top Exam Hint

When revising be clear as to the main theoretical perspectives, i.e. functionalism, Marxism, Weberianism, feminisms, interpretivism, post-structuralism and postmodernism. Produce a separate piece of paper for each theory and stick this on your wall at home. In the weeks leading up to the exam jot down the name of any sociologist and their work that neatly fits into one of the theories and start to memorise these in the final build up to the exam.

● Synoptic Link

The module will examine whether you can make connections with it and other areas of the specification. Max Weber provides a synoptic link with his concept of 'theodicy of privilege/non-privilege' that you have studied in this chapter (section 9). Groups in poverty or hardship will perhaps argue they are 'chosen' and that their 'salvation' will come in the after-life. Their religious experience will be different from that of those in power.

- *Remember* when discussing 'the meaning' of religion that it is the theories of Max Weber and interpretivists that focus on this. Learn their theories thoroughly to be able to answer any question that comes up in relation to this.

- *Make sure* that you fully understand how Weber combines both micro and macro forms of analyses. By focusing on the 'values' of hard work, modesty and the rejection of self-indulgence, he argues that the adoption of Calvinist ideas led to the emergence of capitalism.

- *Remember* that examiners will expect you to be fully on top of the secularisation debate and this means that you must not only be able to define it but also show that there are many conflicting views as to whether such a process exists in the first place.

- *Be clear* as to what 'new religious movements' are and be prepared to connect them to any question that asks you about sects and cults.

- Be clear about what Durkheim means by the 'sacred' and the 'profane'.

- *Draw up a list of the sociological studies* mentioned in this unit. Make revision cards with all the studies on them (one on each side of the card will do) and memorise them for the exam.

- *Be clear* about the problems that this area of sociology poses for methodology (e.g. to what extent is quantitative data useful/not useful when exploring this area).

Key points to remember

- Be absolutely clear about the type of questions that you are facing in the exam. In the two weeks leading up to the exam focus your revision around the past questions.

- The sociology of religion provides a range of synoptic possibilities. Once the exams are over (and the material is still fresh in your mind) transfer all synoptic 'evidence' into new folders in preparation for next year.

- Don't forget that theory is not enough! You need the evidence in the form of the case studies and their findings. You might revise each theory with a variety of case studies as evidence (try ten studies for each theory).

✑ **Coursework Suggestion**

There has been much sociological work that shows that *apparently* women tend to be more 'religious' than men. Explore whether this might be true by carrying out quantitative research using questionnaires or qualitative research using interviews. Remember that when deciding on what questions to pose, you will have to be extremely clear about the definitions you deploy, the sample you use and the theoretical framework you adopt. You will also need to bear in mind that when evaluating your work you can revisit these issues and discuss them as 'methodological problems'.

6.24 Pushing your grades up higher

What do I need to do to get a good grade?

1   Employing an historical perspective when writing about other sociologists will push your grades up, e.g. if you talk about Malinowski's research, identify it as being carried out in the 1950s.

2   Show that you are aware of *where* (geographically) some of these theories and theorists are coming from, e.g. if you talk about Talcott Parsons, refer to him as 'The American structural functionalist . . .'.

3   Mention the methodology of the case study you are referring to and the type of data it produced, i.e. 'adopting positivist methodology, she . . .' or 'the qualitative data he produced . . .'.

4   Your paragraphs (and if possible your sentences) must start with evaluative key words (e.g. 'following on from this . . .' or 'in contrast to this . . .' or 'from this we can see that . . .').

5   Remember to always back up whatever point you are making with evidence. That evidence must be in the form of a case study by a named sociologist.

6   You will always be given credit for knowledge of contemporary issues that you can link to the sociology of religion. That means you *must* in the final weeks before the exam be listening to/watching the news and buying a broadsheet newspaper (e.g. the *Times*) on a weekly basis.

7   When you see the word 'contribution' in the exam, this can be both positive and negative. You will be awarded for commenting on the positive contributions that Marxists have brought but you also need to be able to offer negative ones, i.e. what do Marxists *not* focus on (e.g. 'in the sociology of religion, Marxist contributions tend to be deterministic whereas interpretive sociologists argue from a more individualist perspective . . .')

8   Always remember to use the concepts 'validity', 'reliability' and 'representativeness' when discussing the work of other sociologists. By applying these terms you will show the examiners that you are extremely critical.

Key points to remember

- You must answer every question from a theoretical perspective if you are chasing the highest grades.

- Theory is not enough. You must have *evidence* in the form of the findings that other sociologists have written about.

- Don't forget to use 'sophisticated' language when criticising the theory, case study or concept. Make sure you start those sentences or paragraphs with those key evaluative phrases.

Frequently asked questions

Q. Why does the sociology of religion focus mainly on Christianity?

A. The word 'ethnocentric' means analysing other societies in terms of one's own cultural assumption or bias. The classical sociologists who explored the sociology of religion tended to come from countries where Christianity was the mainstream religion. Although sociologists throughout much of the 20th century tried to avoid such claims, it is only relatively recently that textbooks (with a lot of help from postmodernist theorists and theorists of new social movements) have recognised the enormous diversity of religions.

Q. Do the classical sociologists help me understand contemporary religion?

A. Yes! To fully understand the theories used by sociologists today we have to understand the ideas that these theories have developed from or, in some cases, challenge. Theories, like fashion accessories, can be popular, become dated, recreated or re-emerge albeit in a sometimes more refined form. The classical sociologists wrote about industrial society at a time of immense social, political and economic change. Many commentators argue today, with all the varieties of globalisation processes that exist, huge changes are once again taking place. It is therefore no surprise to see that classical theory has some of the answers to the questions that sociologists pose.

Q. Do I need to know all the variety of different religions to answer well in the exam?

A. No. In this exam you are not being tested on your knowledge of religion. You are, however, being asked to assess the role that such an institution has in the many socialisation processes that exist. In order to do that successfully you need to be able to show that 'religion' is an extremely widely contested concept and therefore it will help to be able to draw on some examples from the variety of religions that exist.

Bibliography

Abbott, D. (1998) *Culture and Identity*, London: Hodder and Stoughton.

Abbott, P. and Wallace, C. (1997) *An Introduction to Sociology: Feminist Perspectives* (second ed.) London: Routledge.

Abbott, P. and Wallace, C. (1990) *An Introduction to Sociology: Feminist Perpectives*, London: Routledge.

Abercrombie, N. and Warde, A. (eds) (1994) *Family, Household and the Life Course*, Lancaster: Framework

Ackroyd, S. and Huges, J. (1983) *Data collection in context*, London: Longman.

Adorno, T. W. (1991) *The Culture Industry*, London: Routledge.

Althusser, L. (1965) *For Marx*, Hamondsworth: Penguin.

Althusser, L. (1971) *Lenin and Philosophy and Other Essays*, London: New Left Books.

Althusser, L. (1971) 'Ideology and Ideological State Apparatuses' in *Lenin and Philosophy and Other Essays*, London: New Left Books.

Althusser, L. (1984) *Essays on Ideology*, London: Verso.

Alvarado, M. et al. (1987) *Learning the Media*, London: Macmillan.

Amos, V. and Parmar, P. (1984) 'Challenging Imperial Feminism', *Feminist Review*, no.17.

Anderson, M. (1971) *Family Structure in Nineteenth Century Lancashire*, Cambridge: Cambridge University Press.

Appadurai, A. (1992) ' Disfunction and Difference in the Global Cultural Economy ' in *Theory, Culture and Society* vol 7, pp. 295-310.

Archard, D. (1993) *Children: rights and childhood*, London: Routledge.

Aries, P. (1973) *Centuries of Childhood*, Harmondsworth: Penguin.

Aronowitz., S. and Giroux, H. (1991), *Postmodern Education Politics, Culture and Social Criticism*, Minneapolis: University of Minnesota Press.

Askew, L. and Ross, C. (1988) *Boy's Don't Cry: Boys and Sexism in Education*, Milton Keynes: Open University Press.

Bainbridge, W. and Stark, R. (1979) 'Cult formation: Three Compatible Models', *Sociology Analysis*, no. 40.

Ball, S. (1994) *Education Reform: A Critical and Poststructuralist Approach*, Buckingham: The Open University.

Ballard, R. (1982) 'South Asian Families' in R. N. Rapoport et al. (eds) *Families in Britain*, London: Routledge and Kegan Paul.

Barker, E. (1984) *The Making of a Moonie: Choice or Brainwashing*, Oxford: Blackwell.

Barker, E. (1995) *New Religious Movements: A Practical Introduction*, London: HMSO.

Barker, M. (1981) *The New Racism*, London: Junction Books.

Barrett, M. and McIntosh, M. (1982) *The Anti-Social Family*, London: Verso.

Barrow, J. (1982) 'West Indian Families: an insider's perspective' in R. N. Rapoport et al. (eds) *Families in Britain*. London: Rouledge and Kegan Paul.

Barthes, R. (1973) *Mythologies*, London: Paladin.

Baudrillard, J. (1983) *Simulations*, New York: Semiotext(e).

Baudrillard, J. (1988) *Selected Writings* (Edited by M. Poster), Cambridge: Polity Press.

Baudrillard, J. (1990) *Fatal Strategies*, New York: Semiotext(e)

Baudrillard, J. (1995) *The Gulf War Did Not Take Place*, Sydney: Power Publications.

Bauman, Z. (1990) *Thinking Sociologically*, Oxford: Blackwell.

Bauman, Z. (1996) ' Culture on Praxis' in S. Hall and P. du Gay (eds) *Questions of Cultural Identity*, London: Routledge.

Beck, U. (1992) *The Risk Society*, London: Sage.

Beck, U. and Beck-Gernsheim, E. (1995) *The Normal Chaos of Love*, Cambridge: Polity Press.

Becker, H. S. (1971) 'Social class variations in the teacher-pupil relationship' in B. R. Cosin et al. (eds) *School and society*, London: Routledge and Kegan Paul.

Becker, H. S. (1951) *Role and Career Problems of the Chicago Public School Teacher* (Doctoral Thesis), University of Chicago.

Beechey, V. (1986) 'Familial Ideology' in V. Beechey and J. Donald (eds) *Subjectivity and Social Relations*, Milton Keynes: Open University Press.

Bellah, R. (1965) 'Religious Evolution' in W. Lessa and E. Voight, *Reader in Comparitive Religion: An Anthropological Approach*. New York: Harper Row.

Bellah, R. (1966) *Civil Religion in America*, New York: Daedalus.

Bellah, R. (1970) *Beyond Belief*, New York: Harper Row.

Belson, W. (1978) *Television Violence and the Adolescent Boy*, Farnborough: Saxon House.

Benn, C. and Simon, B. (1970) *Halfway There*, London: McGraw Hill.

Berger, B. and Berger, P. L. (1983) *The War Over the Family*, London: Hutchinson.

Berger, P. L. (1963*) Invitation to Sociology: A Humanistic Perspective*, Harmondsworth: Penguin Books.

Berger, P. and Luckmann, T. (1967) *The Social Construction of Reality*, New York: Doubleday.

Berger, P. L. (1969) *The Social Reality of Religion*, London: Faber and Faber.

Biggs, S. (1993) *Understanding Ageism*, Milton Keynes: Open University Press.

Blair, M., Holland, J. and Sheldon, S. (eds) (1995*), Identity and Diversity: Gender and the Experience of Education*, Milton Keynes: Open University Press.

Bocock R. (1985) 'Religion in Modern Britain' in R. Bocock and K. Thompson (eds) *Religion and Ideology*, Manchester: Manchester University Press.

Bocock, R. (1993) *Consumption*, London: Routledge.

Boh, K. (1989) 'European Family Life Patterns - a Reappraisal' in K. Boh et al. (eds) *Changing Patterns of European Family Life*, London: Routledge.

Bourdieu, P. and Passeron, J.C. (1977) *Reproduction in Education, Society and Culture,* London: Sage.

Boyd, W. L., and Gibulka, J.G. (1989), *Private Schools and Public Policy: International Perspectives*, London: Falmer Press.

Braverman, H. (1974) *Labor and Monopoly Capital*, New York: Monthly Review Press.

Bretl and Cantor (1988) 'The Portrayal of Men and Women in US Television Commercials', *Sex Roles*, 18, 9/10, pp. 565-609.

Brierly, P. (1991) *Christian England*, London: MARC Europe.

Britton, A. (1989) *Masculinity and Power*, Oxford: Blackwell.

Brown, D. (1975) *Bury my Heart at Wounded Knee*, London: Picador.

Browne, K. (1992) *An Introduction to Sociology*, Cambridge: Polity Press.

Brownmiller, S. (1976) *Against Our Will: Men, Women and Rape*, Harmondsworth: Penguin.

Bruce, S. (1992) 'The Twilight of the Gods: Religion in Modern Britain', *Social Studies Review*, November, 1992.

Bruce, S. (1995) *Religion in Modern Britain*, Oxford: Oxford University Press.

Bruce, S. (1996) *Religion in the Modern World: From Cathedrals to Cults*, Oxford: Oxford University Press.

Bruce, S. (1999) *Choice and Religion: A Critique of Rational Choice Theory*, Oxford: Oxford University Press.

Buckingham, D. (1993) *Children Talking Television*, Lewes: Taylor and Francis.

Burkitt, I. (1991) *Social Selves: Theories of the Social Formation of Personality*, London: Sage.

Carnoy, M., Cardoso, F. H., Castells, M., and Cohen, S. (1993) *The New Global Economy in the Information Age*, Pennsylvania: Pennsylvania State University Press.

Cashmore, E. and Troyna, B. (1990) *Introduction to Race Relations*, London: Sage.

Castells, M. (1997) *The Power of Identity*, Oxford: Blackwell.

Centre for Contemporary Cultural Studies (1982) 'The Empire Strikes Back: Race and Racism in 70s Britain', London: CCCS/Hutchison

Chester, R. (1985) 'The Rise of the Neo-Conventional Family', *New Society*, 9 May.

Chibnall, S. (1977) *Law and Order News: An Analysis of Crime Reporting in the British Press*, London: Tavistock.

Cockett, M. and Tripp, J. (1994) *The Exeter Family Study: family breakdown and its impact on children*, Exeter: University of Exeter Press.

Cohen, S., (1980) *Folk Devils and Moral Panics: The Creation of the Mods and Rockers*, Oxford: Basil Blackwell.

Cohen, S. (1973) *Folk Devils and Moral Panics*, London: Paladin.

Comte, A. (1951) *System of Positive Polity*, London: Longmans Green.

Comte, A. (1853) *The Postive Philosophy of Auguste Comte* (edited by Harriet Martineau), 2 vols, London: Chapman

Craib, I. (1984) *Modern Social Theory: From Parsons to Habermas*, London: Harvester Wheatsheaf.

Craib, I. (1992) *Modern Social Theory* (2nd ed) Hemel Hempstead , London: Harvester Wheatsheaf.

Crewe, I. (1992) ' Changing Votes and Unchanging Voters', *Electoral Studies*, December, 1992.

Crewe, I. (1992) 'Why did Labour lose (yet again)?', *Politics Review*.

Cumberbatch, G. and Negrine, R. (1992) *Images of Disability on Television*, London: Routledge.

Cumberbatch, G. et al. (1990) *Television Advertising and Sex Role Stereotyping,* London: Broadcasting Standards Council.

Curran, P. (1996) 'Rethinking Mass Communications', in J. Curran, D. Morley, and V. Walkerdine (eds) *Cultural Studies and Communications*, London: Arnold.

Curtice, J. and Semetko, H. (1994) 'Does it matter what the papers say?', in A. Heath, R. Jowell, and J. Curtice (eds) *Labours Last Chance? The 1992 Election and Beyond*, Aldershot: Dartmouth.

Davis, K. (1949) *Human Society*, New York: Macmillan and Co.

Dell, D. (1973) *The Coming of Post-Industrial Society*, New York: Basic Books.

Della Porta, D. and Diani, M. (1999) *Social Movements: An Introduction*, Oxford: Blackwell.

Dennis, N. and Erdos, G. (1992) *Families Without Fatherhood*, London: IEA.

Derrida, J. (1991) *A Derrida Reader: Between the Blinds*, Hemel Hempstead, London: Wheatsheaf.

Devine, F. (1992) *Affluent Workers Revisited: Privatism and the Working Class*, Edinburgh: Edinburgh University Press.

Devine, F. and Heath, S. (1999) *Sociological research methods in context*, London: Macmillan.

Dobash, R. E. and Dobash, R. (1979) *Violence Against Wives*, London: Open Books.

Dominick and Rauch (1972) 'The Image of Women in Network TV Commercials', *Journal of Broadcasting*, vol 16.

Donzelot, J. (1980) *The Policing of Families*, London: Hutchinson.

Durkheim, E. (1912) (trans 1961) *The Elementary Forms of Religious Life*, London: Colliers Books.

Durkheim, E. (1938) *The Rules of Sociological Method*, New York: The Free Press.

Durkheim, E. (1979*) Suicide: a study in sociology*, London: Routledge

Dworkin, A. (1981) *Pornography: Men Possessing Women*, New York: Perigee.

Edwards, T. (1997) *Men in the Mirror*, London: Cassell.

Elias, N. (1992) *Time: an essay*, Oxford: Basil Blackwell.

Engles, F. (1972) *The Origin of the Family, Private Property and the State*, New York: Pathfinder Press.

Eversley, D. and Bonnerjea, L. (1982) 'Social Change and Indicators of Diversity' in R. N. Rapoport et al. (eds) *Families in Britain*, London: Routledge and Kegan Paul.

Falk, P. (1994) *The Consuming Body*, London: Sage.

Fallding, H. (1974) *The Sociology of Religion: An Explanation of Unity and Diversity in Religion*, London: McGraw Hill.

Featherstone, M. (1990) *Consumer Culture and Postmodernism*, London: Sage.

Featherstone, M. and Hepworth, M. (1991) 'The Mask of Aging and the Postmodern Life Course' in M. Featherstone et al. (eds) *The Body: Social Process and Cultural Theory*, London: Sage.

Featherstone, M. and Hepworth, M. (1995) 'Images of positive ageing', in Featherstone and Wernick, *Images of Ageing*, London: Routledge.

Ferguson, M. (1983) *Forever Feminine: Women's Magazines and the Cult of Femininity*, London: Heinemann.

Feyerabend, P. (1993) *Against Method* (3rd ed.), London: Verso.

Finch, J. (1989) *Family Obligations and Social Change*, Cambridge: Polity Press.

Finch, J. and Mason, J. (1993) *Negotiating Family Responsibilities*, London: Routledge.

Firestone, S. (1979) *The Dialectic of Sex: the Case for Feminist Revolution*, London: The Women's Press.

Fletcher, R. (1966) *The Family and Marriage in Britain*, Harmondsworth: Penguin.

Foucault, M. (1977) *Discipline and Punish*, Harmondsworth: Penguin.

Foucault, M. (1979) *The History of Sexuality*, vol. 1, London: Penguin.

Freidan, B. (1965) *The Feminine Mystique*, Harmondsworth: Penguin.

Fukuyama, F. (1992) *The End of History and the Last Man*, Harmondsworth: Penguin.

Galtung and Ruge (1981) 'Structuring and selecting news', in S. Cohen and J. Young (eds) *The Manufacture of News*, London: Constable.

Gans, H. (1974) *Popular Culture and High Culture*, New York: Basic Books.

Garfinkel, H. (1967) *Studies in Ethnomethodology*, Cambridge: Polity Press.

Gaskell, J. (1992) *Gender Matters: From School to Work*, Milton Keynes: Open University Press.

Gavron, H. (1966) *The Captive Wife: Conflicts of Housebound Mothers*. Harmondsworth: Penguin.

Gellner, E. (1992) *Post-Modernism, Reason and Religion*, London: Routledge.

Giddens A. (1984) *The Constitution of Society An Outline of the Theory of Structuration*, Cambridge: Polity Press.

Giddens, A. (1986) *Sociology: a Brief But Critical Introduction* (2nd ed.), London: Macmillan.

Giddens, A. (1990) *The Consequences of Modernity*, Cambridge: Polity Press.

Giddens, A. (1991a*) The Consequences of Modernity*, Cambridge: Polity Press.

Giddens, A. (1991b) *Modernity and Self-Identity: Self and Society in the Late Modern Age*, Cambridge: Polity Press.

Giddens, A. (1992) *The Transformation of Intimacy: Sexuality, Love and Eroticism in Modern Societies*, Cambridge: Polity Press.

Giddens, A. (1994) *Beyond Left and Right: the Future of Radical Politics*, Cambridge: Polity Press.

Giddens, A. (1997) *Sociology* (3rd edition), Cambridge: Polity Press.

Giroux, H. and Mclaren, P.(eds) (1994) *Between Borders: Pedagogy and the Politics of Cultural Studies*, New York: Routledge.

Gittins, D. (1993) *The Family in Question: Changing Households and Familiar Ideologies* (2nd ed), Basingstoke: Macmillan.

Glaser, B. G. and Strauss, A. L. (1968) *The Discovery of Grounded Theory: Strategies for Qualitative Research*, Chicago: Aldine and Atherton.

Glasgow University Media Group (1982) *Really Bad News*, London: Writers and Readers.

Glasgow University Media Group(1976*) Bad News*, London: Routledge.

Glass, D. (ed.) (1954) *Social Mobility in Britain*, London: Routledge

Glennon and Butsch, (1982) 'The Family as Portrayed on Television, 1946-1978' in D. Pearl et al, (eds) *Television and Behaviour*, Rockville, MD: National Institute of Mental Health.

Goffman, E. (1959) *Presentation of Self in Everyday Life*, Harmonsworth: Penguin.

Goffman, E. (1963) *Stigma: Notes on the Management on Spoiled Identity*, Harmonsworth: Penguin.

Golding, P. and Murdock, G. (1991) 'Cultural communication and political economy' in J. Curran and M. Gurevitch (eds) *The Mass Media and Society*, London: Arnold.

Goldthorpe, J.H., Llewllyn, C. and Payne, C. (1987) *Social Mobility and Class Structure in Modern Britain*, Oxford: Clarendon Press.

Hall, S. (1992) ' New ethnicities' in J. Donald and A. Rattansi (eds) *Race, Culture and Difference*, London: Sage.

Goode, W. (1963) *World Revolution and Family Patterns*, New York: The Free Press.

Gouldner, A. (1971) *The Coming Crisis of Western Sociology*, London: Heinemann.

Gouldner, A. (1975) *For Sociology*, Harmondsworth: Penguin.

Gramsci, A. (1971) *Selections From the Prison Notebooks of Antonio Gramsci* (edited by Q. Hoare, G. Nowell-Smith), London: Lawrence & Wishart (orig. written 1929-35)

Green, A. (1997) *Education, Globalisation and the Nation State*, London: Macmillan.

Habermas, J. (1989) *Jurgen Habermas on Society and Politics: A Reader* (edited by S. Seidman), Boston: Beacon Press.

Hagell, A. and Newburn, T. (1994) *Young Offenders and the Media: Viewing Habits and Preferences*, London: PSI.

Hall, S. and du Gay, P. (eds) (1996) *Questions of Cultural Identity*, London: Sage.

Hall, S. (1982) *The State and Popular Culture*, Milton Keynes: Open University Press.

Hall, S. and Jacques, P. (eds)(1983) *The Politics of Thatcherism*, London: Lawrence and Wishart.

Hall, S. with Critcher, C., Jefferson, T., Clarke, J., and Roberts, B. (1978) *Policing the Crisis: Mugging, the State and Law and Order*, Basingstoke: Macmillan.

Halsey, A., Health, A. and Ridge, J. (1980) *Origins and Destinations*, Oxford: Clarenden Press.

Hannerz, U. (1996) *Soulside: Inquiries into Ghetto Culture and Community*, New York: Columbia University Press.

Hartmann and Husband (1974) *Racism and the Mass Media*, London: Davis-Poynter.

Hassan, S. (1988) *Combating Cult Mind Control*, Rochester, VT: Park Street Press.

Hebdige, D. (1979) *Subculture: The Meaning of Style*, London: Methuen.

Hechter, M. (1976) *International Colonialism: The Celtic Fringe in British National Development*, London: Collins.

Heelas, P. (1996) *The New Age: Celebrating the Self*, Oxford: Blackwell.

Heidensohn, F. (1996) *Women and Crime* (2nd ed), Basingstoke: Macmillan.

Held, D. (1980) *Introduction to Critical Theory*, London: Hutchinson.

Held, D. (1995) 'Liberalism, Marxism and Democracy' in S. Hall et al. (eds) *Modernity and its Future*, Cambridge: Polity Press.

Herberg, W. (1956) *Protestant, Catholic, Jew*, Garden City NY: Doubleday.

Hey, V. (1997) *The Company She Keeps: An Ethnography of Girls' Friendship*, Buckingham: OUP

Hoggart, R. (1957) *The Uses of Literacy*, London: Chatto and Windus.

Homans, G. (1950) *The Human Group*, New York: Harcourt Brace and World Inc.

Humphreys, L. (1970) *Tearoom Trade*, London: Duckworth.

James, A. and Prout, A. (1990) *Constructing and Reconstructing Childhood*, Lewes: Falmer Books.

Jenkins, R. (1996) *Social Identity*, London: Routledge.

Jhally and Lewis (1992) *Enlightened Racism: The Cosby Show, Audiences and the Myth of the Dream*, Oxford: Westview Press.

Jordan, G. and Weedon, C. (1995) *Cultural Politics: Class, Gender and Race in the Post-Modern World*, Oxford: Blackwell.

Kanapol, B. and Mclaren, P. (1995) *After Postmodernism*, New York: Bergin Garvey.

Kellner, D. (1997) 'Culture' in D. Owen (ed.) *Sociology after Postmodernism*, London: Sage.

Kimmel, A. (1988) *Ethics and values in Applied Social Research*, London: Sage.

Kluckholm, C. (1951) 'The Concept of Culture' in D. Lerner and H. D. Lasswell (eds) *The Policy Sciences*, Stanford: Stanford University Press.

Kohn, M. (1969) *Class and Confomity*, Homewood, IIinois: Darsey Press.

Kuhn, T. (1970) *The Structure of Scientific Revolutions* (2nd edition), Chicago: University of Chicago Press.

Labor, W. (1972) *Language in the Inner City Philadelphia*, Pennsylvania: University of Pennsylvania Free Press.

Labov, W. (1973) 'The Logic of Non-standard English' in N. Keddie (ed.) *Tinker, Tailor: The Myth of Cultural Deprivation*, Harmondsworth: Penguin.

Lacan, J. (1977) *Ecrits: A Selection*, London: Tavistock.

Laing, R. D. (1976) *The Politics of the Family*, Harmondsworth: Penguin.

Laing, R. D. and Esterson, A. (1970) *Sanity, Madness and the Family*, Harmondsworth: Penguin.

Lambert, J. et al. (1984) *The Image of the Elderly on TV*, Cambridge: University of the Third Age.

Land, H. (1995) 'Families and the Law' in J. Muncie et al. (eds) *Understanding the Family*, London: Sage.

Laslett, P. (1965) *The World We Have Lost*, London: Methuen.

Laslett, P. (ed) (1972) *Household and Family in Past Time*, Cambridge: Cambridge University Press.

Layder, D. (1993) *New Strategies in Social Research*, London: Polity Press.

Layder, D. (1994) *Understanding Social Theory*, London: Sage.

Lazarsfeld, P., Berelson, B. and Gaudet, H. (1944) *The People's Choice*, New York: Columbia University Press.

Leach, E. (1964) *Rethinking Anthropology*, London: Althone Press.

Lewis, O. (1961) *The Children of Sanchez*, New York: Random House.

Lewis, O. (1966) *LaVida*, New York: Random House.

Lockwood, D. (1958) *The Blackcoated Worker: a Study in Class Consciousness*, London: Allen and Unwin.

Longmore, F. (1987) 'Screening Stereotypes: Images of Disabled people in TV and Motion Pictures' in A. Gartner and T. Foe (eds) *Images of the Disabled, Disabling Images*, New York: Praeger.

Luckmann, T. (1978) *Phenomenology and Sociology: Selected Readings*, Harmondsworth: Penguin.

Lurie, A. (1998) *Imaginary Friends*, New York: Henry Holt.

Lyotard F. (1993) 'Answering the Question: What is Postmodernism?' in T. Doherty *Postmodernism: A Reader*, Hemel Hempstead: Harvester Wheatsheaf.

Lyotard, J-F. (1984) *The Postmodern Condition*, Manchester: Manchester University Press.

Mac an Ghaill, M. (1988) *Young, Gifted and Black*, Milton Keynes: Open University Press.

Mac an Ghaill, M. (1994) *The Making of Men: Masculinities, Sexualities and Schooling*, Buckingham: OUP.

Mac an Ghaill, M. (1996) 'Sociology of Education, State Schooling and Social Class: Beyond Critiques of the New Right Hegemony', *British Journal of Sociology of Education*, vol. 17, no. 2, June 1996.

Maduro, O. (1982) *Religion and Social Conflicts*, New York: Orbis.

Malinowski, B. (1954) *Magic, Science and Religion*, New York: The Free Press.

Marcuse, H. (1964) *One-Dimensional Man*, London: Routledge & Kegan Paul.

Marris, P. (1996) *The Politics of Uncertainty*, London: Routledge.

Marsh, I. (1996) *Making Sense of Society*, London: Longman.

Marsh, I. (ed.) (1999) *Sociology: Dealing with Data*, Harlow: Longman.

Martin, D. (1976) *A General Theory of Secularisation*, Oxford: Blackwell.

Martin, D. (1978) *A General Theory of Secularisation*, Oxford: Blackwell.

Martin, D. (1990) *Tongues of Fire*, Oxford: Blackwell.

Marx, K. and Engels, F. (1977) *The German Ideology* (edited by C.J. Arthur) London: Lawrence and Wishart (orig. written 1845).

Marx, K. and Engels, F. (1967) *The Communist Manifesto*, Harmondsworth: Penguin (orig. pub. 1848).

Masmoudi, M. (1979) 'The new world information order ', *Journal of Communication*, vol. 29, no. 2, pp.172-85.

May, T. (1993) *Social Research: Issues, Methods and Process*, Buckingham: OUP.

Mayo, E. (1933) *The Human Problems of an Industrial Civilisation*, New Basingstoke: Macmillan.

McCombs and Shaw (1973) 'The Evolution of Agenda-Setting Theory: 25 Years in the Market Place of Ideas', *Journal of Communication*, vol. 43, no. 2.

McLeish, D. (1993) *Key ideas in Human Thought*, London: Bloomsbury.

McLuhan, M. (1963) *The Medium is the Message*, Harmondsworth: Penguin.

McQuail (1972) *The Sociology of Mass Communications*, Harmondsworth: Penguin.

McRobbie, A. (1991) *Settling Accounts with Youth Subcultures* in A. McRobbie, *Feminism and Youth Cultures*, Basingstoke: Macmillan.

Mead, G. H. (1934, 1967) *Mind, Self and Society*, Chicago: University of Chicago Press.

Mead, M. (1935) *Sex and Temperament in Three Primitive Societies*, New York: Morrow.

Meehan, D.M. (1983) *Ladies of the Evening*, New York: Scarecrow Press.

Merton, R. K. (1957) *Social Theory and Social Structure*, New York: Free Press.

Meyrowitz, J. (1984) 'The Adult Child and the Childlike Adult', *Daedalus*, 113(3).

Miles, R. (1989) *Racism*, London: Routledge.

Mills, C. W. (1959) *The Sociological Imagination*, New York: Oxford University Press.

Morgan, D. H. J. (1996) *Family Connections: An Introduction to Family Studies*, Cambridge: Polity Press.

Morley, D. (1980) *The Nationwide Audience*, London: British Film Institute.

Muncie, J. and Weatherell, M. (1995) 'Family Policy and political Discourse' in J Muncie et al. (eds) *Understanding the Family*, London: Sage.

Murdock, G. P. (1949) *Social Structure*, New York: Macmillan.

Newman, D. (1995) *Sociology: Exploring the Architecture of Everyday Life*. London: Pine Forge Press.

Newson, J. and E. (1965) *Patterns of Infant Care in an Urban Community*, Hamondsworth: Penguin.

Nixon, S. (1996) *Hard Looks*, London: UCL Press.

O'Dea, T. and O'Dea Avaid, J. (1997) *The Sociology of Religion* (2nd ed), New York: Prentice-Hall.

O'Rourke, P. J. (1988) *Holidays in Hell*, New York: Vintage Books.

Oakley, A. (1974a) *The Sociology of Housework*, Oxford: Martin Robertson.

Oakley, A. (1974b) *Housewife*, London: Allen Lane.

Oakley, A. (1981) *Subject Women*, Oxford: Martin Robertson.

Oakley, A. (1981) 'Interviewing Women: a contradiction in terms' in H. Roberts (ed.) *Doing Feminist Research*, London: Routledge.

Oakley, R. (1982) 'Cypriot Families' in R. N. Rapoport et al. (eds) *Families in Britain*, London: Routledge and Kegan Paul.

Oliver, M. (1990) *The Politics of Disablement*, London: Macmillan.

Orbach, S. (1986) *Fat is a Feminist Issue*, London: Arrow Books.

Outhwaite, W. (1987) *New Philosophies of Social Science*, Basingstoke: Macmillan.

Pahl, J. (1980) 'Patterns of Money Management Within Marriage', *Journal of Social policy*, vol. 9 (3).

Parsons, T. and Bales, R. F. (1955) *Family, Socialization and Interaction Process*, New York: The Free Press.

Parsons, T. (1973) *The American University*, Cambridge, Massachusetts: Harvard University Press.

Pawson, R. (1999) 'Methodology' in S. Taylor (ed) *Sociology: Issues and Debates*, London: Macmillan.

Pfohl, S. (1992) *Death of the Parasite Café: Social Science (Fictions) and the Postmodern (Culture Texts)*, Basingstoke: Macmillan.

Phillipson, C. (1982) *Capitalism and the Construction of Old Age*, London: Macmillan.

Pickering, W. (1994) *Durkheim on Religion*, Atlanta, Ga: Scholars Press.

Popper, K. (1959) *The Logic of Scientific Discovery*, London: Hutchinson.

Postman, N. (1985) *The Disappearance of Childhood: How TV is Changing Children's Lives*, W H Allen.

Pryce, K (1979) *Endless Pressure*, Harmondsworth: Penguin.

Radcliffe-Brown, A.R. (1938) *Taboo*, Cambridge: Cambridge University Press.

Rapoport, R. (1989) 'Ideologies About Family Forms - Towards Diversity' in K. Boh et al. (eds) *Changing Patterns of European Family Life*, London: Routledge.

Rapoport, R. N. et al (eds) (1982) *Families in Britain*, London: Routledge and Kegan Paul.

Ritchie, J. (1991) *The Secret World of Cults: Inside the Sects That Take Over Lives*, Angus and Robertson.

Robertson, R. (1978) *Meaning and Change: Explorations in the Cultured Sociology of Modern Societies*, Oxford: Blackwell.

Robertson, R. in Bromley, G. ed. (1991) *New Developments in Theory and Research*, Greenwich, Conn: JAI Press.

Robertson, R. (1992) *Globalisation*, London: Sage.

Rose, G. (1982) *Deciphering Sociological Research*, London: Macmillan.

Rosengren, K. E., and Windahl, S. (1972) in McQuail 1972 see also 1989 *Media matters: TV use in childhood and adolescence*, Norwood, New Jersey, Ablex publishers.

Saussure, F. de (1974) *Course in General Linguistics*, London: Fontana (orig. pub. 1915).

Schlesinger, P. (1978) *Putting Reality Together – BBC News*, London: Constable.

Schlesinger, P. and Tumber, H. (1993) 'BBC Crimewatch', *Criminal Justice Matters*, no. 11, Spring 1993, published by Centre for Criminal Justice Studies.

Segal, I. (1983) 'The Heart in The Kitchen' in S. Hall and P. Jacques (eds) *The Politics of Thatcherism*, London: Lawrence and Wishart.

Segal, L. (1990) *Slow Motion: Changing Masculinities, Changing Men*, London: Virago.

Selfe, P. and Starbuck, M. (1997) *Religion*, London: Hodder and Stoughton.

Shakespeare, T. (1994), 'Disabled People: Dustbins for Disavowal?', *Disability and Society*, vol. 9, no. 3, pp. 283-299.

Shilling, C. (1993) *The Body and Social Theory*, London: Sage.

Shor, I. (1986) *Culture Wars: School and Society in the Conservative Restoration 1969-1984*, New York: Methuen.

Signorelli (1989) 'Television and conceptions about sex roles', *Sex Roles*, 21, 5/6, pp. 341-360.

Simon, R. and Nadell, P. (1995) 'In the Same Voice or is it Different? Gender and the Clergy', *Sociology of Religion*, vol. 56, no. 1.

Sklair, L. (1993) *Sociology of the Global System*, Baltimore: John Hopkins University Press.

Smart, C. (1976) *Women, Crime and Criminology*, London: Routledge and Kegan Paul.

Smith, J. (1997) *Different for Girls: How Culture Creates Women*, London: Chatto and Windus.

Smith, R., and Wexler, P. (1995) *After Postmodernism; Education, Politics and Identity*, London: Falmer Press.

Sparks, C. (1998) 'Is there a global public sphere?' in D. K. Thussu (ed.) *Electronic Empires: Global Media and Local Resistance*, London: Arnold.

Stacey, J. (1990) *Brave New Families*, New York: Basic Books.

Stanley, L. (1989) 'Changing Households? Changing Work?' in N. Abercrombie and A. Warde (eds) (1992) *Social Change in Contemporary Britain*, Cambridge: Polity Press.

Stark, R. and Bainbridge, W.S. (1985) *The Failure of Religion: Secularisation, Revival and Cult Formation*, Berkeley: University of California Press.

Stark, R. and Glock, C. (1968) *American Piety: The Nature of Religious Commitment*, Berkeley: California Press.

Strinati, D. (1995) 'Postmodernism and Popular Culture', *Sociology Review*, April 1995.

Swann Report (1985) *Education for All: Report of a Committee into the Education of Children from Ethnic Minorities*, London: HMSO.

Taylor, P. (1997) *Investigating Culture and Identity*, Collins Educational.

Thorne, B. (1982) *Feminist Rethinking of the Family: an overview*, New York: Longman.

Thornton, S. (1995) *Club Cultures, Music Media and Subcultural Capital*, Cambridge: Polity Press.

Tiger, L. and Fox, R. (1972) *The Imperial Animal*, London: Secher and Warburg.

Tischler, H. (1996) *Introduction to Sociology* (5th ed) Fort Worth: The Harcourt Press.

Tomlinson, S. (1983) *Ethnic Minorities in British Schools*, London: Heinemann.

Tonnies, F. (1955) *Community and Association*, London: Routledge & Kegan Paul.

Torres, C. (1973) *Revolutionary Priest*, Harmonsworth: Penguin.

Trenaman, J. and McQuail, D. (1961) *Television and the Political Image*, Methuen.

Troyna, B. (1993) *Racism and Education*, Milton Keynes: Open University Press.

Tuchman, G. (1978) *Hearth and Home: Images of Women in the Mass Media*, New York: Oxford University Press.

Turkle, S. (1996) *Life on the Screen: Identity in the Age of the Internet*, London: Weidenfeld and Nicolson.

Turner, B.S. (1983) *Religion and Social Theory*, Atlantic Highlands, NJ: Humanities Press.

Van Dijk, T. (1991) *Racism and the Press*, London: Routledge.

Varis, T. (1984) 'The International flow of television programmes', *Journal of Communication*, vol. 34, no. 1, pp. 143-52.

Wagner, P. (1994) *A Sociology of Modernity: Liberty and Discipline*, London: Routledge.

Walby, S. (1990) *Theorising Patriarchy*, Oxford: Blackwell.

Walby, S. (1990) *Theorizing Patriarchy*, Sociology, vol. 23 no. 2.

Wallerstein, I. (1991) 'The Construction of Peoplehood: Racism, Nationalism, Ethnicity' in E. Balibar and I Wallerstein (eds) *'Race,' Nation, Class*, London: Verso.

Wallis, R. (1984) *Elementary Forms of the New Religious Life*, London: Routledge.

Warwick, D. (1982) 'Tearoom Trade: Means and Ends in Social Research' in M. Blumer (ed.) *Social Research Ethics*, London: Macmillan.

Weber, M. (1930) *The Protestant Ethic and the Spirit of Capitalism*, London: Allen and Unwin.

Weber, M. (1996) *The Protestant Ethic and the Spirit of Capitalism*, (translated by Talcolt Parsons), Los Angeles, CAL: Roxbury Publishing Co.

Wedge, P. and Prosser, H. (1973) *Born to Fail*, London: Arrow Books.

Westergaard, J. and Resler, H. (1976) *Class in Capitalist Society*, Harmondsworth: Penguin.

Whale, J. (1997) *The Politics of the Media*, London: Fontana.

Williams, G. (1985) *When was Wales*, Harmondsworth: Pelican.

Williams, P. and Dickinson, J. (1993) 'Fear of Crime: Read all about it? The Relationship between Newspaper Crime Reporting and Fear of Crime', *British Journal of Criminology*, no. 33, pp. 33-56.

Williams, R. (1990) *Television, Technology and Cultural Form* (2nd ed), London: Routledge.

Williams, R. (1990) *What I Came to Say*, Cambridge: Cambridge University Press.

Williams, R. (1981) *Culture*, London: Fontana.

Willis, P. (1977) *Learning to labour*, Farnborough: Saxon House.

Willis, P. (1990) *Common Culture: Symbolic Work at Play in the Everyday Lives of the Young*, Milton Keynes: Open University Press.

Willmott, P. (1986) *Social Networks, Informal Care and Public Policy*, London: Policy Studies Institute.

Wilson, B. (1966) *Religion in a Secular Society*, London: CA Watts.

Wilson, W. J. (1987) *The Truly Disadvantaged*, Chicago: University of Chicago Press.

Worsley, P. (1970) *The Trumpet Shall Sound*, London: Palladin.

Wright Mills, C. (1959) *The Power Elite*, New York: OUP.

Yinger, J. (1970) *The Scientific Study of Religion*, London: Macmillan.

Young, M. and Willmott, P. (1962) *Family and Kinship in East London*, Harmondsworth: Penguin.

Young, M. and Willmott, P. (1975) *The Symmetrical Family*, Harmondsworth: Penguin.

Young, M. (1958) *The Rise of the Meritocracy*, Harmondsworth: Penguin.

Zaretsky, E. (1976) *Capitalism, the Family and Personal Life*, London: Pluto Press.

Zweig, F. (1961) *The Worker in an Affluent Society: Family Life and Industry*, London: Heinemann.

Index